MW01620306

LOUISE FISHMAN

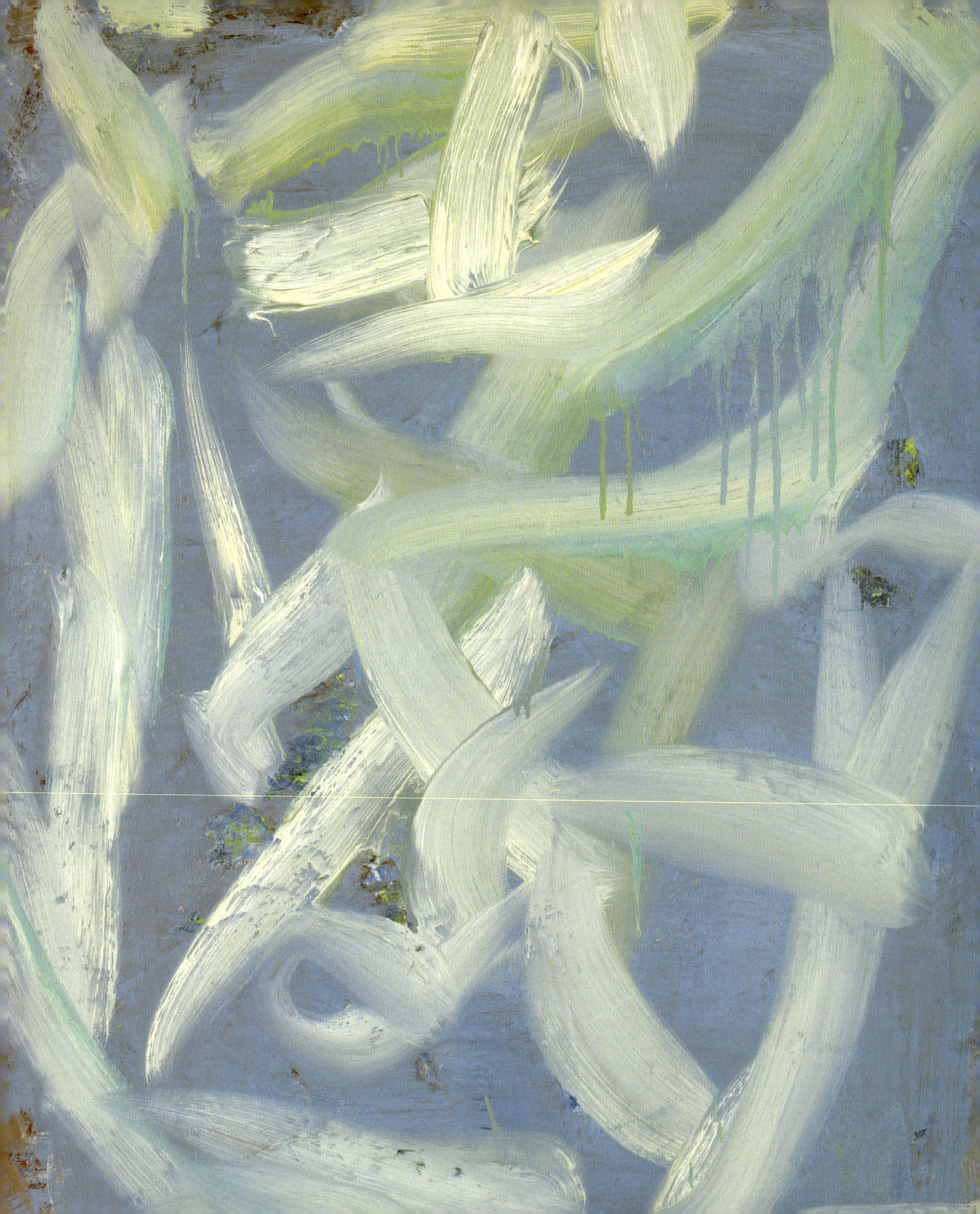

LOUISE FISHMAN

Edited by Helaine Posner

Essays by Carrie Moyer, Helaine Posner, and Nancy Princenthal
With an interview by Ingrid Schaffner

Neuberger Museum of Art
Purchase College, SUNY, Purchase, New York

Institute of Contemporary Art
University of Pennsylvania, Philadelphia

DelMonico Books • Prestel
Munich London New York

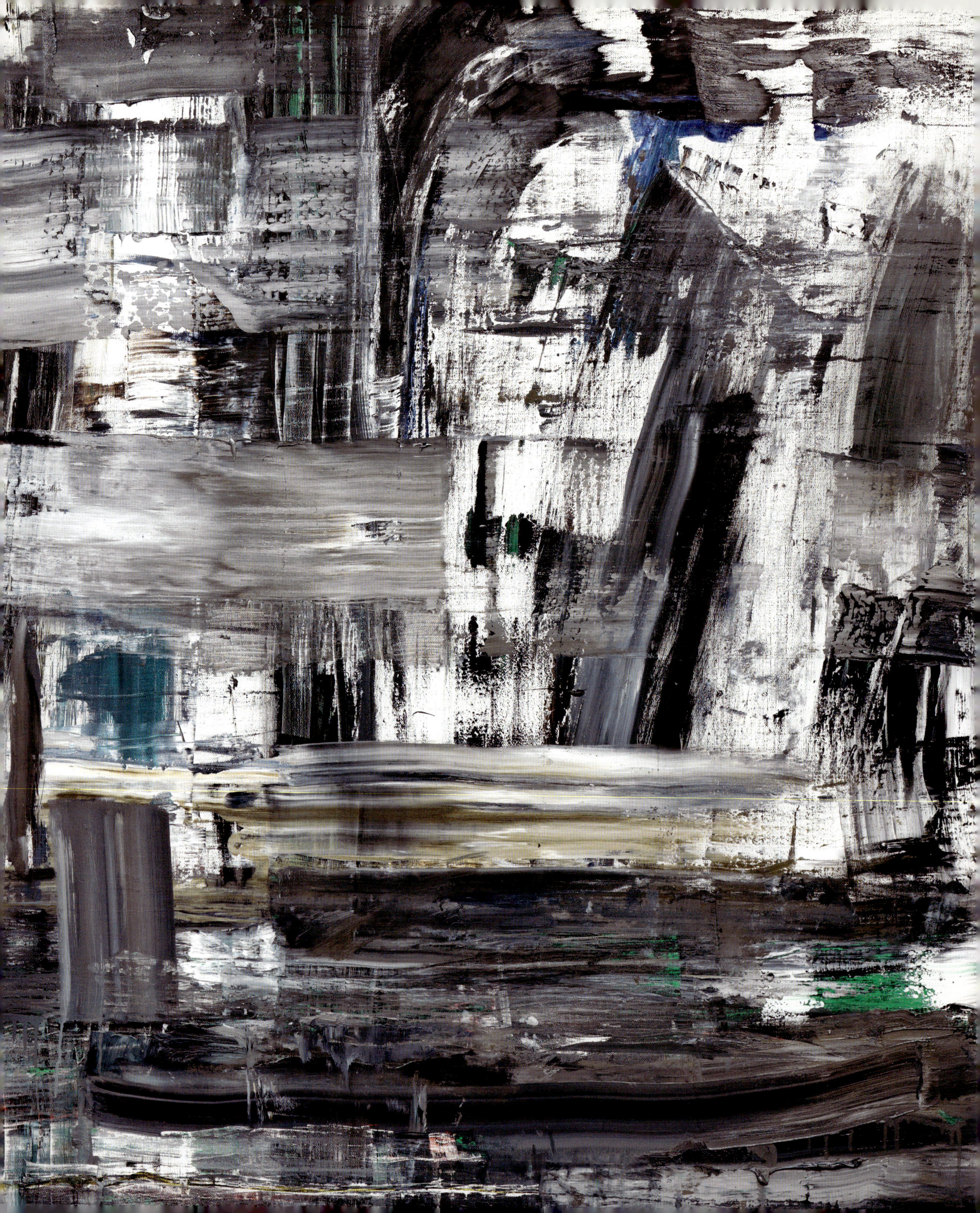

CONTENTS

DIRECTORS' FOREWORDS

The Neuberger Museum of Art prides itself on collaborating with artists whose work is not only of the highest art historical significance and aesthetic quality but also demonstrates critical perspectives that have influenced their peers and had a lasting impact on younger generations. In keeping with this mission we are delighted to present the first museum survey of the work of Louise Fishman. I am deeply grateful for her thoughtful and generous help with this exhibition, and I also offer warm thanks to her spouse, Ingrid Nyeboe, who has likewise provided tremendous support throughout the project.

Projects like this one would not be possible without the dedicated community that supports the museum's exhibitions and programs. For their dedication to the Neuberger and their generous sponsorship of *Louise Fishman: A Retrospective*, profound thanks go to James and Susan Dubin, whose longtime service to the museum, in particular through Susan's work as our current Chair of the Board of the Friends of the Neuberger Museum of Art, is so highly valued and appreciated. I am also grateful to Lauren B. Cramer, Helen Stambler Neuberger and James Neuberger, and Sara and Michelle Vance Waddell for their generous support of this exhibition. Educational programs are funded in part by The Elizabeth A. Sackler Museum Educational Trust. Gratitude is also due to our colleagues at the National Endowment for the Arts for their continued faith in our projects and for funding this exhibition. I also extend thanks to the Friends of the Neuberger Museum of Art and the Purchase College Foundation for their ongoing support.

All of us at the Neuberger have enjoyed working with our institutional collaborators and colleagues on this exhibition. At the Institute of Contemporary Art, University of Pennsylvania, sincere thanks go to Amy Sadao, Director; Ingrid Schaffner, former Chief Curator and current Curator, *Carnegie International*, Carnegie Museum of Art; and Anthony Elms, Chief Curator. We are so pleased to be able to partner with them on exhibiting different aspects of Fishman's work, concurrently, at our respective institutions. We also wish to thank Nancy Doll, Director of the Weatherspoon Art Museum at the University of North Carolina at Greensboro, for hosting the Neuberger Museum retrospective. At Cheim & Read, the gallery that has championed Fishman and her art for many years, particular thanks go to John Cheim, Principal/Head of Exhibitions; Karen Polack, Registrar; and Ellen Robinson, Director of Press and Media.

This catalogue stands among the most authoritative accounts of Fishman's work to date. At our copublisher, DelMonico Books • Prestel, I would like to thank Mary DelMonico, Publisher, Ryan Newbanks, Editor, and Luke Chase, Production Coordinator. Thanks are also due to Amanda Glesmann, who copyedited this publication, and to Rita Jules and Miko McGinty of Miko McGinty Inc., who developed its thoughtful and elegant design. For their insightful catalogue essays many thanks go to Helaine Posner, Chief Curator at the Neuberger Museum of Art; Carrie Moyer, painter, art critic, and Associate Professor of Art at Hunter College, New York; and Nancy Princenthal, a New York–based art critic and former Senior Editor at *Art in America.* I am also grateful to Ingrid Schaffner for her interview with the artist, and to Kimberly Detterbeck, Art Librarian, Purchase College, for producing the Biography and Exhibition History, and Selected Bibliography. Cristina Miranda, Louise Fishman's archivist, provided valuable research assistance.

A project like this would be impossible without the generous support of our private lenders: Tracey and Mark Bilski, Carol A.

Calhoun, Tom Cashin and Jay Johnson, John Cheim, Mike De Paola, The Dicke Collection, Jan and Barry Zubrow, Milton and Sheila Fine, Marc and Jill Fisher, Louise Fishman, The Forman Family Foundation, Stuart and Lisa Ginsberg, James and Janet Kloppenburg, Martha Macks-Kahn, Romita Shetty and Nasser Ahmad, the Speyer Family Collection, and Thomas Whitridge. We are also indebted to our institutional lenders: the Fernando Luis Alvarez Gallery, Stamford, Connecticut; The Art Institute of Chicago; Cheim & Read, New York; the Hood Museum of Art, Dartmouth College, Hanover, New Hampshire; The Jewish Museum, New York; and the Metropolitan Museum of Art, New York.

I would also like to acknowledge our great supporters and colleagues at Purchase College, especially President Thomas J. Schwarz; Provost and Vice President Barry Pearson; and Vice President of Institutional Advancement Jeannine Starr. Warm thanks, as always, is likewise extended to the fantastic staff of the Neuberger Museum of Art for their hard work on this exhibition: Sanjeev Avasthi, Security Supervisor; Jane Barry, Director, Operations and Visitor Services; David Bogosian, Director of Facilities and Chief Preparator; Denise Borsari, Financial Affairs Assistant; Peter C. Cole, Visitor Services Associate; Camilla Cook, Public Programs Manager; Jessica Denaro, Associate Director of Development; Deslyn Downes Dyer, Executive Assistant to the Director; Patrice Giasson, Alex Gordon Associate Curator of Art of the Americas; Suzanne Grady, Marketing Associate; Avis Larson, Assistant Curator; Alison Lowey, Assistant Registrar; Patricia Magnani, Registrar; Carolyn Mandelker, Public Relations Consultant; Rafal Niemojewski, Director of Education and Public Programs; Stephanie Rodriguez, Shop Manager; Jacqueline Shilkoff, Curator of New Media and Director of Digital Initiatives; and Jose Antonio Smith, Associate Preparator. Thank you also to Emma Beiderman, Greg Beise, Matt Harle, Alejandro Lopez, Dan McInerney, and Alex Theodoropoulos; to our Associate Director of Finance, Sarah James; and to Gennelle McNeil, Financial Analyst/Accountant, Campus Foundations and Related Entities, Purchase College.

A special thank you goes to Simon Watson, who first brought the idea of a retrospective of Fishman's work to our attention, initiating a most important project for the Neuberger Museum of Art. My deepest thanks, however, go to Helaine Posner in acknowledgment of her exceptional work on *Louise Fishman: A Retrospective*. It is through Helaine's dedication to the museum and consummate skill as a curator that this exhibition has come to fruition in such a significant and meaningful form.

Tracy Fitzpatrick
Director, Neuberger Museum of Art

My respect for Louise Fishman's work was lit anew by the illuminating *High Times, Hard Times: New York Painting 1967–75* as curated by Katy Siegel with David Reed. Fishman's fabric works were included with pieces by other painters working in constructions, photography, and performance art as well as "music, crafts, carpentry, psychedelic drugs, non-Western cultures, language theory and even geodesic domes." We are honored to expand this inquiry with the current publication and concurrent exhibitions at the Neuberger Museum of Art, Purchase College, and the Institute of Contemporary Art, University of Pennsylvania (ICA). All are investigations into Fishman's work to expand the boundaries of Abstract Expressionism, notably through the incorporation of the artist's politicization.

ICA focuses on the unknown and maintains an overriding interest in nudging through lines separating artist studio and exhibiting space. *Paper Louise Tiny Fishman Rock* presents the "tiny" paintings and folded paper books Fishman has steadily created alongside larger canvases. Never-before-seen objects from the artist's studio as well as painting experiments on metal and even carpet samples represent a simultaneous, companion vein of creativity that illuminates our understanding of the artist's full production.

I am grateful to work again with The Edna W. Andrade Fund of the Philadelphia Foundation. I thank Chief Curator Helaine Posner, Director Tracy Fitzpatrick, and the Neuberger Museum of Art for this fruitful collaboration. Special acknowledgments are due to Mary DelMonico and Ryan Newbanks at DelMonico Books • Prestel. My thanks to Karen Polack and Ellen Robinson from Cheim & Read for providing essential assistance with images and information and also to Ingrid Nyeboe, Louise's spouse, who helped organize so much on behalf of the studio that this project is hers as well.

ICA's research-based, artist-centric program is made possible by the vision of our Board of Overseers who support and encourage our focus on underrepresented and overlooked artists and exhibition, publication, and public programs that focus on urgent art in new and experimental forms. Led by President Andrea Laporte, ICA's Overseers welcome a program that challenges their expectations and is inspired by artists' risk-taking. I remain in awe of their faith in our ever-changing work and their generosity.

I thank the University of Pennsylvania's President Amy Gutmann, Provost Vincent Prince, and Vice Provost of Academic Affairs Anita Allen for ensuring that ICA flourishes as an essential component of the university and crossroads between the campus, the City of Philadelphia, and the wider world.

ICA's staff shared in my wish to make this last collaboration with our longtime Chief Curator, and Guest Curator of *Paper Louise Tiny Fishman Rock*, the very best of our efforts. For their admiration of the artist's importance, the curator's impeccable work, and in recognition of their endless contributions, I gratefully acknowledge colleagues Mandy Bartram, Registrar; Jeffrey Bussmann, Associate Director of Development for Individual Gifts; Robert Chaney, Director of Curatorial Affairs; Eliza Coviello, Administrative Coordinator & Assistant to the Director; Lauren Downing, Curatorial Administrative Assistant; Anthony Elms, Chief Curator; Shannon Freitas, Business Administrator; Samantha Gibb Roff, Director of Development; William Hidalgo, Visitor Services Coordinator & Program Technician; Becky Huff Hunter, Communications Associate; Charlotte Ickes, Whitney-Lauder Curatorial Fellow; Jessica Kaminski, Catalogues and Prints Coordinator; Jill Katz, Director of Marketing & Communications; Alex Klein, Dorothy and Stephen R. Weber (CHE '60) Curator; Kate Kraczon, Associate Curator; Paul Swenbeck, Chief Preparator/Building Administrator; Gee Wesley, Spiegel-Wilks Curatorial Fellow; and Christina Yu, Development Assistant.

Guest Curator Ingrid Schaffner conceived of this project, organized *Paper Louise Tiny Fishman Rock* for ICA, and ensured the fruitful collaboration with the Neuberger Museum of Art. So I offer my final thanks to her alongside the power couple of Louise Fishman and Ingrid Nyeboe.

Amy Sadao
Daniel W. Dietrich, II Director,
Institute of Contemporary Art

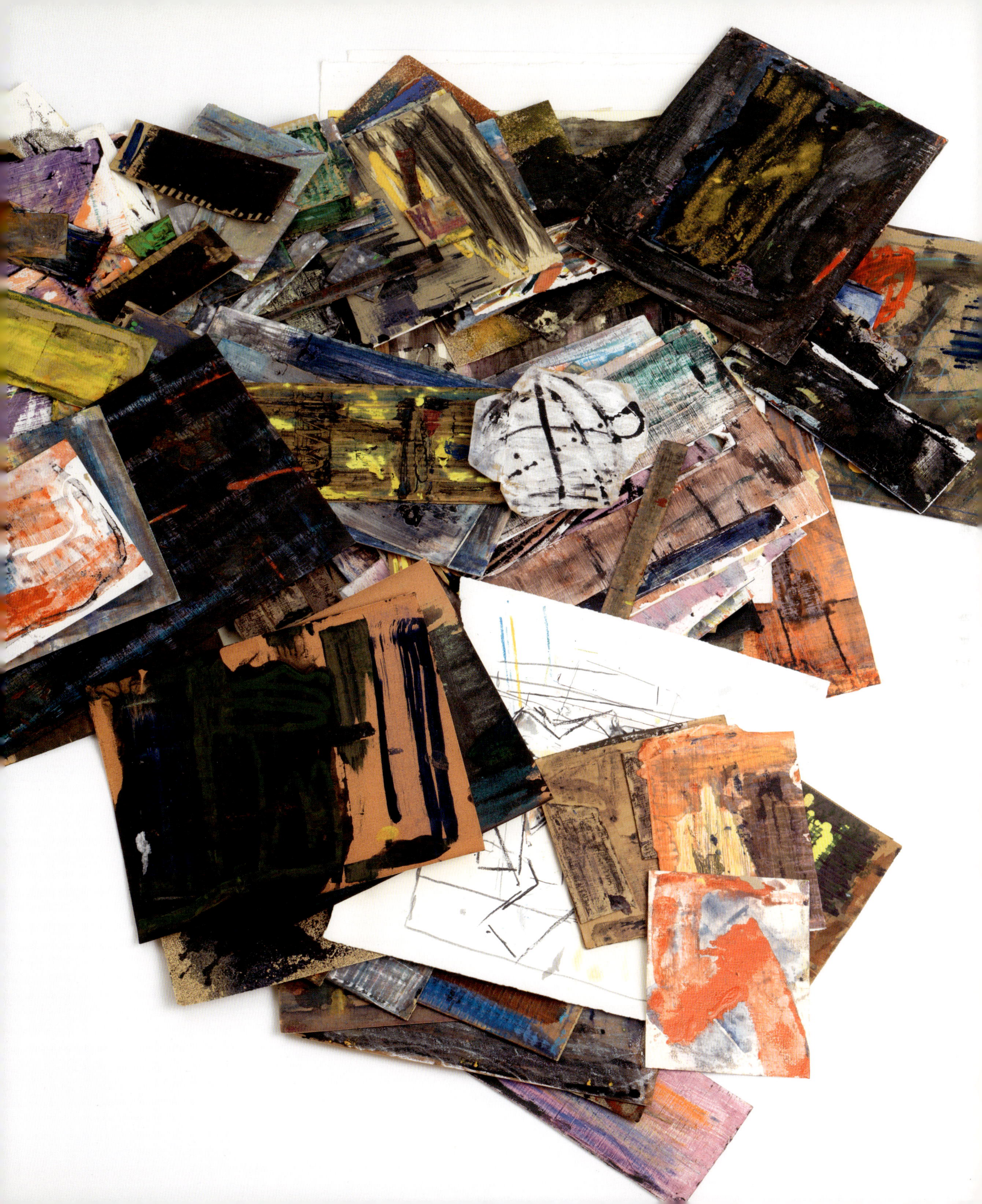

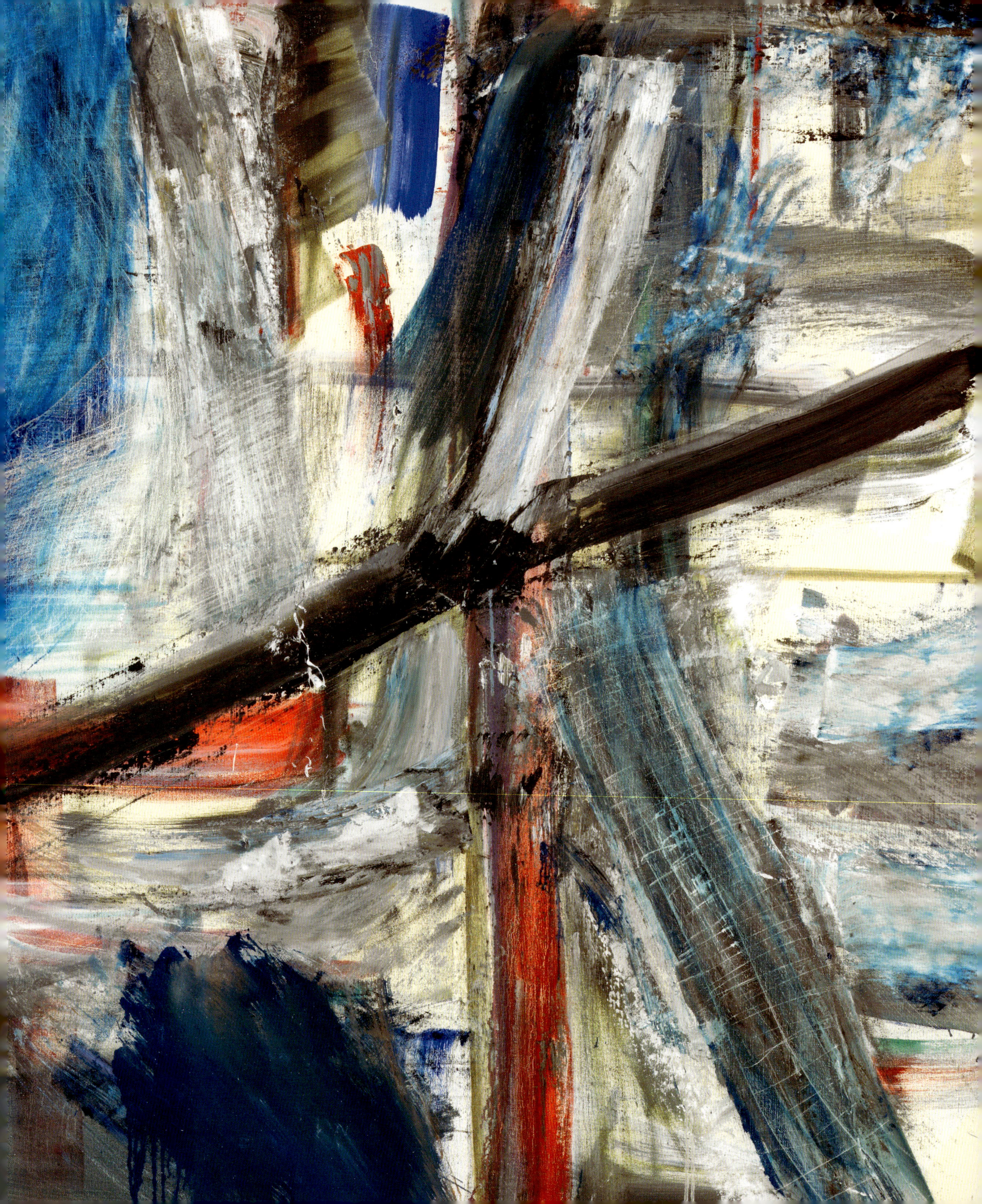

LOUISE FISHMAN
THE ENERGY IN THE RECTANGLE

HELAINE POSNER

According to conventional wisdom, in the 1940s and 1950s a group of male painters living in New York and working in a heroic style on a monumental scale essentially cornered the market on gestural abstraction. If that's true then it raises the question: What's left for an artist to express after the triumph of Abstract Expressionism? And what, if anything, could a woman contribute to the territory so decisively demarcated by Jackson Pollock's ejaculatory drips, Willem de Kooning's fractured women, and Franz Kline's bold, black strokes (FIG. 1)? American painter Louise Fishman's powerful body of work offers a robust response. Both embracing and redefining the aggressively masculine tradition of Abstract Expressionism, she has employed its formal language to create large-scale, gestural abstractions that share the physicality, dynamism, and emotional force of that movement while remaining visually poetic and intimate in tone. As critic Michael Brenson has noted, Fishman's work is "tough without being macho, . . . modest, no matter how grand the aim."[1] Fishman herself observes, "I've always thought of myself as an Expressionist painter. I associate it with a certain kind of passion and a certain kind of marking. A kind of immediacy."[2] The artist seems to revel in the act of painting; in the materiality of oil paint roughly applied by brush, palette knife, or serrated trowel; in the

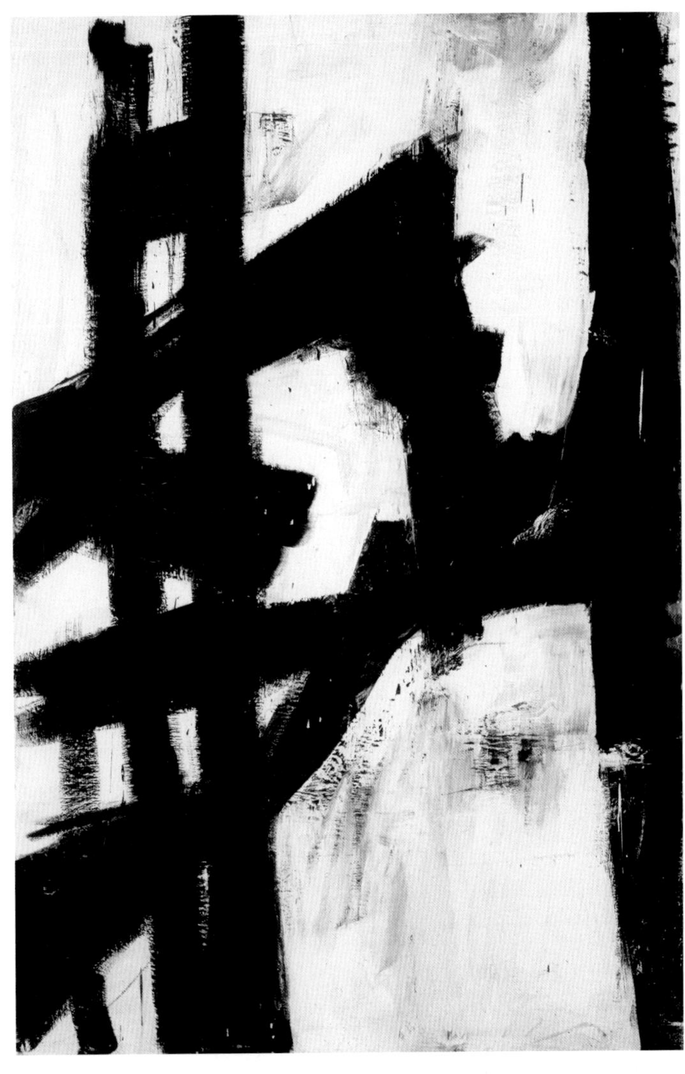

FIGURE 1
Franz Kline (1910–1962), *New York, N.Y.*, 1953
Oil on canvas, 79 x 50½ in. (200.6 x 128.2 cm)
Albright Knox Gallery, Buffalo, Gift of Seymour H. Knox, Jr., 1956

OPPOSITE: Detail of *Crossing the Rubicon*, 2012 (pl. 102)

texture of densely built-up and scraped-down surfaces; in the agile, sweeping gesture. Over the course of a career spanning more than fifty years she has used these tools and techniques to create works that express a broad range of emotions, from explosive anger and profound mourning to, more recently, joyful exuberance. Her work seems to pulsate with life.

Fishman has enduring respect for the Abstract Expressionists and cites them as among her greatest influences. She is not the only woman to lay claim to this male-dominated tradition but, unlike other well-known female practitioners of this style, such as Lee Krasner and Joan Mitchell (FIG. 2), she approaches this gendered form of painting as an active feminist and a lesbian. Speaking of abstraction's appeal, Fishman has recalled, "painting gave me the same feeling of tremendous freedom I had experienced playing ball" as a tomboy in school. She explains: "I was an abstract painter from the start and it was abstraction as much as painting that thrilled me. . . . I saw all those painters [the Abstract Expressionists] as rogues, outside the normal course of things. I knew by the time I got to art school that I was a lesbian. . . . I felt that abstract expressionist work was an appropriate language for me as a queer. It was a hidden language, on the radical fringe, a language appropriate to being separate. In sports I didn't have to explain myself. And in art I didn't have to unless I used figurative art and content. And like baseball, painting was a powerful activity that didn't narrowly define me."[3] It seems that Fishman identified with Abstract Expressionism as a means by which to both express and protect herself as a young artist in the 1950s. It was a choice that served her well, and since the late 1990s she has taken this style of painting to new heights.

Louise Fishman was born in Philadelphia in 1939 and grew up with two practicing women artists. Both her mother, Gertrude Fisher-Fishman, and her paternal aunt, Razel Kapustin, studied at the Barnes Foundation in Merion, Pennsylvania, where they had access to the work of European Modernists such as Henri Matisse, Paul Cézanne, Pierre-Auguste Renoir, Chaim Soutine, and Georges Rouault. Her mother was an abstract painter whose sophisticated, richly colored works particularly

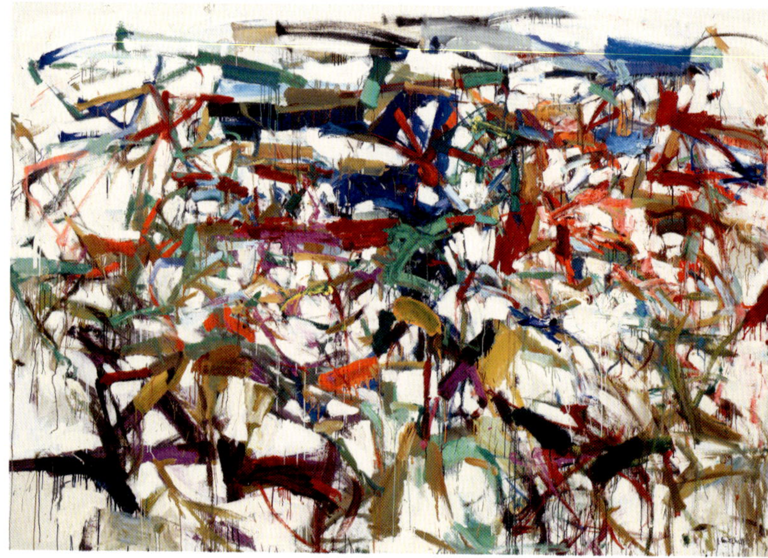

FIGURE 2
Joan Mitchell (1925–1992), *Ladybug*, 1957
Oil on canvas, 77⅞ x 108 in. (197.8 x 274.3 cm)
The Museum of Modern Art, New York

reflect the influence of Matisse. Fishman's aunt, a Social Realist painter, briefly studied in New York with Mexican muralist David Alfaro Siqueiros; Jackson Pollock was among her classmates. She later turned to Jewish themes as her main subjects and maintained an active professional life. As a young girl Fishman spent time in her mother's library, poring over artists' monographs published by the Barnes; reading catalogues her parents had received from the Museum of Modern Art, New York, as a membership benefit; and leafing through issues of *ARTnews*. She was always looking at images but had not yet resolved to become an artist.[4]

Fishman entered art school in 1956, attending the Philadelphia College of Art, the Pennsylvania Academy of Fine Arts, and the Tyler School of Fine Arts, where she earned Bachelor of Fine Arts and Bachelor of Science degrees in 1963. At Tyler, which she describes as "a real academy," she learned oil painting techniques and created still lifes and figure paintings from live models. Although she felt some frustration in this conservative setting, she valued the rigorous training she received from the Tyler faculty and ascribes her respect for traditional materials and methods in part to them. In 1965 Fishman received a Master of Fine Arts degree from the University of Illinois, Urbana-Champaign, then hopped in her Nash Rambler and drove straight to New York City.

The 1960s was a time of great social, political, and cultural upheaval, and New York was the place to be. Fishman quickly became involved with the emerging women's liberation movement, as well as with the movement for lesbian and gay rights, and attended consciousness-raising sessions organized by the radical feminist group known as Redstockings along with meetings of Upper West Side W.I.T.C.H. (Women's International Terrorist Conspiracy from Hell). While feminism raised her awareness and inspired her activism, it was the advent of lesbian feminism that changed her life. As she recently declared, "I knew I was home! I felt like I was walking in my own shoes for the first time."[5] This realization prompted her to question the impact of "all the male stuff in my history" and to make major changes in her art.[6] By the late 1960s Minimalism had eclipsed Abstract Expressionism as the dominant mode of art making, and for about six years, from 1964–70, Fishman followed suit, making a series of hard-edged grid paintings inspired by the work of Sol LeWitt and Ellsworth Kelly (SEE FIG. 3). From this point on, the grid became a constant in her work. Then, in an attempt to eliminate all references to the prevailing male-dominated styles from her art, she abandoned painting altogether and began experimenting with materials and techniques traditionally associated with women, craft, and the handmade. Fishman cut up her canvases

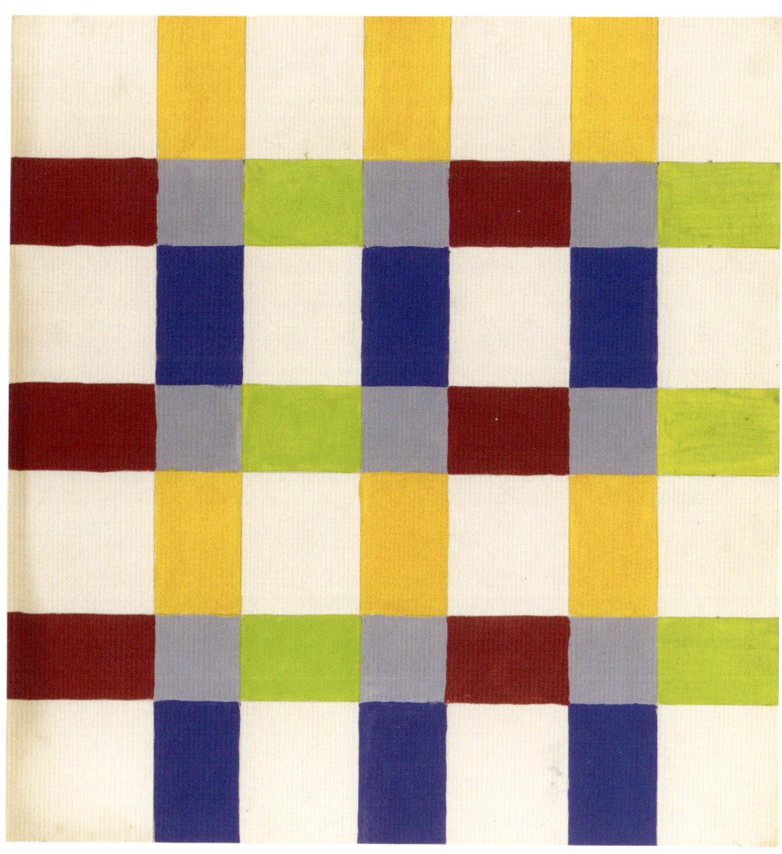

FIGURE 3
Louise Fishman, *Untitled*, 1968
Gouache and graphic on paper, 17½ x 19 in. (44.5 x 48.3 cm)

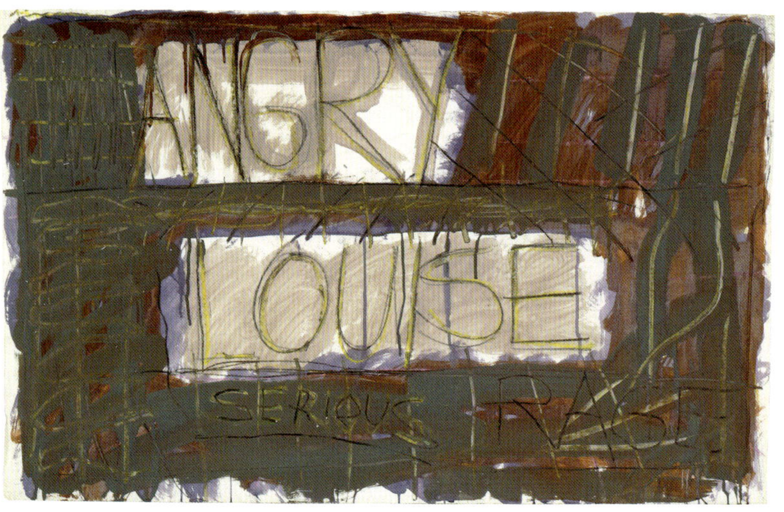

FIGURE 4
Louise Fishman, *Angry Louise*, 1973
Acrylic on paper, 26 x 40 in. (66 x 101.6 cm)
Pl. 12

and wove or stitched the squares together with thread, creating small-scale, quilt-like, gridded collages (SEE PL. 6). She admired the work of Eva Hesse, whose organic sculptures made of malleable materials such as latex and rubber breathed life into Minimalism's geometric forms. Following this example, Fishman relaxed her compositions and broadened her range of materials, even adopting the use of liquid rubber. She continued to use the grid, but it was now the scaffold for a more personal, intimate form of expression.

From 1970 to 1974 Fishman belonged to a consciousness-raising group that included artists Harmony Hammond, Patsy Norvell, and Jenny Snider; dancer Trisha Brown; and anthropologist Esther Newton, among others. They met weekly in SoHo, the new center of the downtown art scene, to talk about their work in the context of feminism. They began these sessions by choosing a topic, such as the challenges facing women artists in a male-dominated culture, and each member of the group then addressed the subject based on her own experience. For Fishman, strong feelings emerged during these meetings, including a deep-seated sense of both personal and collective rage. It was a moment of crisis. As Fishman's spouse, graphic designer Ingrid Nyeboe, recalls: "It wasn't just about a lack of recognition. It was the knowledge that in the seventies women really were second class citizens. The rage level for both straight and lesbian women was so thick you could cut it with a knife. The fact that you knew your life had been adjunct to the culture was unbearable. Your contribution went unacknowledged. What had I accomplished, what had my mother and grandmothers accomplished? It's like ripping yourself apart and putting yourself back together again."[7]

Fishman's rage provided the fuel for a series of works that were her most personal to date. The Angry Paintings of 1973 were unlike anything she had done before, and their ferocity frightened her. She spontaneously scrawled "Angry Louise" on a sheet of paper, surrounded the words with agitated slashes of green on a blood-red ground, and finished with the inscription "Serious Rage" (FIG. 4). Expressing her anger on paper proved to be a transformative experience; Fishman believed she might never again return to abstract painting. She followed *Angry Louise* with a series of works intended to capture the anger felt by various members of her consciousness-raising group, by her mother and aunt, and by art world acquaintances, noted feminists and literary figures, and other women she admired. This impassioned sorority included *Angry Harmony* (for Hammond), *Angry Gertrude* (for her mother and Gertude Stein), *Angry Razel* (for her aunt), *Angry Paula* (for gallerist Paula Cooper), and *Angry Marilyn* (for her heroine, the iconic actress Marilyn Monroe). All told there are thirty of these emphatic works, each bristling with explosive energy (SEE PLS. 9–17). Despite her concerns about where they might lead, these portraits ultimately brought Fishman back to painting.[8]

Although it took nearly five years for Fishman to return to the medium that had been her first love, when she did so she made a total commitment, one that has lasted nearly forty years. She at first worked in oil on linen, applying paint thickly with a palette knife to achieve a highly tactile, almost sculptural effect. As she remarked shortly after returning to painting: "I thought of [the paint] like clay. . . . I was trying to make paintings that felt like objects."[9] And although their subject matter is not overt, Fishman's densely painted, small-scale abstractions of the late 1970s to early 1980s are instilled with meaning. Around the time they were completed, Fishman, though not religious, had become interested in exploring her Jewish roots and identity. She studied Yiddish, read Jewish history and literature (including Elie Wiesel's Holocaust memoir and texts on mystical Judaism), and gave her works titles that reference Jewish folklore, such as *Golem* (PL. 28) and *Tabernacle*. According to the artist, *Ashkenazi* (PL. 26), a bold, symmetrical composition in black, white, and red, is intended to resemble an altar flanked by candles.

In 1987 Fishman bought a farmhouse in upstate New York that continues to serve as a studio and second home. This new residence had a salutary effect on her life and work. After she settled there her paintings began to echo the natural environment in its various forms and phenomena, recalling, as Jill Weinberg and Bernard Lennon have noted, "earth, rocks and stones, water, trees, the light in the woods and the space of the fields."[10] *Headwaters* (PL. 35), a tightly composed, compact painting built of thick, tumbling slabs of green, orange, black, and white, captures the force of a waterfall breaking over bedrock. In contrast, *Stand of Beech* (PL. 36), a thinly painted grid of whitish-grey, turquoise, and pink rectangles, seems bathed in an otherworldly glow evoking moonlight in the trees. In fact, Fishman's paintings tend to gravitate between two poles: alternating between gesture and geometry, they may be earthy or ethereal, intensely physical or quietly spiritual.[11]

In a career typified by experimentation and change, Fishman's next body of work constituted a striking formal departure along with a return to lifelong interests. In the spring of 1988 she traveled to Eastern Europe accompanied by a friend who was an artist, collector, and Holocaust survivor. They visited the region's major cities, including Warsaw, Budapest, and Prague, as well as the sites of the former Nazi extermination camps at Auschwitz and Terezín. The experience affected Fishman profoundly and, upon her return, she created a group of nineteen elegiac paintings collectively titled *Remembrance and Renewal*. They are spare, rectilinear compositions in subtle shades of dark blue, green, and black paint applied in thin washes with broad strokes. Fishman's luminous, hovering blocks of color and deeply somber palette recall Mark Rothko's late work as well as his memorable statement, issued with Adolph Gottlieb, that subject matter is valid only if it is "tragic and timeless."[12] The surfaces of these mournful paintings are layered but smooth, with just the slightest traces of texture provided by the handful of silt laced with human remains that she gathered from the Pond of Living Ashes at Auschwitz and applied to these canvases in a coating of beeswax combined with layers of thinned paint. After visiting the concentration camps she had questioned whether the act of painting could ever hold any meaning, but as she recalls, "when I used the wax and ashes it felt like I had company in the studio. I had these voices with me and I could paint."[13] In a spirit of renewal she gave the paintings Hebrew titles that refer to Passover, a holiday commemorating the emancipation of the Israelites from slavery in ancient Egypt and the reaffirmation of their faith. For example, *Haggadah* (PL. 40) is named for the traditional book of prayers and rituals for the Passover Seder, while *Bitter Herb* (FIG. 5) refers to one of the symbolic foods consumed at that meal. Taken together, the *Remembrance and Renewal* paintings serve as a memorial to the many who were lost and as a testament to the endurance of those who survived. As a body of work it is at once wholly material and oddly transcendent.

Fishman faced another crisis in 1990, when her studio in upstate New York was destroyed by fire and some of her works—as well as all of her tools and equipment—were lost. She developed chronic fatigue syndrome as a result of the trauma and found herself unable to paint. In an effort to recover her health and regain her focus she traveled to New Mexico, where she spent time with painter Agnes Martin. She was inspired by the artist's serene grid paintings and quiet presence, and she realized that for Martin the grid was more than a simple compositional device, it was a form of meditation. This notion resonated with Fishman, who had practiced Buddhist meditation on a daily basis for years. She decided to return to the grid as a tool for balancing structure and spontaneity in her art. Fishman began to paint with renewed strength and confidence, creating large-scale, vertically oriented works such as *Sanctum Sanctorum* and *Valles Marineris* (both 1992; PLS. 48, 49), a canvas painted primarily with a roller that features shimmering blocks of pale green framed by a gray-black grid that alternately suggests flatness and depth.[14]

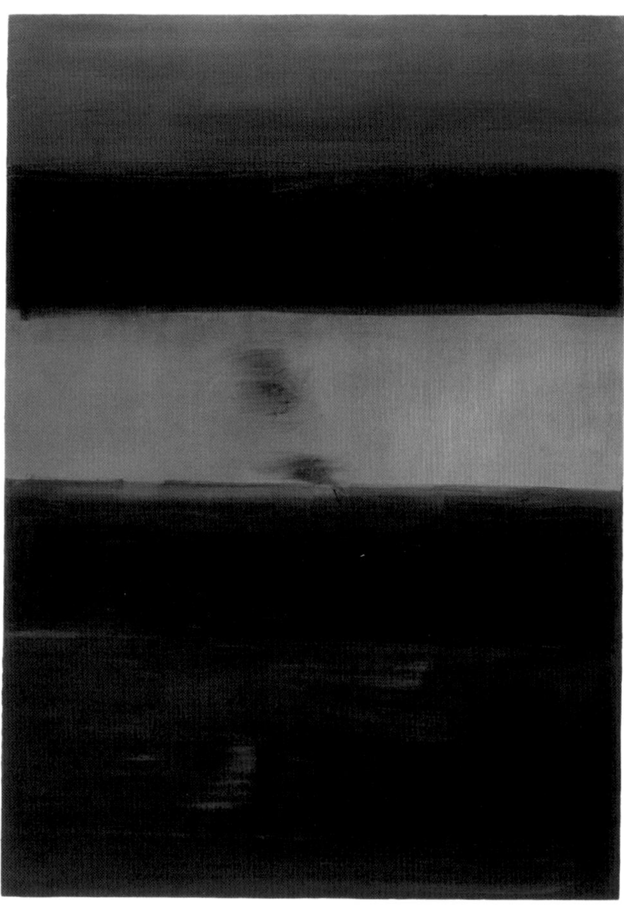

FIGURE 5
Louise Fishman, *Bitter Herb*, 1988
Oil on linen, 65 x 45 in. (165.1 x 114.3 cm)
Courtesy of Fernando Luis Alvarez Gallery, Stamford, Connecticut
Pl. 38

Fishman first became aware of the importance of the picture plane—the extreme foreground or point of visual contact between the picture and viewer—and the grid's potential as a flattening device in Karl Sherman's design class at the Philadelphia College of Art in the mid-1950s. Sherman encouraged his students to focus on the dynamics of the canvas as a whole. He believed that different points in a painting's rectangular surface contain different energy levels, with some areas highly active and others inert. Fishman absorbed these ideas and later observed of her process: "As I make a mark I am aware of the impact on every square inch of the painting."[15] For the artist, composition became a sort of dance on the surface of the canvas as she recorded her movements with each mark.

Fishman's increasingly ambitious works of the 1990s display a vigorous physicality that is expressed, in part, through a lively interplay between gesture and grid. The dazzling *Blonde Ambition* (1995; PL. 52), a boldly graphic, black-and-white painting whose composition Fishman describes as a collapsing grid, captures the look and vitality of a signature Franz Kline but is inspired by a far different source. Fishman watched Madonna's 1990 Blond Ambition World Tour on television and immediately identified with the pop icon in her athleticism and her toughness. She recalls: "I saw this little Tom Boy dancing around and thought 'she's like me!' "[16] Madonna also emulated Marilyn Monroe, who is the other blond in the painting. In this work a stark-white grid veers diagonally toward the left, resembling a figure with arms outstretched and head tossed backward; the gritty white paint, textured with sand, is as thick as plaster.

The radiant *For There She Was* and *The Sunrise Ruby* (PLS. 65, 67) are densely painted, tactile works whose surfaces have been built-up, scraped-down, and built-up again in a process the artist likens to an "archaeological dig."[17] Both canvases are nearly square in format, their gestural brushstrokes aligned with rectilinear grids. Here Fishman's palette, newly colorful, comprises glowing yellows and reds and rich earth tones that seem to spring from natural forms and forces. Although more of the land than of the sea, these works evoke the luminous, nearly abstract seascapes of British painter J. M. W. Turner, a connection that deepens in Fishman's more recent paintings, as will be discussed below. Perhaps more significantly, they point to Fishman's wholehearted embrace of the postwar American tradition of large-scale gestural abstraction, which, by the time these canvases were painted, in the late 1990s, she had begun to make her own.

Although Fishman may be best known for a highly physical painting process that produces gestural, expressive marks that follow the movement and extension of her body, she has also, since 1997, worked with calligraphic markings to chart what she calls the "language of the hand."[18] Her interest in such forms derived in part from a study of Hebrew characters and Chinese and Japanese calligraphy, which she admires as much for their aesthetics as for the meanings they convey. Of course, the impact of Pollock's, Mark Tobey's, and Bradley Walker Tomlin's sinuous lines cannot be ignored. Not surprisingly, the calligraphic mark first appeared in Fishman's drawings, later joining gesture and the grid as structural elements for her paintings. *In Paul's Hands* (PL. 72), made in memory of the late writer and translator Paul Schmidt, features an interweaving of radiant yellow and green calligraphic strokes that creates an amplified sense of movement within the grid. And in *Slippery Slope* (PL. 92) a network of fluid black lines graces a field of Prussian blue.

Fishman is aware of a shared "quality of expression" across the work of the artists who have most greatly impacted her. Her sources include the canvases of modernists such as Rouault, Soutine, Kline, and Alberto Giacometti and nineteenth- and mid-twentieth-century American poetry (FIGS. 6, 7). In *The Art of Losing* (PL. 79), a large-scale, brooding work named for a poem by Elizabeth Bishop and dedicated to a lost love, a grid constructed of thick black bands drips down a translucent blue-white plane, giving the impression that, as critic Faye Hirsch puts it, "the whole painting is weeping."[19] The heavy black contours and cool, glowing light suggest stained glass and recall the work of Rouault and Soutine, as well as that of De Stijl artist Piet Mondrian, whose work Fishman had the opportunity to view at the

Barnes Foundation and the Philadelphia Museum of Art when she was a student. Notably, Fishman has also looked farther afield, drawing inspiration from medieval crucifixes and religious masterworks such as Rogier van der Weyden's *Descent from the Cross* (ca. 1435) and Matthias Grünewald's *Isenheim Altarpiece* (1512–16). Like these works, her paintings can be very sculptural. *Zero at the Bone* (PL. 99), for example, is a dense composition of thickly applied bands of earth and mineral colors whose materiality is palpable. It is a powerful work in the Abstract Expressionist mode whose "vitality stems from an appreciation of European culture merged with American spontaneity and force," according to critic Jonathan Goodman.[20] As in *The Art of Losing*, this painting is inspired by poetry as well as the history of art. The phrase "zero at the bone," the last line of a poem by Emily Dickinson, describes an intense sensation akin to a chilling fear.

Fishman's new work took an exhilarating turn after she traveled in fall 2011 to Venice, where she spent two months as artist in residence at the Emily Harvey Foundation. During her stay she took hundreds of photographs and painted numerous small watercolors. She was inspired by the color, light, and atmosphere of the city, with its ubiquitous waters and luminous blue skies. Naturally, she sought out the work of the great Venetian painters such as Titian, Tintoretto, Giorgione, and Veronese, and she has likened the thrill of walking in their footsteps to the experience of traversing "sacred ground."[21] Fishman made this journey with Nyeboe, who was then her new love and six months later would become

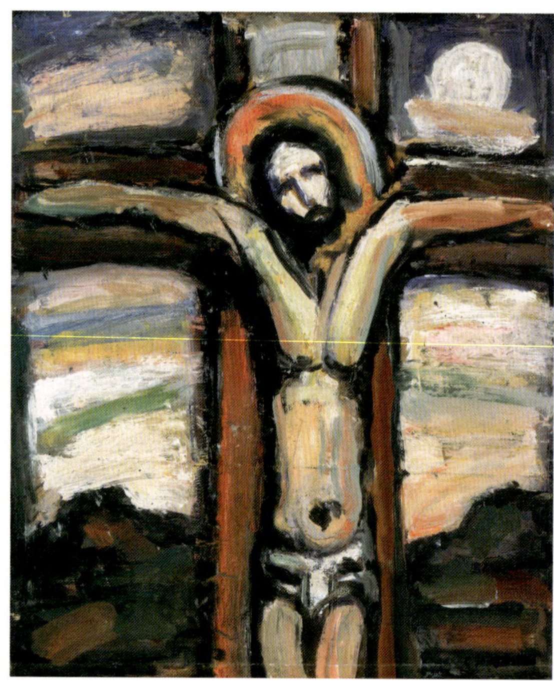

FIGURE 6
George Rouault (1871–1958), *Christ*, ca. 1938
Oil on canvas, 19⅜ x 15⅞ in. (49.2 x 40.3 cm)
Philadelphia Museum of Art, The Samuel S. White III and Vera White Collection, 1967

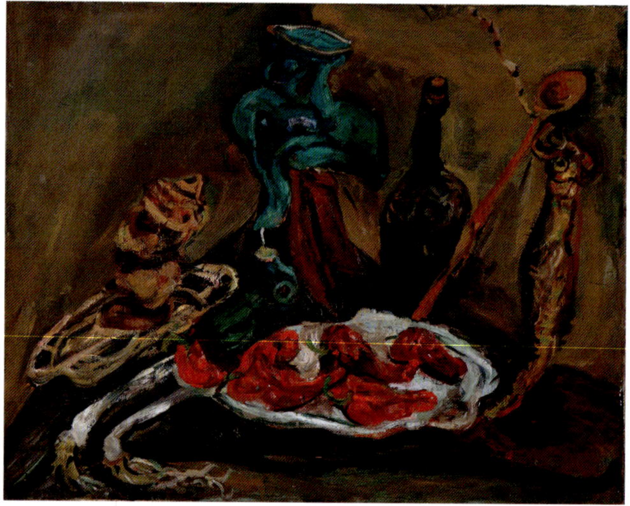

FIGURE 7
Chaim Soutine (1893–1943), *Fish, Peppers, Onions (Poissons, poivres et oignons)*, ca. 1919
Oil on canvas, 23⅝ x 28¹⁵⁄₁₆ in. (60 x 73.5 cm)
The Barnes Foundation, Philadelphia, BF2042

her spouse. It was a creatively rich and personally fulfilling time.

Fishman returned to her New York studio and immediately began making paintings that were based on the Venice watercolors yet quite different in their materials, scale, and impact. She describes the new works as having an "odd theatricality about them . . . this quality of everything moving up and out, explosively," a condition she sees as a direct response to Titian's *Assumption of the Virgin* (FIG. 8).[22] *Serenissima* (PL. 105) is titled for the name Venice bore for more than one thousand years as a city-state; it translates as "most serene republic." Paradoxically, it is a highly dynamic work in which all parts appear to be in perpetual motion, broad stokes of paint radiating from the center of the canvas with amazing force. By contrast, *Crossing the Rubicon* (PL. 102), which is named for Julius Caesar's proverbial point of no return, is animated by vibrant slashes of color that appear to gravitate toward the middle of the composition and spin. Unlike her earlier, densely painted and composed canvases, Fishman's Venetian works appear to open up and let in air and light, breathing new life into her art.

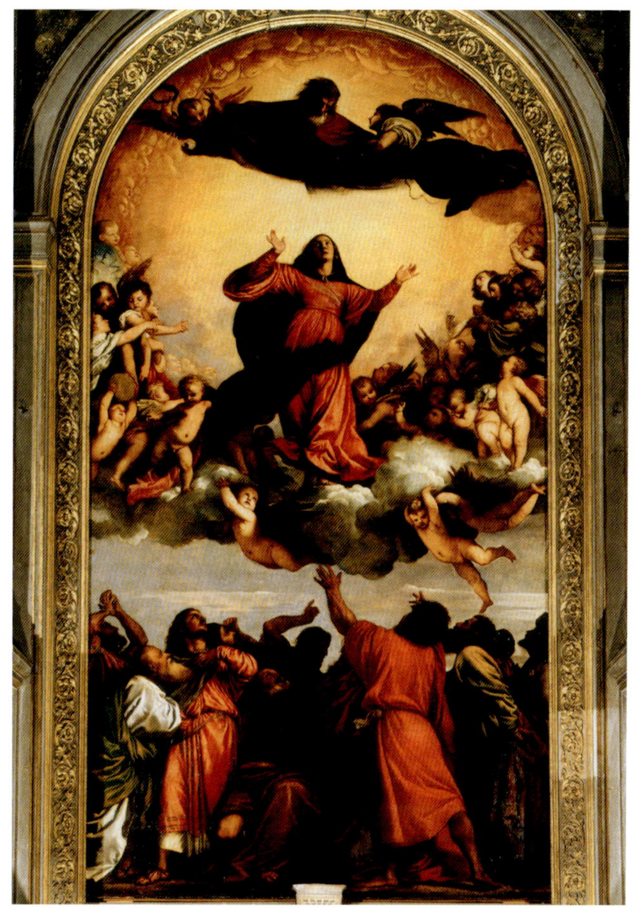

FIGURE 8
Titian (Tiziano Vecellio; ca. 1488–1576), *The Assumption of the Virgin*, 1516–18
Oil on panel, 270 x 140 in. (685.8 x 355.6 cm)
Chiesa di Santa Maria dei Frari, Venice

And then there are the blues in these works—the phthalos, ultramarines, and related tones, occasionally interrupted by blazing bands of red. Although Fishman had used blue before, the vibrant hues of her Venetian paintings are something new. Filled with allusions to the Italian city, they echo the brilliant shades of Titian, the iridescence of a Murano glass vase, the sky, and the Venetian Lagoon and the reflections in its waters. Fishman has said that in Venice the air itself feels as if it's colored.[23] In addition, there is a play among the blues in these works that suggests the dancing of light on all surfaces. But despite their ethereal blend of color and light, these large-scale gestural abstractions retain the physicality, grandeur, and emotional punch that mark the best of the Abstract Expressionist tradition, qualities Fishman continues to pursue in her most recent work.

There was another shift in Fishman's work after she went to London in fall 2014 for the opening of an exhibition of her Venice watercolors. While there she had the chance to see several important museum shows, including presentations of the late works of Rembrandt and Turner at the National Gallery and at Tate Britain (FIG. 9), respectively, and an installation of John Constable's paintings at the Victoria

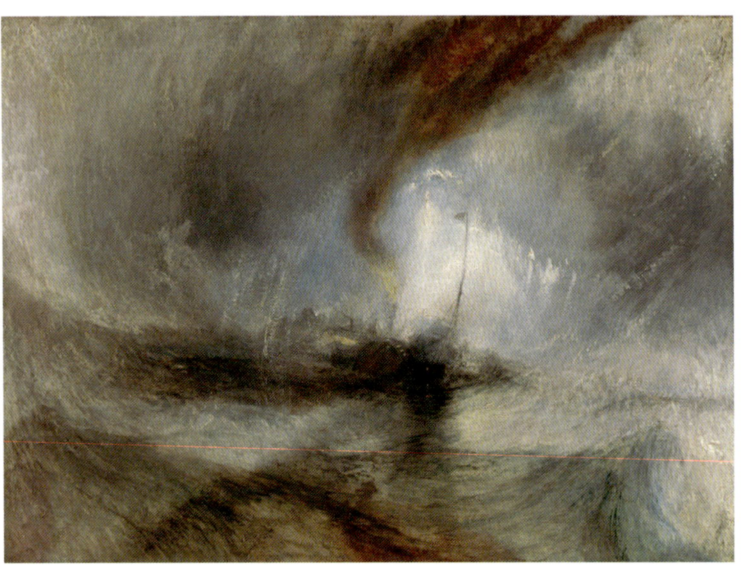

FIGURE 9
Joseph Mallord William Turner (1775–1851), *Snow Storm – Steam-Boat off a Harbour's Mouth*, exhibited 1842
36 x 48 in. (91.4 x 121.9 cm)
Tate Gallery, London

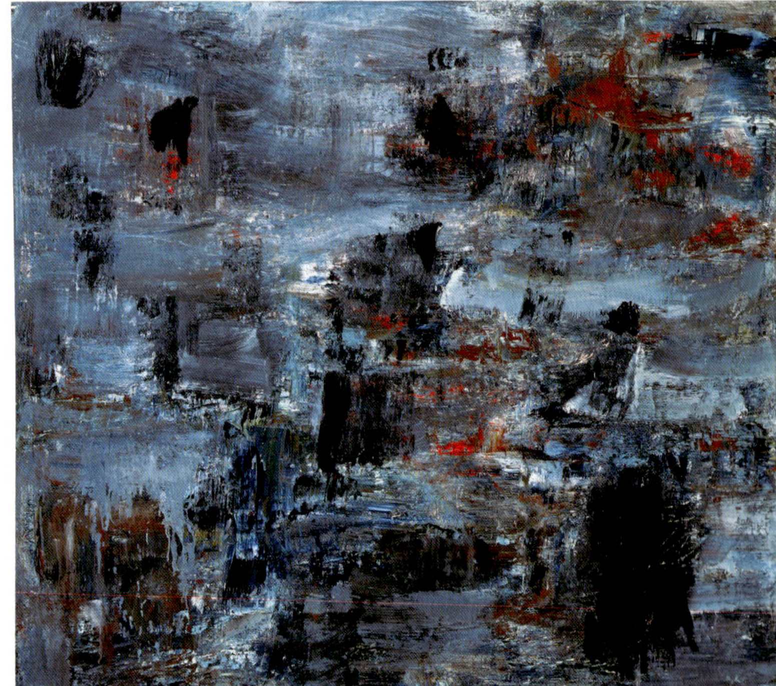

FIGURE 10
Louise Fishman, *For There She Was*, 1998
Oil on linen, 76¼ x 82 in. (193.7 x 208.3 cm)
Collection of Romita Shetty and Nasser Ahmad
Pl. 65

and Albert Museum. Though each artist made a strong impression she felt a special kinship with Turner, who is known for his views of Venice. *Margate* (2015, PL. 114) is Fishman's homage to the British master, who studied and painted in Margate, Kent, a seaside town to which he returned throughout his life. In this work a small slash of red is tossed about by churning stokes of blue, green, and white, recalling Turner's portrayals of natural phenomena such as light, rain, and wind in scenes of ships battered by stormy seas in a manner also reminiscent of *For There She Was* (FIG. 10) and *The Sunrise Ruby*, Fishman's works from the late 1990s mentioned above. Yet in *Margate* the affinity goes further, as Fishman captures the intensity of a Turner seascape and, remarkably, distills it to its essence. Likewise, in *Kreisleriana* (PL. 113), a celebratory work named for a piano composition by Robert Schumann and dedicated to his fellow Romantic composer Frédéric Chopin, Fishman captures the substance of gestural abstraction with a few broad, raw, vertical strokes of bold color. Over the course of a career spanning more than five decades she has fully mastered these and other masters of the arts, interpreting their work through the lens of her own experience.

Although Fishman has successfully worked within the largely masculine idiom of Abstract Expressionism and acknowledges a debt to a number of major male artists from the Renaissance through Modernism, her work is most profoundly shaped by the fact of having come of age as a woman artist in the 1960s and 1970s. That was a time when feminism made significant inroads into the social consciousness and, in terms of art, opened the door to a wide-ranging pluralism, seen in works that explore multiple materials, styles, subjects, and ideas. In a long career marked by both experimentation and consistency, Fishman pushed formalist abstraction beyond the standard notions of purity and universality that defined much modernist art. One of her great contributions, along with peers such as Elizabeth Murray, Mary Heilmann, Suzan Frecon, and Pat Steir, has been her determination to introduce content into this traditionally male bastion and make room for firsthand experience and personal expression.[24] While Fishman's paintings do not openly tell the story of her life, they arise from her personal, political, and cultural experiences to form a body of work that offers deep aesthetic rewards while both redefining and expanding the scope of abstraction.

Notes

1. Michael Brenson, "Louise Fishman," in *Louise Fishman*, exh. cat. (Elkins Park, PA: Tyler Galleries, Tyler School of Art, 1993), unpaginated.
2. Louise Fishman in Carter Ratcliff, Hayden Herrera, Sarah McFadden, and Joan Simon, "Expressionism Today: An Artists' Symposium," *Art in America* 70, no. 11 (December 1982): 66.
3. Louise Fishman in Holland Cotter, "Art after Stonewall: Twelve Artists Interviewed—Louise Fishman," *Art in America* 82, no. 6 (June 1994): 59–60.
4. Carrie Moyer, "A Restless Spirit," *Art in America* 100, no. 9 (October 2012): 128. I am indebted to Carrie Moyer for confirming many details of Louise Fishman's biography.
5. Louise Fishman, conversation with the author, March 13, 2015.
6. "Zero at the Bone: Louise Fishman Speaks with Carrie Moyer," *Art Journal* 71, no. 4 (Winter 2012): 39.
7. Ingrid Nyeboe, conversation with the author, March 13, 2015.
8. Writer and artist Catherine Lord makes this point in her essay "Their Memory is Playing Tricks on Her: Notes Toward a Calligraphy of Rage," in *WACK!: Art and the Feminist Revolution*, exh. cat., ed. Cornelia Butler and Lisa Gabrielle Mark (Los Angeles: The Museum of Contemporary Art, 2007), 445.
9. Miriam Seidel, "Material Imperatives," *Art in America* 81, no. 9 (September 1993): 94–99.
10. Jill Weinberg and Bernard Lennon, *Louise Fishman: Paintings 1987–1989*, exh. cat. (New York: Lennon, Weinberg, Inc., 1989), unpaginated.
11. An exhibition titled *Louise Fishman: Between Geometry and Gesture* was presented at Galerie Kienzle & Gmeiner, Berlin, in 2008.
12. Adolph Gottlieb and Mark Rothko, Letter to Edward Alden Jewell, art editor for the *New York Times,* June 7, 1943. Reprinted as appendix A in *Adolph Gottlieb: A Retrospective*, ed. Lawrence Alloway and Mary Davis MacNaughton (New York: Adolph and Esther Gottlieb Foundation in association with The Arts Publisher, Inc., 1981), 169.
13. Fishman, conversation with the author, March 13, 2015.
14. *Valles Marinaris* is a one of a group of paintings by Fishman referring to the planet Mars.
15. Louise Fishman, conversation with the author, March 16, 2015.
16. Ibid.
17. Louise Fishman in Nathan Kernan, "A Field of Stones," in *Louise Fishman,* exh. cat. (New York: Cheim & Read, 1998), unpaginated.
18. Louise Fishman in Sharon L. Butler, "In Conversation: Louise Fishman with Sharon Butler," *The Brooklyn Rail*, October 4, 2012, http://www.brooklynrail.org/2012/10/art/louise-fishman-with-sharon-butler.
19. Faye Hirsch, "The Disputatious Abstraction of Louise Fishman," in *Louise Fishman: The Tenacity of Painting, Paintings from 1970 to 2005*, exh. cat. (Hanover, NH: Dartmouth College, 2007), unpaginated.
20. Louise Fishman in Jonathan Goodman, "Louise Fishman," *The Brooklyn Rail*, October 4, 2012, http://www.brooklynrail.org/2012/10/artseen/louise-fishman-artseen.
21. Fishman, conversation with the author, March 16, 2015.
22. Fishman in Butler, "In Conversation."
23. Fishman, conversation with the author, March 16, 2015.
24. I am indebted to my colleagues Eleanor Heartney, Nancy Princenthal, Sue Scott, and Susan Sterling for their insights into feminism and abstraction.

PLATES I

Works are courtesy of the artist and Cheim & Read, New York, unless otherwise noted.

PLATE 1. *In and Out*, 1968. Acrylic on canvas, 66 x 50 in. (167.6 x 127 cm)

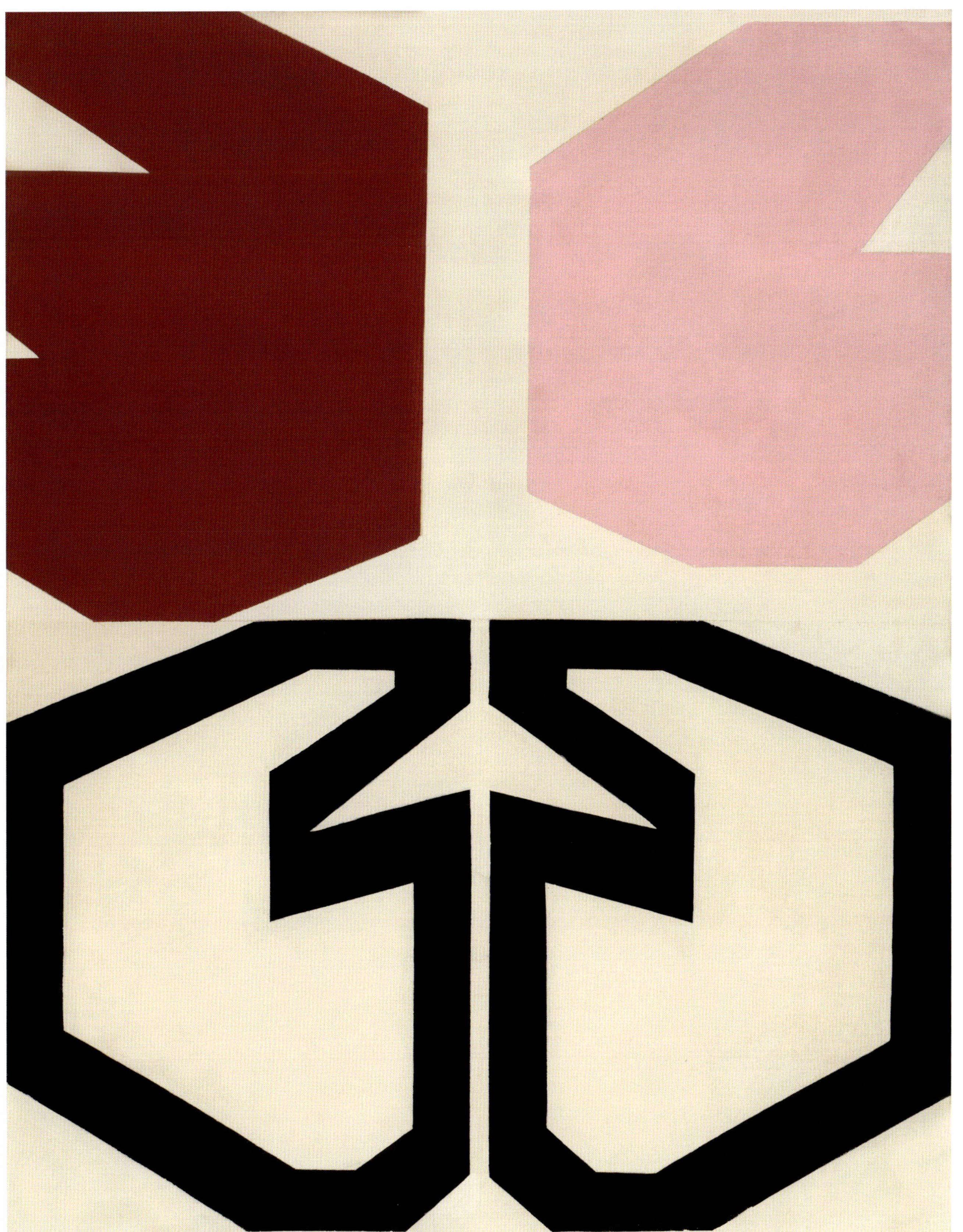

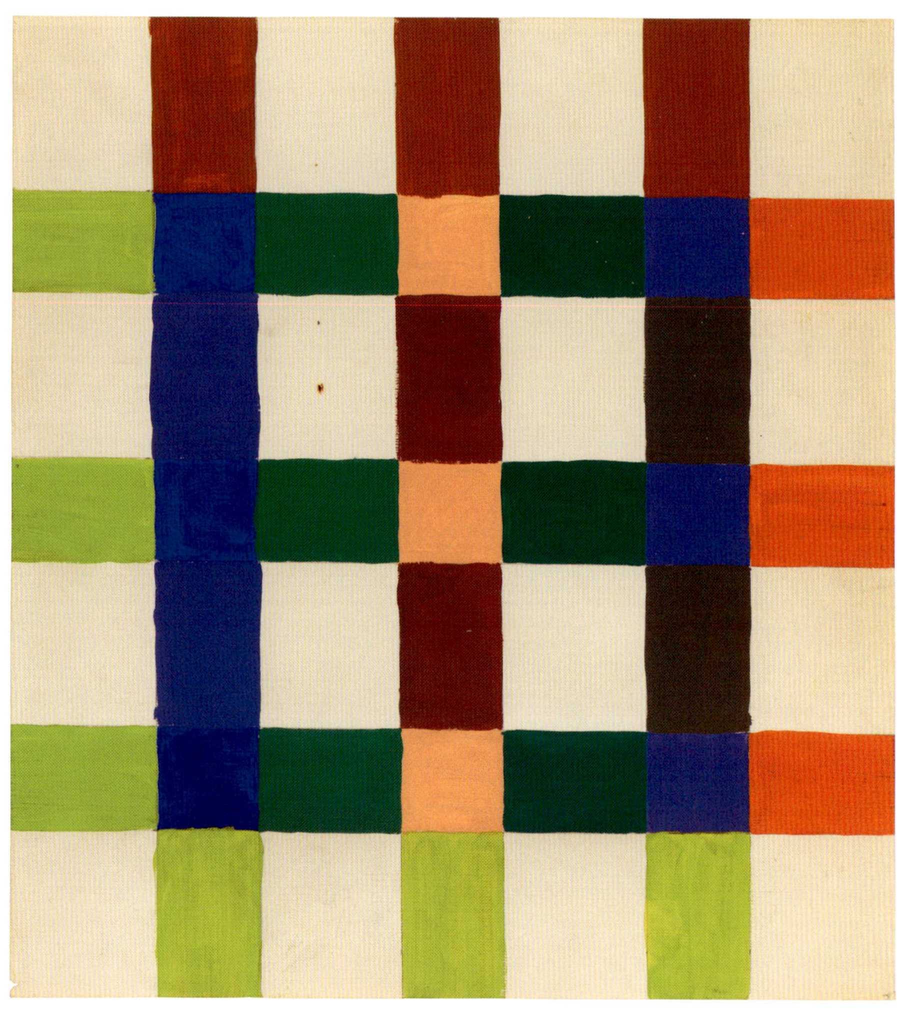

PLATE 2. *Untitled*, 1968. Gouache and graphite on paper, 19 x 17 in. (48.3 x 43.2 cm)
PLATE 3. *Untitled*, 1970. Acrylic and pastel on canvas, 66 x 51 in. (167.6 x 129.5 cm). Collection of Carol A. Calhoun

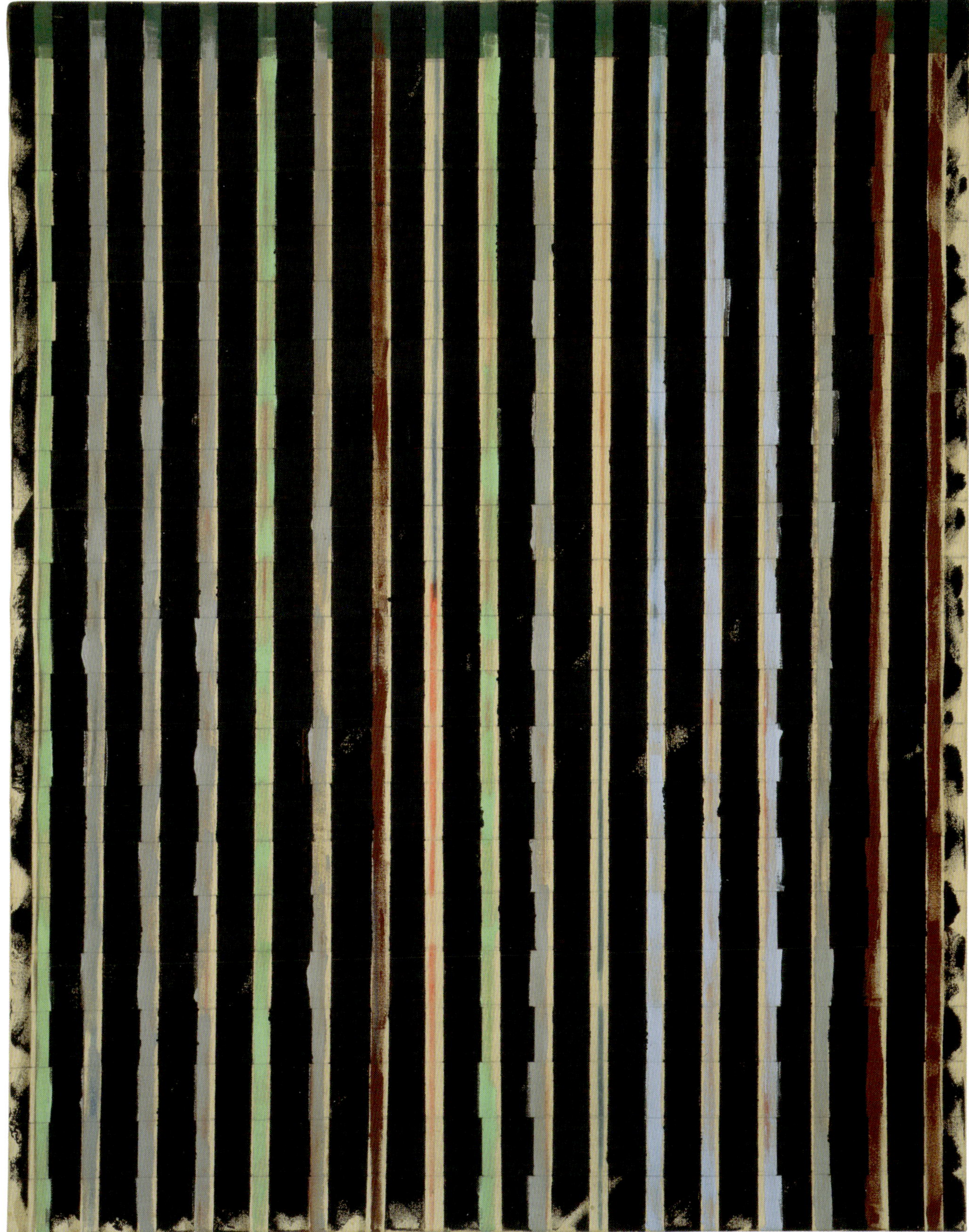

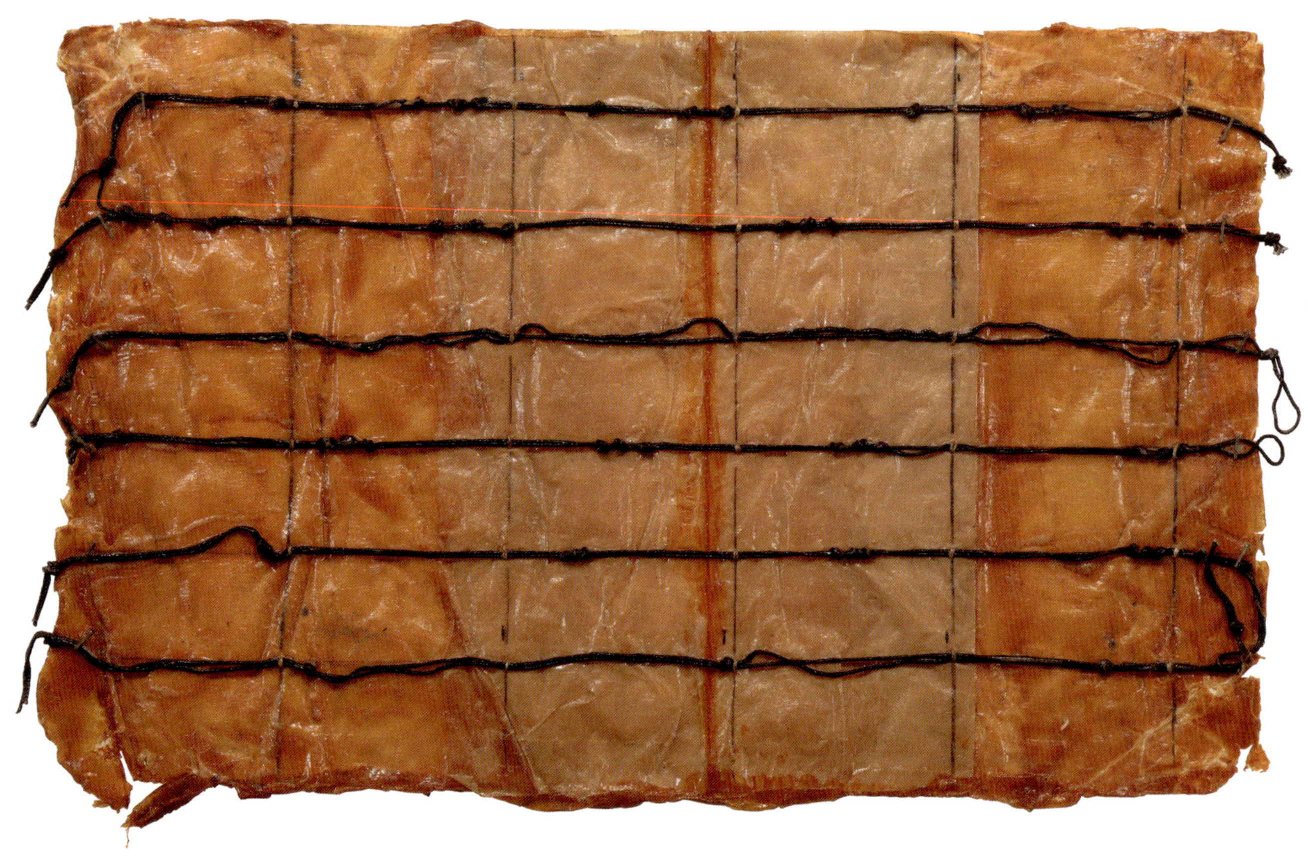

PLATE 4. *Untitled*, 1971. Rubber, graphite, string, and staples on tracing paper, 14 x 21 in. (35.6 x 53.3 cm)

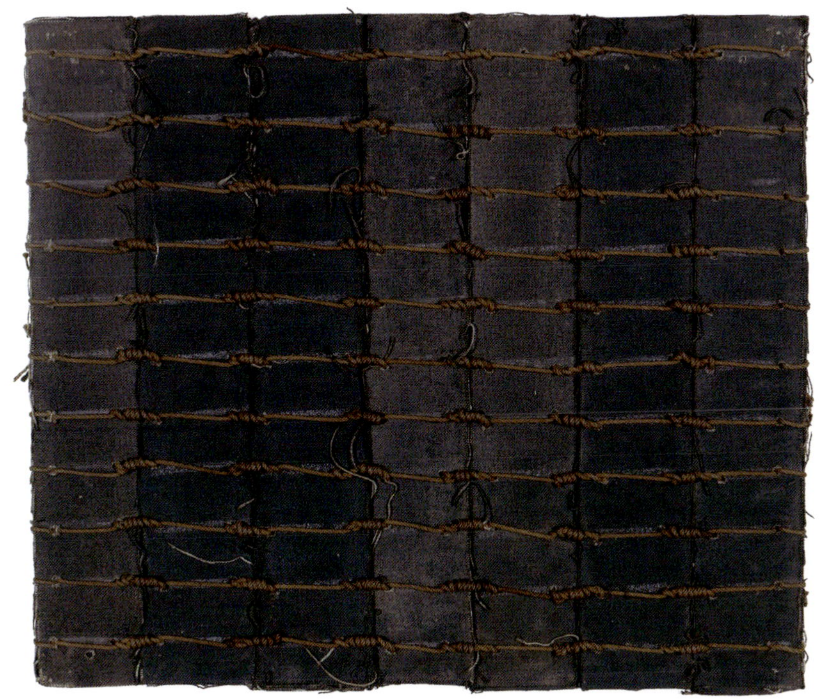

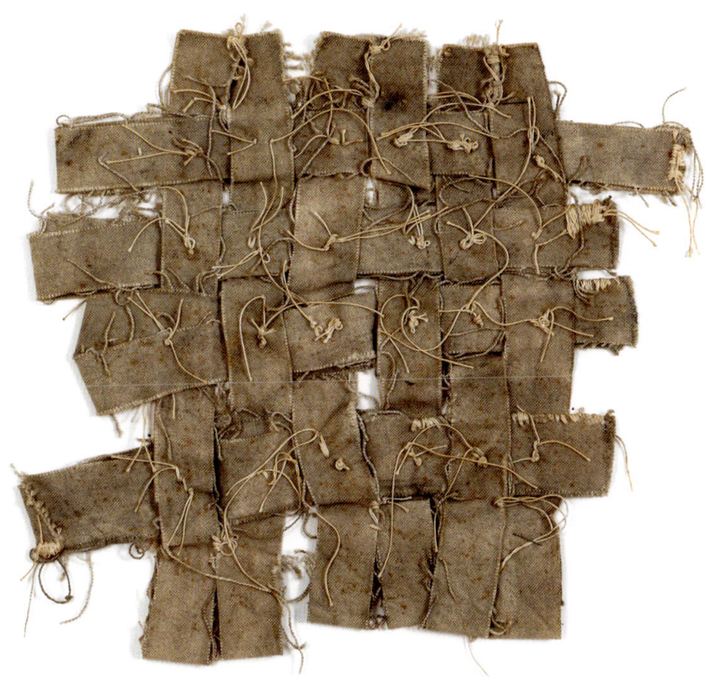

PLATE 5. *Untitled*, 1971. Acrylic on canvas with chalk and string, 12 x 13½ in. (30.5 x 34.3 cm)
PLATE 6. *Untitled*, 1971. Canvas and string, 10 x 10 in. (25.4 x 25.4 cm). Collection of Lynne and Bertram Strieb, Philadelphia

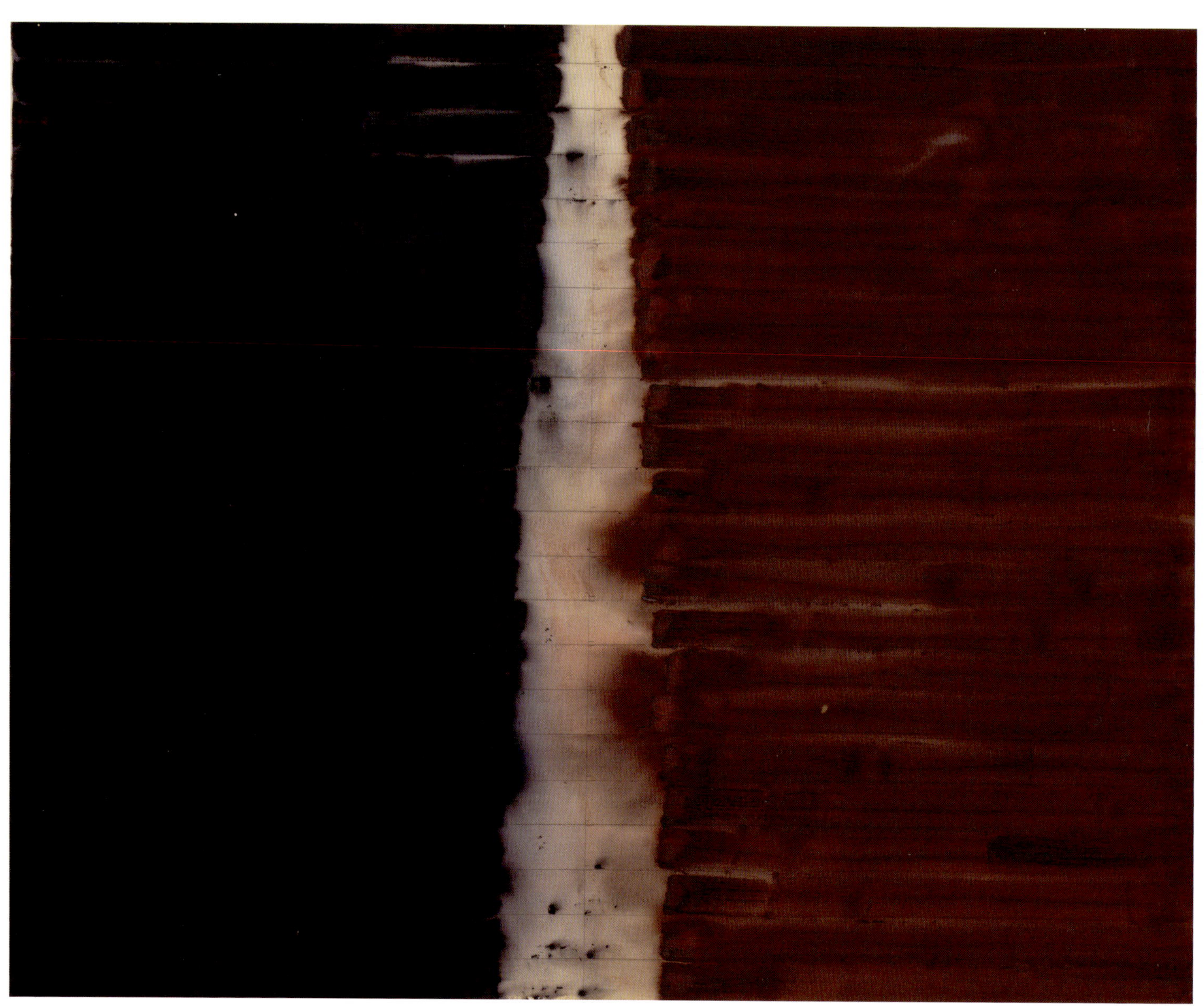

PLATE 7. *Untitled*, 1971. Acrylic and graphite on canvas, 65 x 78 in. (165.1 x 198.1 cm)

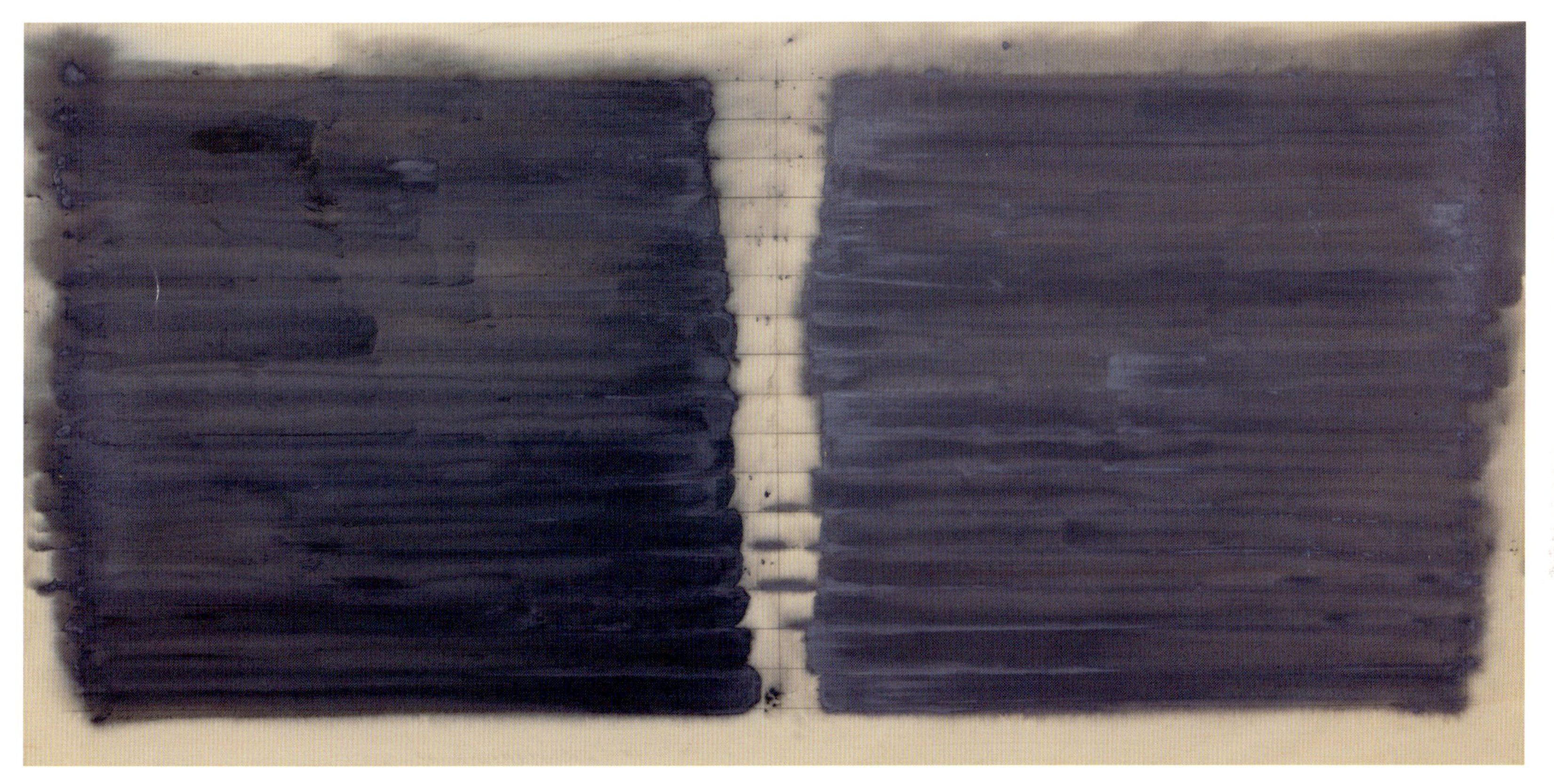

PLATE 8. *Untitled*, 1971. Acrylic and graphite on canvas, 48 x 94 in. (121.9 x 238.8 cm)

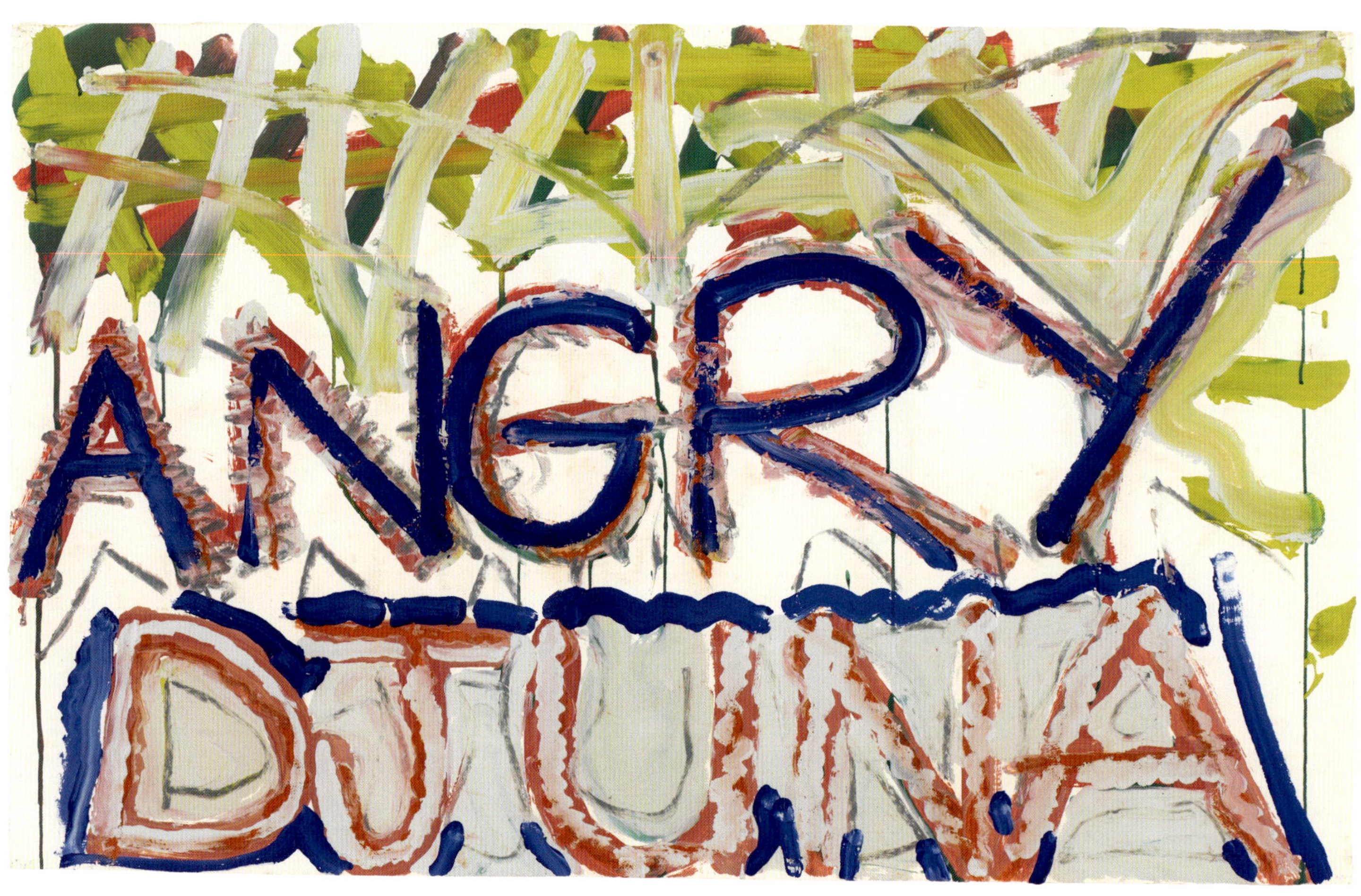

PLATE 9. *Angry Djuna*, 1973. Acrylic on paper, 26 x 40 in. (66 x 101.6 cm)

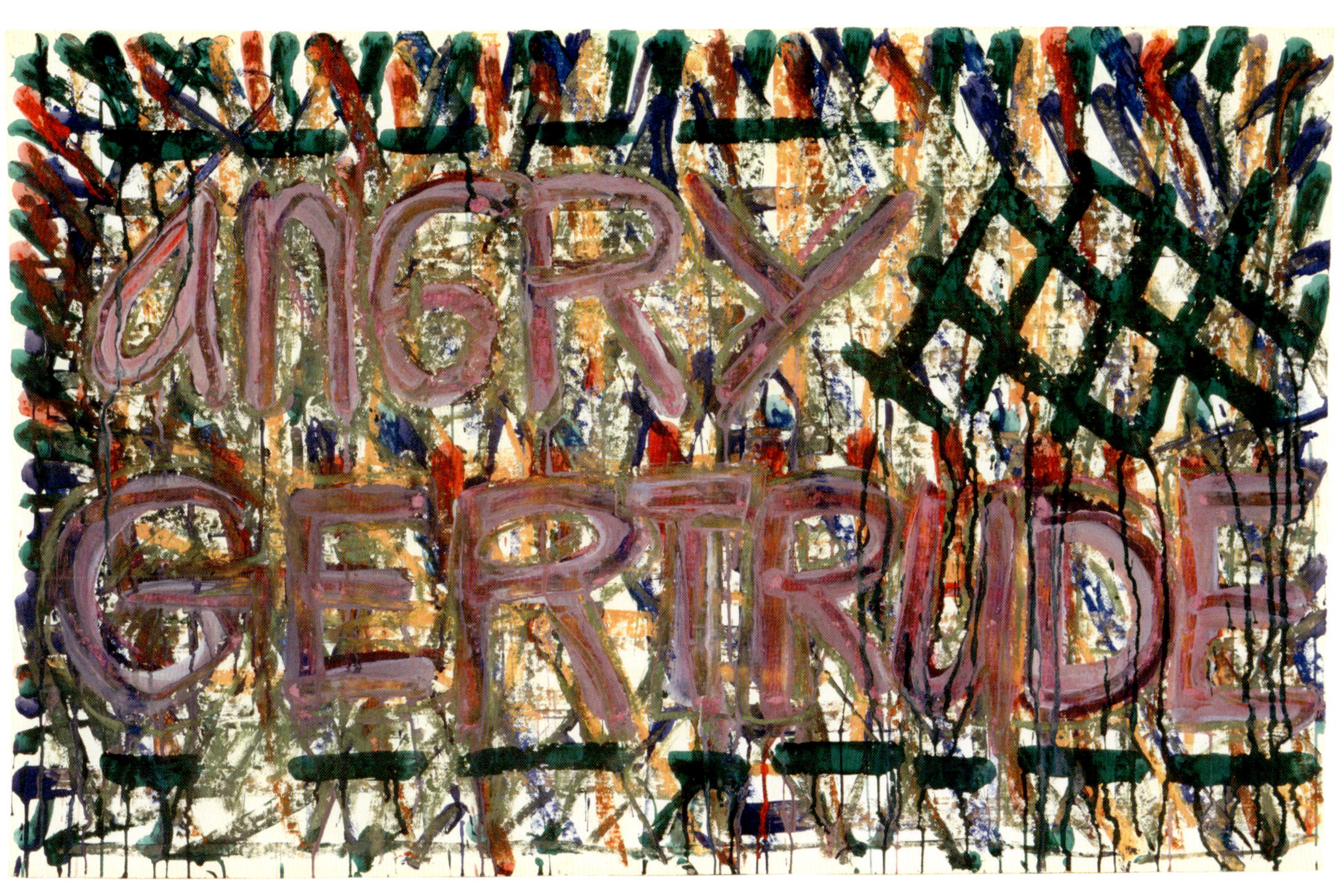

PLATE 10. *Angry Gertrude*, 1973. Acrylic on paper, 26 x 40 in. (66 x 101.6 cm)

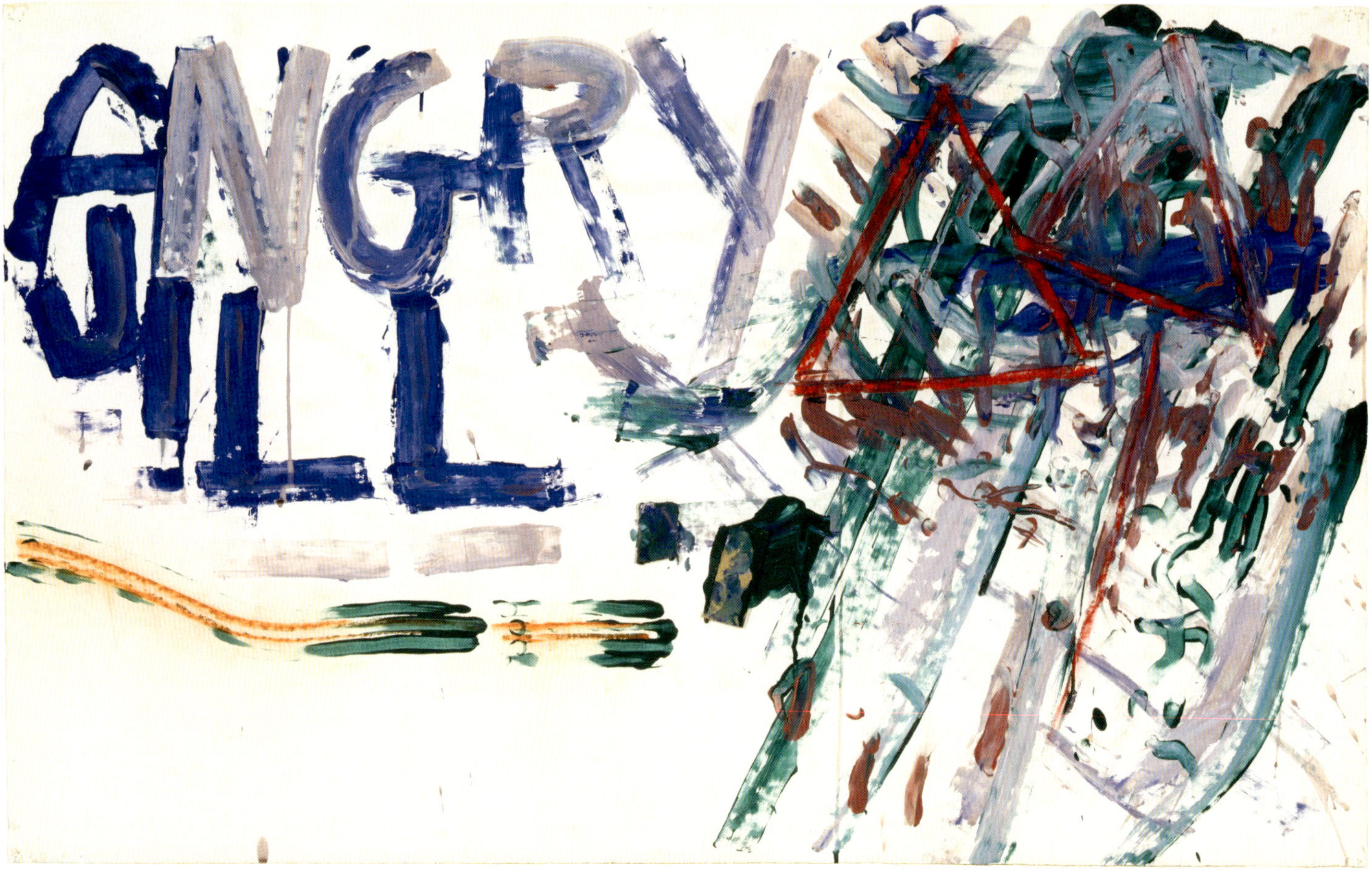

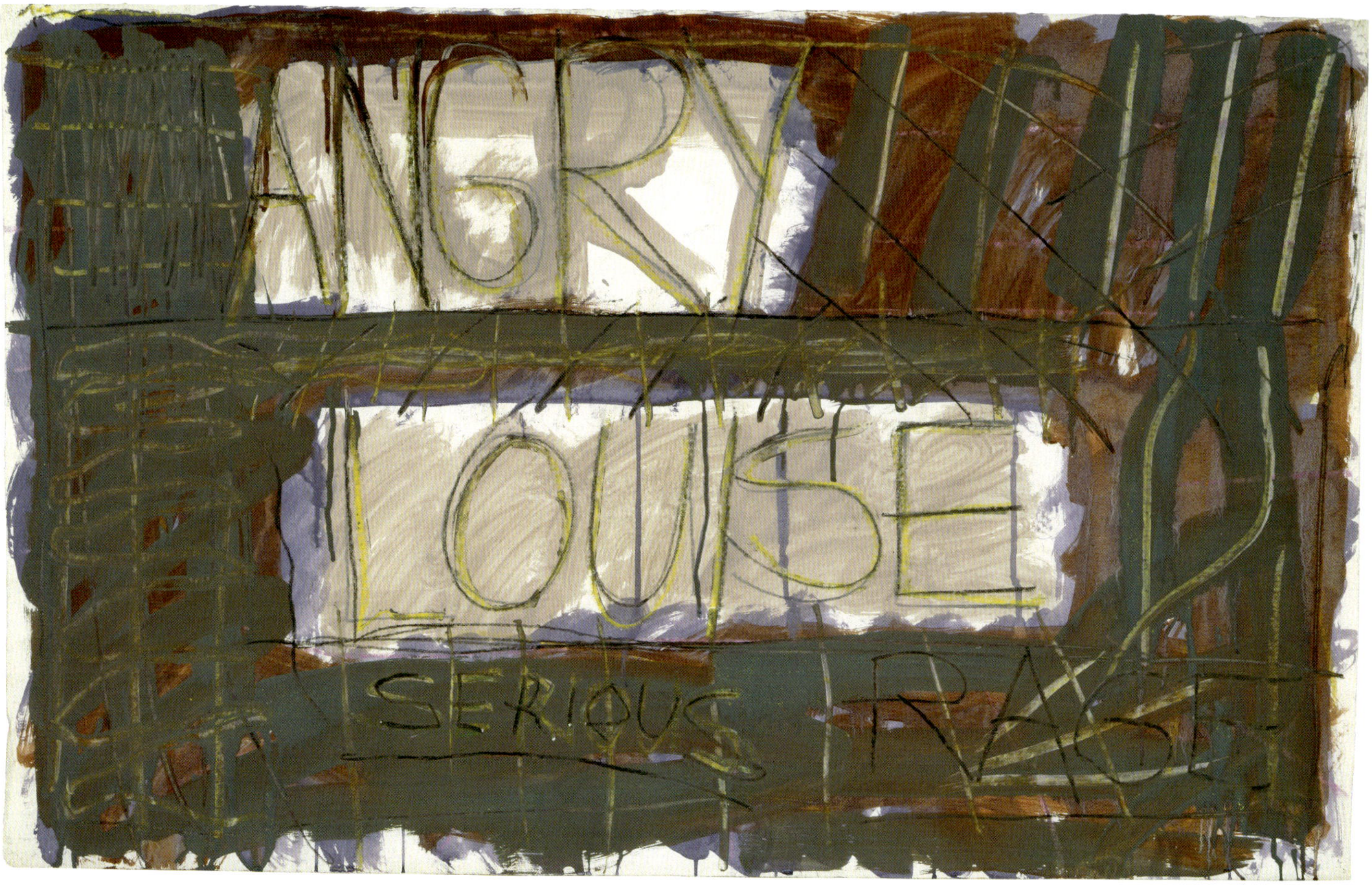

PLATE 11. *Angry Jill*, 1973. Acrylic on paper, 26 x 40 in. (66 x 101.6 cm)
PLATE 12. *Angry Louise*, 1973. Acrylic on paper, 26 x 40 in. (66 x 101.6 cm)

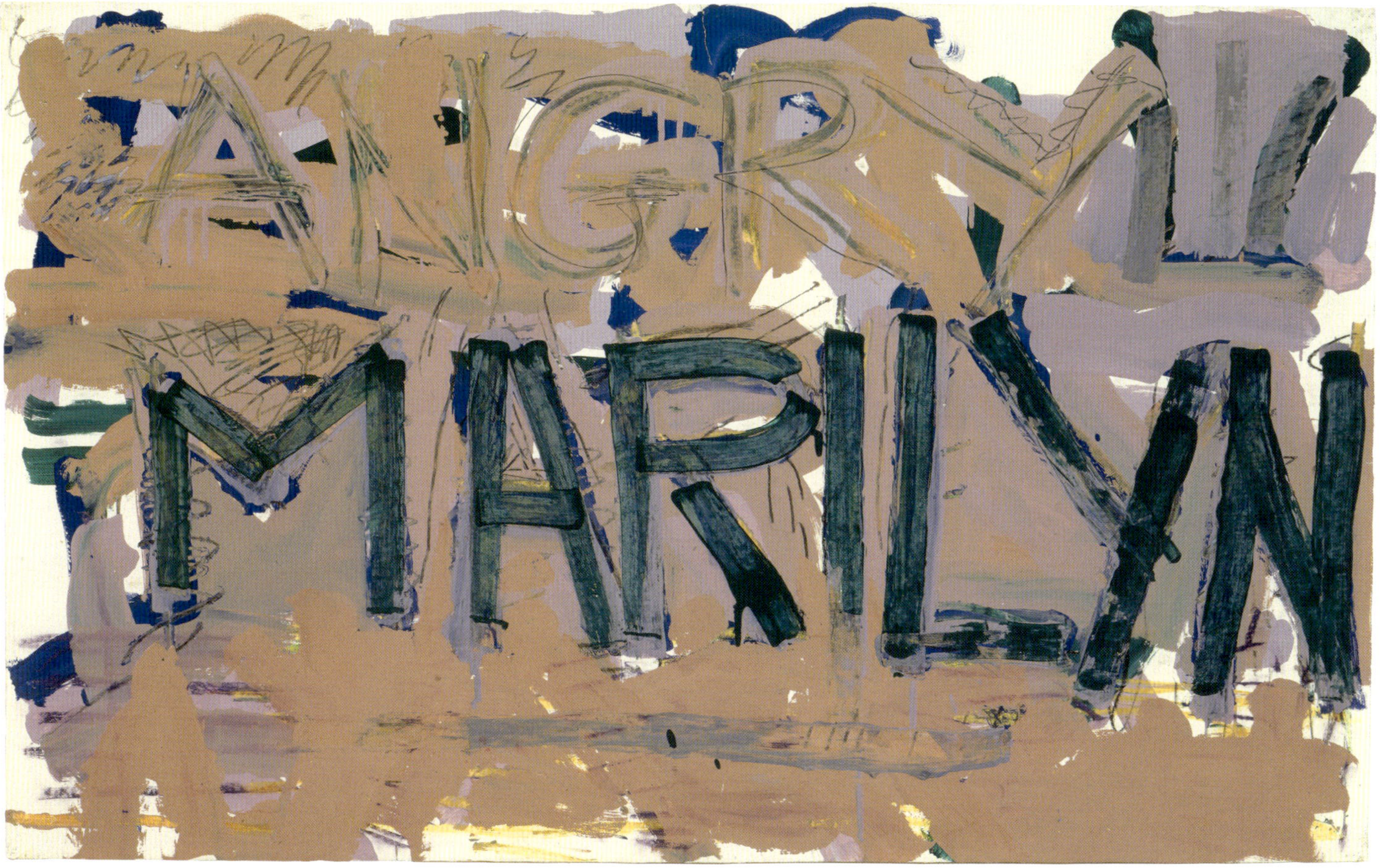

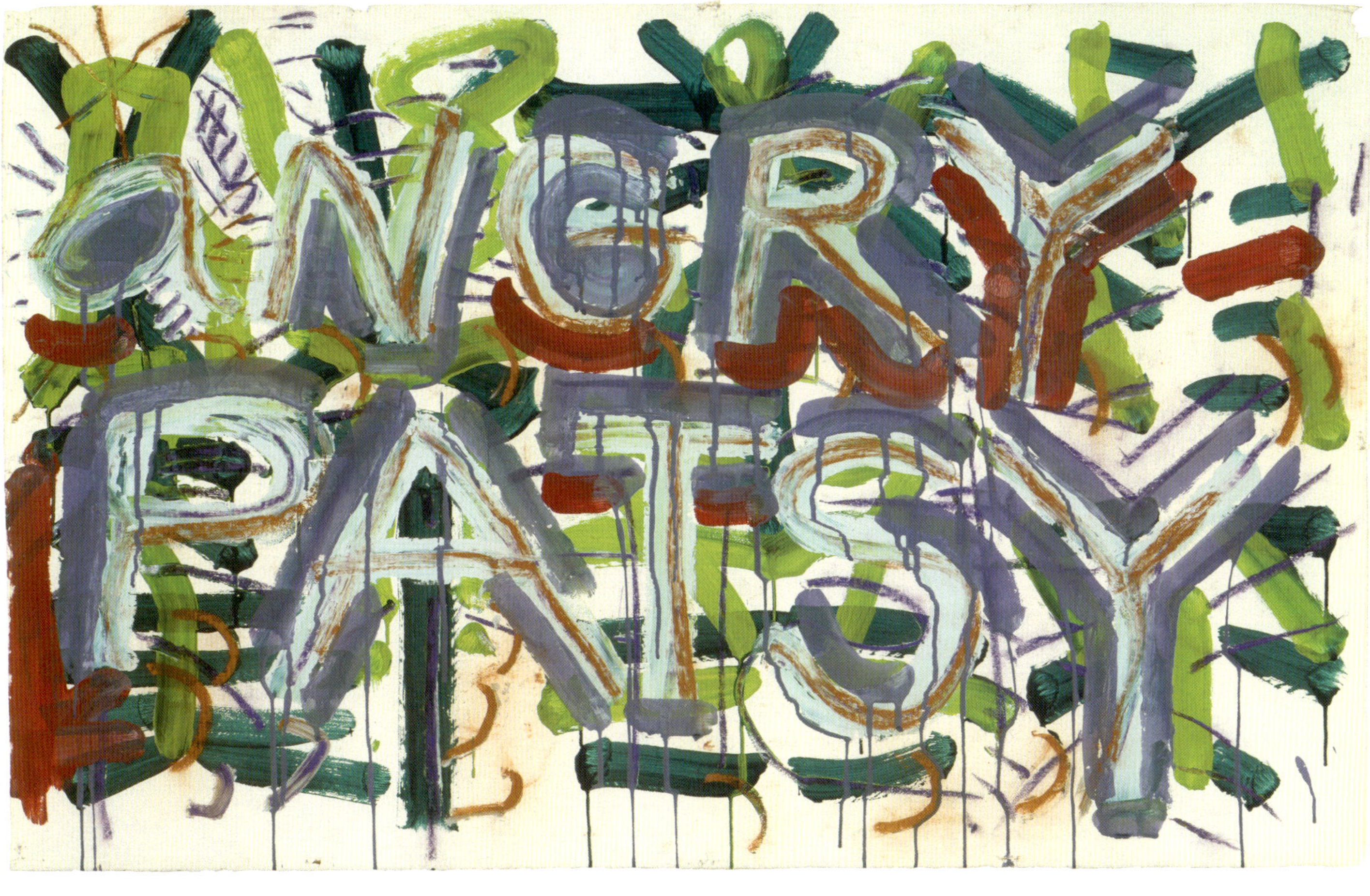

PLATE 13. *Angry Marilyn*, 1973. Acrylic on paper, 26 x 40 in. (66 x 101.6 cm)
PLATE 14. *Angry Patsy*, 1973. Acrylic on paper, 26 x 40 in. (66 x 101.6 cm)

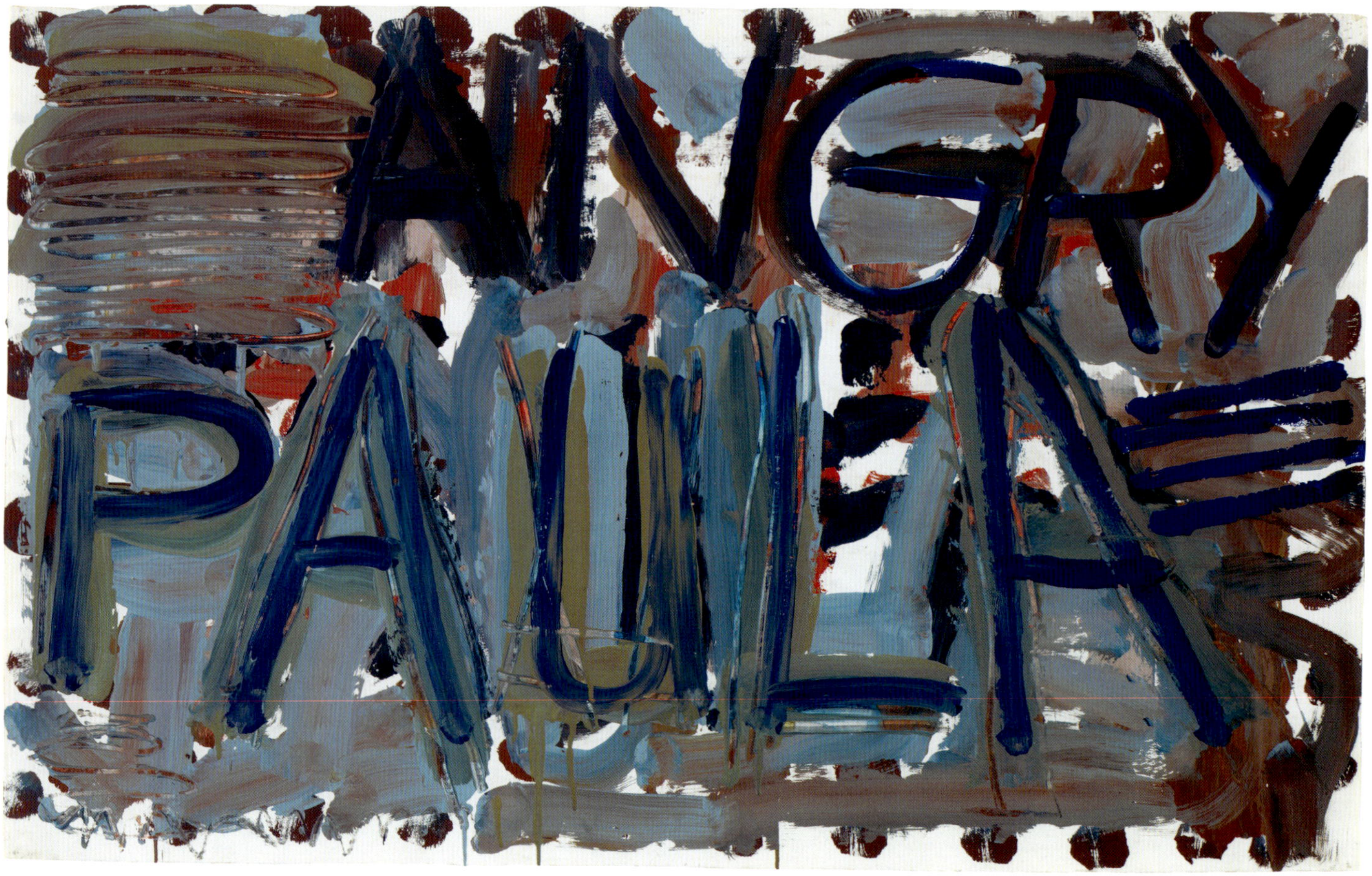

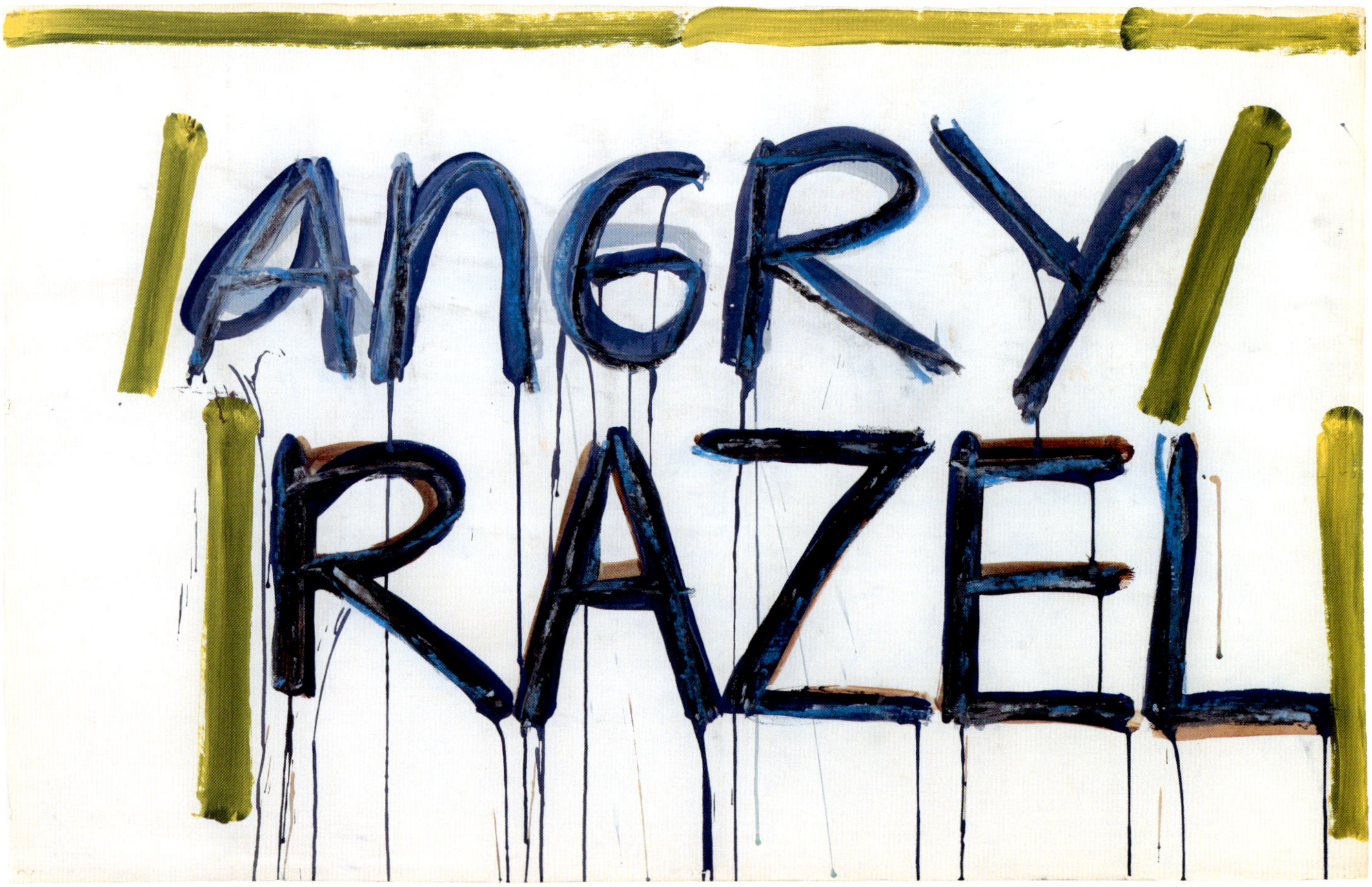

PLATE 15. *Angry Paula*, 1973. Acrylic on paper, 26 x 40 in. (66 x 101.6 cm)
PLATE 16. *Angry Razel*, 1973. Acrylic on paper, 26 x 40 in. (66 x 101.6 cm)

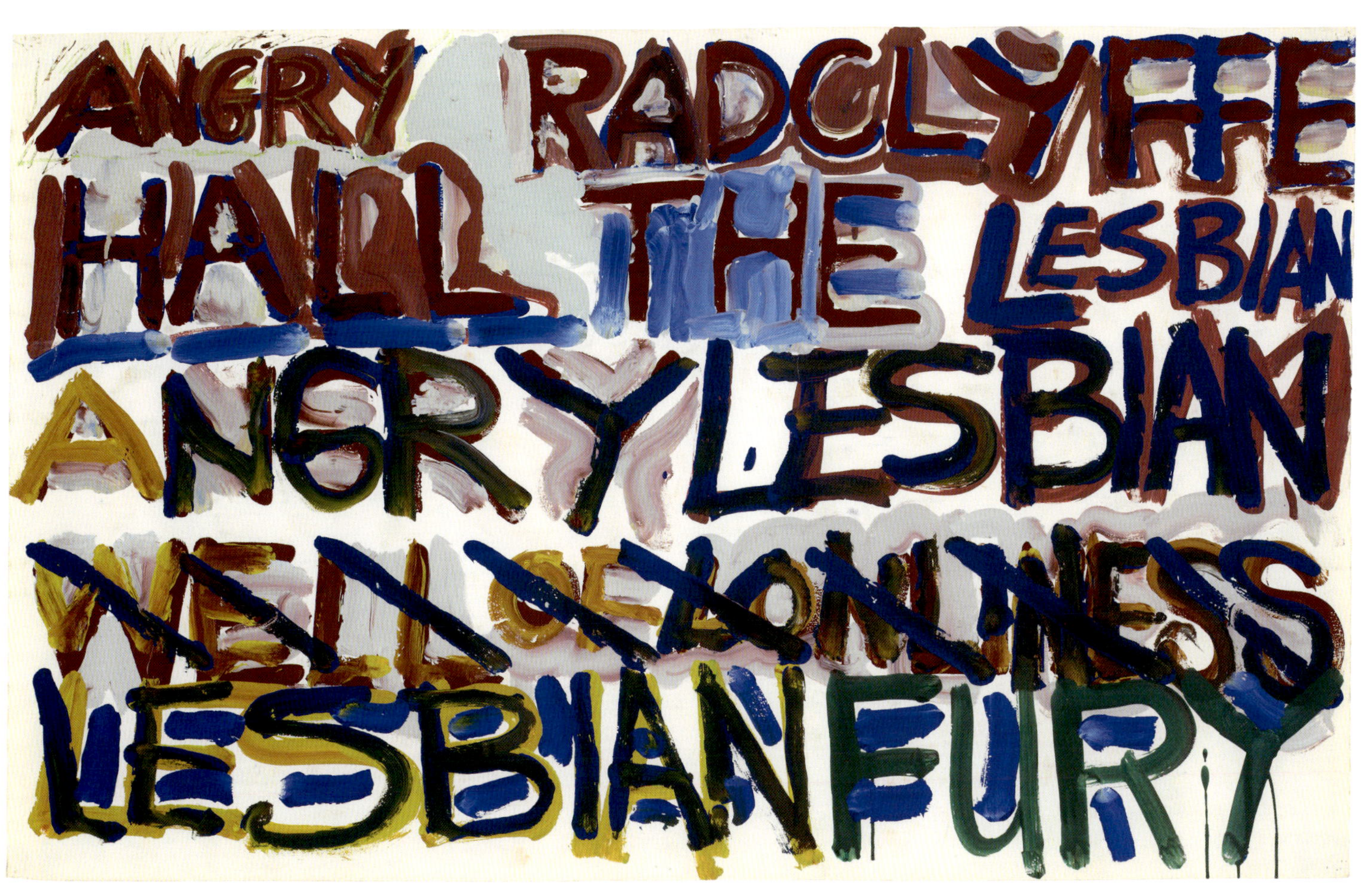

PLATE 17. *Angry Radclyffe Hall*, 1973. Acrylic on paper, 26 x 40 in. (66 x 101.6 cm)

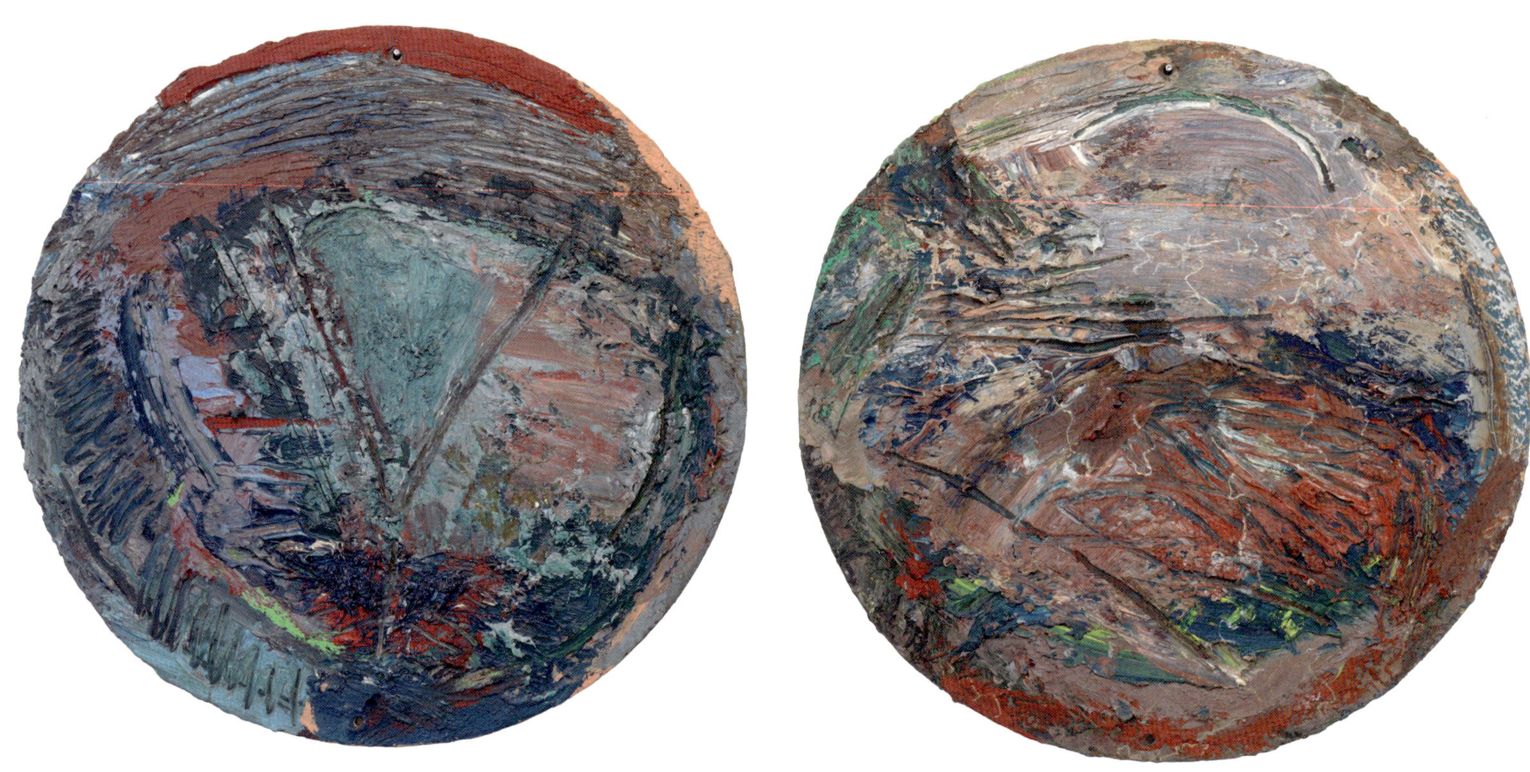

PLATE 18. *Bianca's Repose*, 1973. Oil on Masonite; two panels, each: 11½ x 11½ in. (29.2 x 29.2 cm); overall: 11½ x 23 in. (29.2 x 58.4 cm)

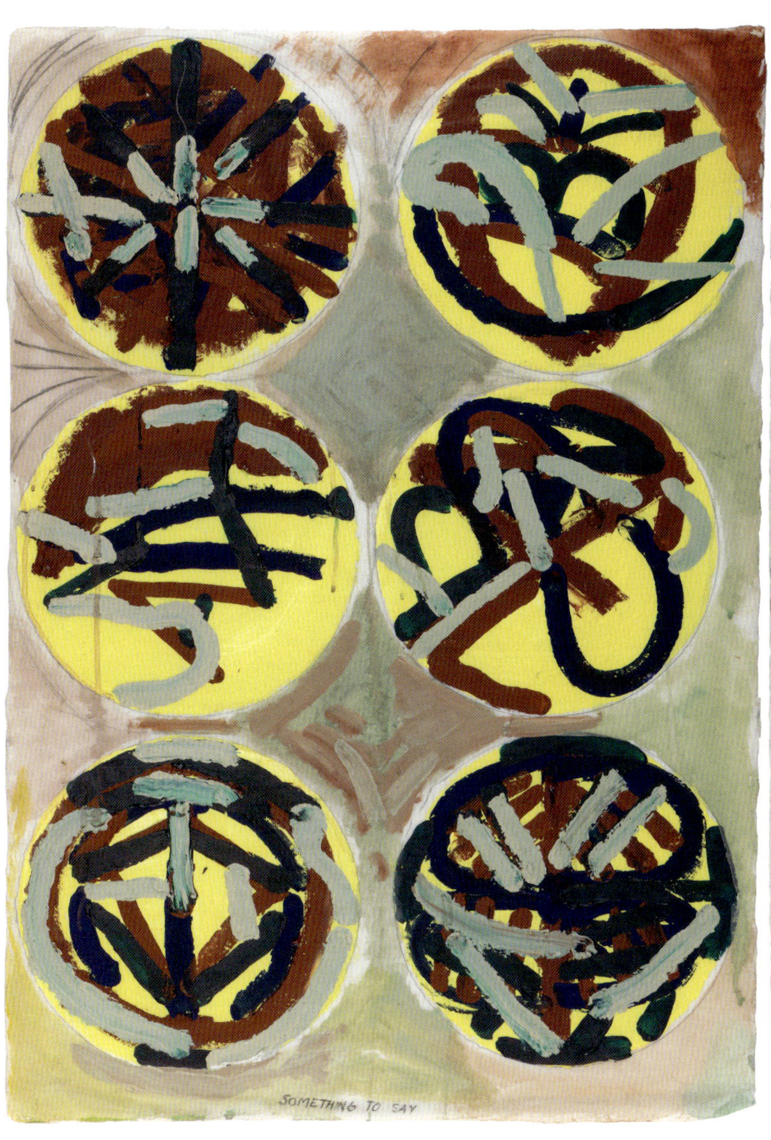

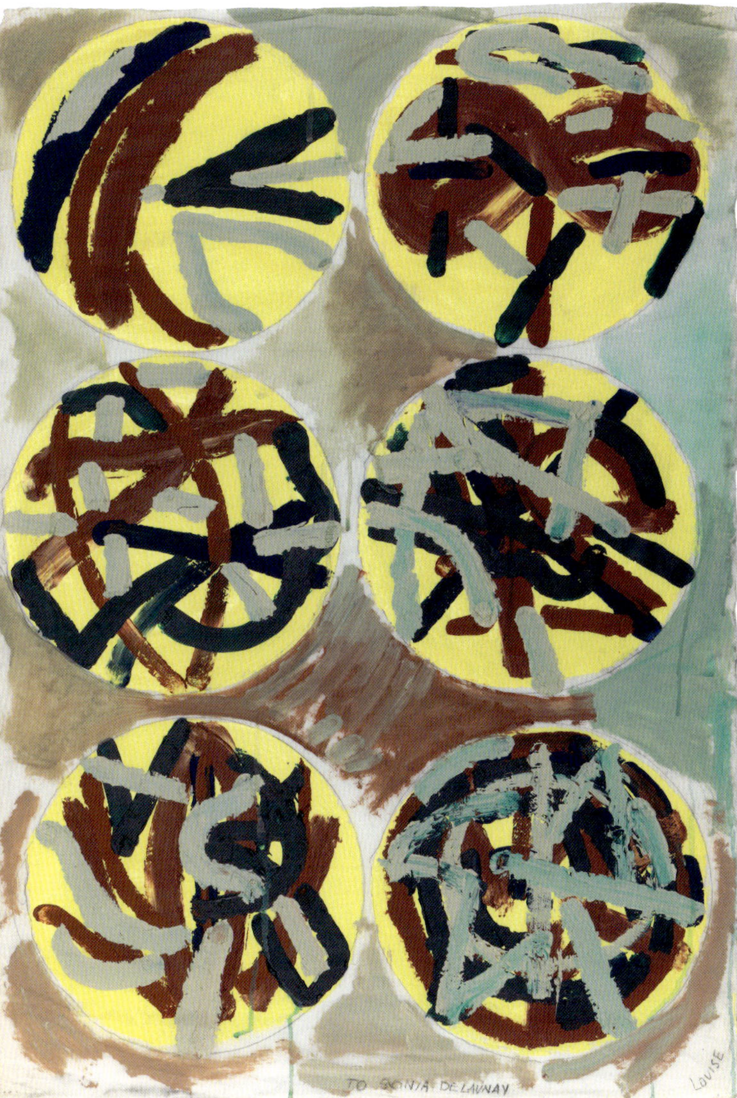

PLATE 19. *Something to Say to Sonia Delaunay*, 1973. Acrylic on rice paper, overall: 25 x 37 in. (63.5 x 94 cm)

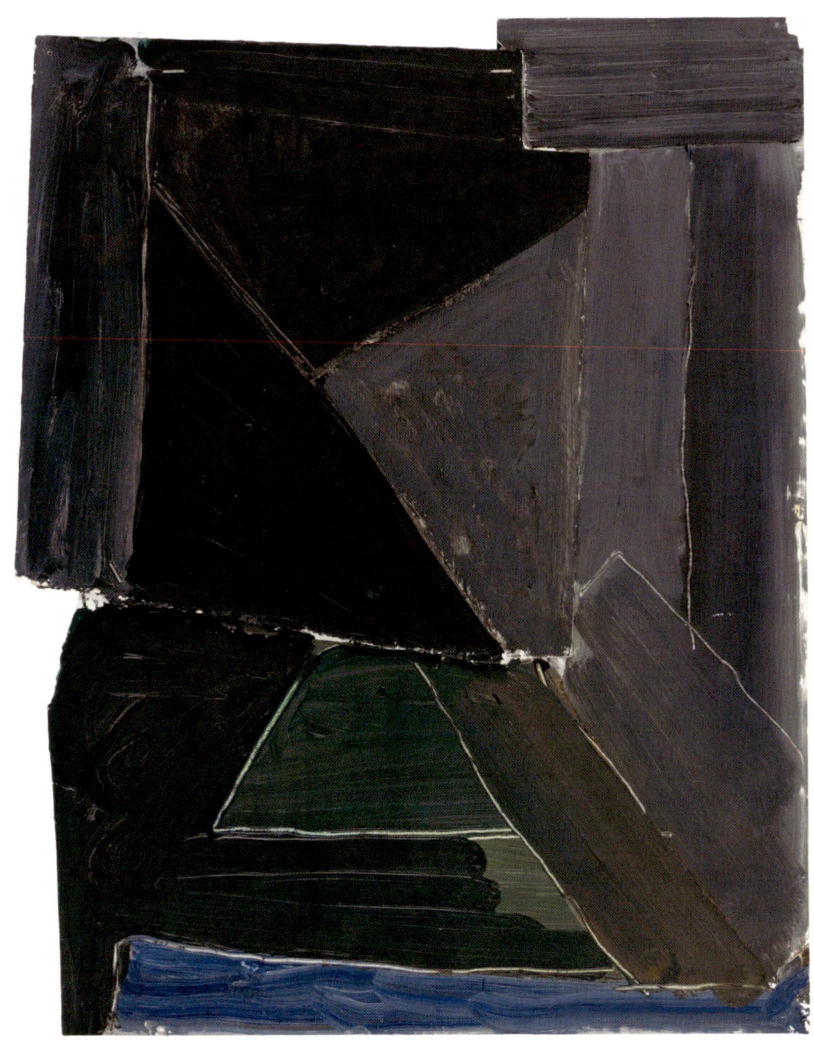

PLATE 20. *Untitled*, 1973. Oil and staples on paper and cardboard, 20 x 16¾ in. (50.8 x 42.5 cm)

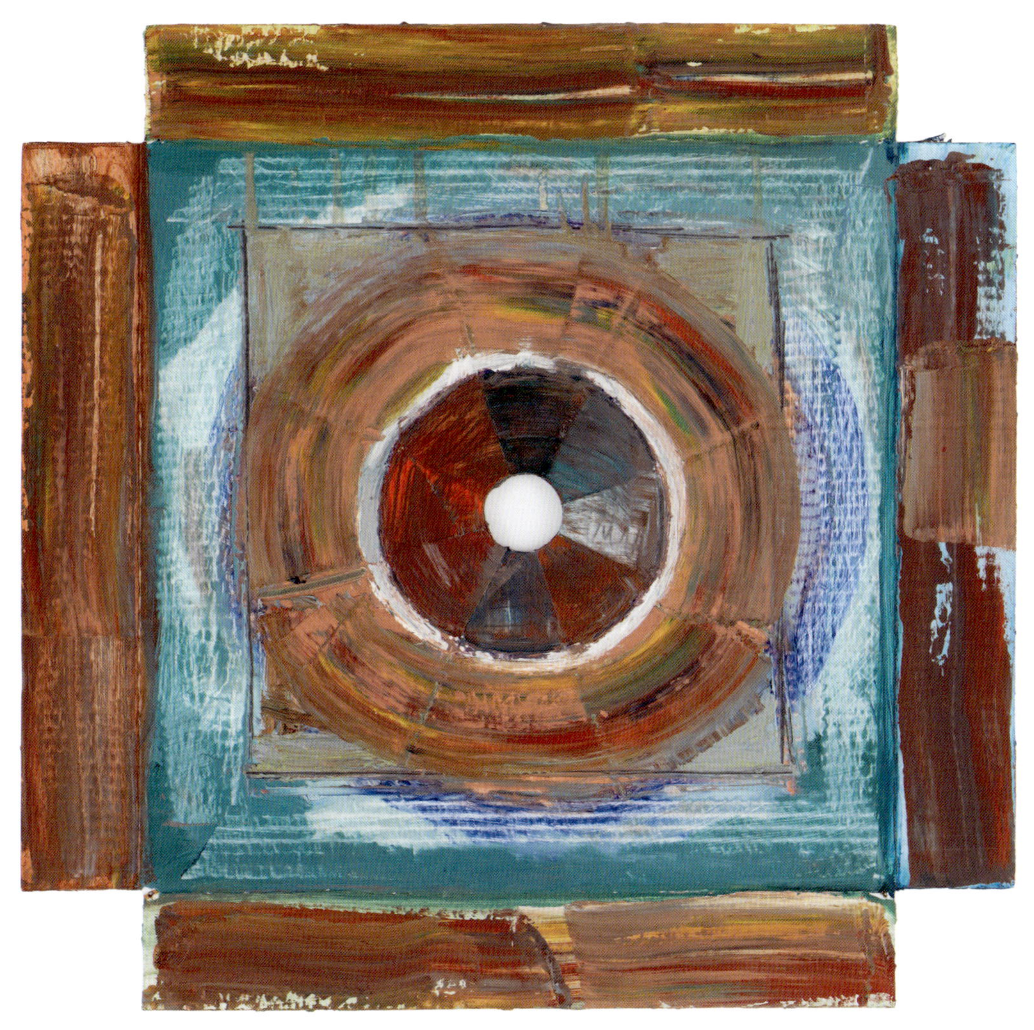

PLATE 21. *Untitled*, 1973. Oil and graphite on cardboard, 19 x 19 in. (48.3 x 48.3 cm)

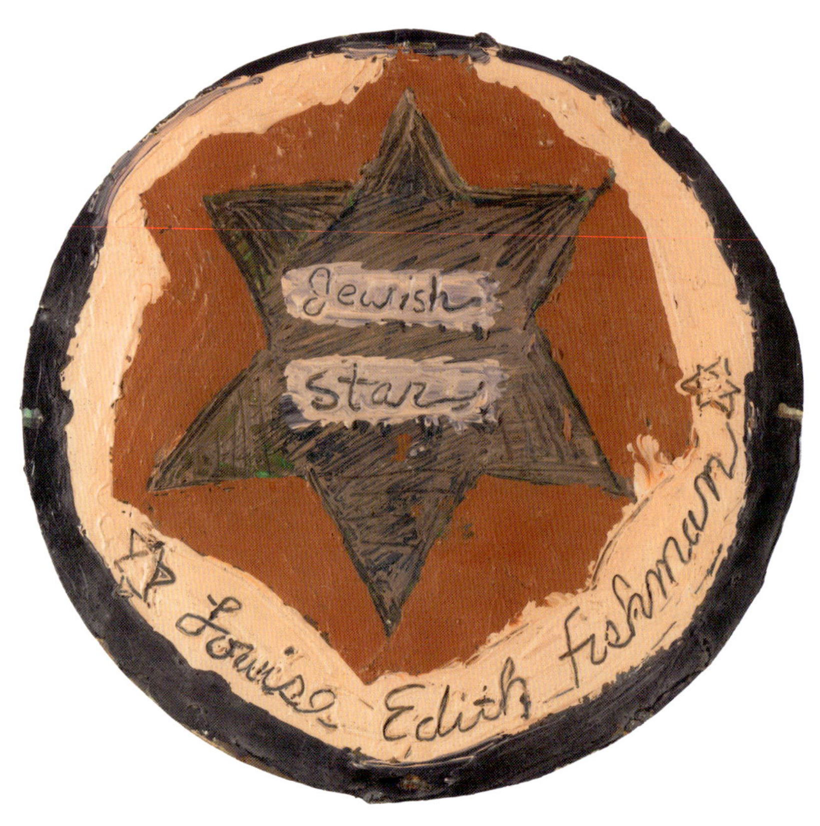

PLATE 22. *Jewish Star Painting*, 1973–74. Graphite and acrylic on paper, 11¼ x 11¼ in. (28.6 x 28.6 cm)

PLATE 23. *Caryatid*, 1974. Oil and wax on wood, 30¼ x 17¼ in. (76.8 x 43.8 cm)

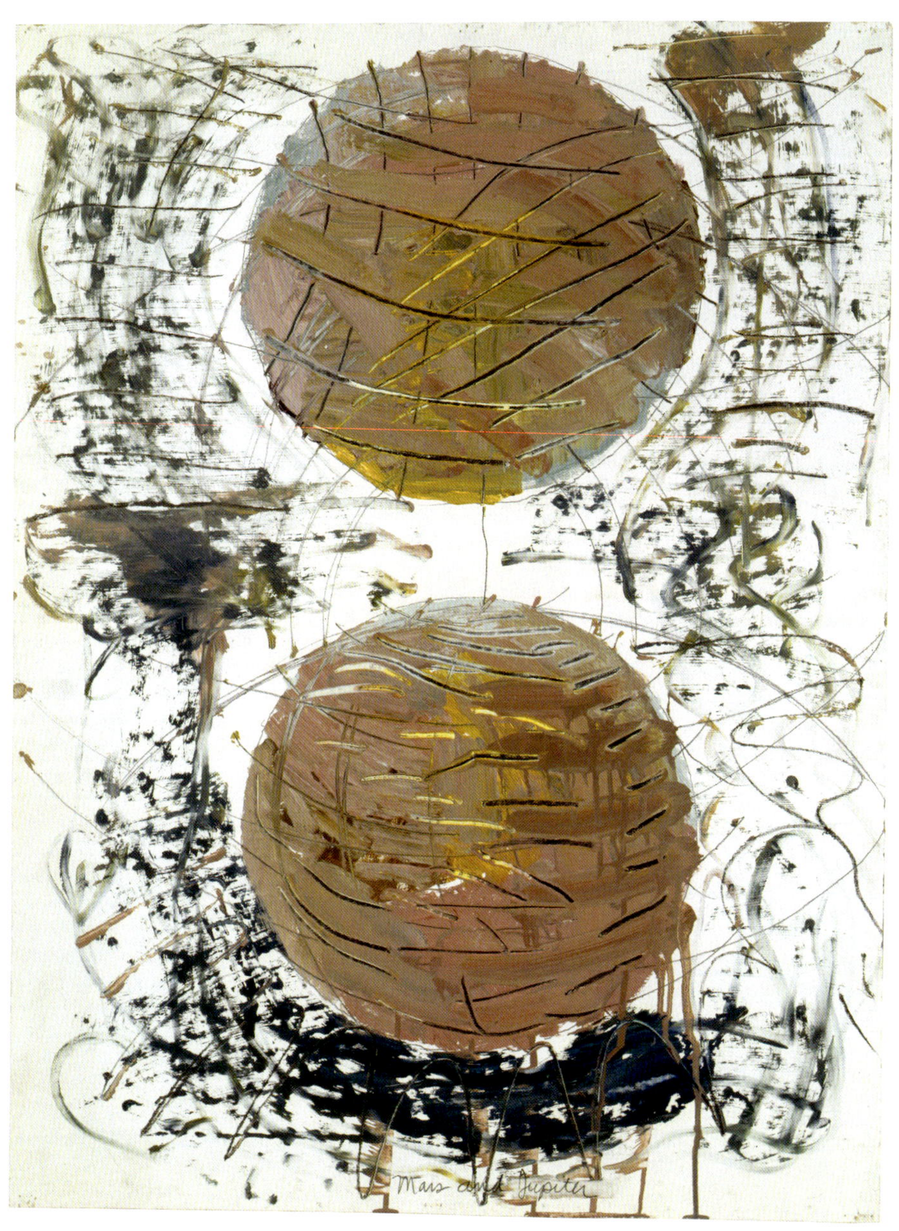

PLATE 24. *Mars and Jupiter*, 1974. Oil and charcoal on gessoed paper, 30 x 22 in. (76.2 x 55.9 cm)

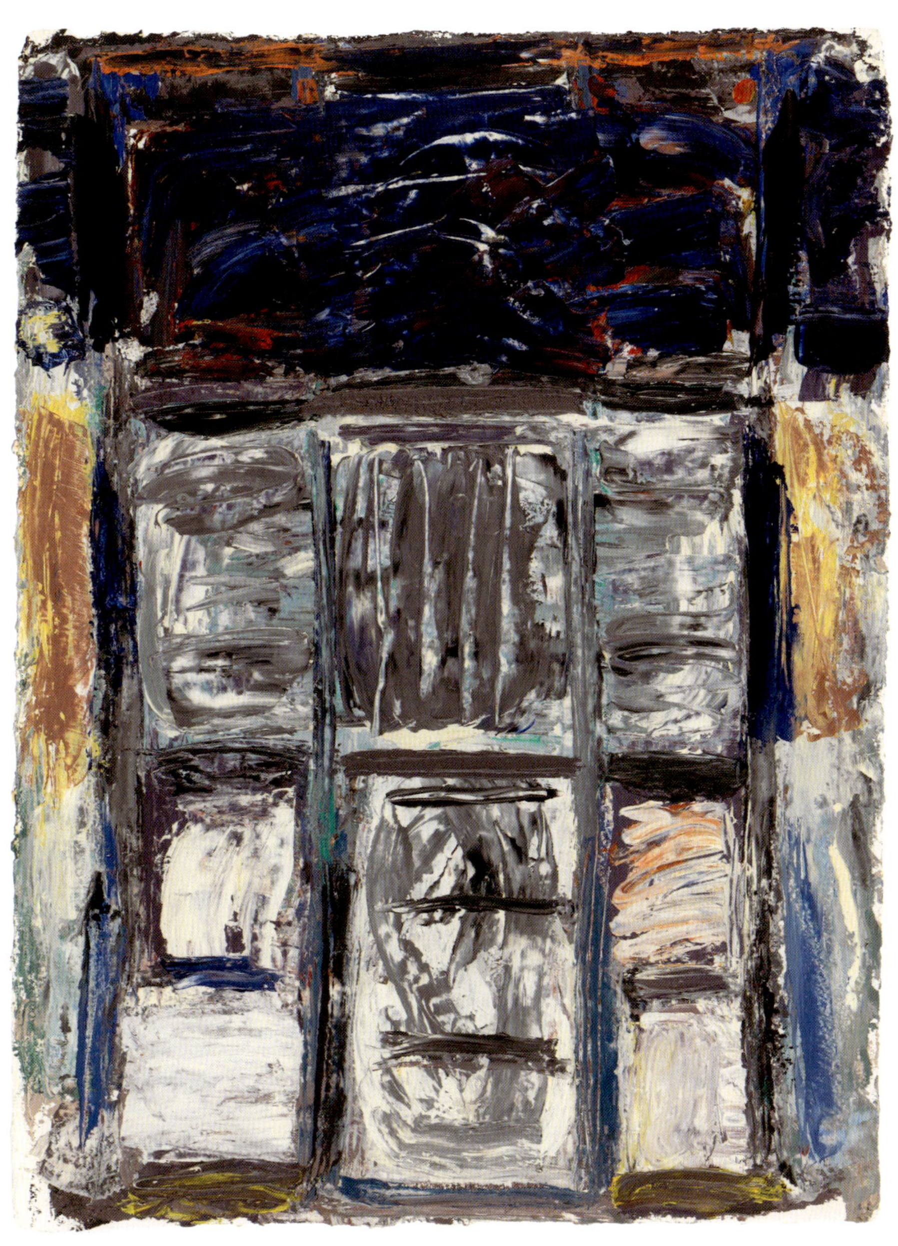

PLATE 25. *Untitled*, 1975–76. Oil on primed paper, 31¼ x 22¾ in. (79.4 x 57.8 cm)

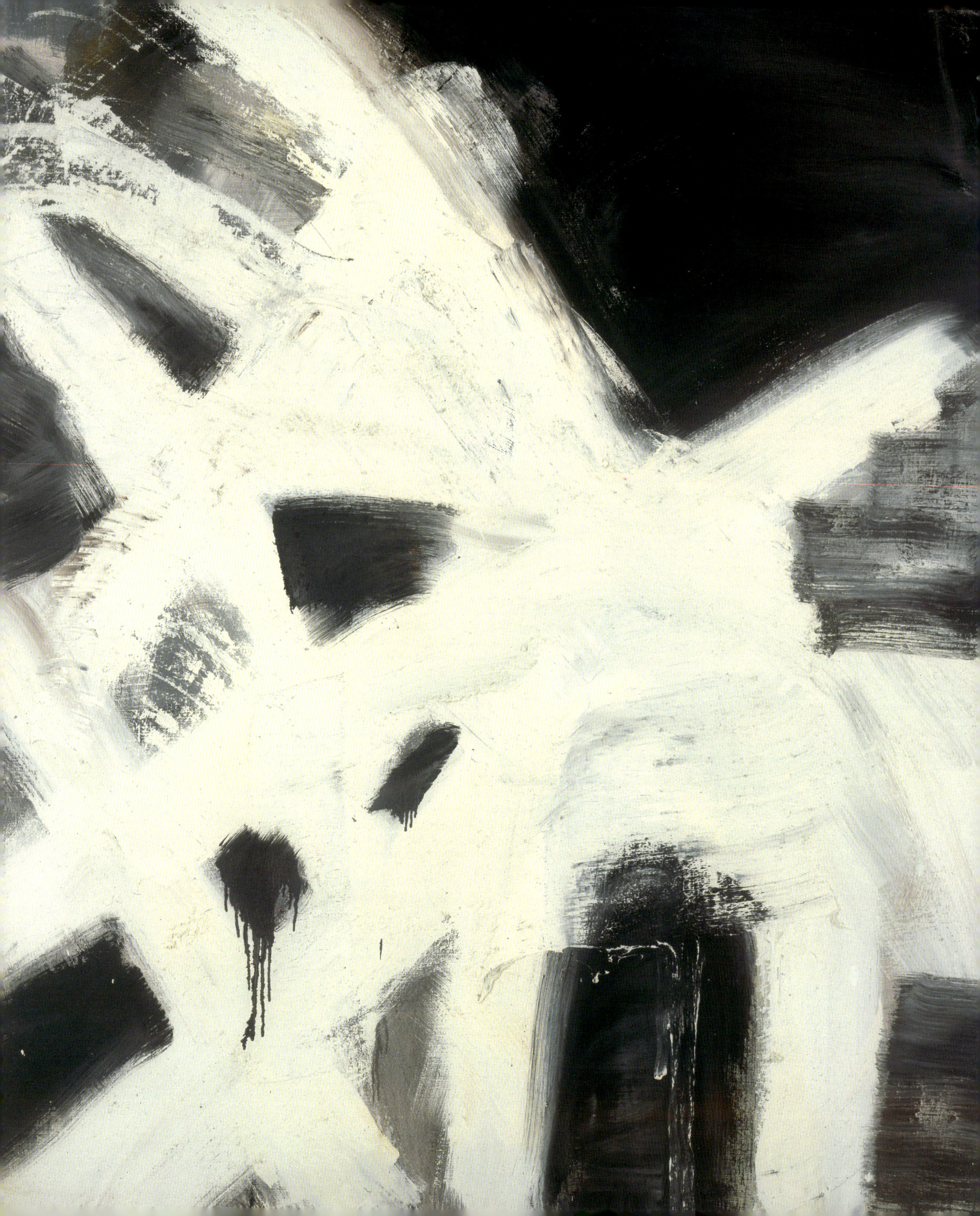

LOUISE FISHMAN LANGUAGE LESSONS

NANCY PRINCENTHAL

Drawing in part on the spare geometries of Minimalism, the graphic elegance of the Hebrew alphabet, and the domestic art of hand sewing, Louise Fishman early on developed a form of abstraction that can be said to operate like language. Alternately structural, metaphorical, and literal, the linguistic features of Fishman's paintings contribute to a flexible idiom that is deeply personal—and widely, gloriously resonant.

Having experimented widely, Fishman arrived, by the mid-1960s, at a series of hard-edged shapes and patterns that included checkerboards and plaids. An untitled watercolor of 1968 (PL. 2), for instance, features horizontal and vertical stripes of varied colors woven into a loose Tattersall pattern, its points of intersection luminous and semitransparent. The artist's touch is apparent in this textile-like composition, and the rich colors are idiosyncratically complicated, but the format is coolly impersonal. That would soon change. By the end of the decade, Fishman was cutting up her own grid-based paintings, as well as canvases she dyed in the kitchen sink, and assembling the small squares into hand-stitched paintings that reflected the influence of the then-rising feminist movement, into which she had entered with enthusiasm.

David Deitcher writes that the stitched-together canvases combine "an act of symbolic self-mutilation (tearing apart her own paintings)" with a foray into techniques newly promoted by women artists, and argues that these paintings relate "to fellow Redstockings member Patricia Mainardi's 1970 polemic, 'The Politics of Housework.' "[1] But far from promoting techniques that have traditionally been identified as feminine, Mainardi's essay, which is very funny (and still all too apt), calls housework what it is—repetitive, time-consuming, boring, and unpleasant—and tartly observes the many ways men avoid it. She left it to others to transform domestic chores, and related crafts, from signs of constraint into emblems of pride. In a 1973 article called "Household Images in Art," first published in *Ms.* magazine, Lucy R. Lippard discussed the overturning of taboos by women artists, and noted that " 'Female techniques' like sewing, weaving, knitting, [and] ceramics," which had long been avoided, were now being embraced.[2] If Fishman's cut-and-stitched paintings reflected this shift, their embrace was decidedly wary; in the spirit of Mainardi's essay, Fishman's sewing exercises are plainly effortful and stubbornly, proudly untidy. An untitled painting of 1971 comprises strips of cloth that have been painted in dour shades of gray and dark blue and marked with short, vertical strokes of white chalk, then bound together with string. Another such painting is hung loosely from a

OPPOSITE: Detail of *Blonde Ambition*, 1995 (pl. 52)

row of grommets, like an old coat (FIG. 11). In several other works, the cloth has uneven borders. In almost all, threads dangle, and there is throughout a feeling of rough handling. A reluctant seamstress—she later said, "I spent my life avoiding sewing and anything else that had to do with 'women's tasks'"[3]—Fishman turned hand-stitching toward a transformation of the grid from a paradigm of minimalist painting into a statement of hard-fought resistance to its heavily male authority.

Along with an expression of female identity, there can be seen, in these regularly stitched and ruled fields (particularly those drawn on with chalk) an additional, implicit element: a line of text that seems to run beneath the surface, not quite linguistic but nonetheless organized like handwriting. This textual association is reinforced by other works of the same period in which the cut-up canvases are stitched and stapled into canvas books. And by 1972, Fishman had moved from incipient to manifest text. *Letter to My Mother about Painting* (FIG. 12) is a five-part work in which each component is two-sided, bearing the title's words within heavily marked fields. The

FIGURE 11
Louise Fishman, *Untitled*, 1971
Acrylic, glue, grommets, canvas, and thread, 17 x 10½ in. (43.1 x 26.6 cm)

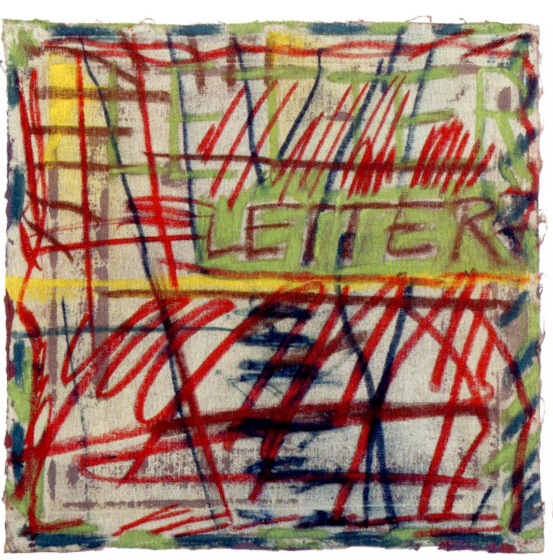

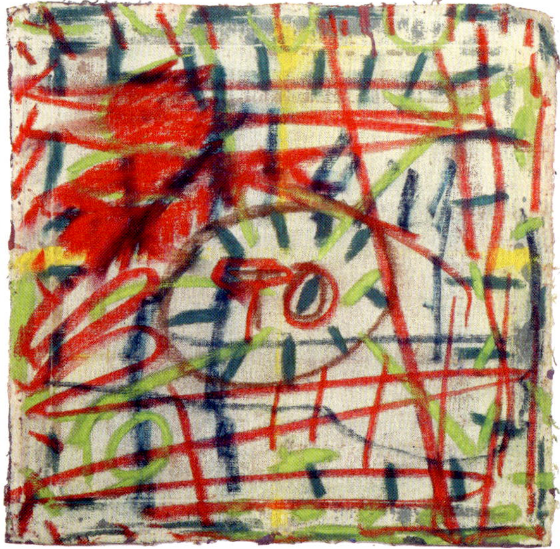

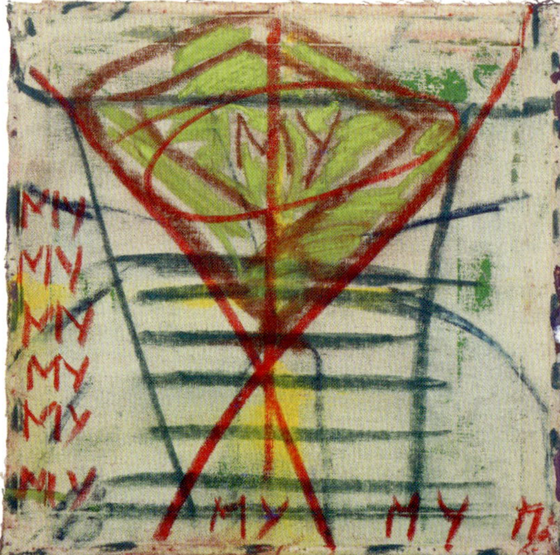

FIGURE 12
Louise Fishman, *Letter to My Mother about Painting*, 1972–73
Oil on canvas; six double-sided panels, each: 13¾ x 14 in. (34.9 x 35.6 cm); overall: 13¾ x 84 in. (34.9 x 213.6 cm)

FIGURE 13
Bruce Nauman (b. 1941), *My Name as Though It Were Written on the Surface of the Moon*, 1968
Fluorescent light, $11\frac{13}{16}$ x $216\frac{9}{64}$ x $2\frac{3}{4}$ in. (30 x 549 x 7 cm)
Stedelijk Museum Amsterdam

same year, she painted two versions of *Louise 5 Times*, watercolor drawings in which she repeats her first name in tidy rows. These works suggest an obstinate child sent to the blackboard—or, perhaps, an insubordinate student of Bruce Nauman, countering the two attenuated signatures he rendered as neon signs, in the late 1960s (see FIG. 13), with her own, hand-drawn and inky dark.

If anger is only implicit in these last works, it is inescapable in Fishman's most extensive body of word-based compositions, the thirty Angry Paintings she made in 1973. Created in acrylic on paper and seemingly bigger than their fairly modest dimensions (each is twenty-six by forty inches), they name lesbian novelists and poets, social and cultural critics, a few painters, and, notably, the artist herself, each subject qualified by the same emotion. The titular words of *Angry Louise* (PL. 12) are roughly scrawled on a neutral patch of ground and hounded on all sides by thickly applied, blood-red slashes of paint. In other examples, the words—most lettered in screaming caps—are inscribed in several layers and surrounded by furious brushwork, the palette in some cases grim and in others jubilant. The letters of "angry" in *Angry Djuna* (for Djuna Barnes; PL. 9) grow in size, and the "Y" is explosive, but more like fireworks than gunfire. In *Angry Gertrude* (PL. 10), the words are nearly buried in a thicket of brushstrokes, many of them green, which

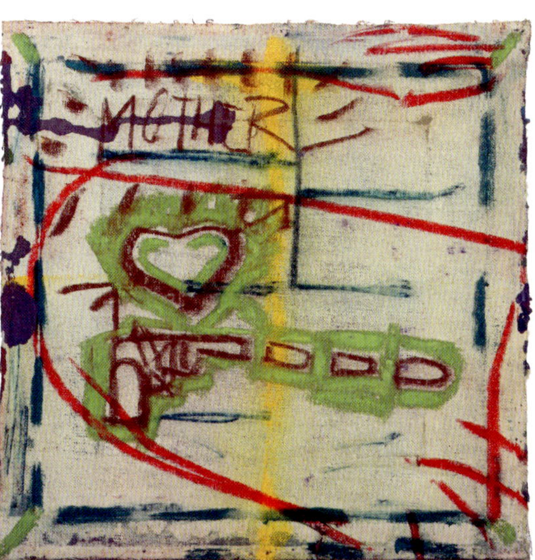

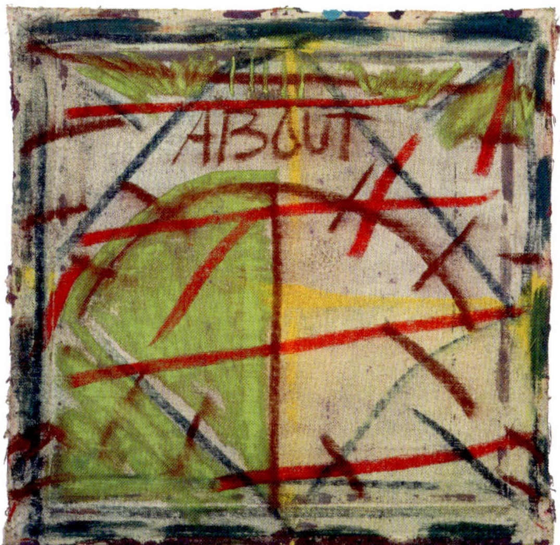

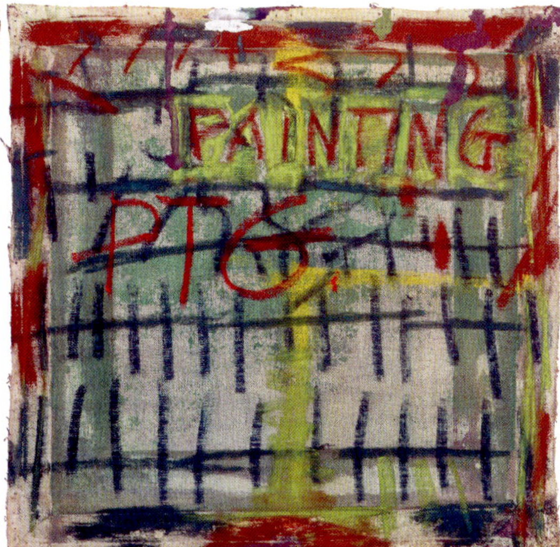

supports the impression of a prickly hedge: a reference, perhaps, to Gertrude Stein's notoriously thorny prose (although this work also refers to Fishman's mother, Gertrude). In *Angry Jill* (PL. 11), the words are shoved into the painting's upper left quadrant, harried by a scrum of brushstrokes going every which way, anarchic and somehow ruefully funny, like Jill Johnston's writing. On the other hand, *Angry Radclyffe Hall* (PL. 17), which also shouts "Angry Lesbian" and "Lesbian Fury," is a clarion call suitable for carrying aloft in a street demonstration. The words "Well of Loneliness," which refer to Hall's landmark 1928 novel of lesbian love, judged obscene at the time of its writing, appear in this painting only to be crossed out: solitary and isolated no more, Fishman and her friends were speaking up, in force.

"I was very angry for most of my early life," Fishman recalled twenty-five years later.[4] But these word-based paintings were more than expressions of personal rage; they were impelled by her friendships in the women's movement, which at first were largely with writers rather than painters. "In 1973 I was doing calligraphic paintings," she has said, "writing on unstretched canvas. I was trying to mimic my friends," who were all "writers, anthropologists, and other kinds of academics. They formed writing groups. . . . I felt so excluded that I started making marks—as if I were drawing fake writing."[5] But it seems clear, too, that at this moment of newly aroused awareness of the grip of patriarchy and—although the women's movement was a little slow to embrace this message—homophobia, only plain words would do to give full voice to Fishman's ire.

While fully formed words entered Fishman's work (and receded from it) mainly for topical reasons, the connection between language and picture-making has been a sustained concern—and not hers alone. It is not for nothing that we speak of "reading" a painting, even, or especially, when it is abstract. In the period when Fishman's work was developing, a number of artists had been exploring this conjunction. Jasper Johns's gridded alphabets, which reconcile pictorial to linguistic structure; Robert Indiana's sign paintings, which constituted a kind of supergraphics using found poetry; and the cascades of cursive writing in Cy Twombly's big canvases were all at hand, although none offer precise precedents for Fishman's approach. Her active ambivalence toward language is perhaps most consonant with that of poet Henri Michaux, who wrote: "If I am set on taking the way of lines rather than of words, it's in order to enter into relation with what is most precious to me, most true, most withdrawn, most 'mine.' . . . Written things are never impoverished or *rustic* enough."[6] This belief that words are too replete with fixed meaning, too settled and full to be useful for visual artists, accords with Fishman's. Although "writing is one of the ways thought becomes phenomenal,"[7] as philosopher Vilém Flusser writes, there are other "gestures" by means of which thinking can be articulated (to use Flusser's phrase). In Fishman's work, it can be said that the written gesture cedes ground to the visual without vacating the field entirely.

Although she has made no word-based paintings since 1973, the enduring presence of language in Fishman's work is connected to several kinds of writing. "In retrospect, I've always had an interest in calligraphy, starting with Hebrew, a language that I didn't understand,"[8] she has said. Of course, Hebrew was compelling not just for its visual form, but also for the history, culture, and religion it represents. Raised in a Conservative Jewish family by parents from Orthodox backgrounds (her father, who taught in a yeshiva, was the son of a Talmudic scholar), Fishman attended synagogue regularly as a child. Her work's first explicit acknowledgment of Judaism is in titles for paintings of the late 1970s, a period when she read Holocaust literature extensively, along with other related material, including Yiddish writing in translation.[9] In *Ashkenazi* (1978, PL. 26), the grid returns, this time more as an emblem than a structure; expressionistic brushwork, both scumbled and scribbly, and iconic colors—red, white, blue, and black—describe and activate rectangles that stride forth as independent figures. By contrast, the two tumbling circular forms in *Golem* (1981, PL. 28) seem inescapably organic. Heavily drawn in black, they are both internally subdivided, like fetal cells: we sense that, as with the Golem of Jewish mystical tradition, mere matter is becoming animate, though whether it is to be a living being or a spoken word isn't yet clear.

In 1987 Fishman moved to a farmhouse in rural upstate New York, and natural references flourished. *Stand of Beech* (PL. 36) is more grid than grove, but the whiteness of beech bark seems to glow in the deeply shaded ground; *Headwaters* (PL. 35) is a smaller canvas whose cataract of colors spills over patches of stony gray. But the bucolic influence was countered by a spring 1988 trip to Warsaw, Prague, and Budapest, during which Fishman visited Auschwitz and Terezín. Later that year, following her return, she created nineteen paintings named for components of the Passover Seder plate. *Bitter Herb* (for the Seder, the herb is commonly horseradish, eaten to remember the bitterness of slavery; PL. 38) is a large (sixty-five by forty-five-inch) painting, simple and commanding, organized by horizontal bands of dark green, blue, and gray. *Karpas #4* (the title refers to an herb or a vegetable, generally parsley, dipped in salt water for similar reasons; PL. 41) is a more modest composition, in chalky blue against saline gray, held lightly in place by the ghost of a grid. *Haggadah* (PL. 40) is named for the handbook that guides participants through the Seder, telling the Passover story in prose, song, and prayer. This painting's central, branching form—an open book?—spreads its wings over the smallish canvas, casting it in cool, dark shadow.

Together, these paintings suggest the lineaments of ritual held in place by narrative—by a history heard so early and often that, like a song popular in one's childhood, it is learned before its meaning is understood, much less examined. Fishman's Seder paintings put that examination, undertaken in adulthood, into the context of a centuries-old process of inquiry. "While the series refers directly to her experience of visiting the camps, and therefore to a specific Jewish experience, the Jewishness of Fishman's paintings in general is more ineffable, constituting a kind of visual cognate of Talmudic disputation,"[10] Faye Hirsch writes. The dialogic, amicably contentious nature of such scholarship, deeply familiar to Fishman, structures these paintings not just as interrogations of cultural history, but also as spirited engagements with the tenets of modernist abstraction, which likewise have been endlessly—and productively—debated without ever being resolved.

By the late nineties, Fishman was using linear gestures that alluded not only to calligraphy of several varieties but also, as Hirsch writes, "to Chinese scholars' rocks of the kind she collects, with their fluid shapes, holes, and concavities that, as she sees it, can almost look like writing"; the artist was influenced as well by Bradley Walker Tomlin and, especially, Mark Tobey, who was himself inspired by Chinese and Japanese calligraphy.[11] It is relevant, too, that earlier in the decade Fishman, heading West following a devastating 1990 studio fire, had met with Agnes Martin in Galisteo, New Mexico. Martin's grids of the sixties, and the

FIGURE 14
Agnes Martin (1912–2004), *Night Sea*, 1963
Oil on canvas with gold leaf, 72 x 72 in. (183 x 183 cm)

horizontal and vertical bands of the following decades (SEE FIG. 14), were understood by Fishman—whose involvement with Zen Buddhism dates to the 1970s[12]—as a form of meditation. Indeed, Martin was deeply engaged with various Eastern and other mystical spiritual practices; a writer's hand can also be seen in the penciled lines that run throughout her work. In spite of Martin's protests, most observers have made a further connection between her abstractions and the natural world. "The work of Agnes Martin," Melissa E. Feldman observes, "renewed Fishman's interest in the grid, but as a breathing system as opposed to a minimalist vise." Feldman further describes Fishman's use of the grid as "'organic' in that it represents repetition and continuity found in nature, a waterfall or the rings of a tree, for example."[13] A similar approach to the grid, and a similar resolution of the linear with the calligraphic, were put forward in the late eighties by Brice Marden, whose *Cold Mountain Series* (1988–91; FIG. 15) is inspired by the T'ang-dynasty poet Han Shan. Though their meandering, linear organization refers, Marden says, to the meditative wandering of Zen monks, these paintings also can be seen as descendants of his early grids.[14]

By the 1990s, Fishman, too, had stretched the grid almost beyond recognition. But following her trip to New Mexico she returned to its more familiar form in earnest. In *Valles Marineris* (PL. 49), which is named for a system of canyons on Mars, heavy, black strokes, patient as bandaging, define a rectilinear network whose internal squares are scraped to the canvas—the painting's flinty substrate. The fragments of a grid that appear in *Burnt Bridges* (PL. 53) suggest an almost architectural scaffold, and also the strokes of a system of signage. Big and commanding (it is ninety inches high), *Blonde Ambition* (1995, PL. 52) deploys bold, curving marks that seem bent to the use of not only verbal signs but also of body language. Against

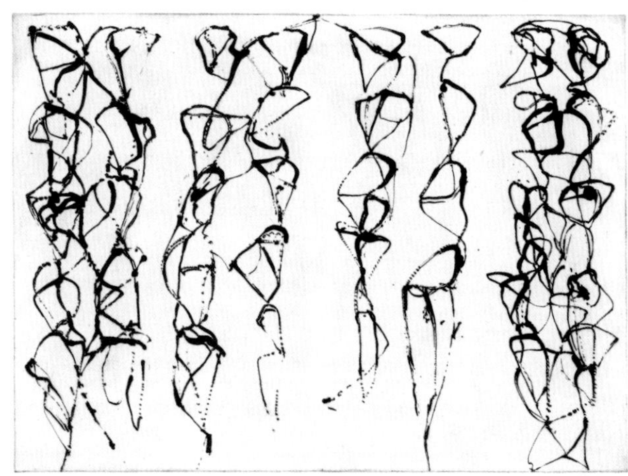

FIGURE 15
Brice Marden, *Zen Study 3 (Early State) from Cold Mountain Series*, 1990
Etching and lift ground aquatint, printed in black; plate: 20 11/16 x 27 3/16 in. (52.6 x 69.1 cm); sheet: 27 3/8 x 35 1/4 in. (69 x 89.6 cm)
The Museum of Modern Art, New York; Linda Barth Goldstein Fund

a matte black ground, the heavy, slightly gritty strokes of bright white in this painting have the sweep of road markings—they were applied with rollers—and suggest a figure on stage under spotlights: it is possible to see arms stretched wide, a head thrown back. The muscularity of *Blonde Ambition* can be attributed in part to a concert of the same name by Madonna, which Fishman had seen before making this painting, and to Marilyn Monroe, who had long been an inspiration to Madonna, and to Fishman as well.[15]

No such figurative associations are invited by *The Art of Losing* (PL. 79), in which a freshet of cold blue at right gleams amid the dark, heavy contours that structure the canvas. Some straight and others bent, these contours again suggest rudimentary letterforms, and also a maze: we are invited to trace—to read—the composition's passages and blockages as a wordless narrative. In *Moon and Movies* and, especially, *Green in the Body* (PLS. 81, 85), there are similar passages, these less congested; the latter painting offers a palette of greens, some lit up by juicy yellow, that powerfully evoke the upward, sun-seeking inclination of springtime growth. And written language remains a reference point, sometimes plainly stated. *Longhand* (FIG. 16) names the cursive penmanship that is its motor: against a dark ground, white brushstrokes dance upward through the big, vertical canvas with whiplash speed.

In other paintings of the late nineties and since, linear structure abates; the imperative of these works is that of the paint and its application, and of unbounded color. Again referring to the landscape (and, perhaps, to the work of Joan Mitchell, which has been a sustained source of inspiration), such paintings as *April* (FIG. 17) and *The Sunrise Ruby* reveal the character of the brush—hairy, flexible, vestigially

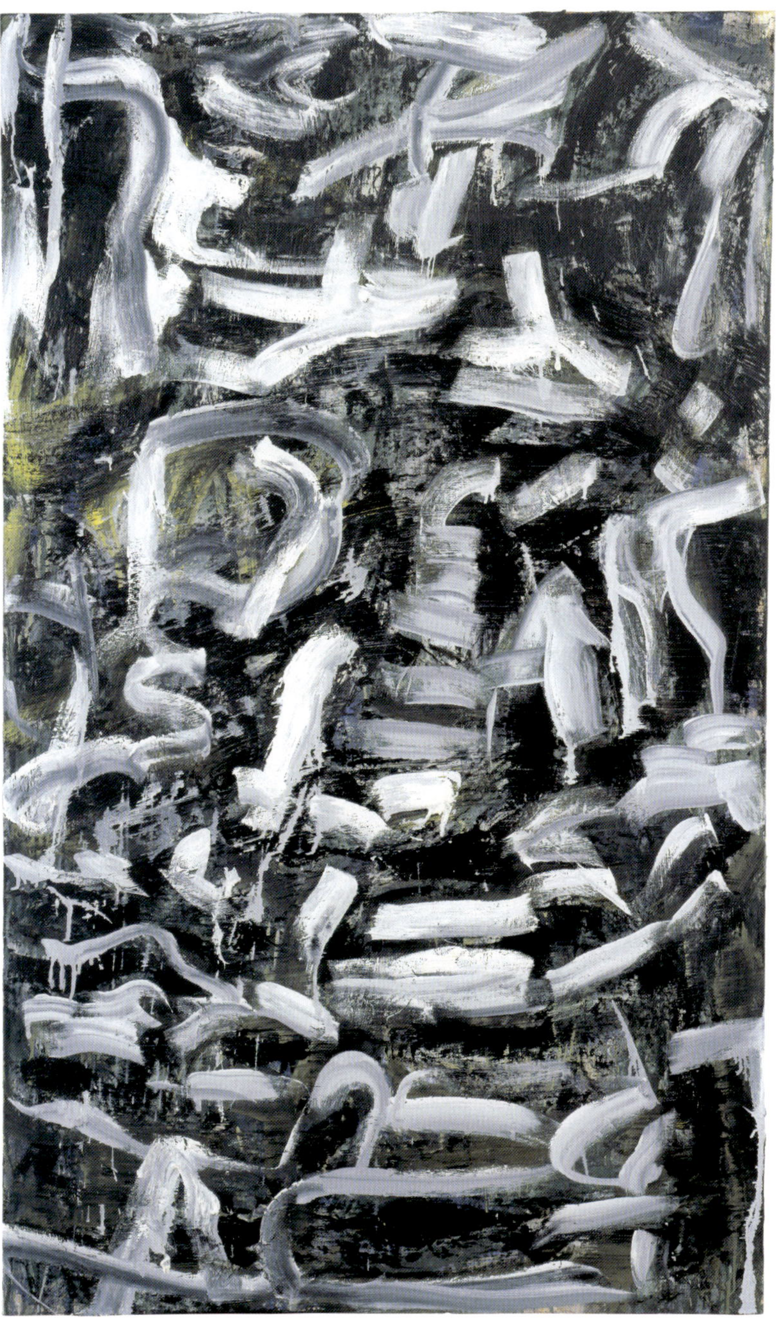

FIGURE 16
Louise Fishman, *Longhand*, 2007
Oil on linen, 66 x 39 in. (167.6 x 99 cm)

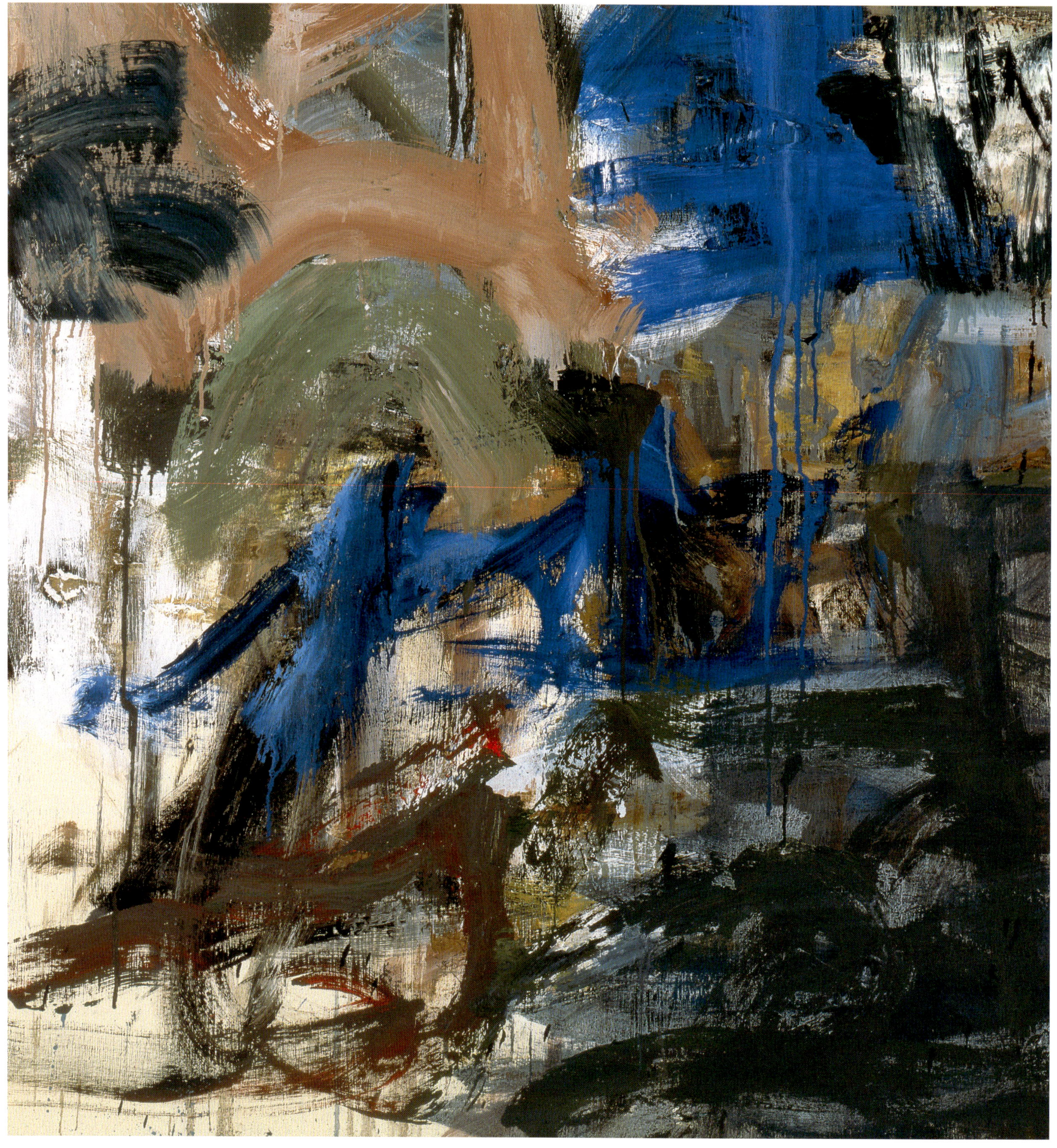

FIGURE 17
Detail of *April*, 1998 (pl. 61)

animal—as well as of the artist's hand. Fishman's more recent works continue to speak of material and process. The blades of knives and the teeth of trowels, along with the resilience and weave of the linen or canvas support and the saturation of the paint's pigment, are all given voice. Colors sing, strokes dance. Lately, air and light, as well as high-keyed palettes and glorious complications of deliberate gesture and barely controlled accident, have set the canvases in joyous motion.

The freedom of these recent paintings is grounded in a discipline long since internalized. When she was a teenager, Fishman was a competitive athlete. "I pitched hardball on the boys' team and I played varsity basketball in high school for four years," she recalls. "Playing sports was the only time I felt at home. . . . It wasn't until I started going to art school in 1956 that there was anything remotely as interesting to me as playing ball." It isn't the rigors of training and competition that she remembers; instead, she says, "painting gave me the same feeling of tremendous freedom I had experienced playing ball." That freedom is of a particular kind: It is born of immersion in an activity—and a language—that is bounded, rule-driven, in some ways arbitrary, and profoundly satisfying once absorbed and mastered. It allows for a kind of expression independent of words. "In sports I didn't have to explain myself. And in art I didn't have to unless I used figurative art and content," Fishman observes.[16] That is to say, abstraction, like sports, offers a kind of linguistic community—a community of understanding that can be as satisfying as those organized around faith, or other forms of identity: gender, culture, profession, age. It is a language for expressing things that are unsayable any other way. Few artists have put it to use with greater fluency.

Notes

1. David Deitcher, "Vitruvian Woman," in *Louise Fishman*, exh. cat. (New York: Cheim & Read, 2006), unpaginated.
2. Lucy R. Lippard, "Household Images in Art" (1973), reprinted in Lippard, *From the Center: Feminist Essays on Women's Art* (New York: E. P. Dutton, 1976), 57. In a reluctant summary of such characteristics originally published in 1971, Lippard listed "a uniform density, or overall texture, often sensuously tactile and repetitive or detailed to the point of obsession. . . ." See "Prefaces to Catalogues of Women's Exhibitions (Three Parts)" (1971–75), also reprinted in *From the Center*, 49.
3. Louise Fishman in Carrie Moyer, "Zero at the Bone: Louise Fishman Speaks with Carrie Moyer," *Art Journal* 71, no. 4 (Winter 2012): 40.
4. Louise Fishman quoted in Holland Cotter, "Art after Stonewall: Twelve Artists Interviewed—Louise Fishman," *Art in America* 82, no. 6 (June 1994): 60.
5. Fishman in "Zero at the Bone," 40–41.
6. Henri Michaux, *Drawing Papers 14: Emergences/Resurgences*, trans. Richard Sieburth (New York: The Drawing Center, 2000), 12. Ellipsis in the original.
7. Vilém Flusser, "The Gesture of Writing," in *Gestures*, trans. Nancy Ann Roth (Minneapolis: University of Minnesota Press, 2014), 21.
8. Fishman in "Zero at the Bone," 41.
9. These details were confirmed by Ingrid Nyeboe, Fishman's spouse. Nyeboe, email to the author, June 5, 2015.
10. Faye Hirsch, "The Disputatious Abstraction of Louise Fishman," in *Louise Fishman: The Tenacity of Painting, Paintings from 1970 to 2005*, exh. cat. (Hanover, NH: Dartmouth College Studio Art Exhibition Program, 2007), unpaginated.
11. Ibid.
12. Nyeboe, email to the author, June, 2015.
13. Melissa E. Feldman, *Louise Fishman*, exh. cat. (New York: Robert Miller Gallery, 1993), unpaginated.
14. "Brice Marden on *Cold Mountain*," San Francisco Museum of Modern Art video interview, February 20, 2007, www.sfmoma.org/explore/multimedia/videos/125.
15. The name of Madonna's tour spelled "blonde" without the "e." Nyeboe notes that Fishman's addition of an "e" in this artwork's title was a "secret reference" to Marilyn Monroe, another famous blonde. Ingrid Nyeboe, email to the author, June 23, 2015.
16. All quotations of Fishman's reflections on sports and painting in this paragraph are from Fishman in "Art After Stonewall," 59.

PLATES II

PLATE 26. *Ashkenazi*, 1978. Oil on linen, 32 x 48 in. (81.2 x 122 cm)

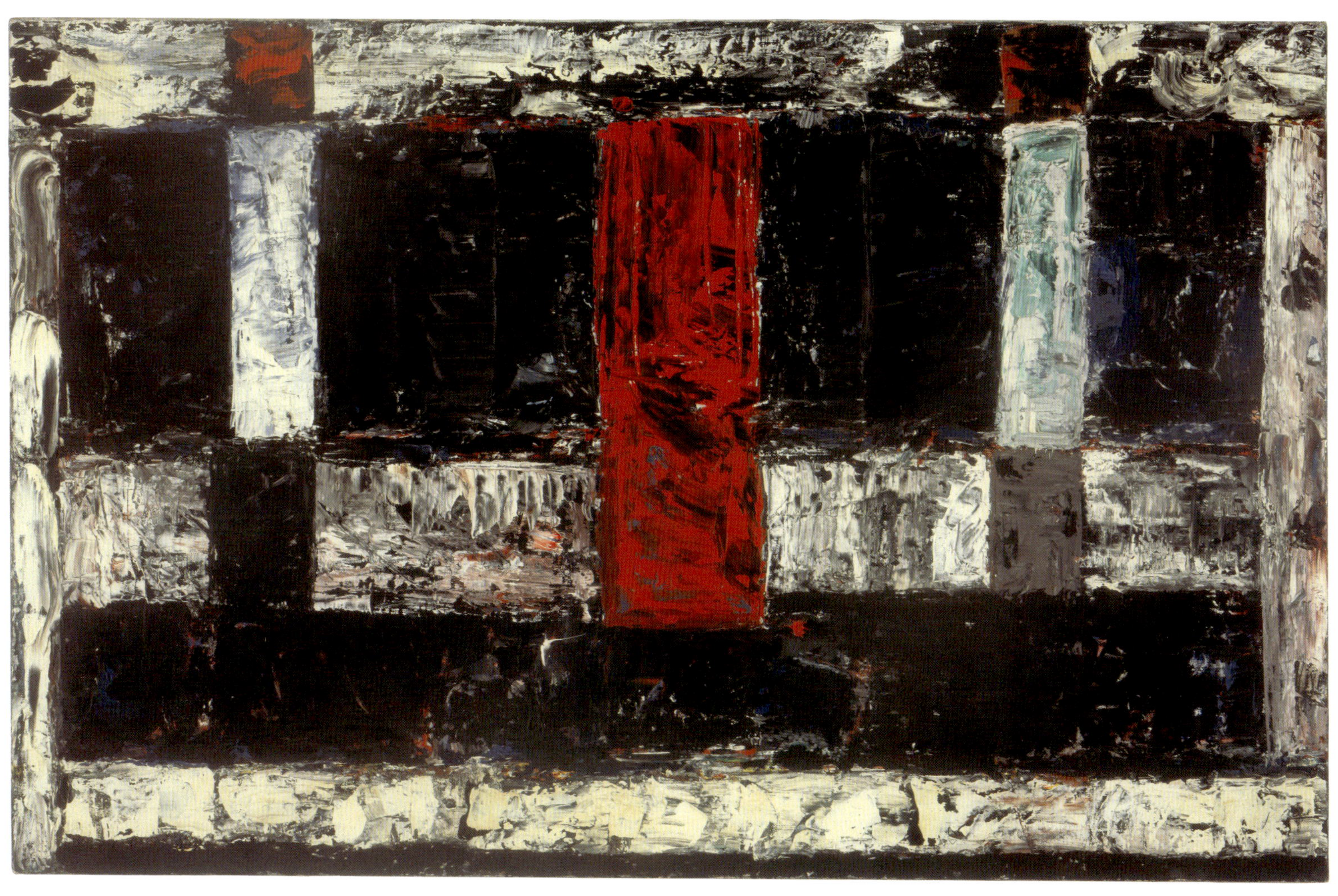

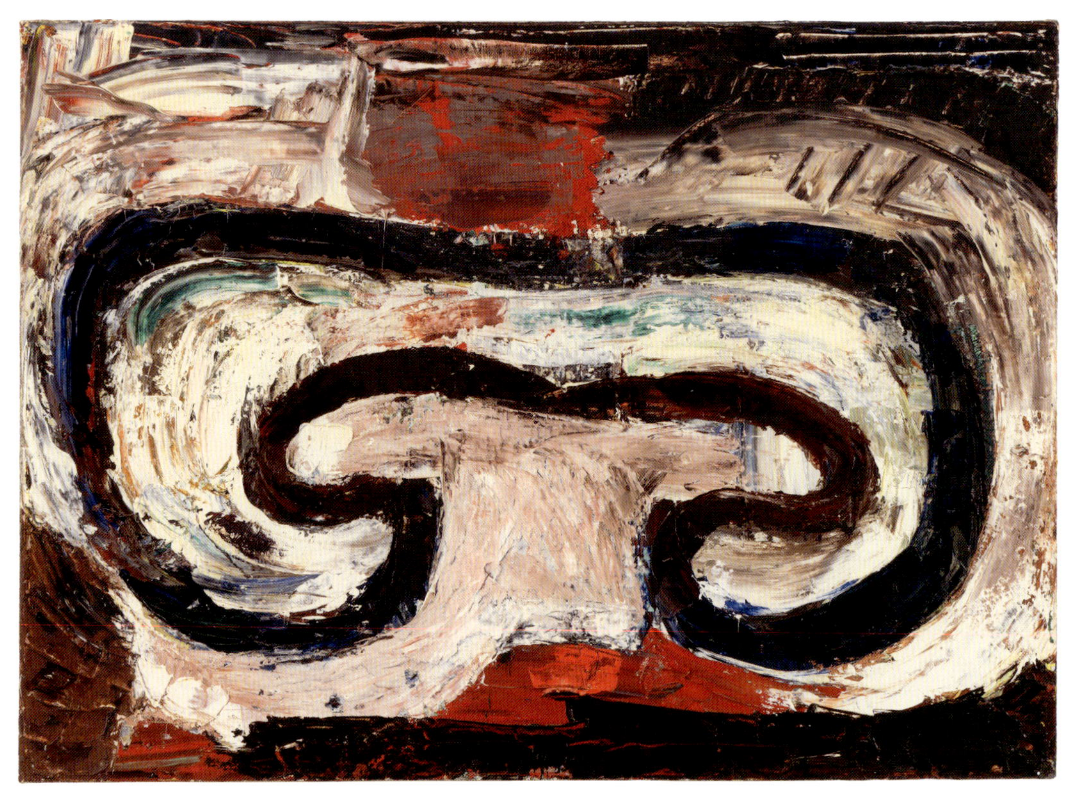

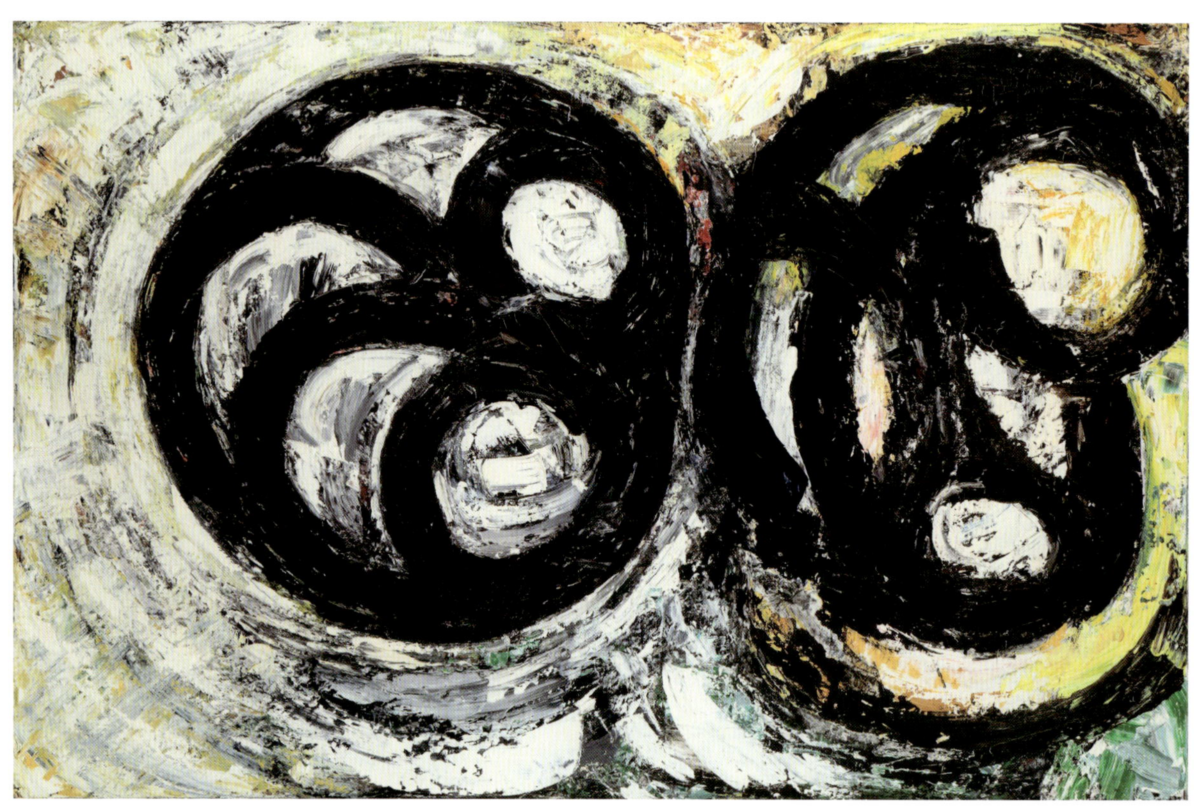

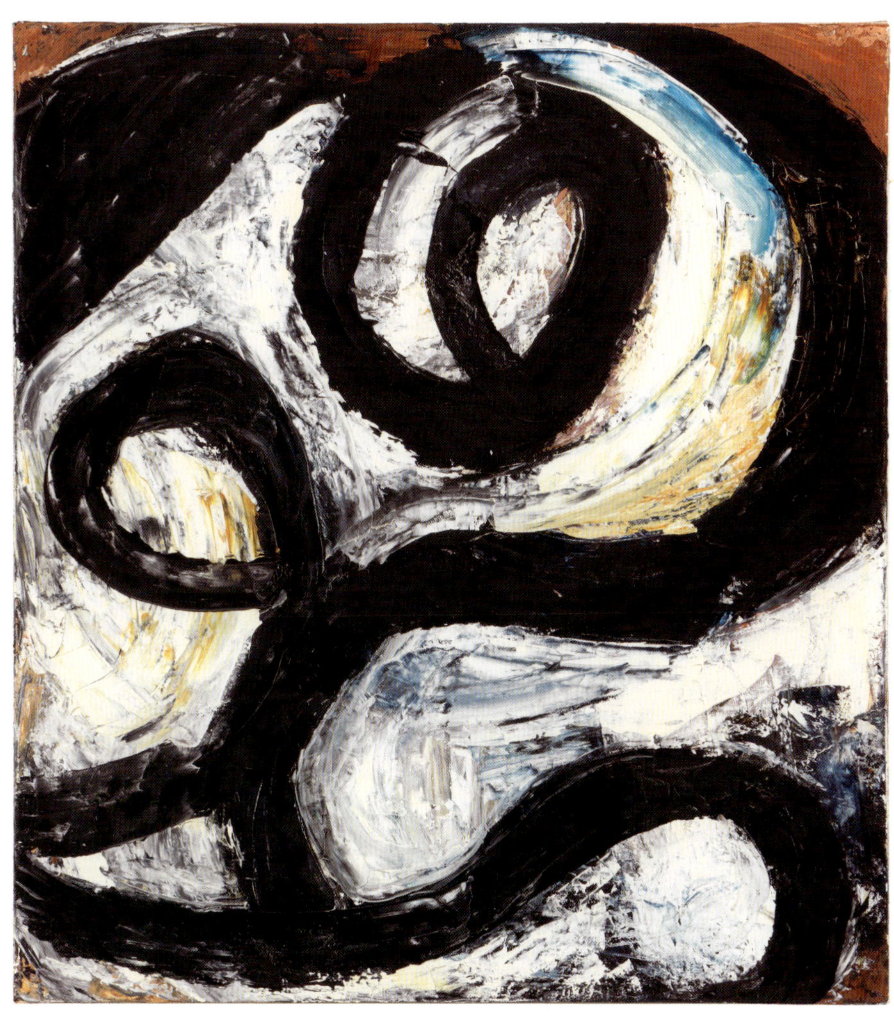

PLATE 27. *MacDowell Series #4 (Red Lodge)*, 1980. Oil on linen, 23 x 32 in. (58.4 x 81.3 cm)
PLATE 28. *Golem*, 1981. Oil on linen, 32 x 48 in. (81.3 x 121.9 cm). The Jewish Museum, New York, Gift of Francine and Samuel Klagsbrun, 1991-56
PLATE 29. *Navigation*, 1981. Oil on linen, 25 x 22 in. (63.5 x 55.9 cm)

PLATE 30. *Grand Slam*, 1985. Oil on canvas, 56 x 40 in. (142.2 x 101.6 cm). The Metropolitan Museum of Art, New York, Edith C. Blum Fund, 1986.387

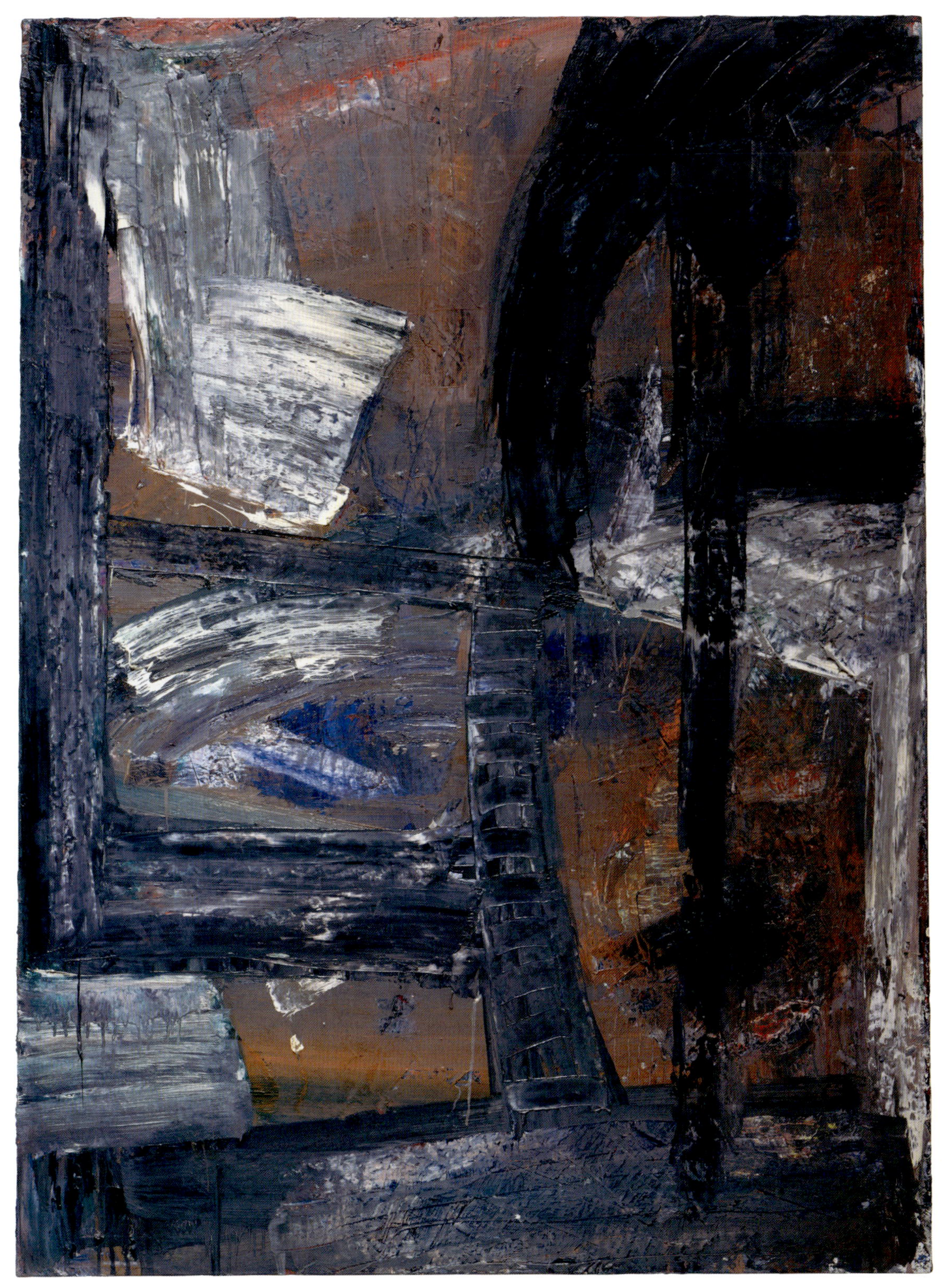

PLATE 31. *Roughneck*, 1985. Oil on linen, 47 x 41 in. (119.4 x 104.1 cm). Private collection

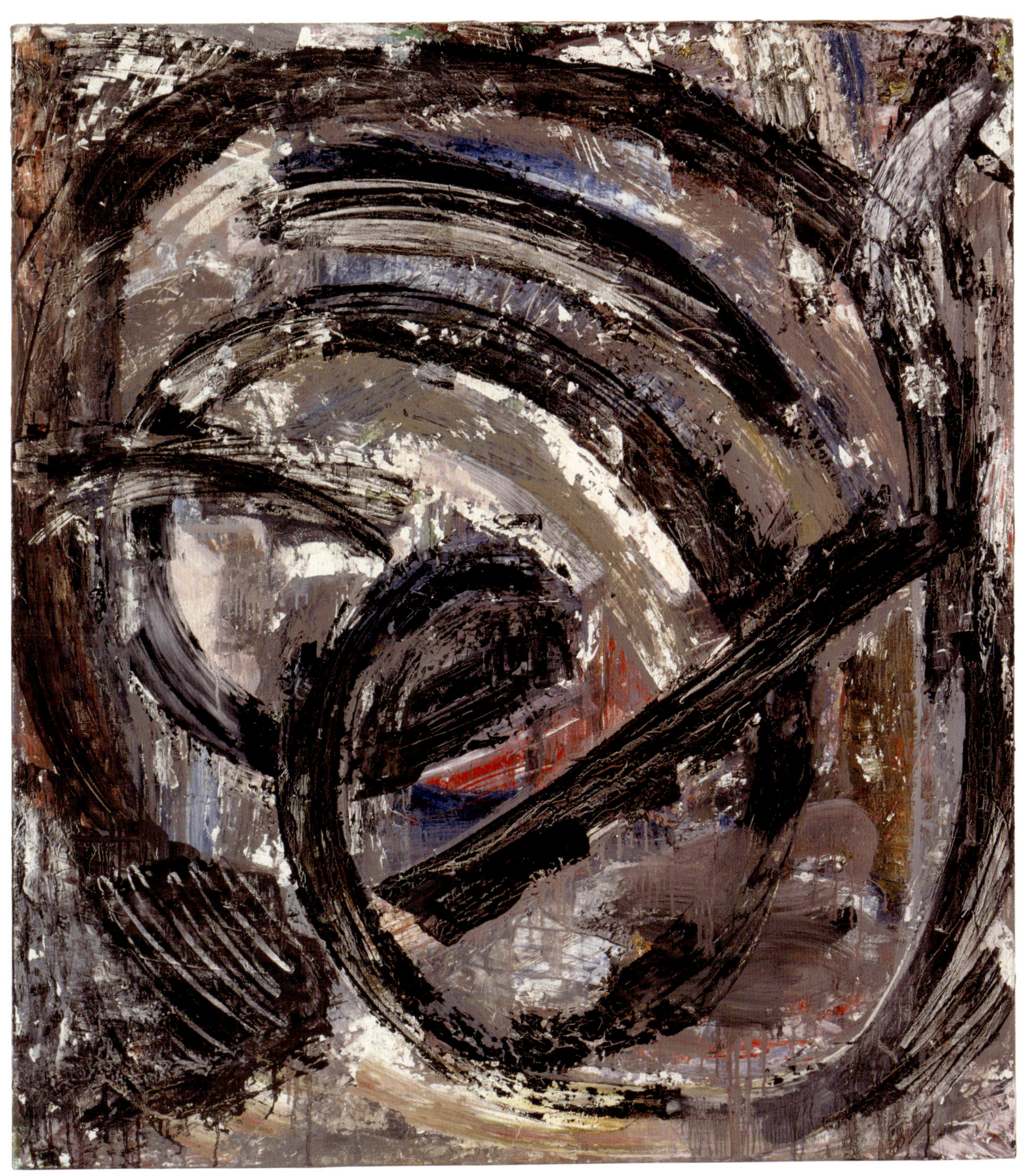

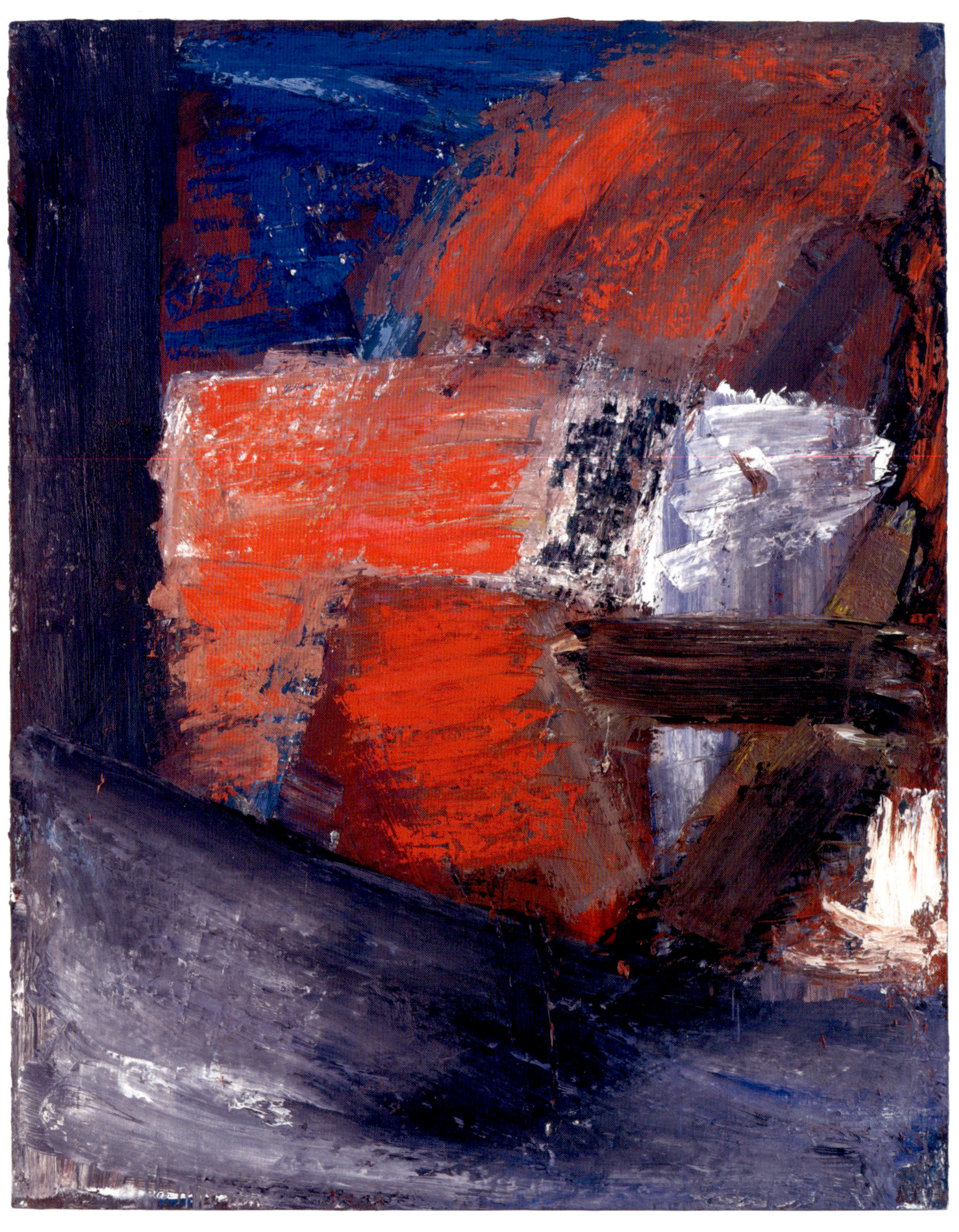

PLATE 32. *Cinnabar and Malachite*, 1986. Oil on linen, 50 x 39 in. (127 x 99.1 cm). Private collection
PLATE 33. *Colophon*, 1987. Oil on linen, 77 x 54 in. (195.6 x 137.2 cm). Private collection

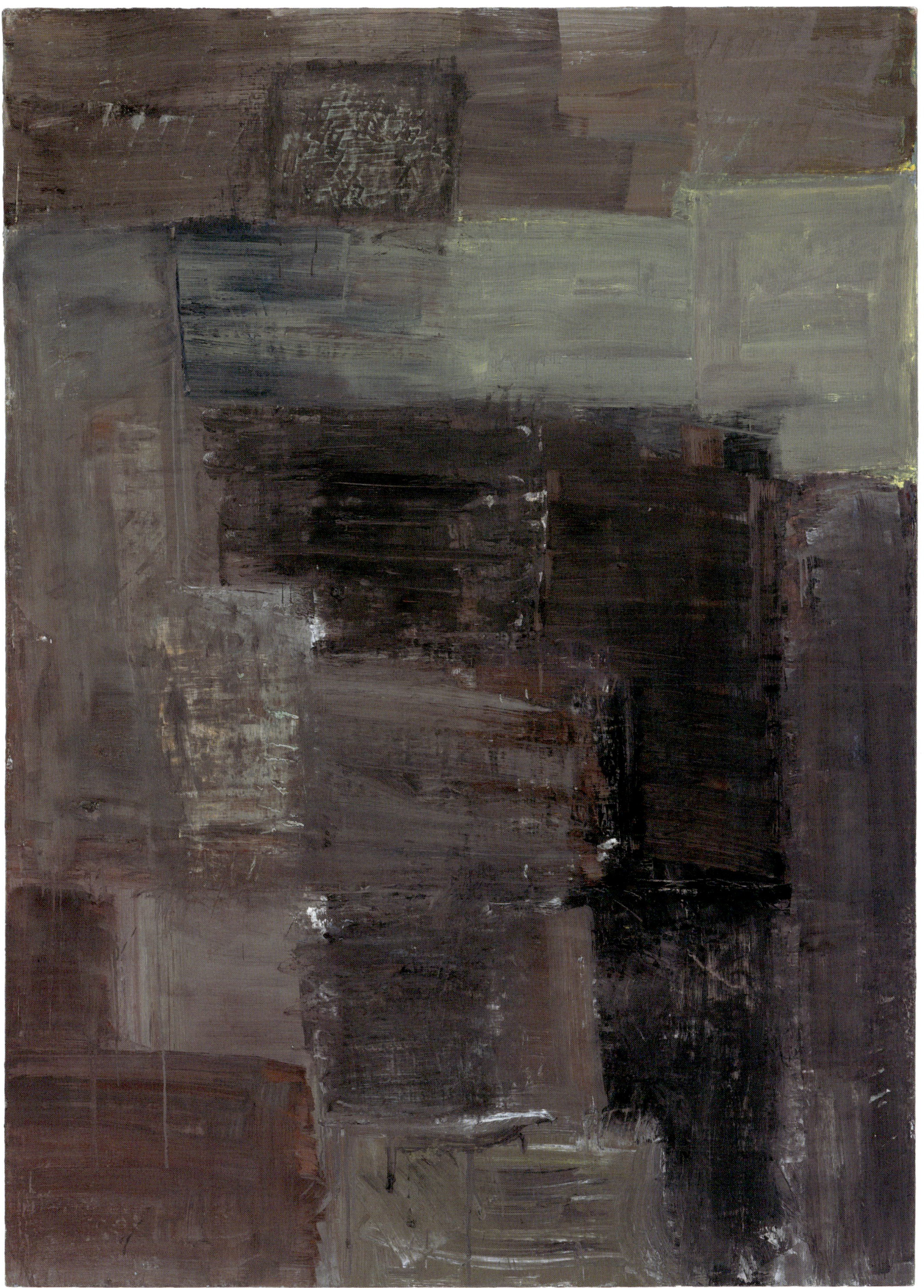

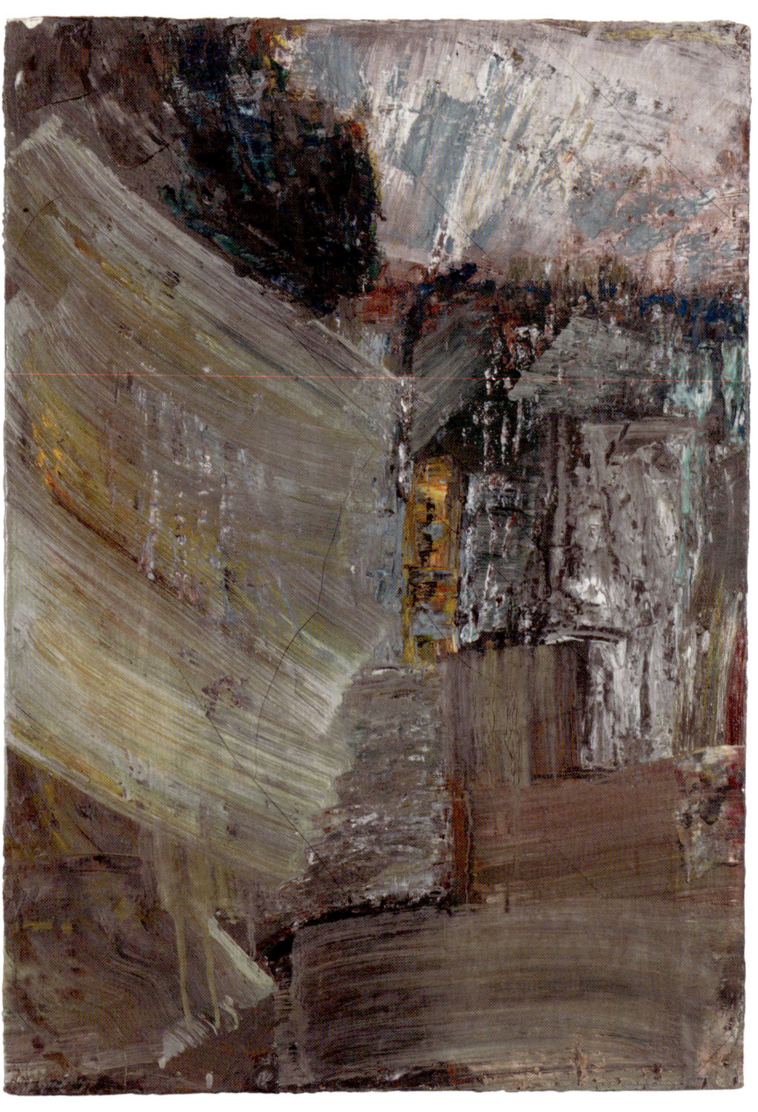

PLATE 34. *Double Dutch*, 1987. Oil on linen, 25 x 17 in. (63.5 x 43.2 cm). Collection of John Cheim

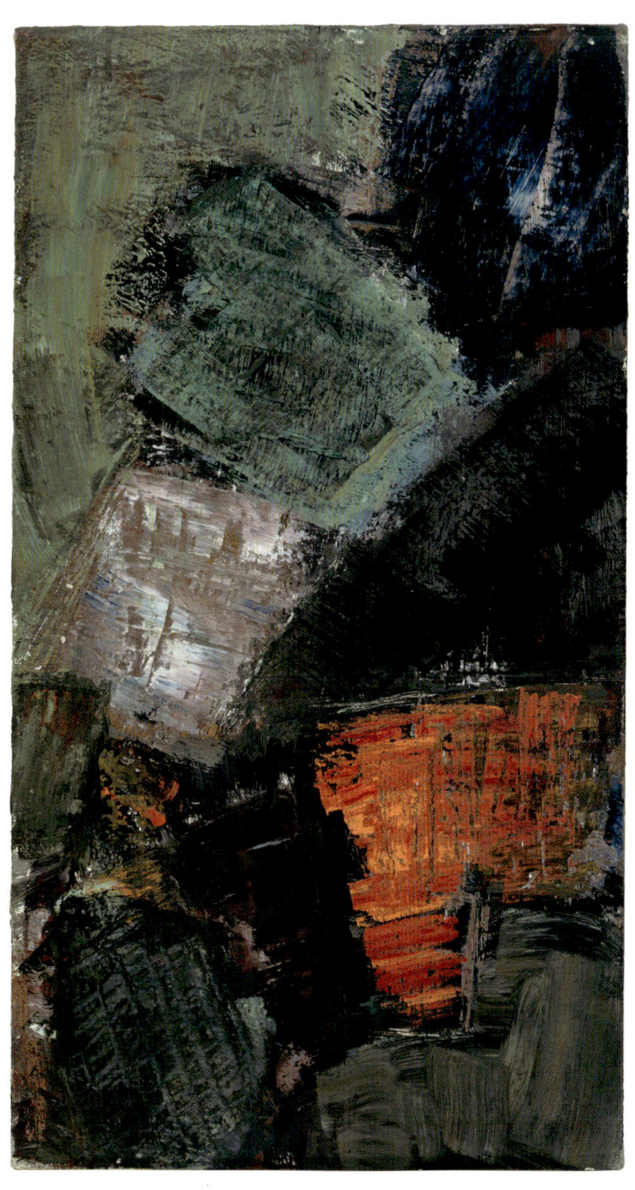

PLATE 35. *Headwaters*, 1987. Oil on canvas, 32 x 17 in. (81.2 x 43 cm). Private collection

PLATE 36. *Stand of Beech*, 1987. Oil on canvas, 65 x 50 in. (165.1 x 127 cm)

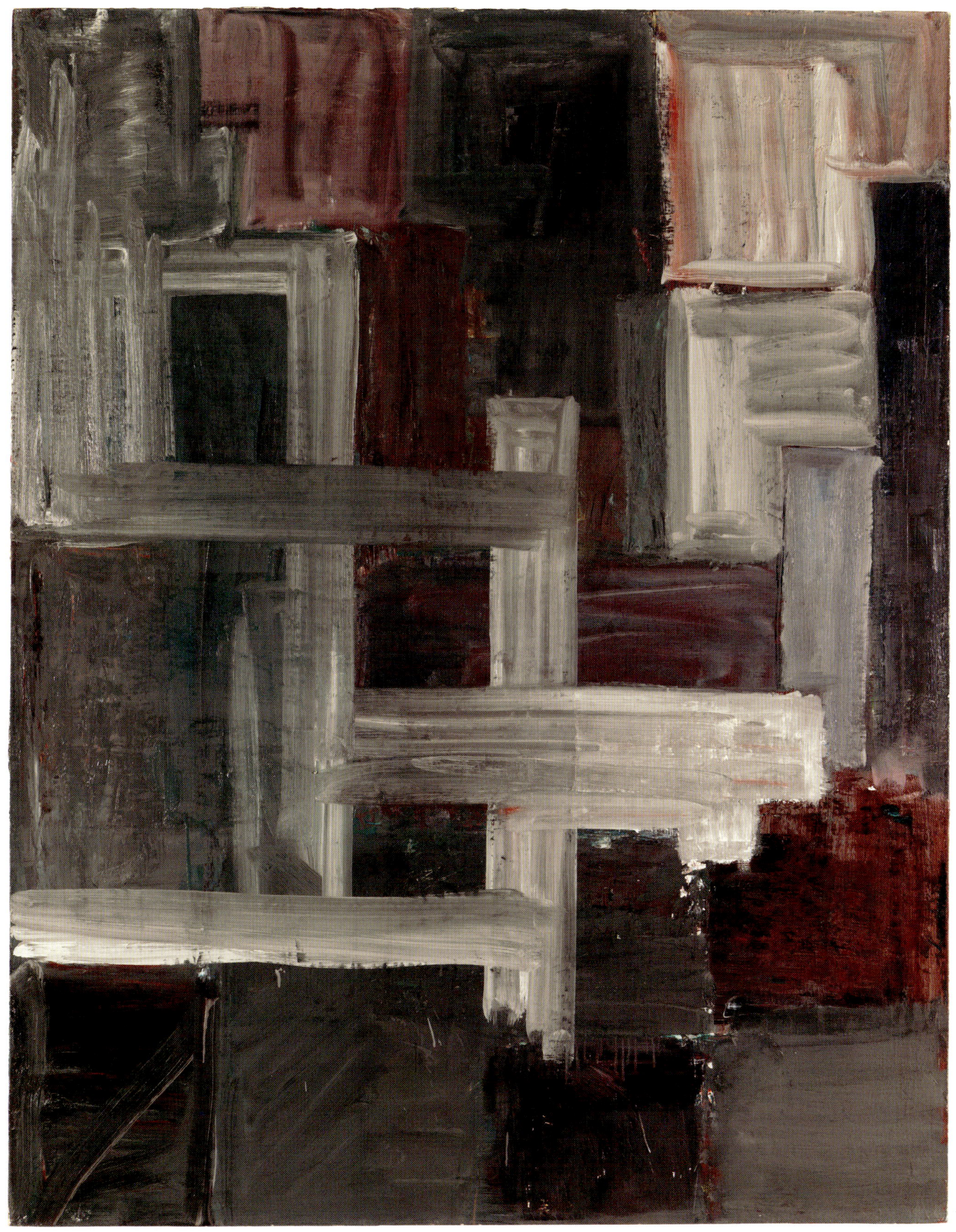

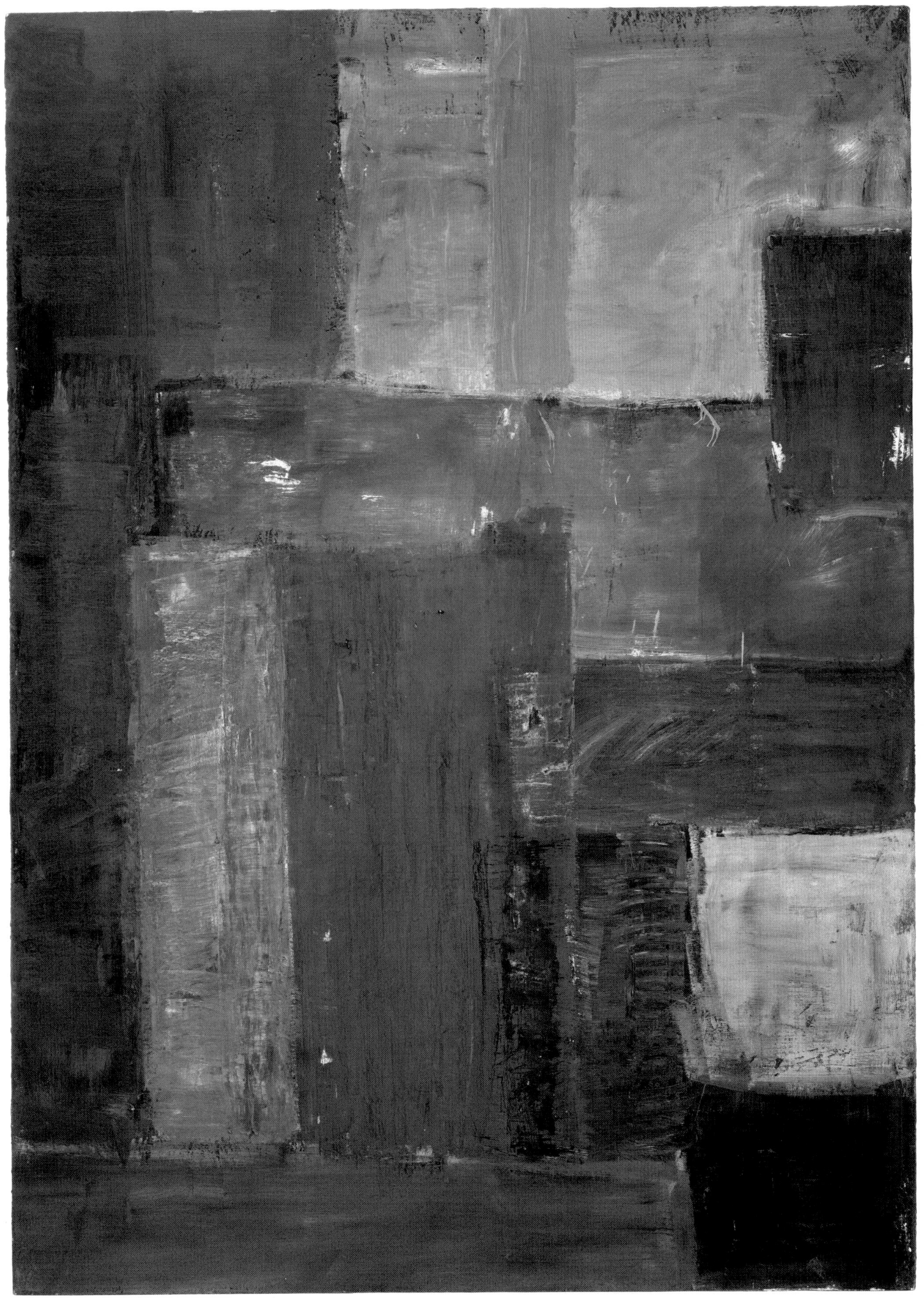

PLATE 37. *Dortn*, 1987–88. Oil on linen, 77 x 54 in. (195.6 x 137.2 cm). Private collection
PLATE 38. *Bitter Herb*, 1988. Oil on linen, 65 x 45 in. (165.1 x 114.3 cm). Courtesy of Fernando Luis Alvarez Gallery, Stamford, Connecticut

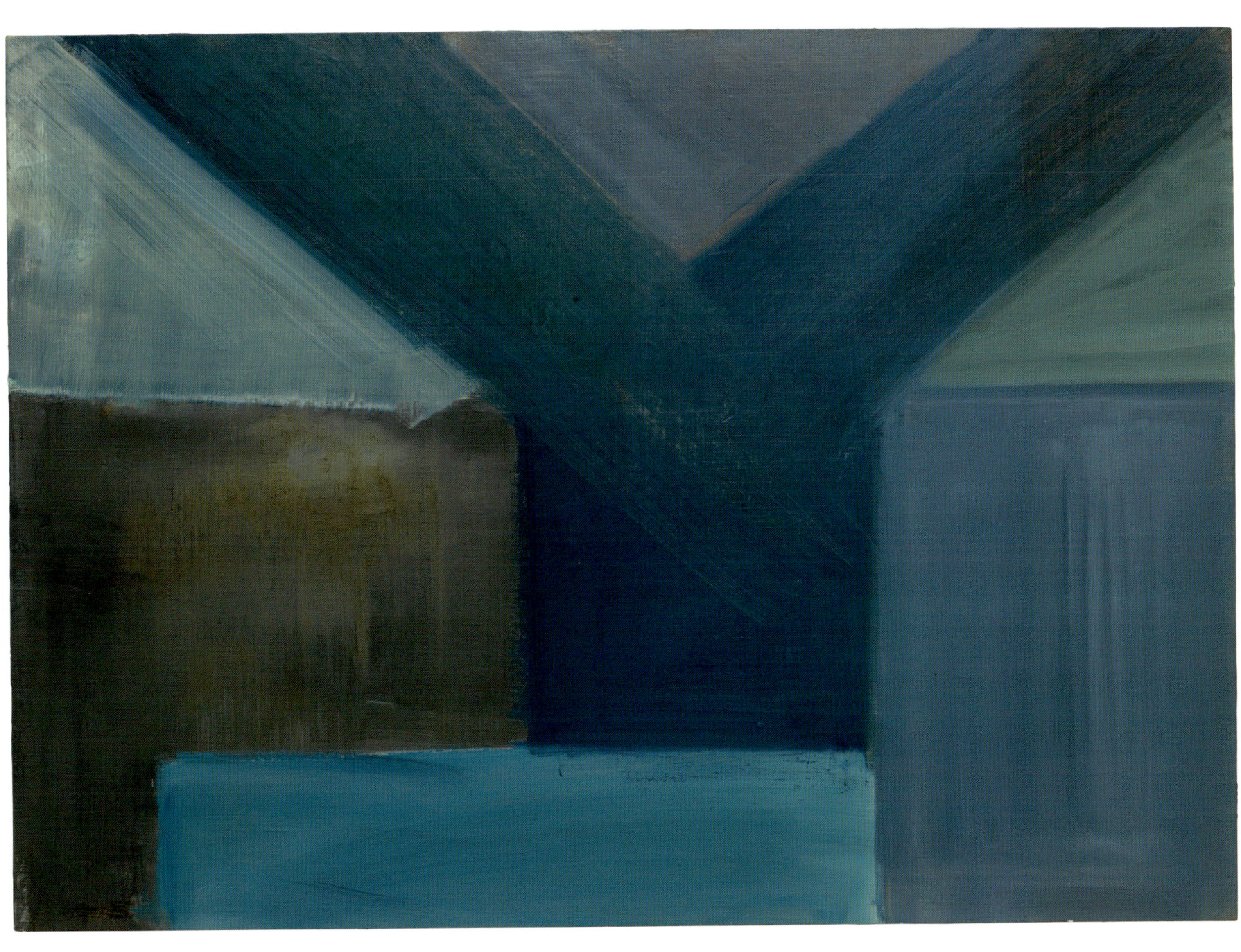

PLATE 39. *Four Questions*, 1988. Oil on canvas, 65 x 45 in. (165.1 x 114.3 cm)
PLATE 40. *Haggadah*, 1988. Oil on linen, 37 x 50 in. (94 x 127 cm). Collection of Stuart and Lisa Ginsberg

PLATE 41. *Karpas #4*, 1988. Oil on linen, 32½ x 24 in. (82.6 x 61 cm)

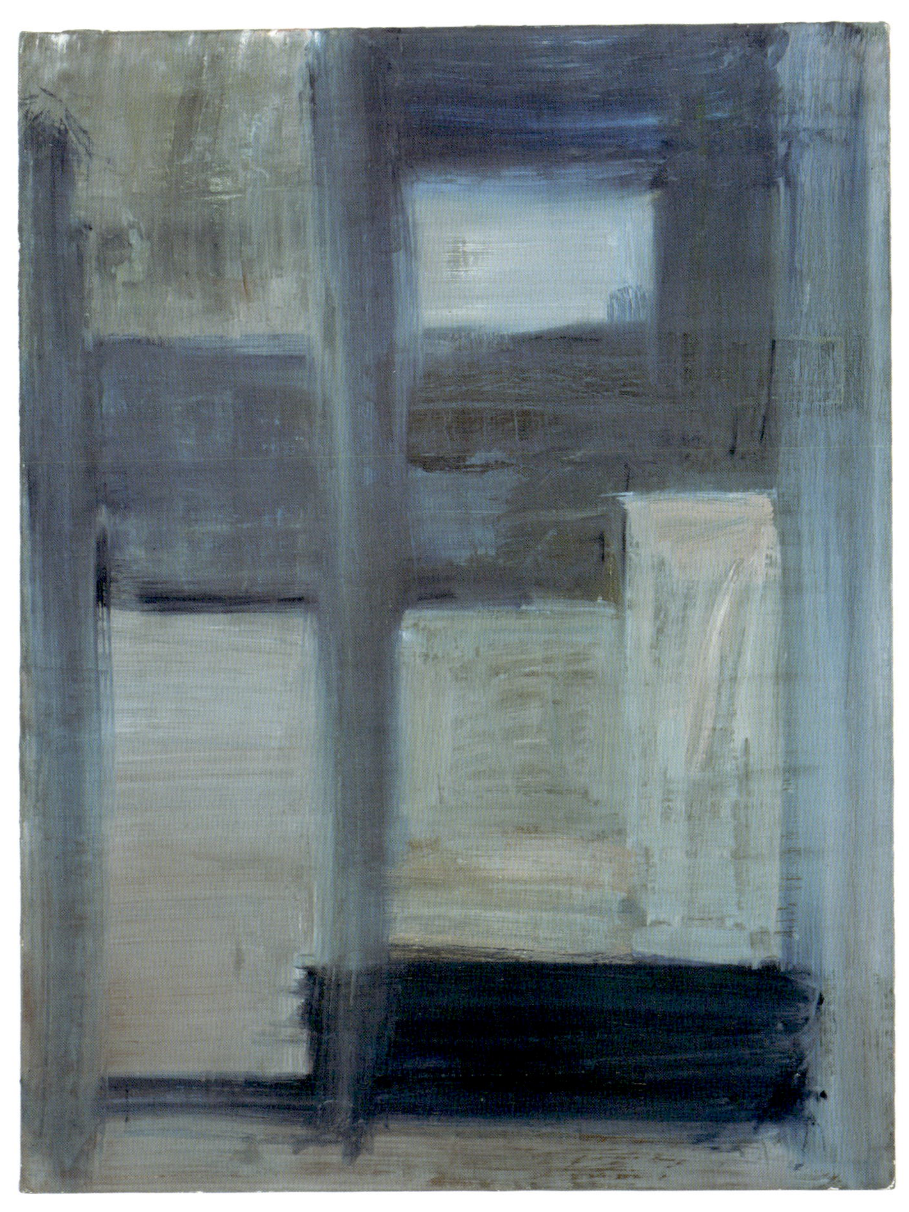

PLATE 42. *Untitled*, 1989. Oil on paper, 31 x 24 in. (78.7 x 61 cm)

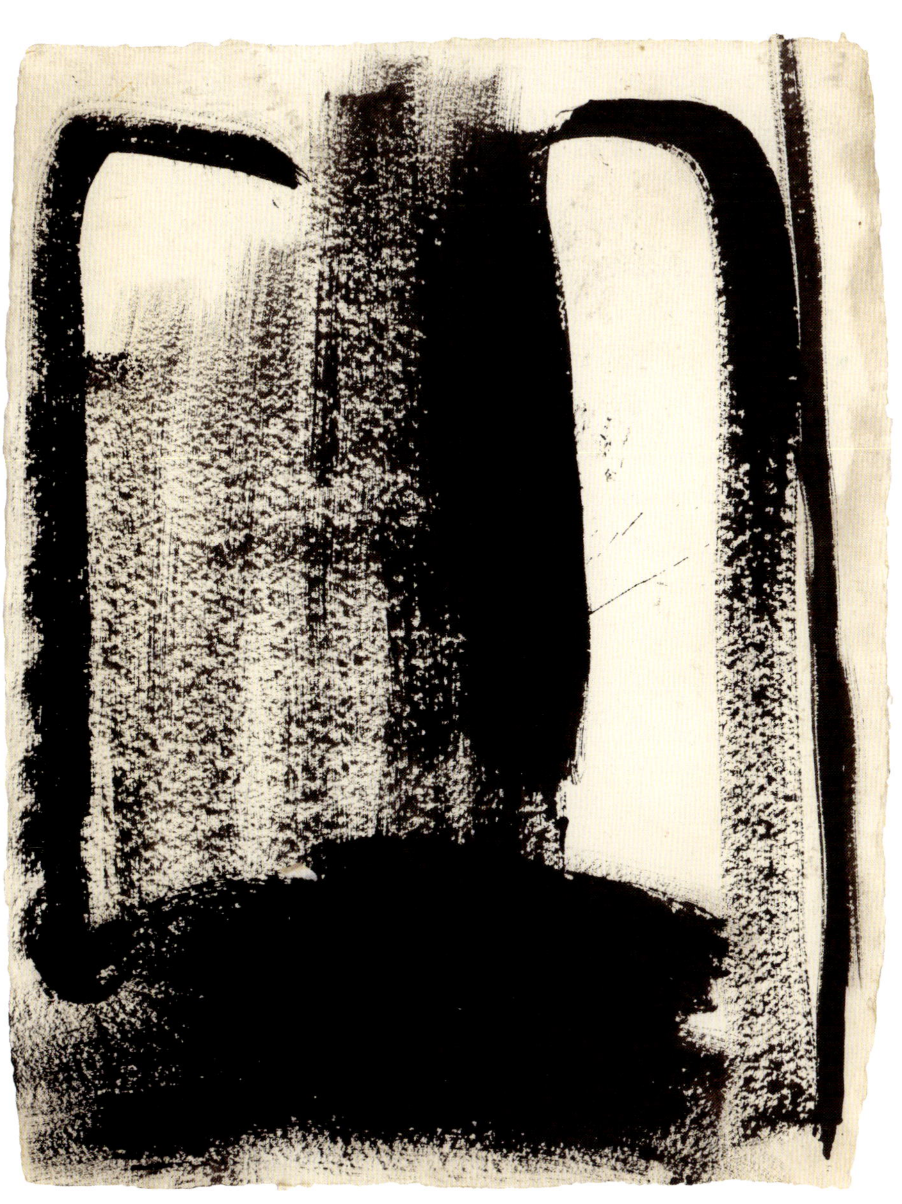

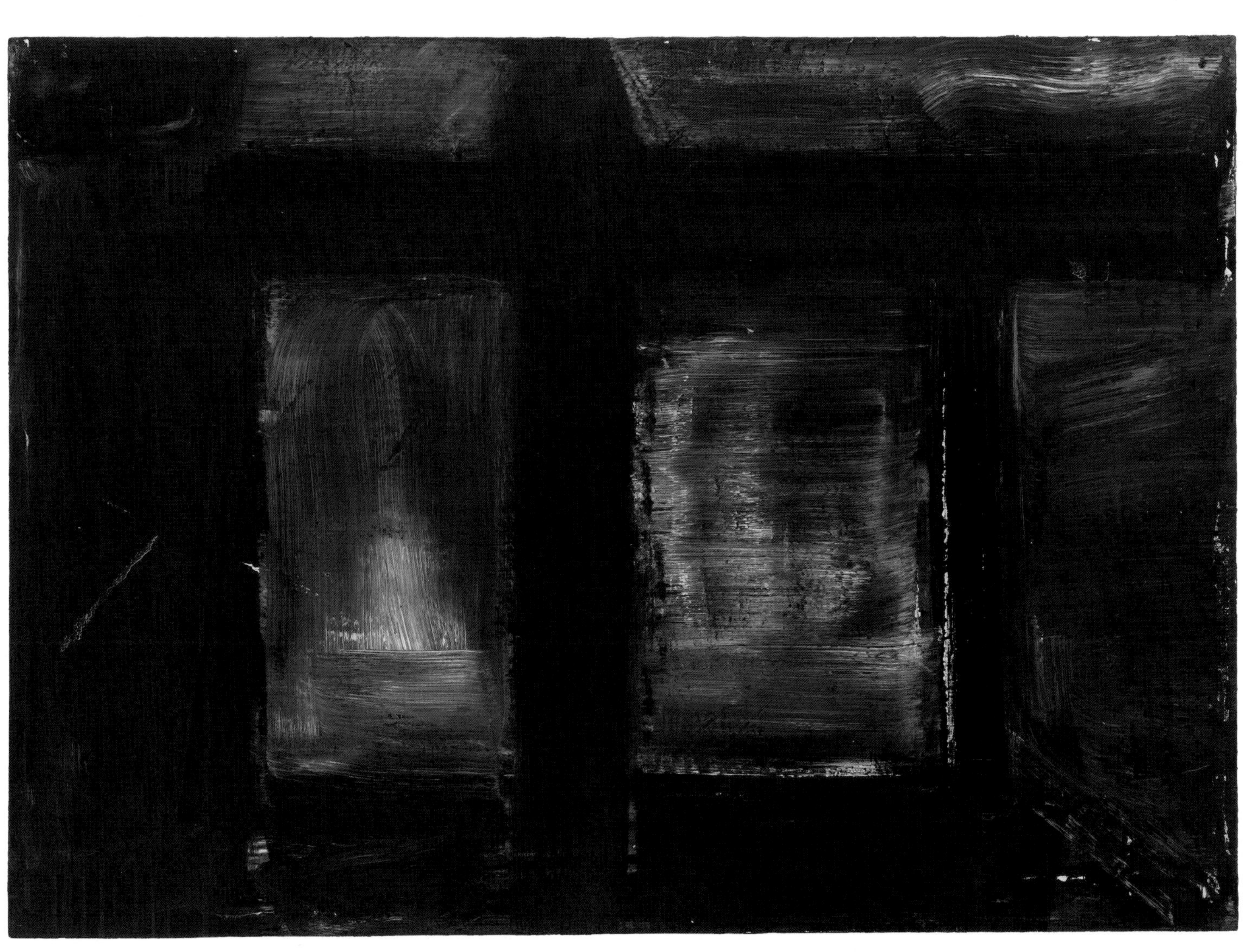

PLATE 43. *Beast in the Jungle*, 1990. Oil on linen, 65 x 58 in. (165.1 x 147.3 cm). Private collection
PLATE 44. *Dybbuk*, 1990. Oil on linen, 37 x 50 in. (94 x 127 cm)

PLATE 45. *Untitled*, 1990. Oil on paper, 31 x 22¾ in. (78.7 x 57.8 cm)

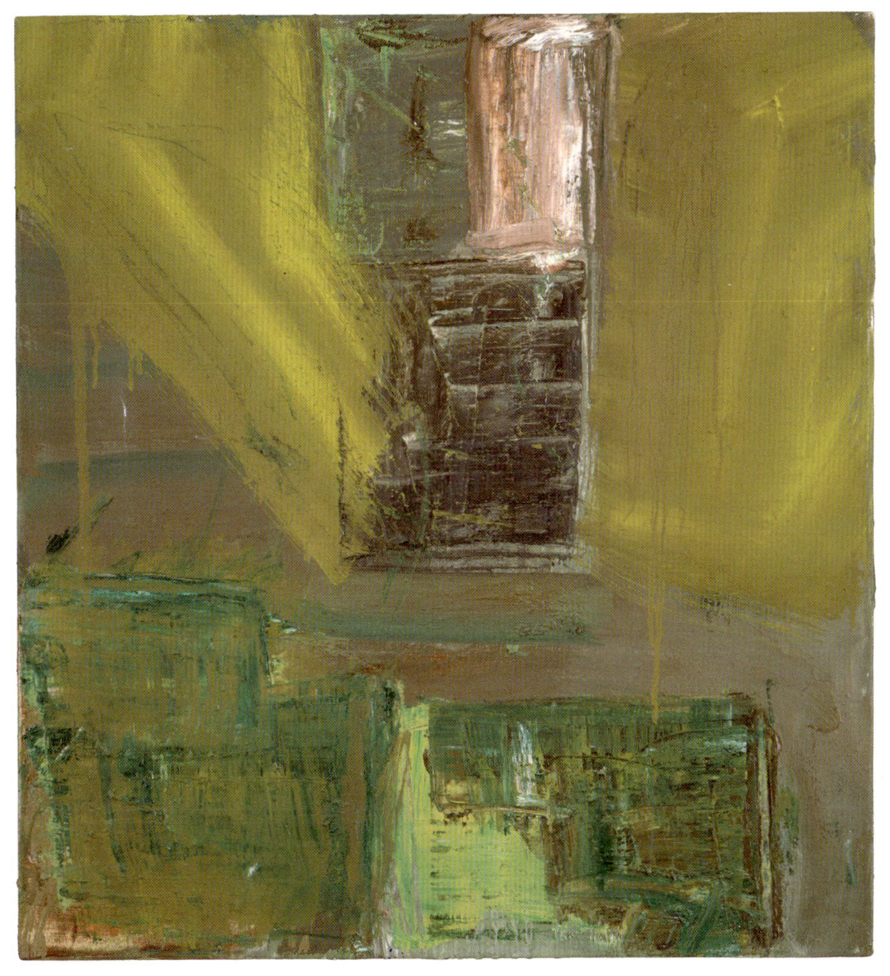

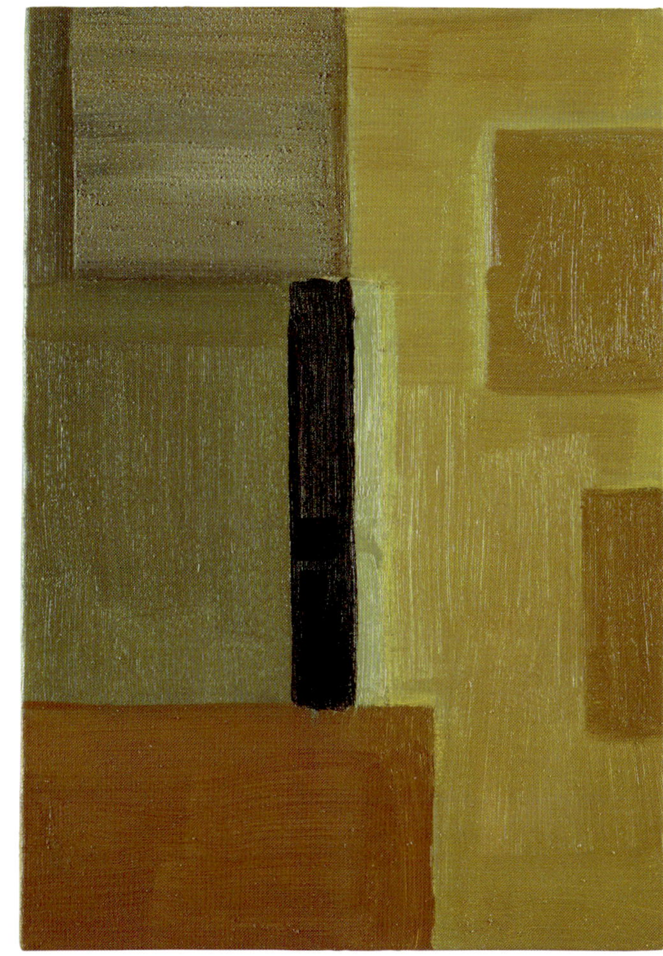

PLATE 46. *Dukkha*, 1991. Oil on linen, 20 x 18 in. (50.8 x 45.7 cm)
PLATE 47. *Samahdi*, 1991. Oil on linen, 19 x 13 in. (48.3 x 33 cm)

PLATE 48. *Sanctum Sanctorum*, 1992. Oil on linen, 90 x 62 in. (228 x 157.5 cm)

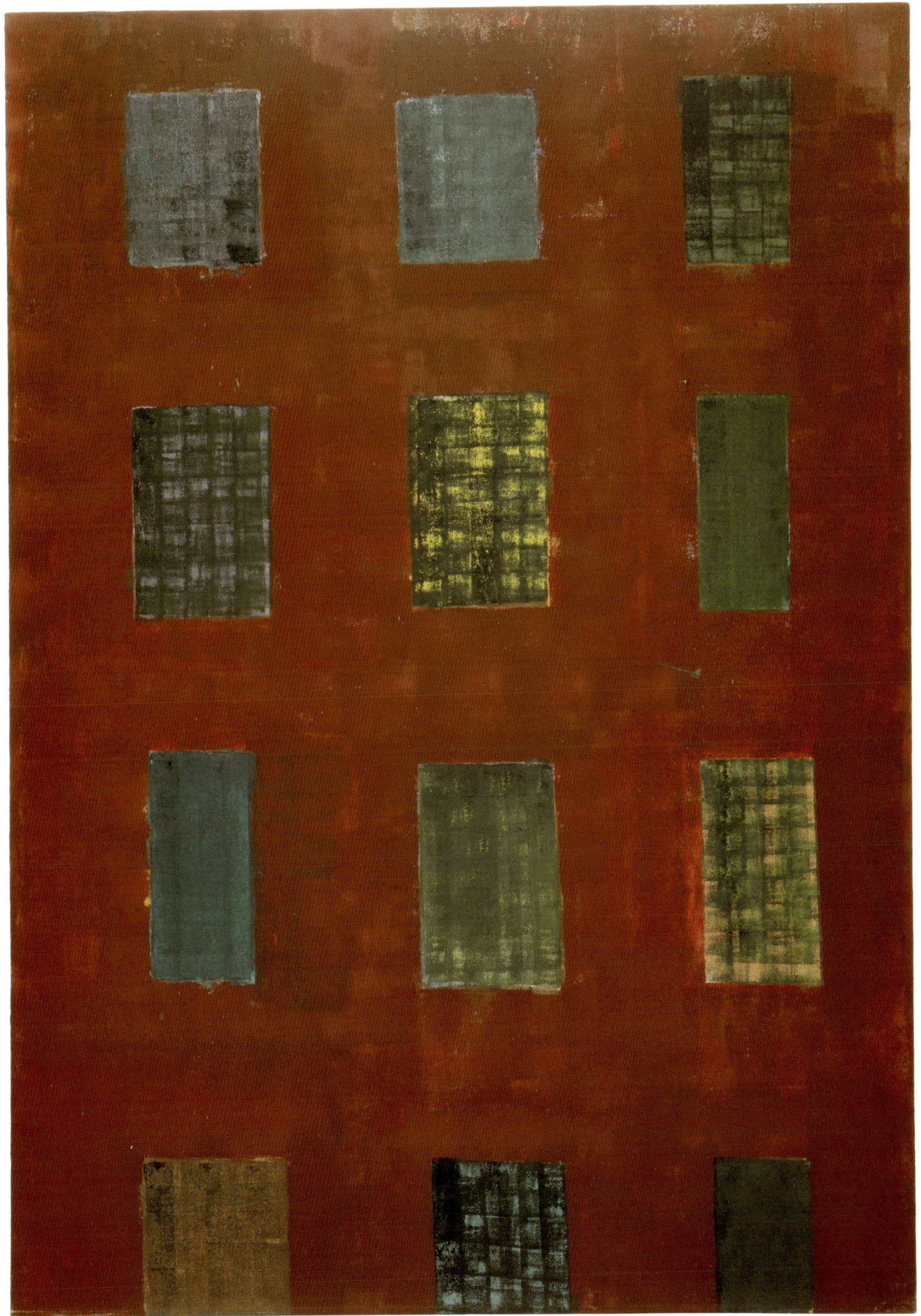

PLATE 49. *Valles Marineris*, 1992. Oil on linen, 90 x 62 in. (228 x 157.5 cm)

PLATE 50. *Iron Sharpens Iron*, 1993. Oil on linen, 110 x 70 in. (279.4 x 177.8 cm). The Art Institute of Chicago, gift of Robert Miller and Sarah Wittenborn Miller

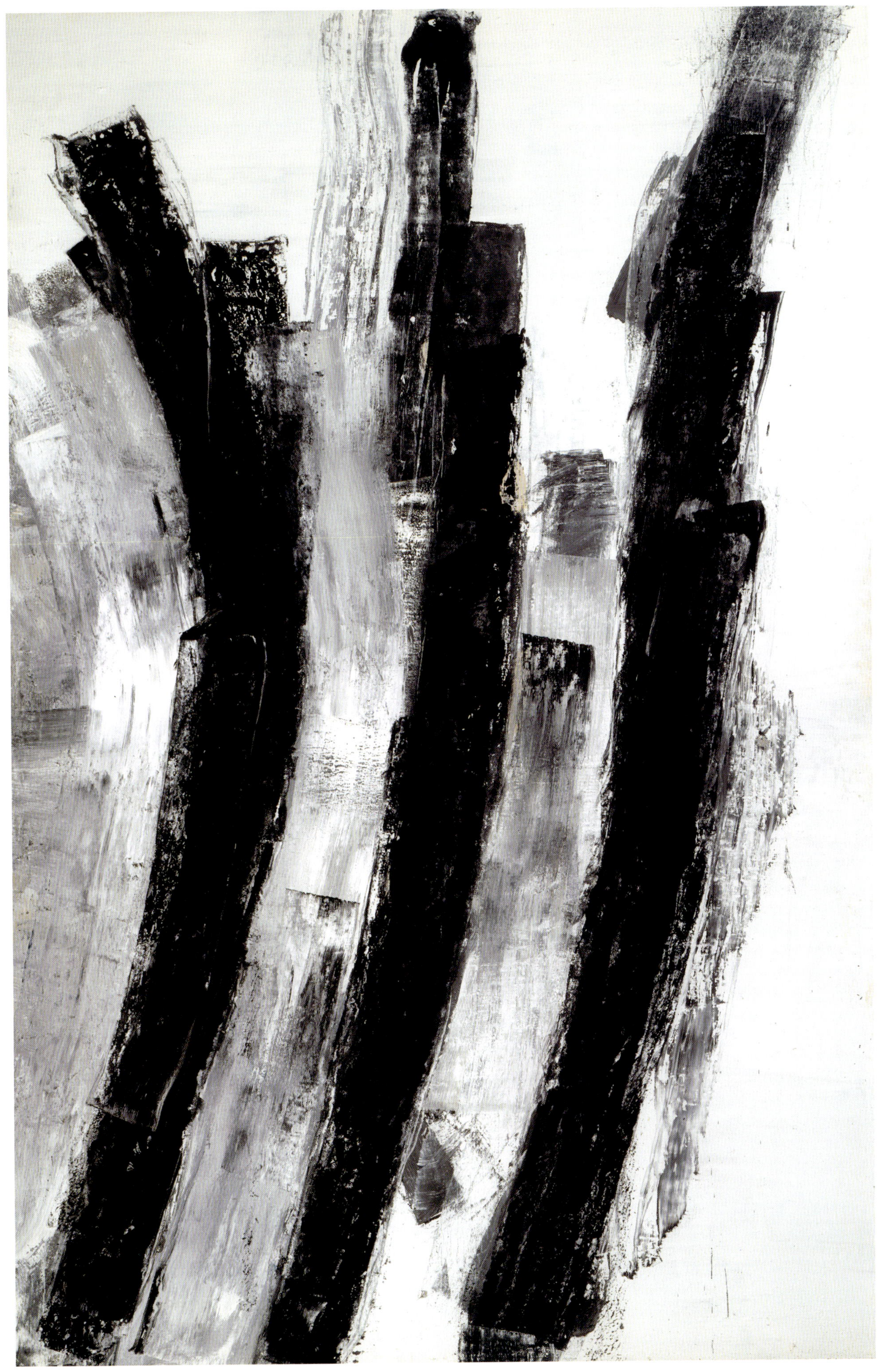

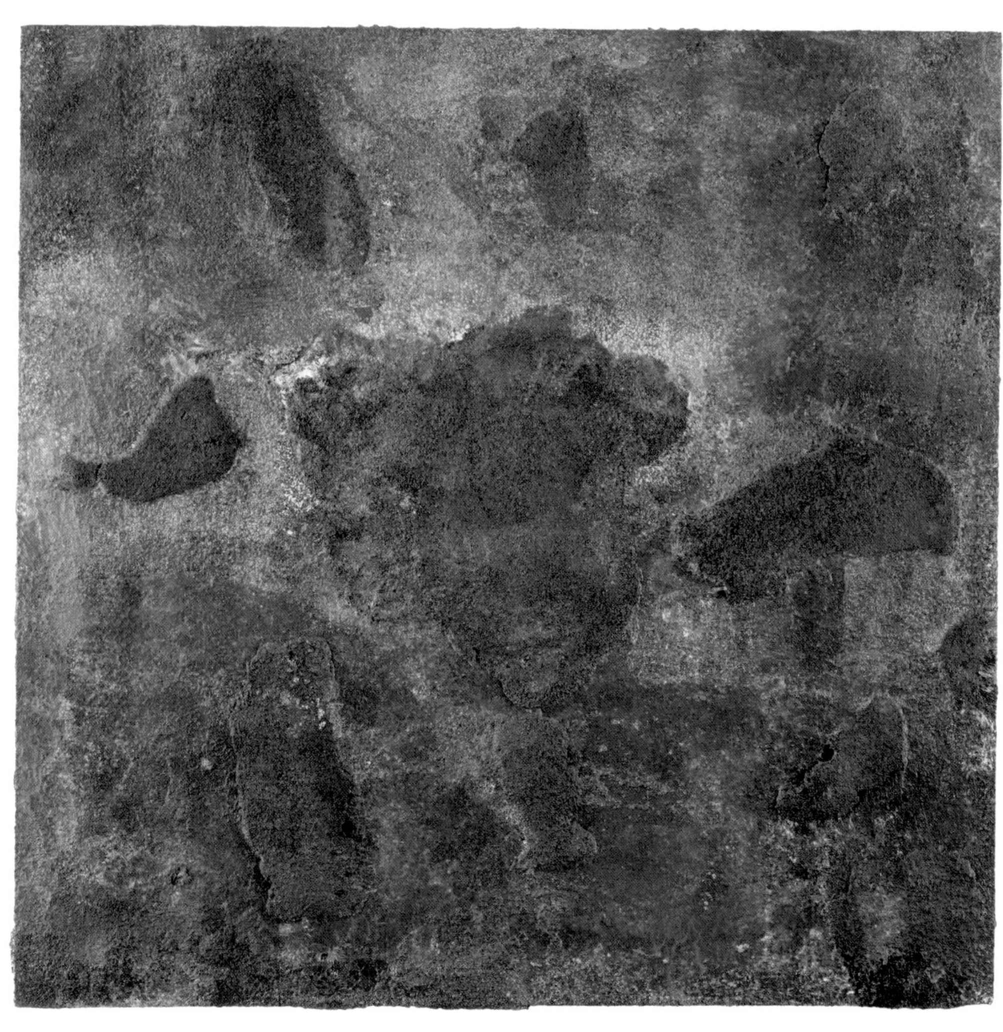

PLATE 51. *Walking with Maydl*, 1993. Oil on board, 12 x 12 in. (30.5 x 30.5 cm)
PLATE 52. *Blonde Ambition*, 1995. Oil on linen, 90 x 65 in. (228.6 x 165.1 cm)

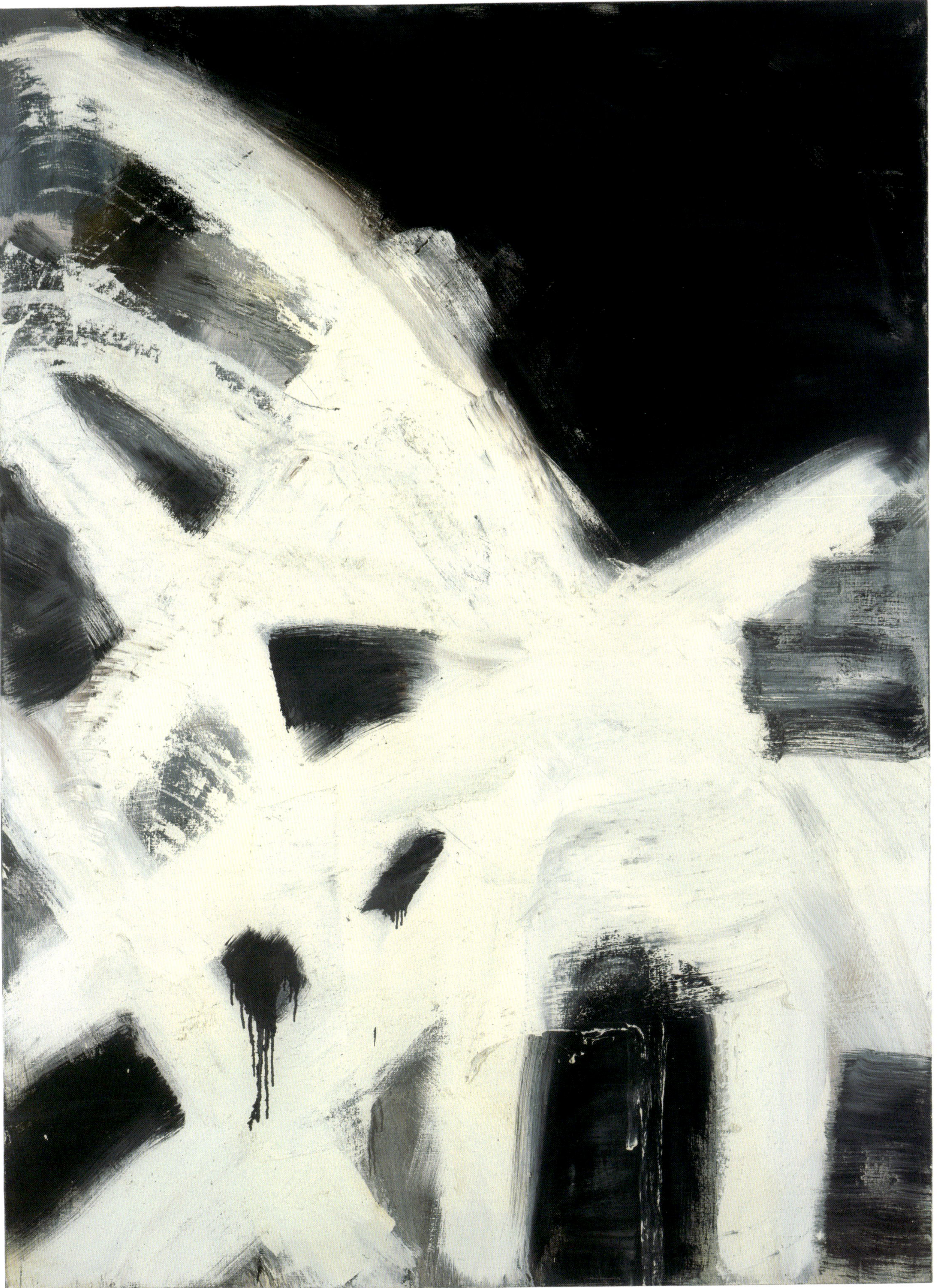

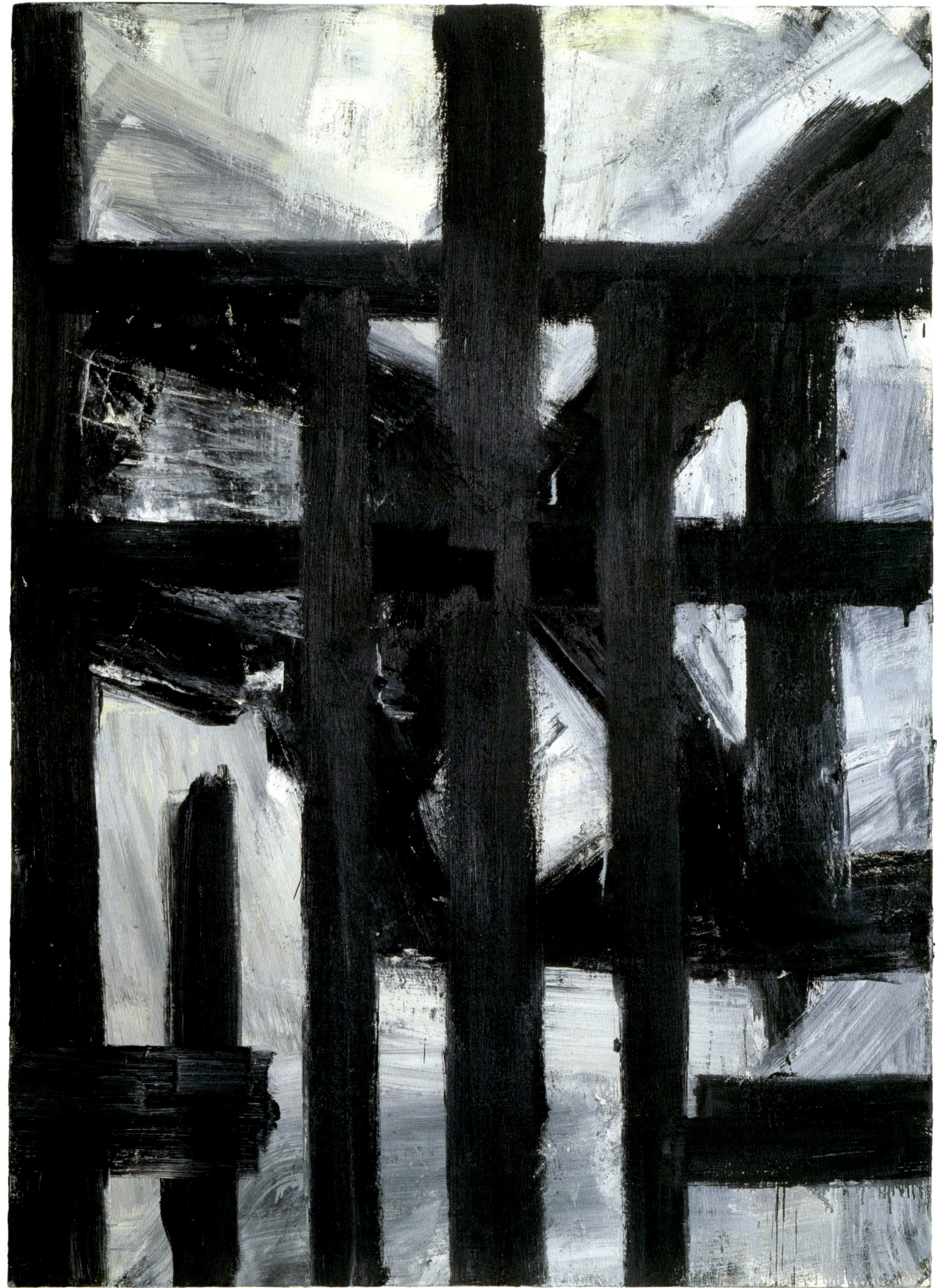

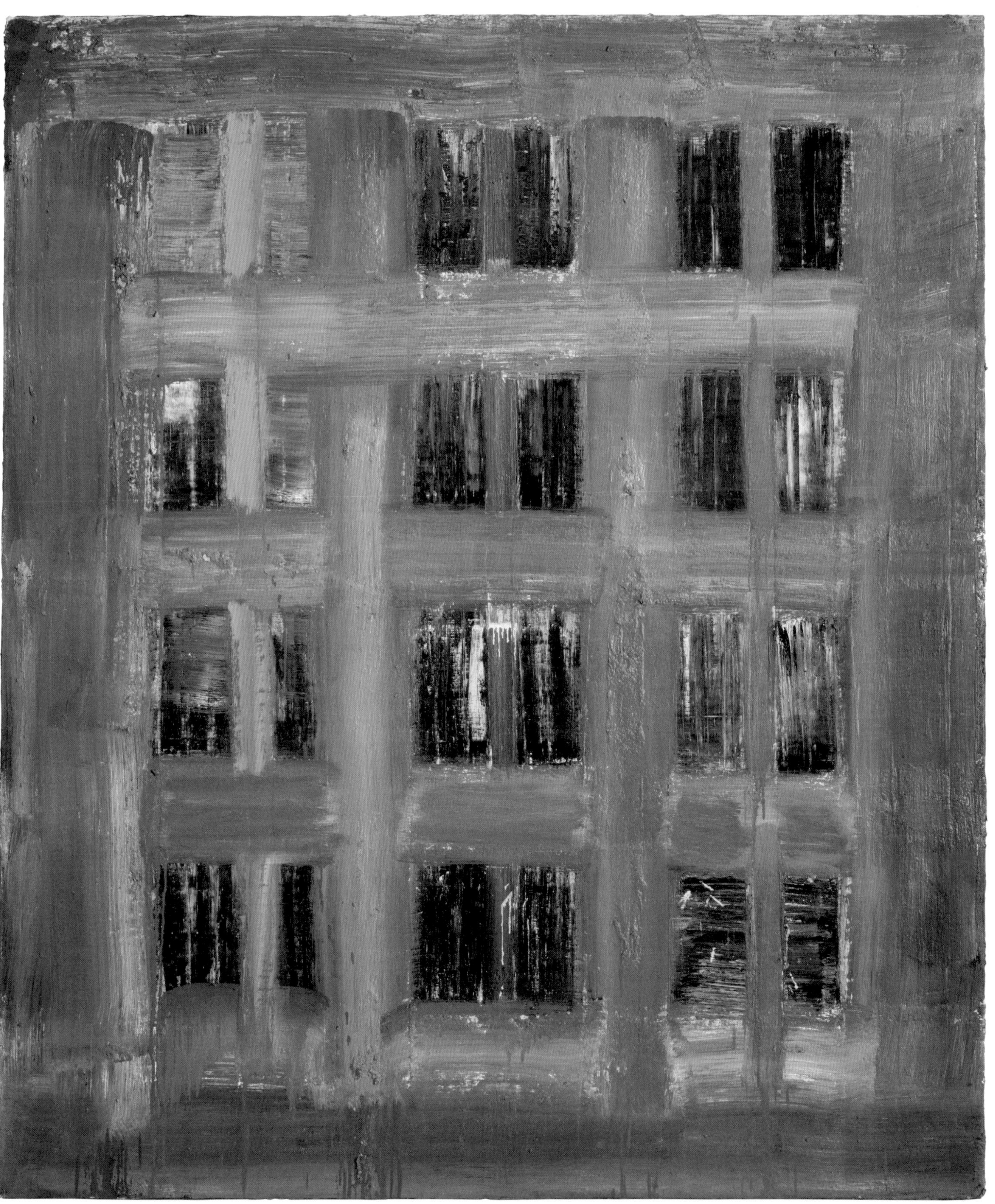

PLATE 53. *Burnt Bridges*, 1995. Oil on linen, 84 x 61 in. (213.4 x 154.9 cm). Speyer Family Collection, New York
PLATE 54. *North Light*, 1995. Oil on linen, 70 x 58 in. (177.8 x 147.3 cm)

PLATE 55. *Hill Censer*, 1996. Oil on linen, 47 x 51 in. (119.4 x 129.5 cm)

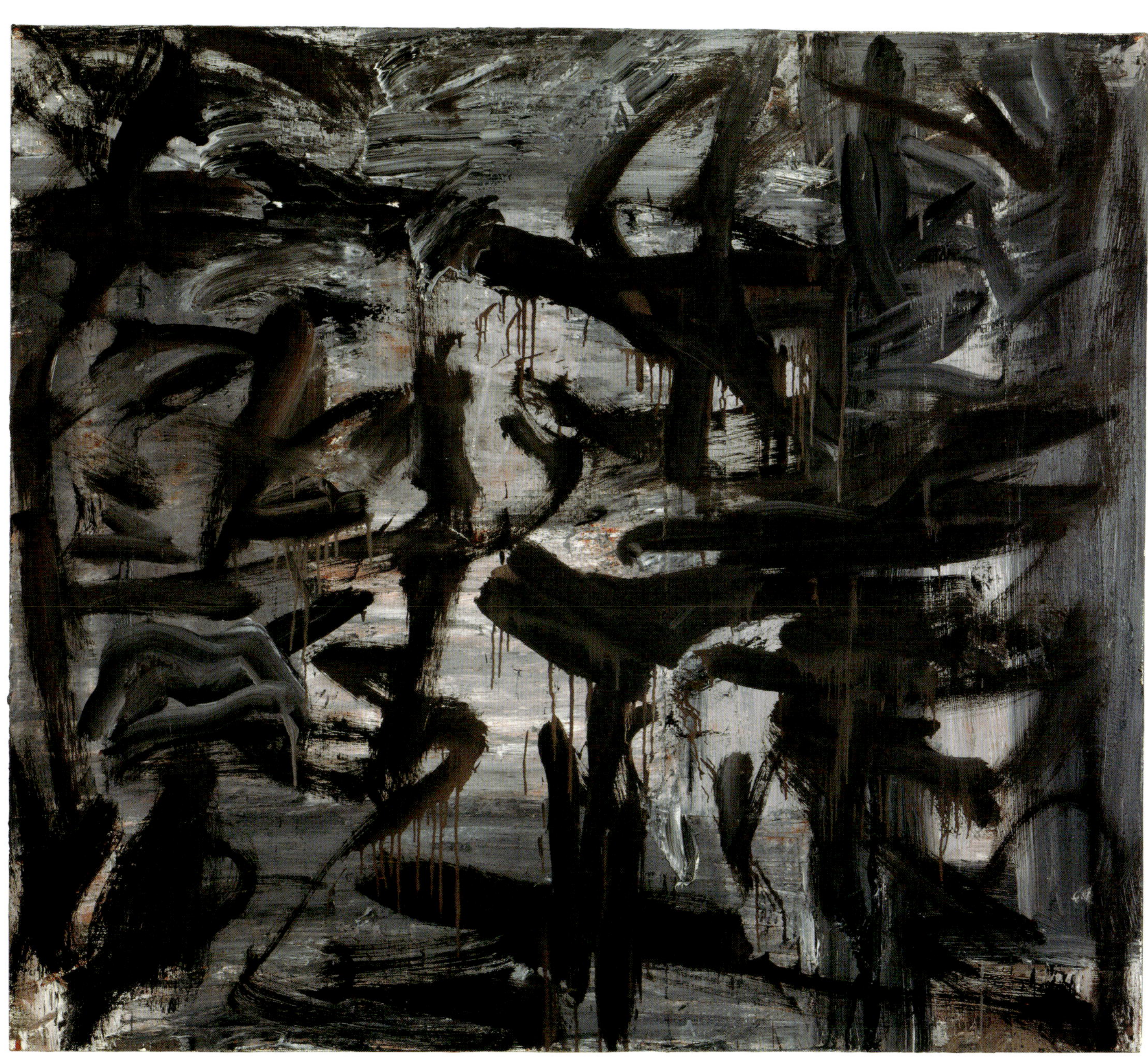

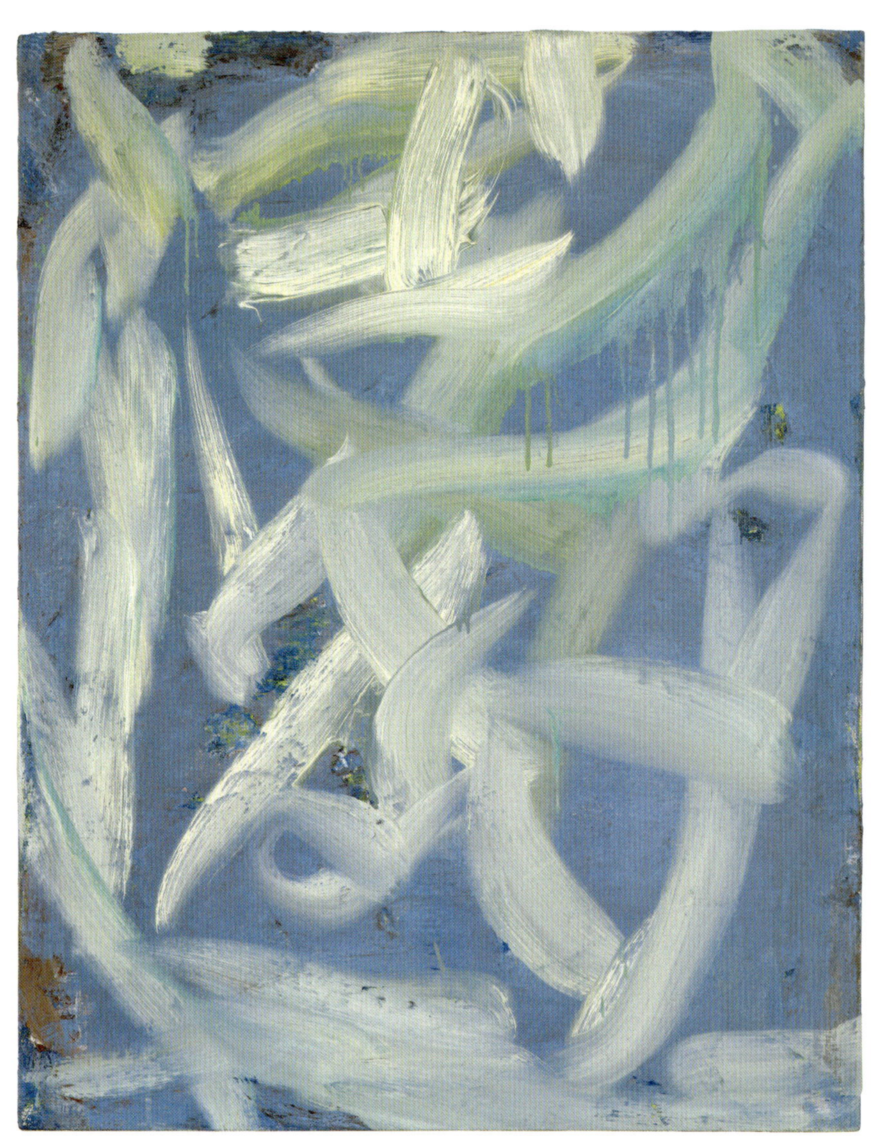

 PLATE 56. *Heavy Is the Root of the Light,* 1997. Oil on linen, 30 x 23 in. (76.2 x 58.4 cm)

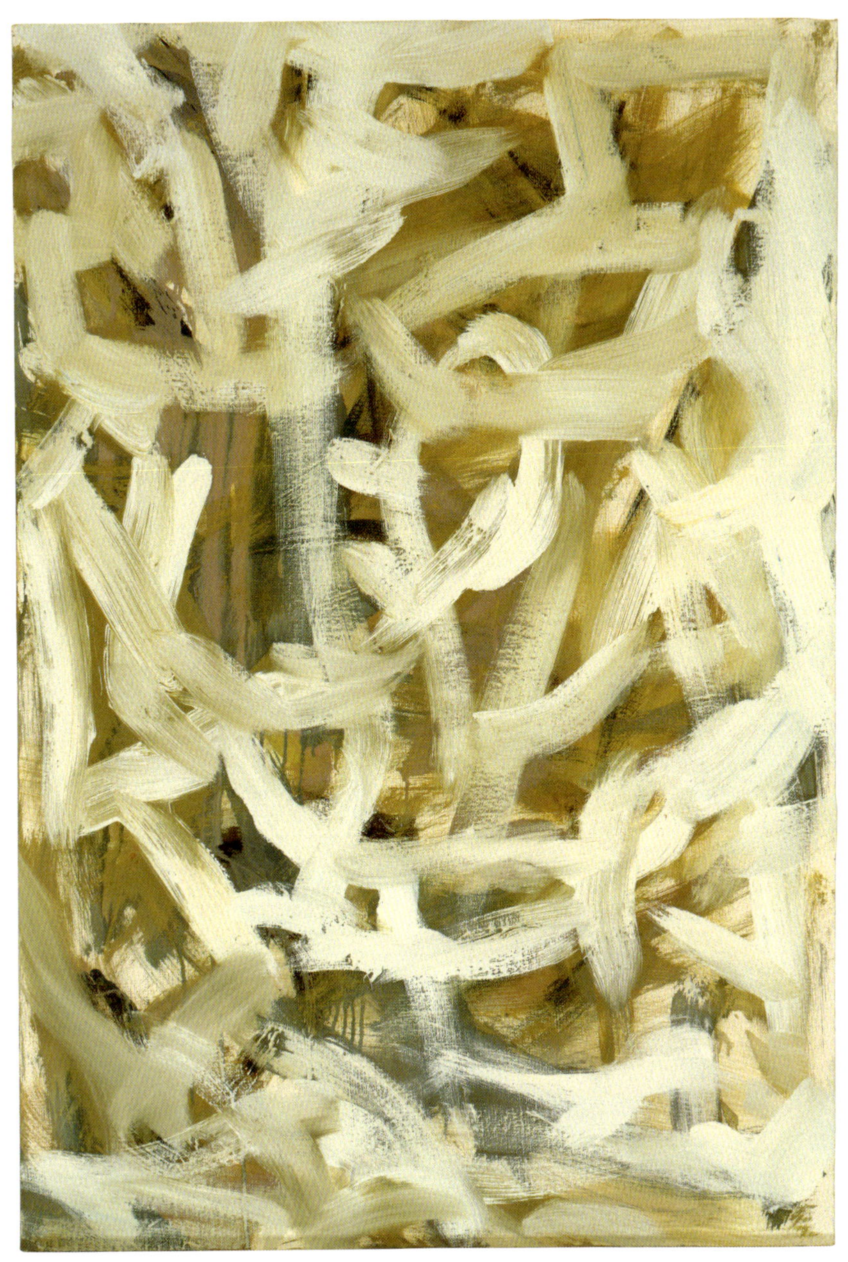

PLATE 57. *Know the White*, 1997. Oil on linen, 36 x 24 in. (91.4 x 61 cm). Private collection

PLATE 58. *Narrow Fellow in the Grass*, 1997. Oil on linen, 50 x 65 in. (127 x 165.1 cm). Private collection

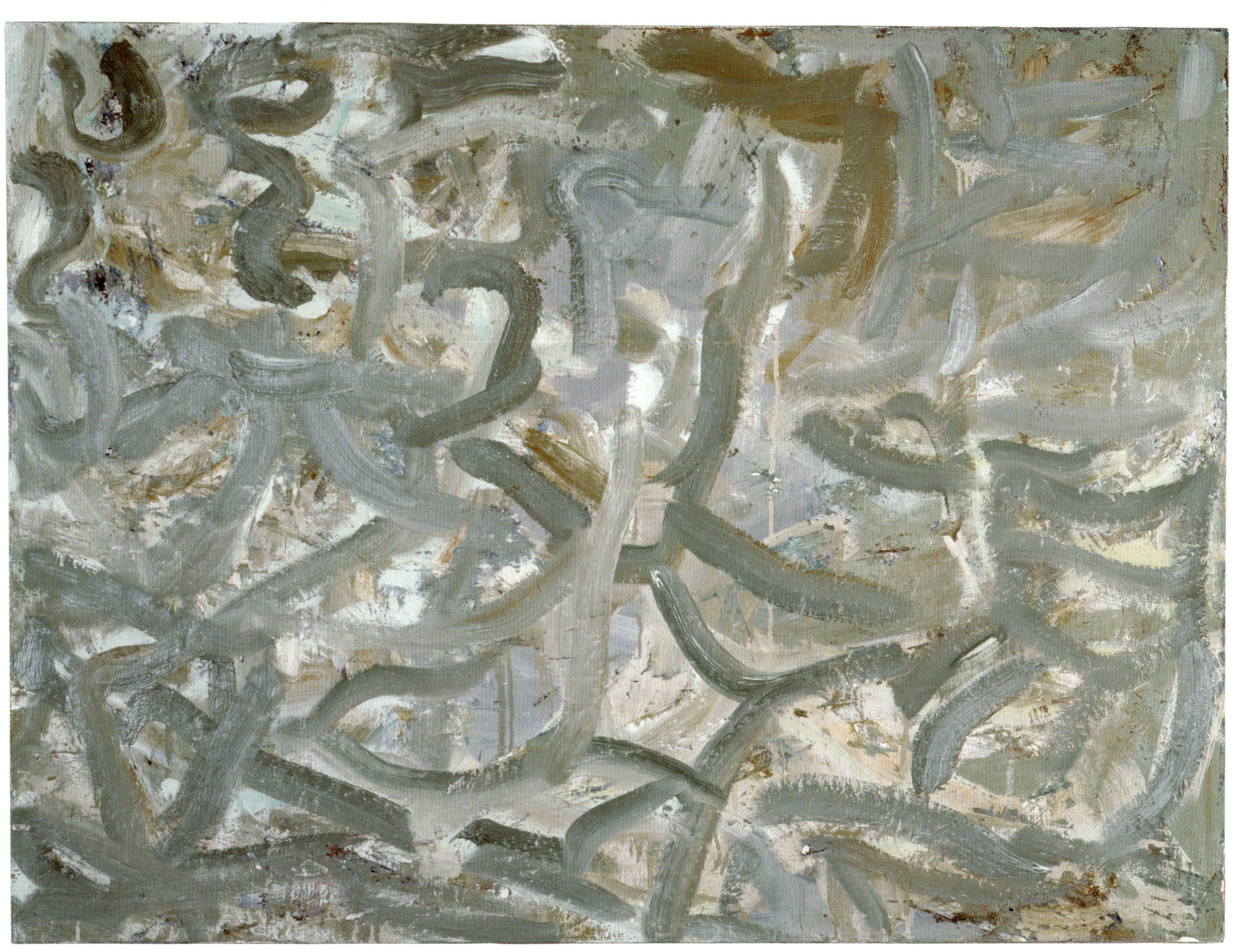

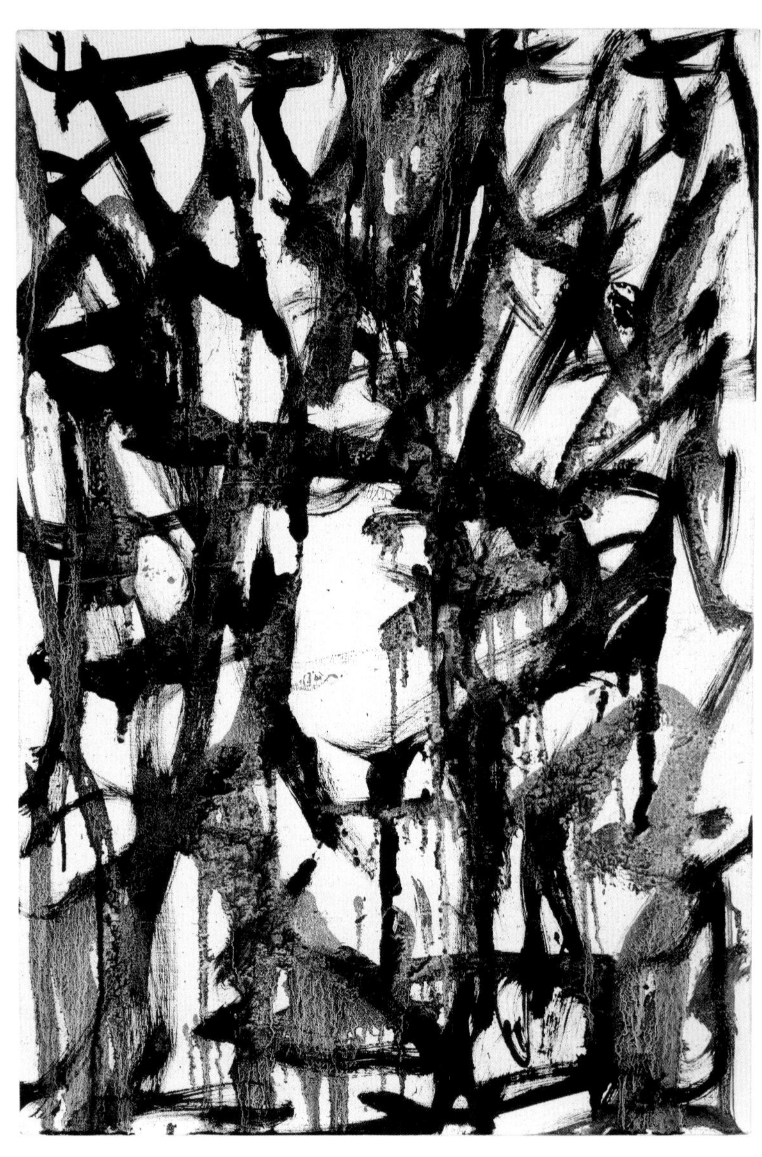

PLATE 59. *Tossed As It Is Untroubled*, 1997. Oil on canvas, 30¼ x 20¼ in. (76.8 x 51.4 cm). Private collection

PLATE 60. *Untitled*, 1997. Oil and ink on paper, 30 x 18 in. (76.2 x 45.7 cm)

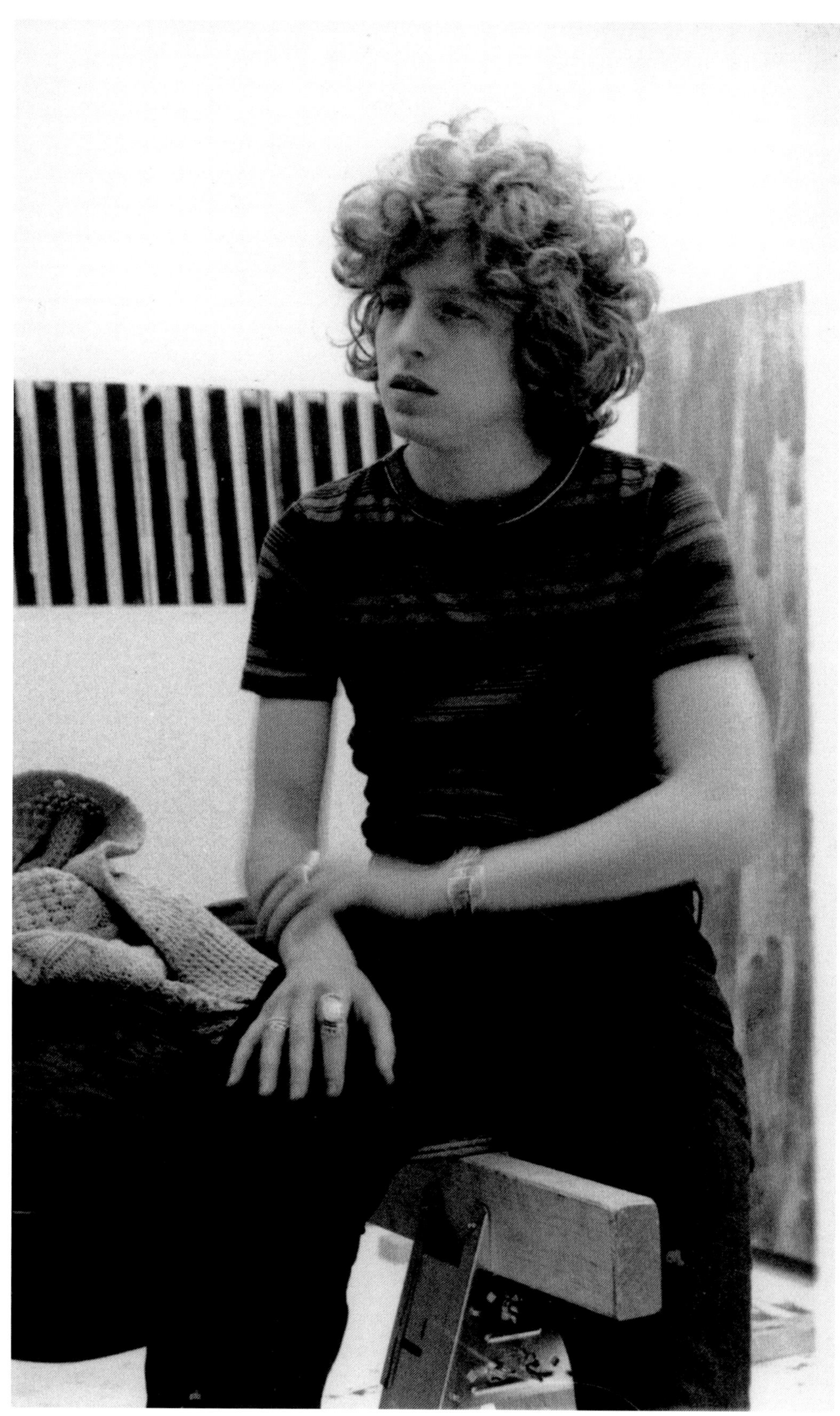

Louise Fishman in her SoHo studio, 1970. Photograph by Shirley Davidson

LOUISE ISN'T ANGRY ANYMORE. SHE'S PAINTING

CARRIE MOYER

The first time Louise Fishman laid brush to canvas, she knew that she wanted to make paintings; that's what she wanted to do for her entire life.[1] She was good at it, a fact her fellow students and teachers recognized immediately. It was 1956 and Fishman was in her first year of art school. Pursuing her childhood fantasy of becoming a professional basketball player wasn't in the cards—that career didn't exist for women. She came out as a lesbian the same year and was immediately placed in therapy by her parents. Fishman's first lover had seduced her by declaring that all artists are queer. Her father must have had the same thought; he stopped paying for his daughter's art school tuition. Eventually she received her BFA and BS degrees from Temple University's Tyler School of Art in Elkins Park, Pennsylvania. As an undergrad she would often travel to New York from the Philadelphia area, where she had lived since childhood, to go to galleries on Fifty-Seventh Street, half hoping to run into some of the famous painters she'd read about. Endearingly, she thought of them as "peers."[2]

Fishman was ten years old in 1949, when the romantic image of Jackson Pollock was first transmitted into the American consciousness via *Life* magazine. With their striking individuality and self-seriousness, New York School painters such as Pollock came to represent the mediated embodiment of independence and freedom, among other postwar American ideals. Coming from an educated Jewish family, Fishman had been exposed to modern art from an early age: her aunt, Razel Kapustin, had a lifelong career as a professional painter, and her mother, Gertrude Fisher-Fishman, gradually developed into a serious painter as well. Fishman remembers getting her hands on her mother's copies of *ARTnews* and excitedly poring over "De Kooning Paints a Picture" (1953; FIG. 18) and similar pictorials showing Franz Kline and

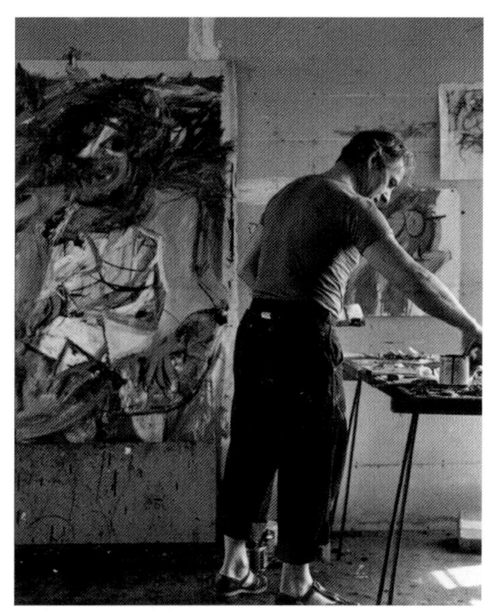

FIGURE 18
Willem de Kooning painting in his East Hampton, Long Island studio, 1953. Photograph by Tony Vaccaro

Philip Guston in their studios, surrounded by their work.

After graduating in 1965 with an MFA from University of Illinois, Urbana-Champaign, Fishman moved to New York City and set up a studio. In search of like-minded women, she eventually gravitated toward consciousness-raising groups. As she has often said in interviews, it was her immersion in the nascent women's and gay liberation movements that provoked a complete rupture in life as she had known it. In the studio, the use of taped edges, staining, and acrylic paint, along with the other conventions of Post-painterly abstraction that lingered from her graduate school years, were purged entirely from her work. It was a period of introspection, isolated from the art world at large but nurtured and supported by the women in her artists' group. As she has noted, her new paintings were hard won. They were "raw, alienated and always looked wrong. Very few things were allowed to stay in the pictures. I kept moving things around, similar to moving furniture."[3]

It was only sixty years ago that the first American women artists began making it through the gauntlet of obstacles to professional visibility and commercial success. Well before Fishman had entered art school and declared herself queer, the American arts press had shifted its gaze from the dour, middle-aged men of the New York School to a handful of up-and-comers. According to Katy Siegel, "The 'new' or 'second' generation of the New York School," which included women, "has often been cast as feminine or feminized in relation to the first generation of abstract expressionist artists, with a range of connotations, both positive and negative, attaching to that term: lyrical, emotionally expressive, and also of lesser historical impact, developing out of previous art rather than harshly breaking with older figures such as Willem de Kooning and Jackson Pollock."[4] A notable example is "Women Artists in Ascendance: Young Group Reflects Lively Virtues of U.S. Painting," a four-page illustrated feature in a 1957 issue of *Life* magazine that featured Nell Blaine, Helen Frankenthaler, Grace Hartigan, Joan Mitchell, and Jane Wilson, coiffed and gracefully posed with their work. A handful of women artists featured in a mainstream magazine does not a revolution make, especially when their outfits have been coordinated with their paintings. As Daniel Belasco writes, "The women of the New York School were damned for being feminine, yet they stood out as radicals, their attire and attitudes contradicting the domestic stereotypes and expectations of 1950s America."[5] Their qualified "admission" to the sweat lodge of Abstract Expressionism was mainly symbolic, as it did little to relieve the naturalized sexism that constrained all women, in or outside the studio. Closer to home, Fishman has told a story of going to New York City as a young woman with one of her classmates. After shopping for art supplies, they headed for the Cedar Tavern. Far in the back, they saw Milton Resnick, Joan Mitchell, and a few others sitting around a table. Resnick called them over . . . "Hey what's in your package?" As Fishman approached, he motioned for her to come sit on his lap. She turned around and walked away.[6]

Unlike disciplines whose evolutionary narratives are less burdened by pedigree and the father-son drama, painting is characterized by a degree of self-reflexivity that puts genealogy at the center of how it is discussed, taught, and, especially, sold. For Fishman, the tomboy-turned-artist, figures such as Kline or de Kooning, who combined a deeply felt painterly athleticism with a kind of virile, photogenic aloofness, were obvious role models. Closer to home, Fishman could look to Aunt Razel, a successful artist who had opted out of having children. Then there was Joan Mitchell: Fishman remembers being especially smitten with the photographs that accompanied the artist's work in Irving Sandler's 1957 *ARTnews* profile.[7] Yet Mitchell was ultimately too heteronormative to identify with, more of an aspirational love object to be admired for her ambition. These days, open dialogue about gender and sexual identity allows us to see how Fishman might have taken on the swagger of male painters and sought out female painters as companions. But in the mid-twentieth century her identity as a lesbian and an abstract painter made her doubly invisible.

In her groundbreaking 1990 essay "Patrilineage," Mira Schor anticipated the impact that the growing number of significant, publicly recognized women artists would have on the construction of art history. Schor wrote: "Artists working today, particularly those who have come of age since 1970, belong to the first generation that can claim artistic matrilineage, in addition to the patrilineage that must be understood as a given in patriarchal culture."[8] Changing demographics, combined with the steady recuperation of marginalized artists to art history, makes claiming a "matrilineage" for one's particular studio practice ever more feasible. Since the publication of Schor's essay, the need for validating role models has become something akin to an article of faith. Unlike the male modernists, who were all about killing their fathers with their "masterpieces," women artists are now looking for radical "art mothers" who grant permission—permission to be alienated, angry, political, sexual, loud, gauche, out of step, or just plain weird. In other words, permission to do whatever it takes to make the work ring true.

Louise Fishman's involvement with consciousness-raising in the early 1970s marked a dramatic break with the historical structures that could not "see" her. It upended nearly everything about her studio practice, including her relationship with art history as a woman artist. Many different types of work resulted from the intense period of self-interrogation that followed, including the well-known Angry Paintings on paper and a series of small tondos clogged with manic brushstrokes. The various bodies of work possessed an awkward interiority as well as an acute sense of necessity. In response to feminist claims that domestic crafts represented a form of bona fide female art, Fishman created a series of deconstructed paintings she made by dying and cutting up

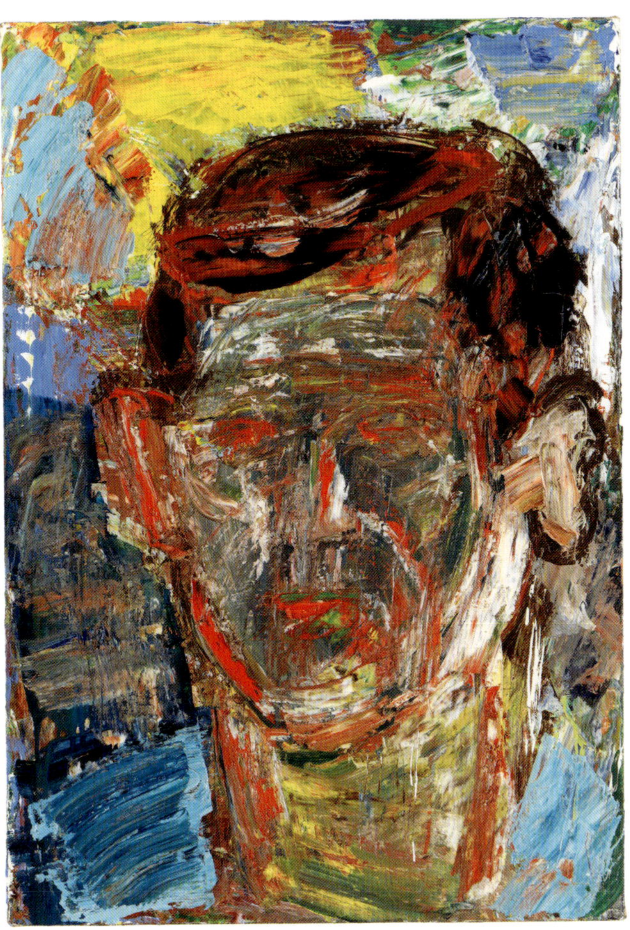

FIGURE 19
Louise Fishman, *Portrait of Myself as a Man,* ca. 1983
Oil on canvas, 25⅛ x 17³⁄₁₆ in. (63.8 x 43.6 cm)

canvas squares and sewing them together into small wall pieces. Looking back, the artist recalls: "I decided to stitch—which I hated. I spent my life avoiding sewing and anything else that had to do with 'women's tasks.' I thought, okay, I'm going to embrace this . . . I hate it, but I'm going to figure out what it is."[9]

Paradoxically, the culmination of Fishman's self-critique and experimentation was a return to traditional oil painting on stretched canvases. The fact that she felt a sense of permission to return to conventional methodologies says a lot about her alienation from the art world, a sentiment that was shared by many painters well into the 1990s, when the medium became a convenient whipping boy for critical theorists and gestural abstraction was demoted to a general sign for painting. As Elizabeth Murray said, "I think the greatest part about being a woman in the world of painting is that I'm not really part of it. I can do whatever the hell I want."[10] Perhaps this feeling of estrangement made it easier for feminist artists to introduce the subject of identity—specifically their own ethnicity and sexuality—to the otherwise anodyne realm of abstract painting. In a 1977 issue of *Heresies* magazine entitled "Feminism, Art, and Politics," Harmony Hammond rallies for the radical, revelatory potential of abstraction: "If our lives and our art are connected," she writes, "and if 'the personal is political' in the radical sense, then we cannot separate the content of our work from the form it takes. As abstract artists, we need to develop new abstract forms for revolutionary art."[11]

The late twentieth-century critical reassessment of Abstraction Expressionism—through which it was recast as a pictorial code for hyper-inflated male egos and American triumphalism rather than a movement of "universal" sentiments and humanist ideals—would seem to make it an improbable mode for a lesbian-feminist artist to adopt. Yet because it was where she found her own authentic voice, Fishman returned to the discredited language of gestural abstraction, rejecting the popular tropes of painting—feminist, formalist, minimalist, or otherwise—favored by her peers in the late 1970s and 1980s. One is reminded of Harold Rosenberg's "The American Action Painters," from 1952, in which he notes: "With a few important exceptions, most of the artists of this vanguard found their way to the present work by being cut in two. Their type is not a young painter but a re-born one. The man may be over forty, the painter around seven. The diagonal of a grand crisis separates him from his personal and artistic past."[12] Fishman's journey back to the formal language and customary materials of modernist abstract painting was equally transformational, if guided by different impulses. Certainly, values such as authenticity, honesty, autonomy, and individuality, once attached to Abstract Expressionism, resonate with the goals of any consciousness-raising group. In the essay on the women painters of the New York School cited above, Daniel Belasco further suggests that "radical feminism may have some of its intellectual roots in the Abstract Expressionist rhetoric of individual freedom and morality."[13] He goes on to write: "The feminist art movement of the 1960s developed in the United States simultaneously with the canonization of Abstract Expressionism and the elimination of women from its history. This was not a coincidence. Many radical feminists, such as Shulamith Firestone and Kate Millett, started out as and remained artists. These younger women, born in the late 1930s and 1940s, aimed to achieve the command and freedom of the male abstract painters."[14]

Taking this idea one step further, Fishman's series *Remembrance and Renewal*, for which

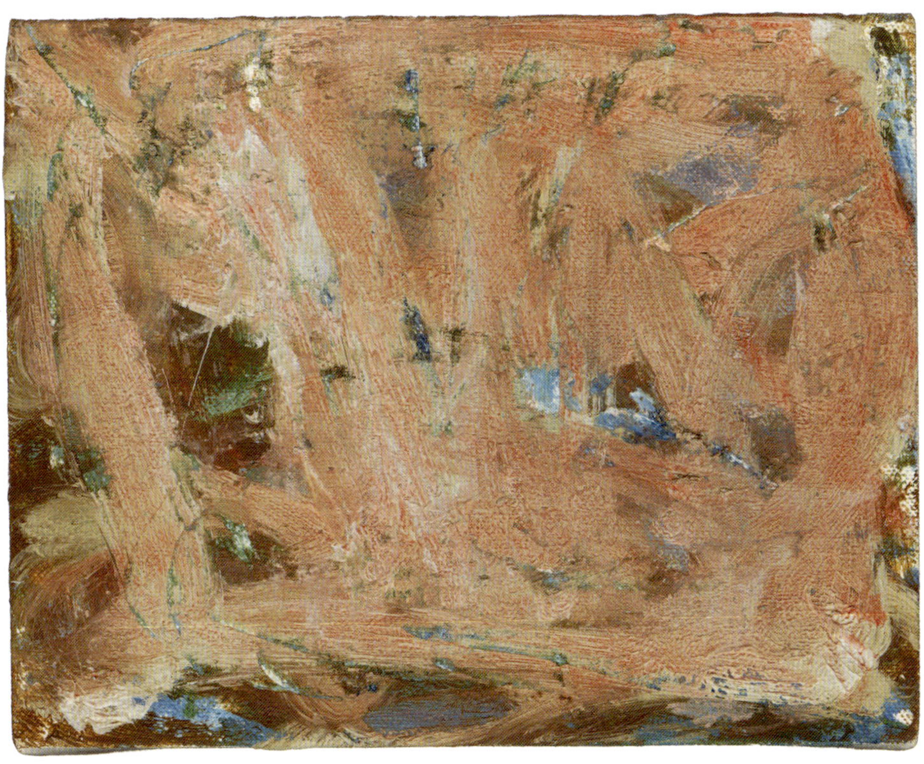

FIGURE 20
Louise Fishman, *The Spreading Wide My Narrow Hands*, 1997
Oil on linen, 8¼ x 10 in. (21 x 25.4 cm)
Collection of Ingrid Nyeboe

oil paint and beeswax were mixed with human ashes gathered at Auschwitz, could be seen to "complete" the unfinished business of Abstract Expressionism. Instead of generalizing the horror of the Holocaust through metaphor, Fishman's pictures force us to confront its material remains. Fishman's stubborn confidence in a kind of gravitas and the language of gesture has sometimes caused her pictures to appear detached from—even oblivious to—the zeitgeist that moves through contemporary painting. It isn't that her paintings are anachronistic, however; it's that they're not ironic. Her investment in notions of originality and authenticity is palpable. If anything, Fishman's paintings reveal how unfamiliar we are with the idea of interpreting painting without the distancing scrim of critical meta-narrative. Her account of meeting Agnes Martin, an artist who was truly an elder colleague and fellow traveler, makes her stance clear. By the time of their encounter, Fishman, who was in her forties, had developed her own singular voice and an audience who embraced it. She recalls:

> [Agnes] showed me paintings in her studio after we got to know each other, and then she started showing me drawings. I'd always loved her work and was fascinated by her. I was really beside myself just being around her. When I first saw her, she was sitting in her rocking chair, not saying much. And I thought, It's like sitting with the Buddha. So I'll

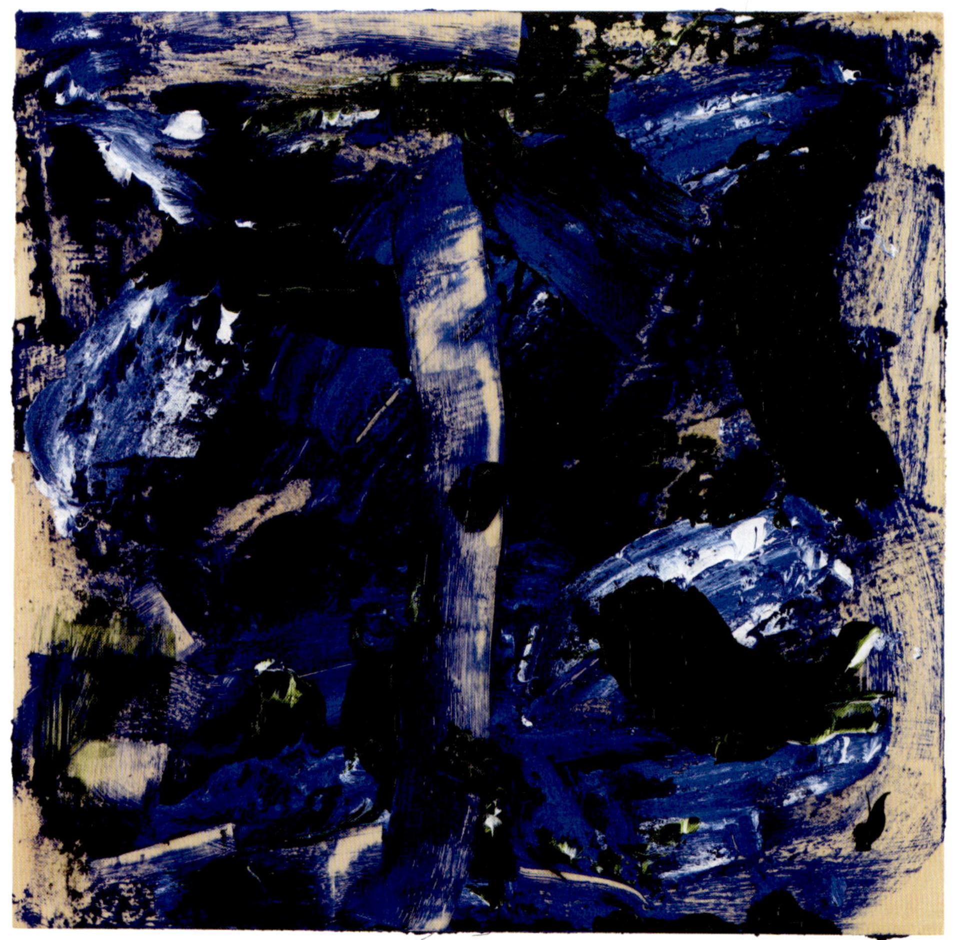

FIGURE 21
Louise Fishman, *Lille Skagen*, 2014
Oil on linen, 16 x 16⅛ in. (40.6 x 40.9 cm)
Collection of Ingrid Nyeboe

just meditate. That's what she seems to be doing. [*Laughter*][15]

As Fishman nears eighty, her career trajectory looks more and more like the prototypical "painter's journey," an outcome that was hard to envision when abstraction was valorized as an intellectual position, uncomplicated by the messiness of identity. She's been variously referred to as a "lesbian painter," a " feminist painter," and/or a "Jewish painter." It's as if her kind of abstraction needed to be qualified to ameliorate the critical discomfort of being faced with unironic painting. By following the current of her own work (and without anyone's permission), Fishman has developed a muscular, painterly abstraction that compels us to see the gesture as highly individual, rather than as a proxy for "feeling." In her paintings, the emotions conveyed by the formal idiom of Abstract Expressionism become straightforward, stripped of both the movement's original existential burden and the overworked interpretations that followed. As a result Fishman has also become a kind of role model, demonstrating to younger artists how to work through the internecine self-consciousness that bogs down painting and the discourse surrounding it. While the rest of the art world catches up, Fishman's painting keeps getting more and more expressive and capacious. Now she just wants to be called a painter, plain and simple.

The author wishes to thank Sheila Pepe for her sharp mind and good-humored assistance.

Notes

1. Louise Fishman, conversation with the author, June 14, 2015.
2. Ibid.
3. Ibid.
4. Katy Siegel, "Contextually Boundless," in *"The heroine Paint": After Frankenthaler*, ed. Katy Siegel (New York: Rizzoli, forthcoming).
5. Daniel Belasco, "The Best of Everything: Women in the New York School," in *"The heroine Paint": After Frankenthaler*, ed. Siegel (forthcoming).
6. Fishman, conversation with the author, June 14, 2015.
7. Ibid.
8. Mira Schor, "Patrilineage" in *Wet: On Painting, Feminism, and Art Culture* (Durham, N.C.: Duke University Press, 1997), 98.
9. Louise Fishman in Carrie Moyer, "Zero at the Bone: Louise Fishman Speaks with Carrie Moyer," *Art Journal* 71, no. 4 (Winter 2012): 40.
10. Elizabeth Murray quoted in *High Times, Hard Times: New York Painting, 1967–1975*, ed. Katy Siegel (New York: Independent Curators International, 2006), 86.
11. Harmony Hammond, "Feminist Abstract Art—A Political Viewpoint," in "Feminism, Art, and Politics," ed. Joan Braderman, Harmony Hammond, Elizabeth Hess, Arlene Ladden, Lucy Lippard, and Mary Stevens, special issue, *Heresies: A Feminist Publication on Art and Politics* 1, no. 1 (January 1977): 70, http://heresiesfilmproject.org/wp-content/uploads/2011/09/heresies1.pdf.
12. Harold Rosenberg, "The American Action Painters," in *The Tradition of the New* (1959; repr., New York: Da Capo Press, 1994), 22. Rosenberg's essay was originally published in *ARTNews* 51, no. 8 (December 1952): 22–23, 48–50.
13. Belasco, "The Best of Everything."
14. Ibid.
15. Fishman in Moyer, "Zero at the Bone," 38.

PLATES III

PLATE 61. *April*, 1998. Oil on linen, 76 x 46 in. (193 x 116.8 cm). Collection of John Cheim
OVERLEAF: PLATE 62. *August*, 1998. Oil on linen, 76 x 46 in. (193 x 116.8 cm). Private collection
PLATE 63. *September*, 1998. Oil on linen, 76 x 46 in. (193 x 116.8 cm). Private collection

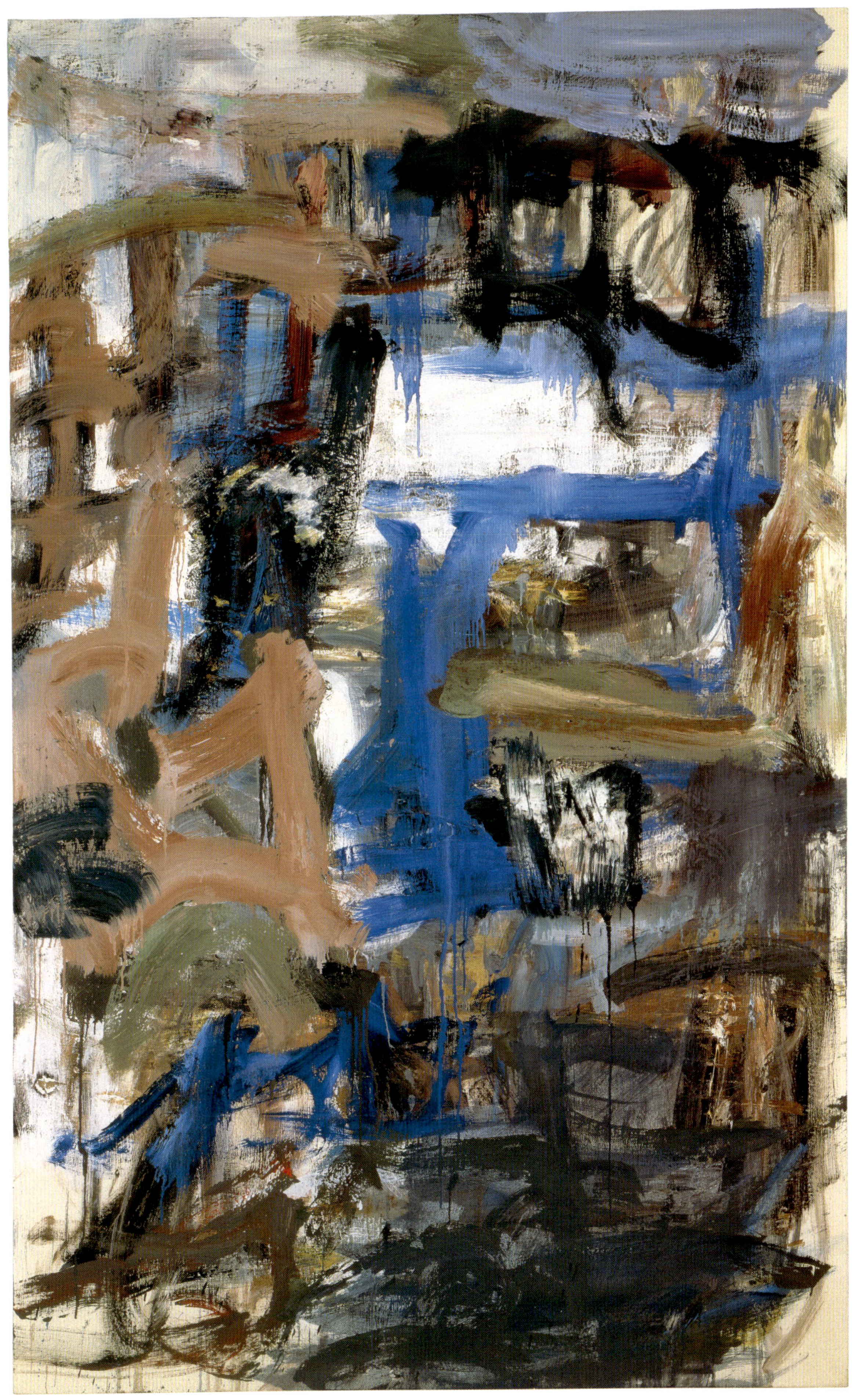

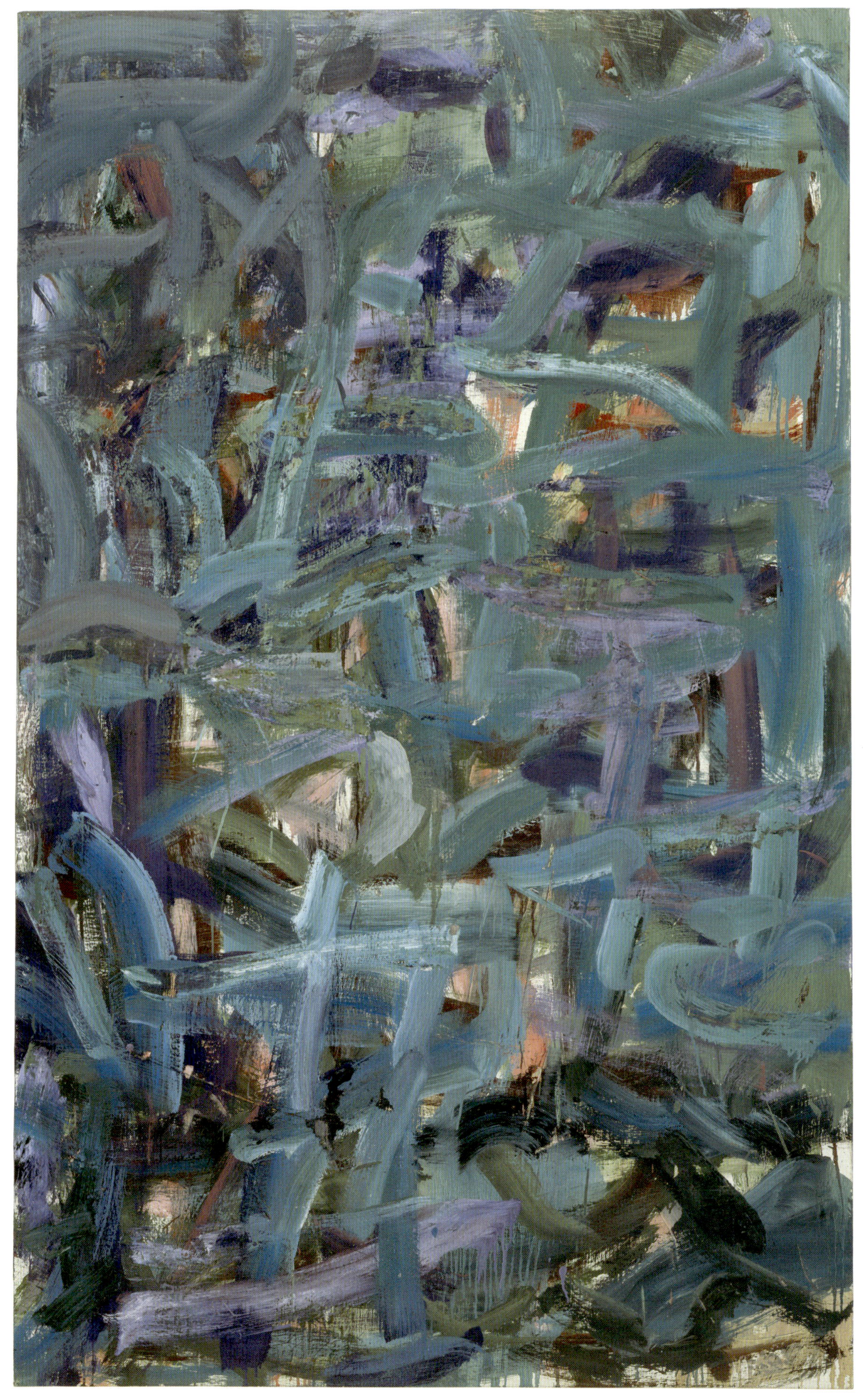

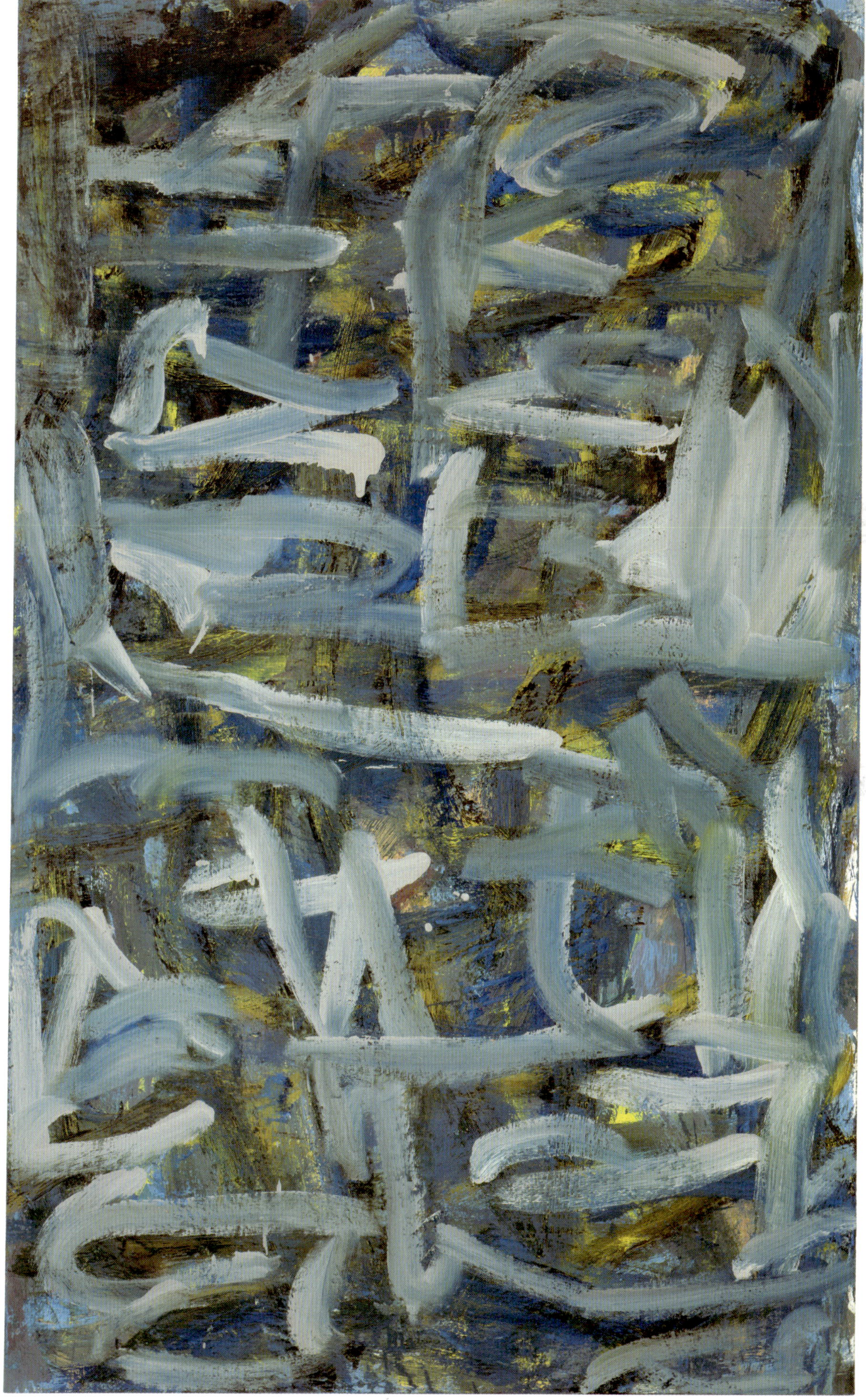

PLATE 64. *October*, 1998. Oil on linen, 76 x 46 in. (193 x 116.8 cm). Private collection

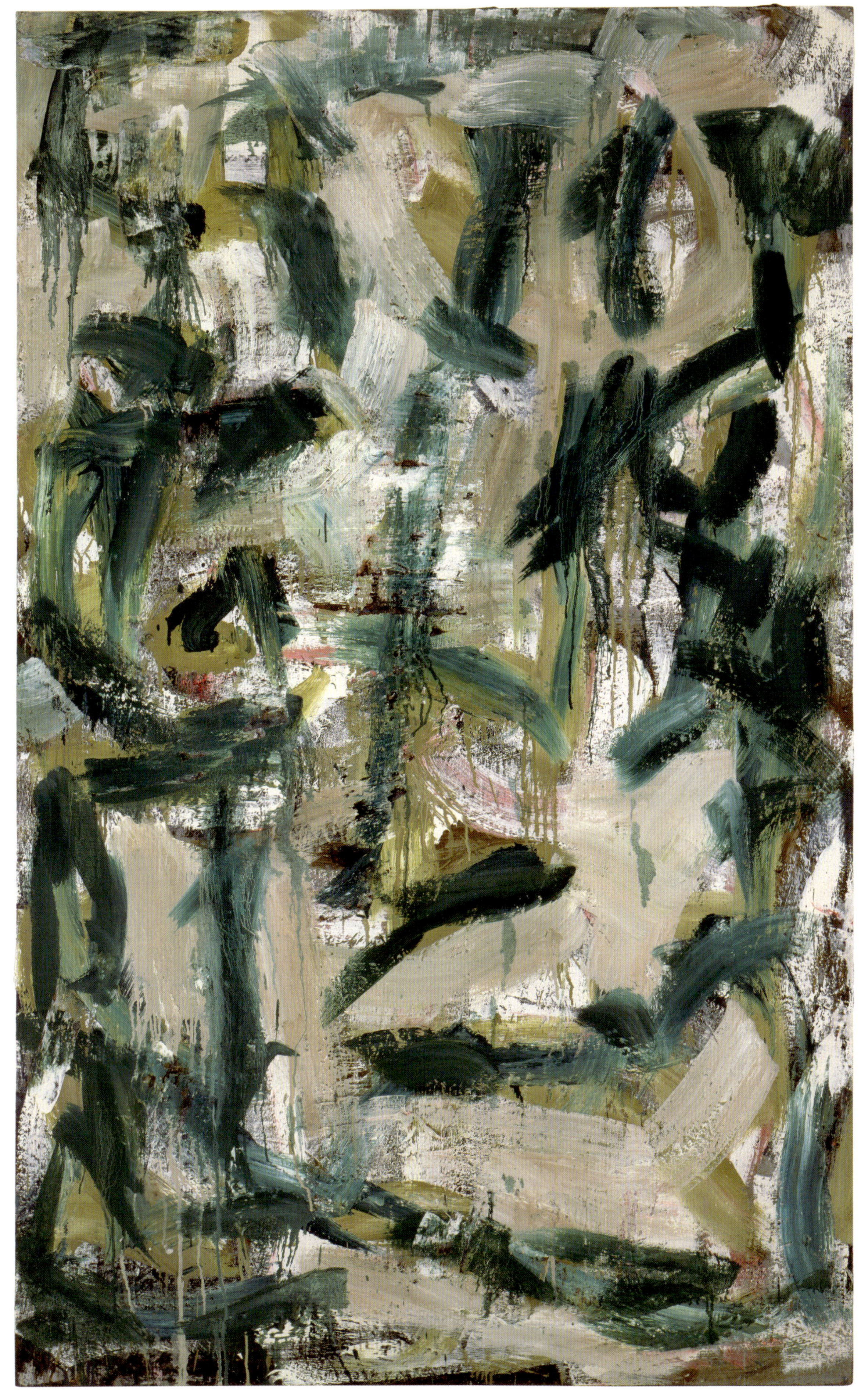

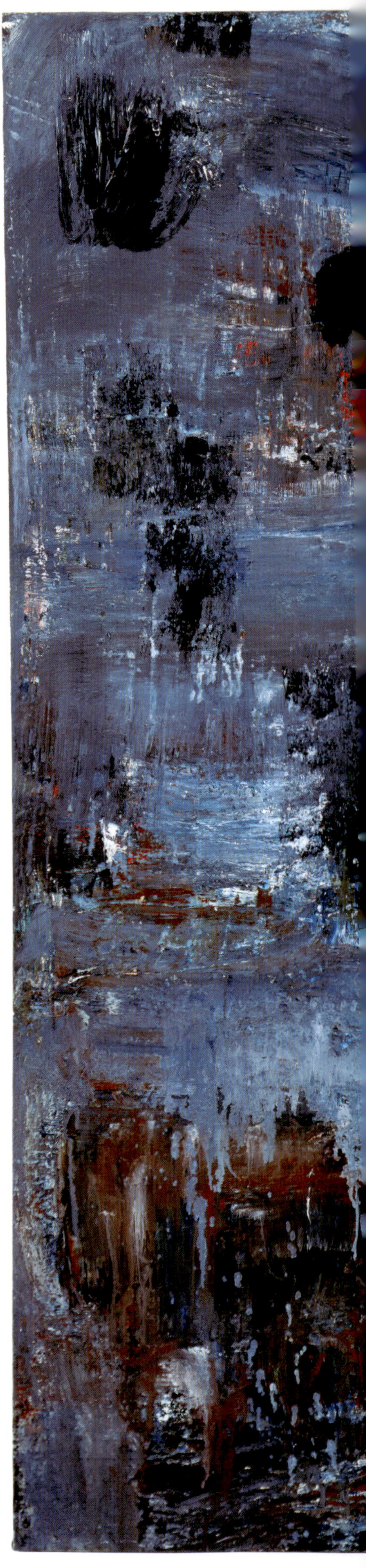

PLATE 65. *For There She Was*, 1998. Oil on linen, 76¼ x 82 in. (193.7 x 208.3 cm).
Collection of Romita Shetty and Nasser Ahmad

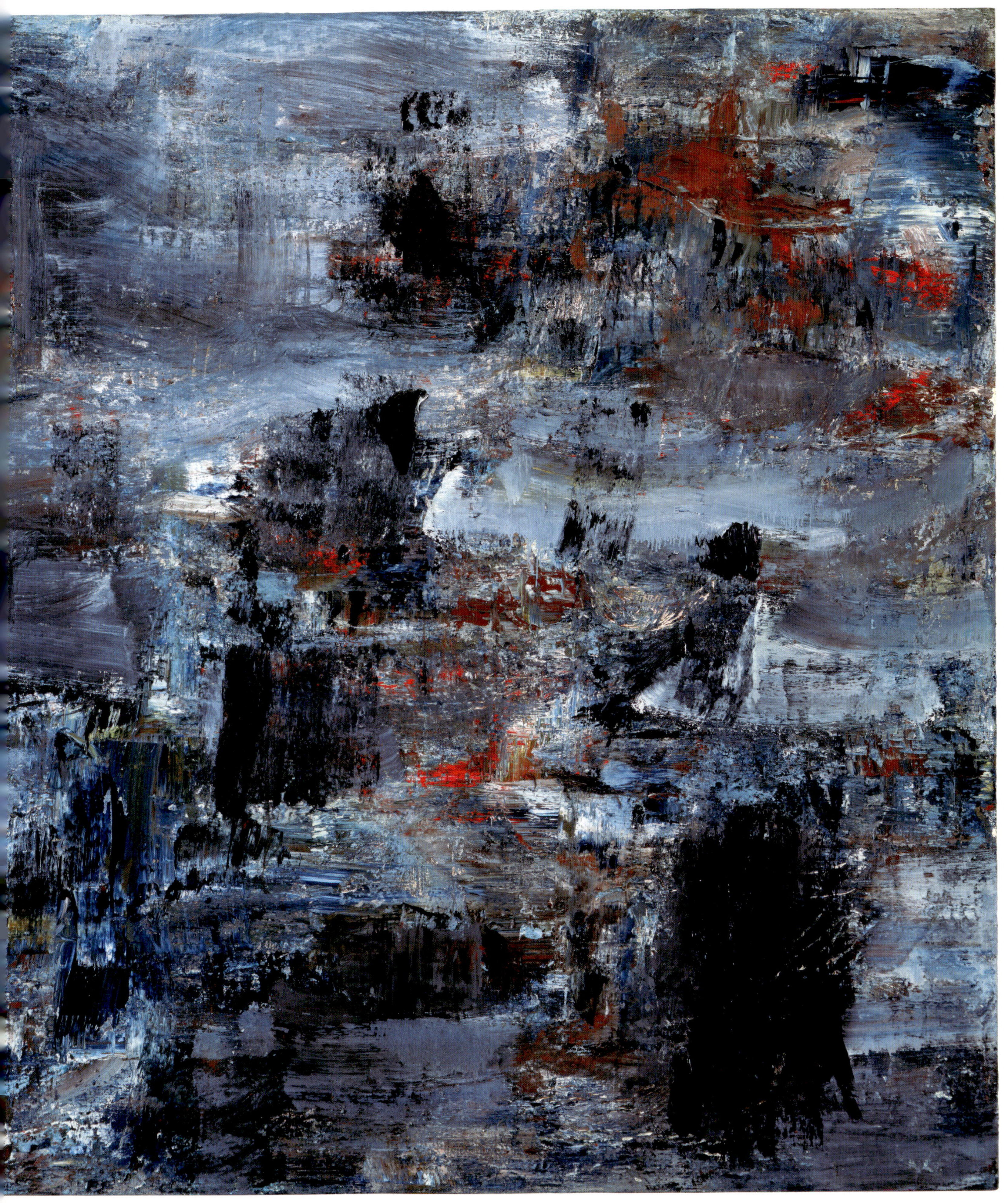

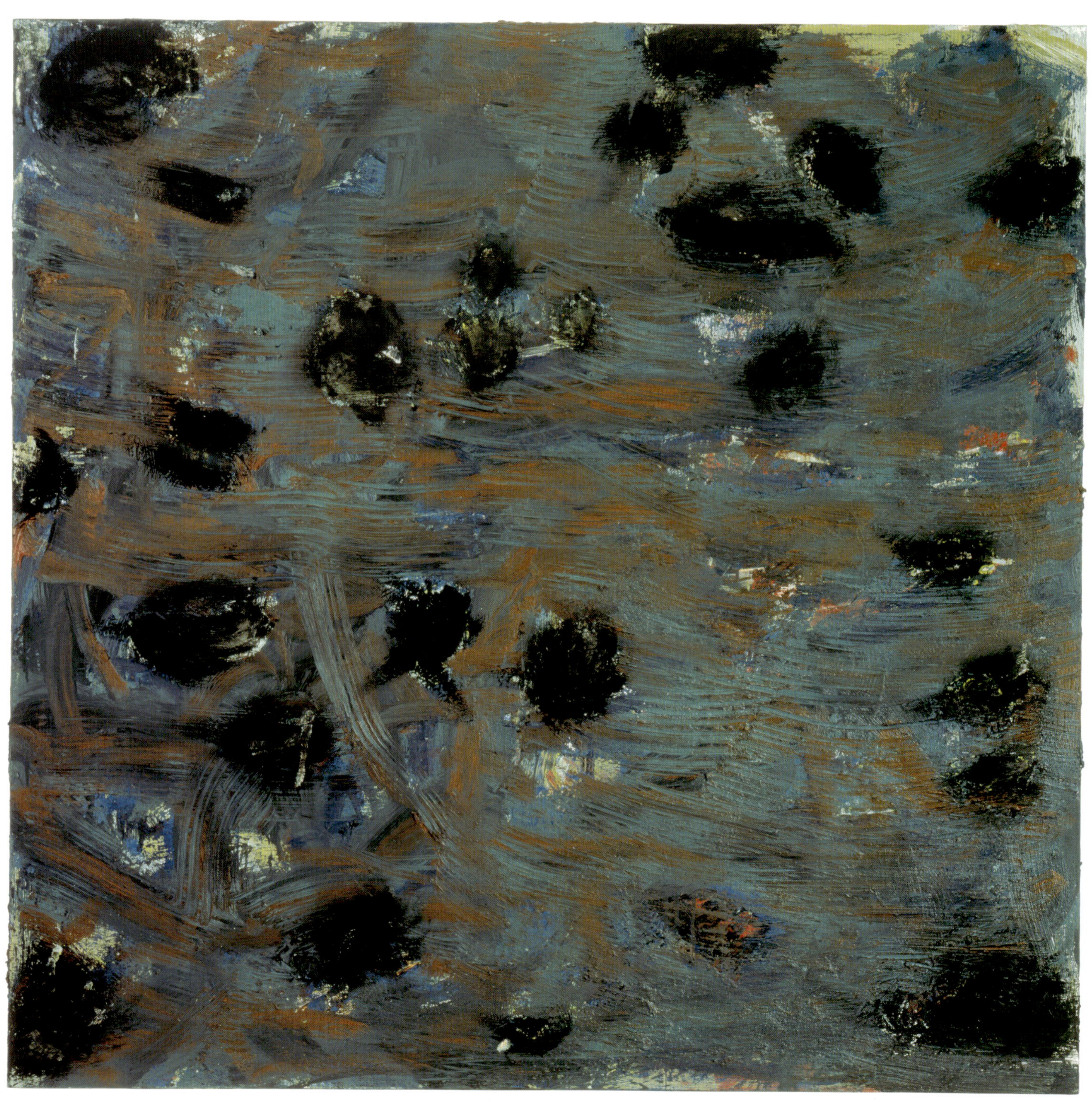

PLATE 66. *Look Back*, 1998. Oil on linen, 58 x 58 in. (147.3 x 147.3 cm)

PLATE 67. *The Sunrise Ruby*, 1999. Oil on linen, 82 x 75⅞ in. (208.3 x 192.7 cm). Collection of Martha Macks-Kahn

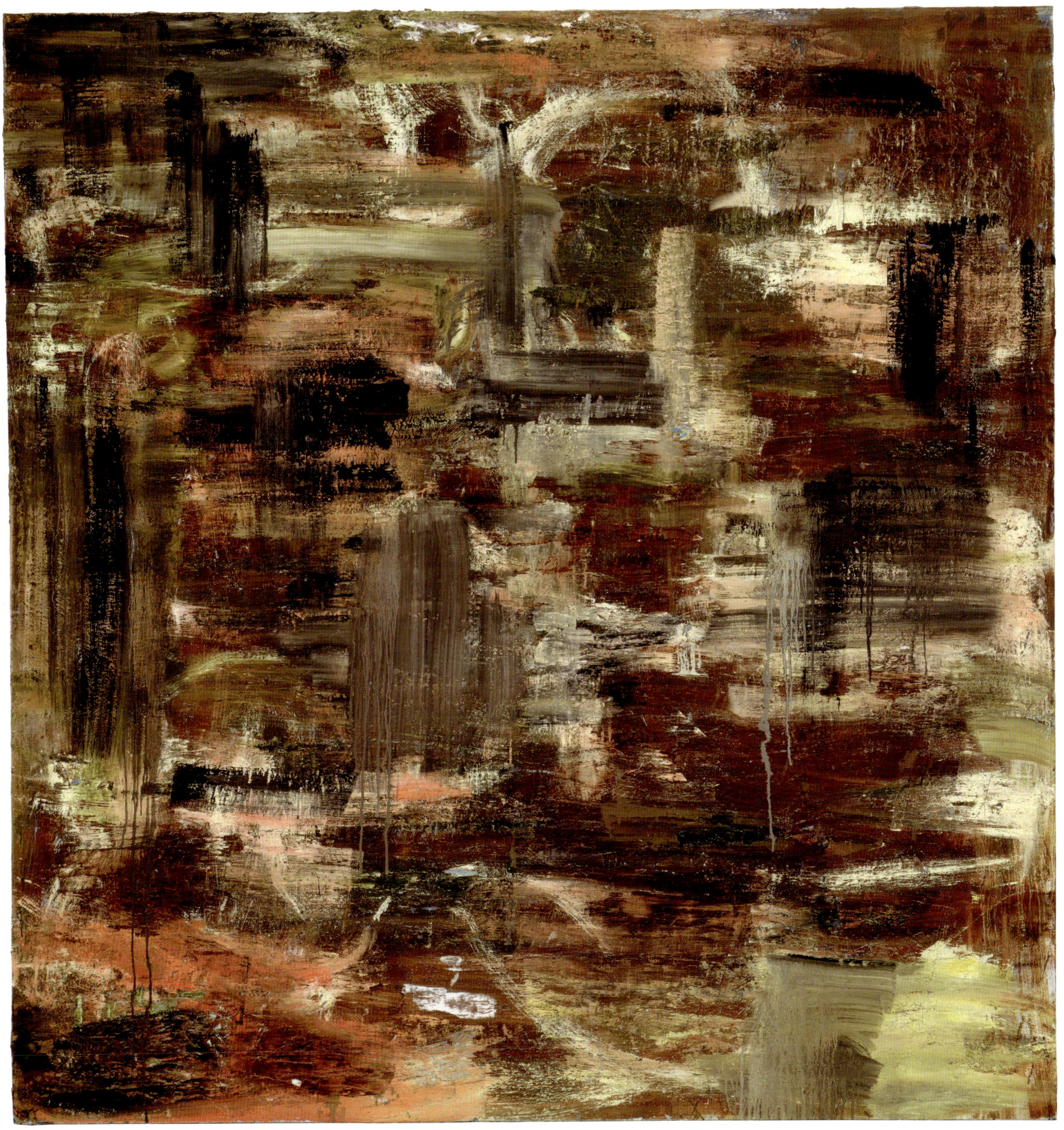

PLATE 68. *Untitled*, 1999. Oil and watercolor on paper, 23 x 19 in. (58.4 x 48.3 cm)

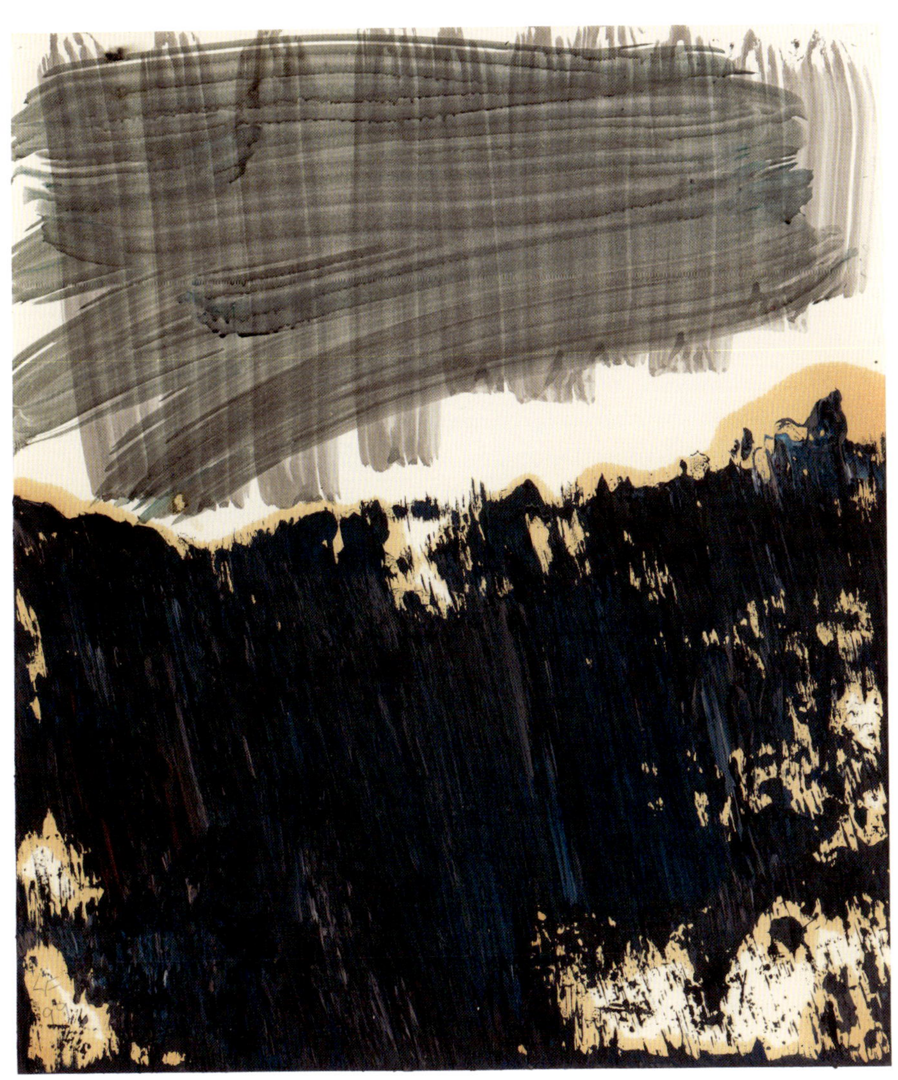

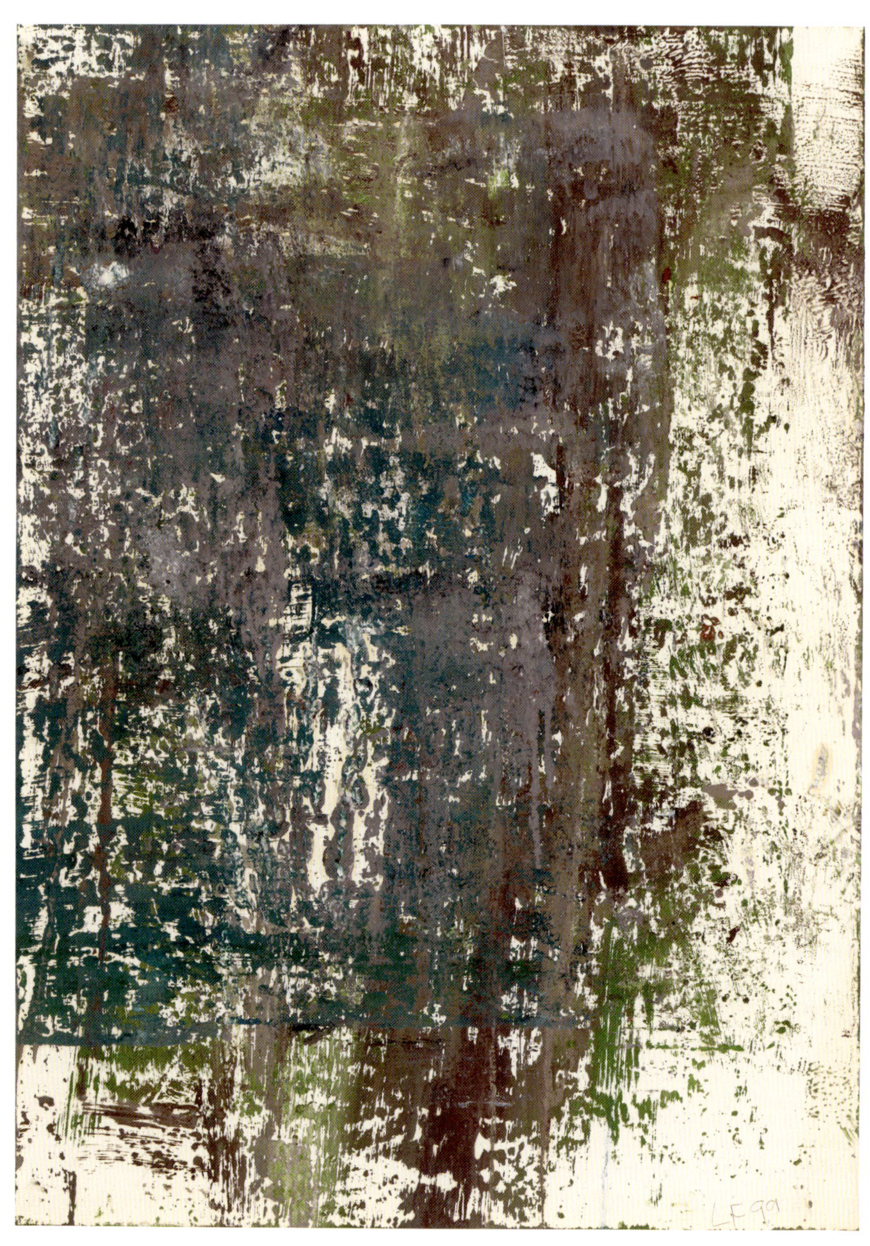

PLATE 69. *Untitled*, 1999. Oil on paper, 36 x 25 in. (91.4 x 63.5 cm)

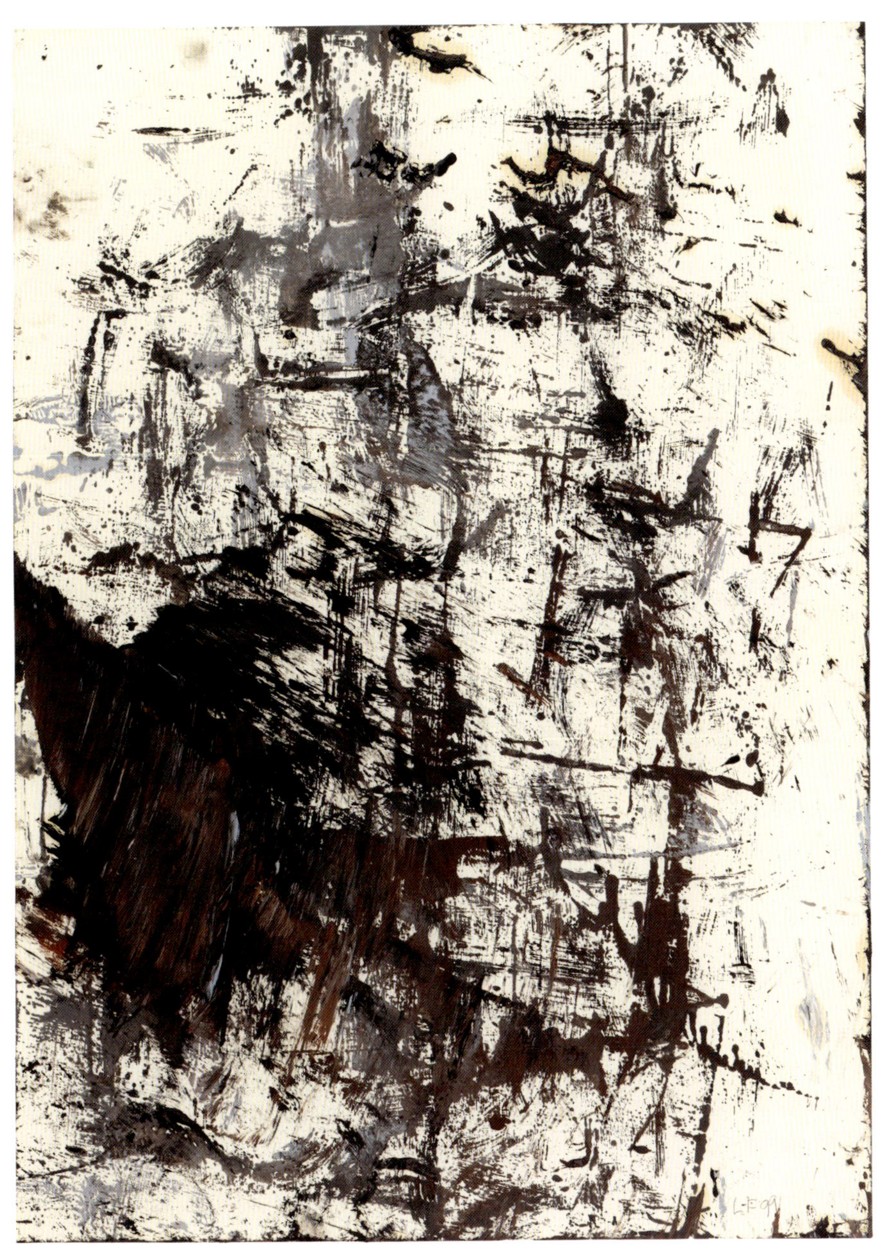

PLATE 70. *Untitled*, 1999. Oil on paper, 36 x 25 in. (91.4 x 63.5 cm)

PLATE 71. *Flying Solo*, 2000. Oil on linen, 65¼ x 60¼ in. (165.7 x 153 cm). Private collection

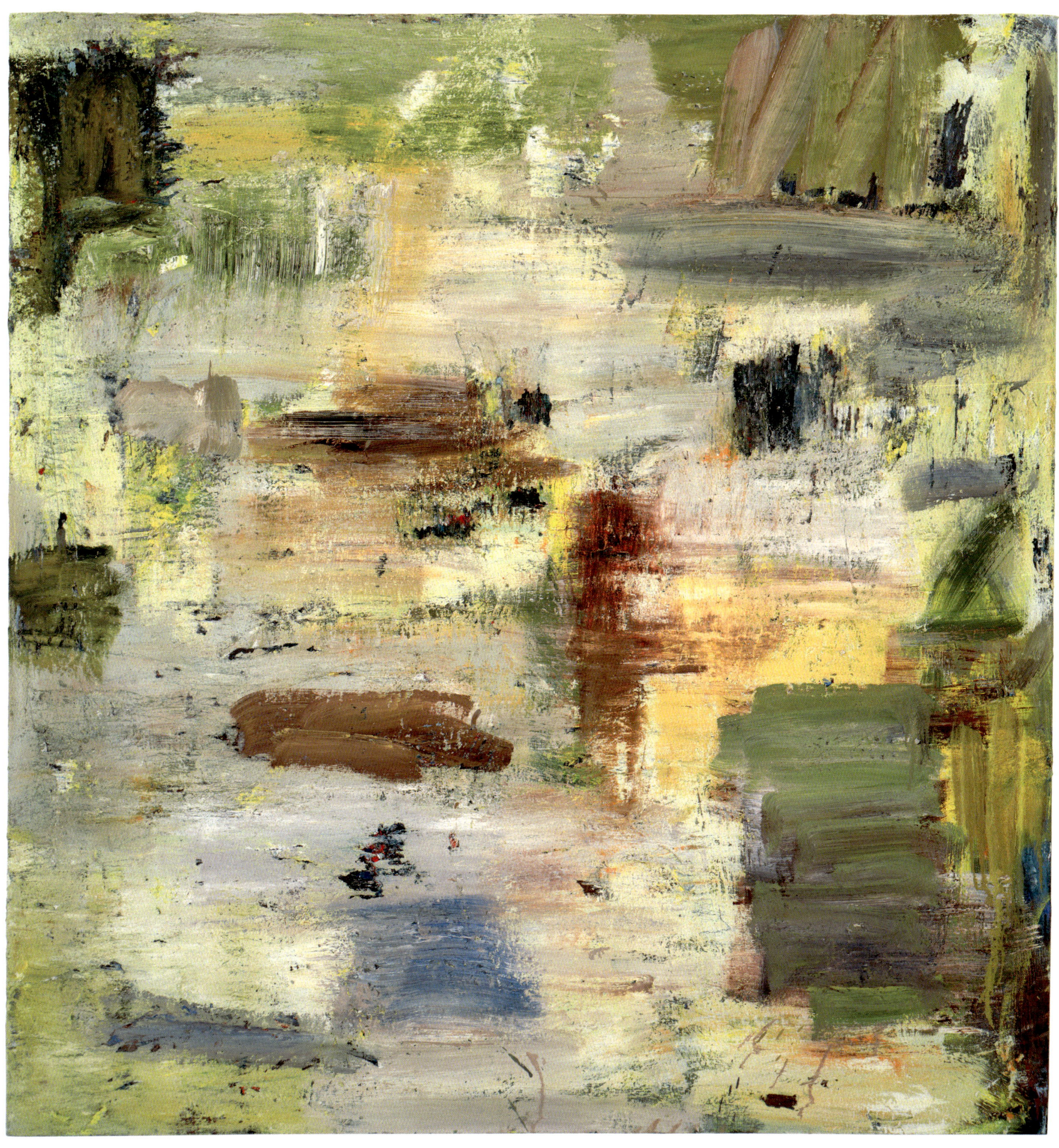

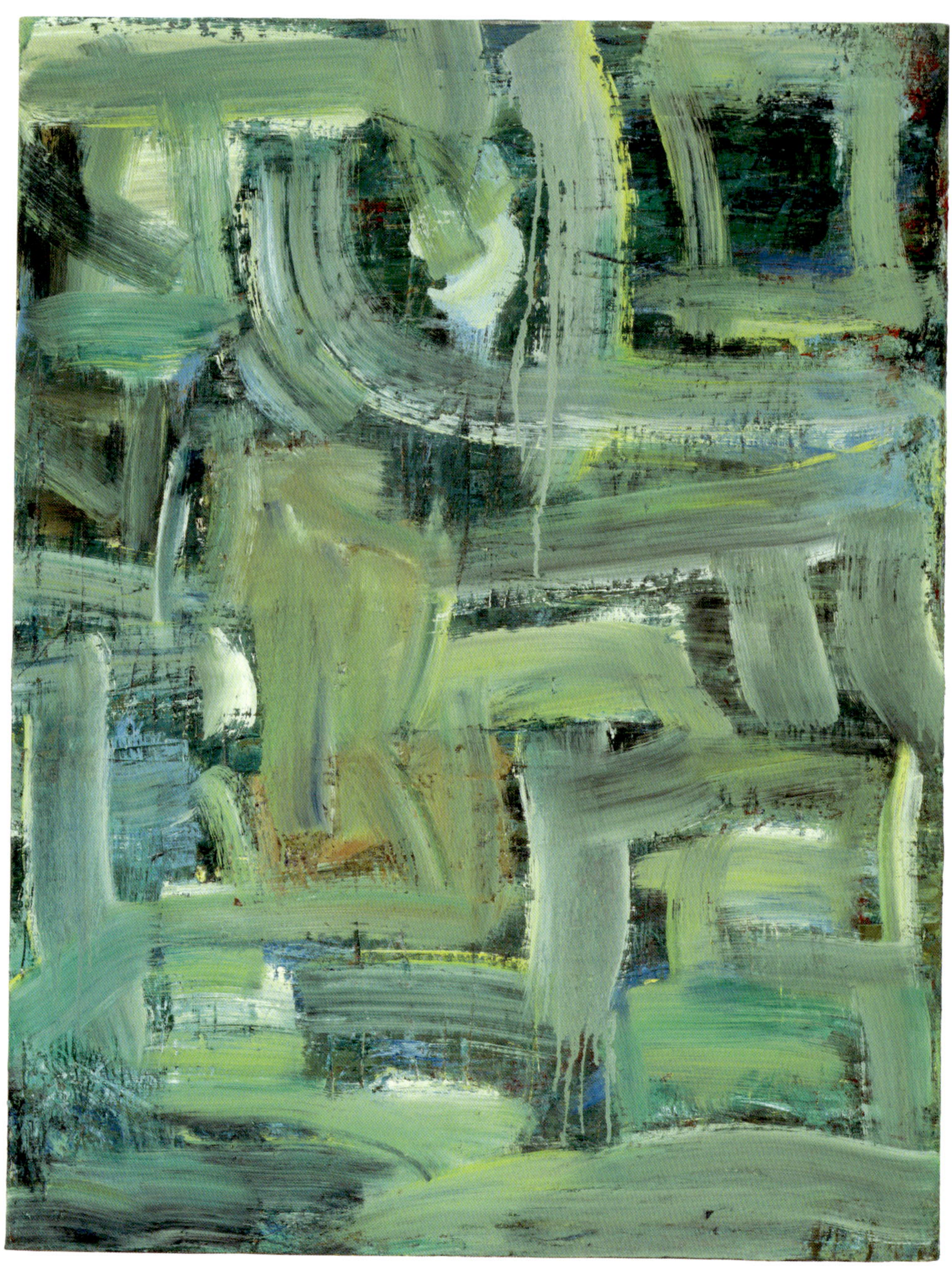

PLATE 72. *In Paul's Hands*, 2000. Oil on linen, 40 x 30½ in. (101.6 x 77.5 cm). Collection of Thomas Whitridge

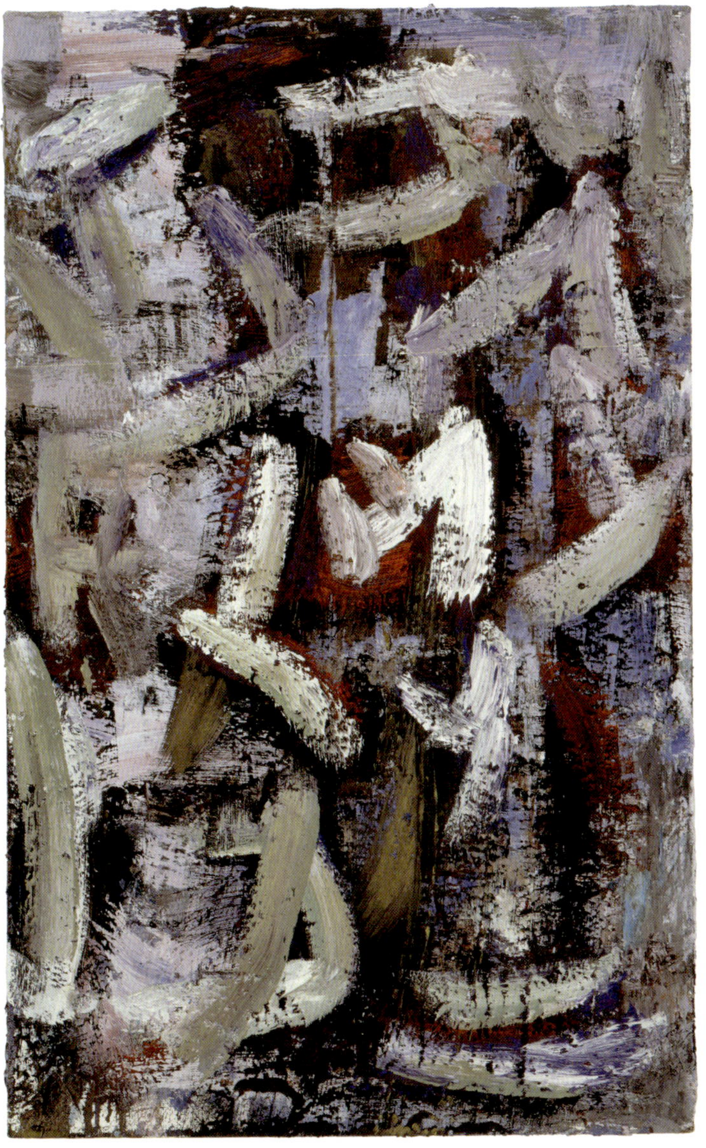

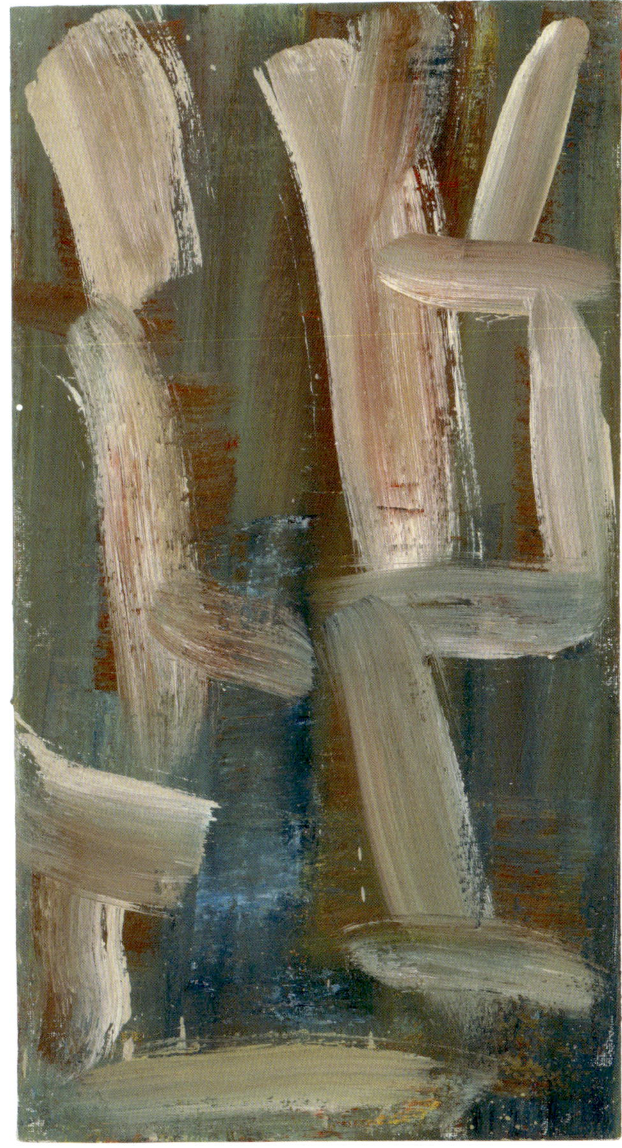

PLATE 73. *Lesson of the Master*, 2000. Oil on linen, 30¼ x 18¼ in. (76.8 x 46.4 cm). Collection of Tracey and Mark Bilski
PLATE 74. *Pisser*, 2000. Oil on jute, 31 x 16 in. (78.7 x 40.6 cm)

PLATE 75. *That Iron String*, 2000. Oil on linen, 38 x 38 in. (96.5 x 96.5 cm). Collection of Milton and Sheila Fine

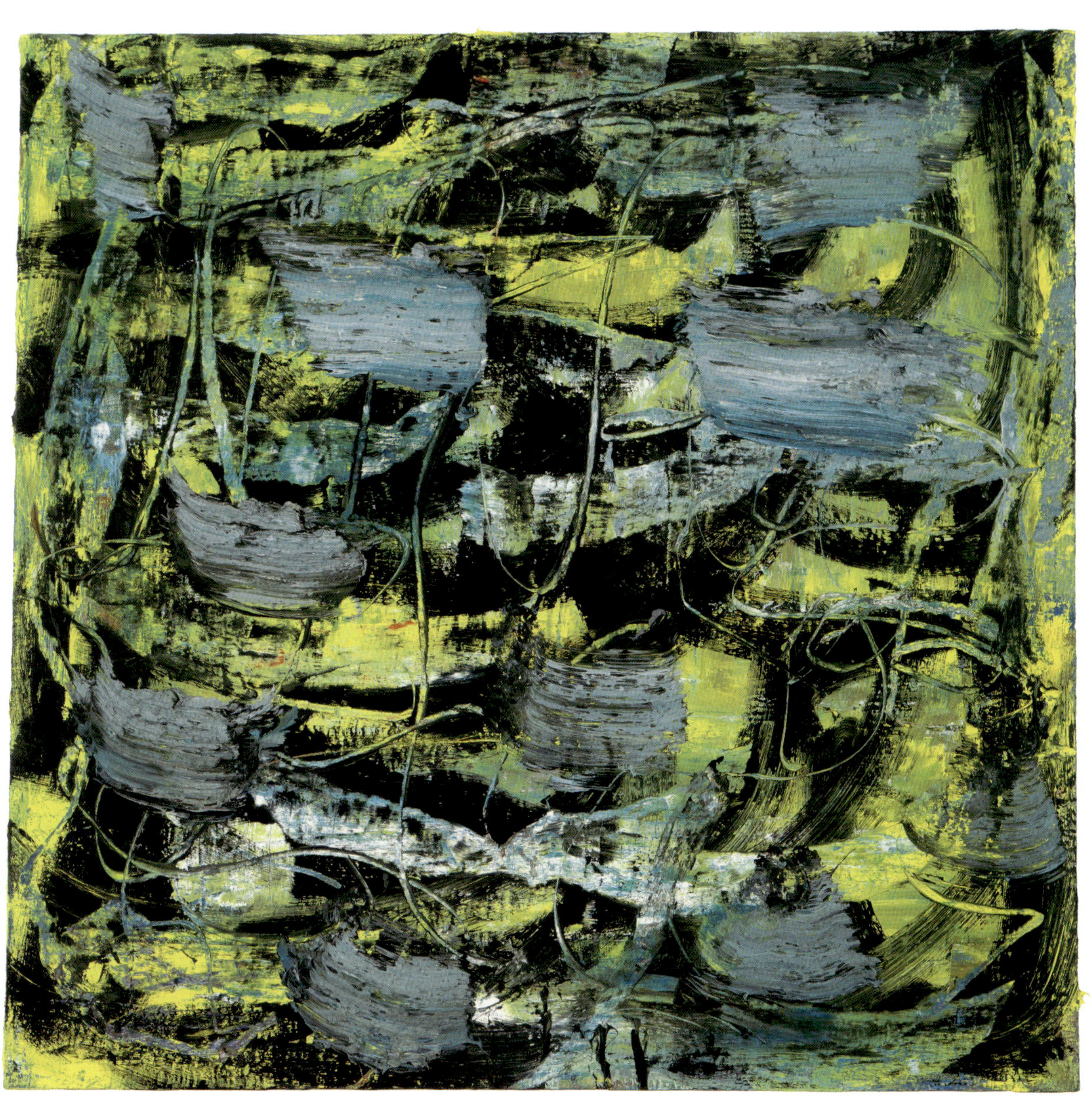

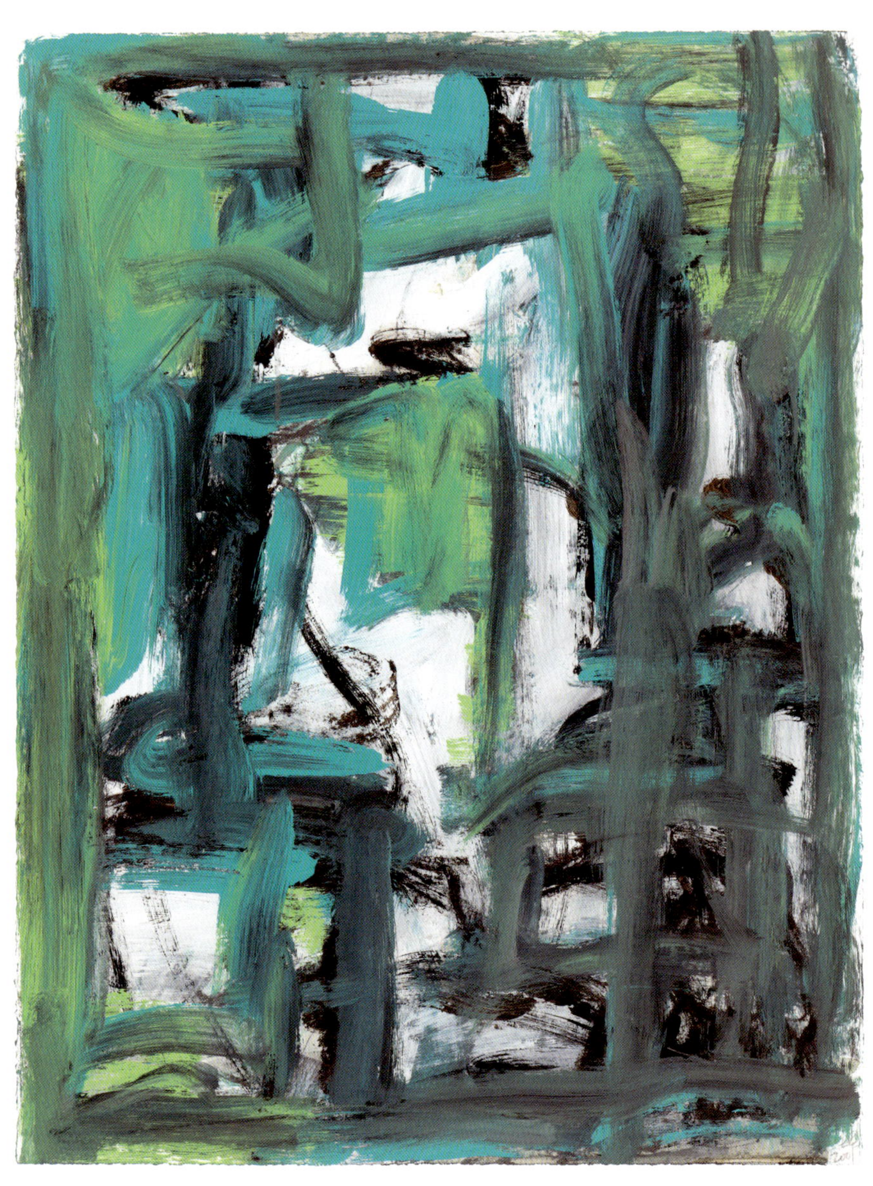

PLATE 76. *Untitled*, 2001. Oil on paper, 30 x 22¼ in. (76.2 x 56.5 cm)
PLATE 77. *My City*, 2002. Oil on linen, 80 x 70 in. (203.2 x 177.8 cm)

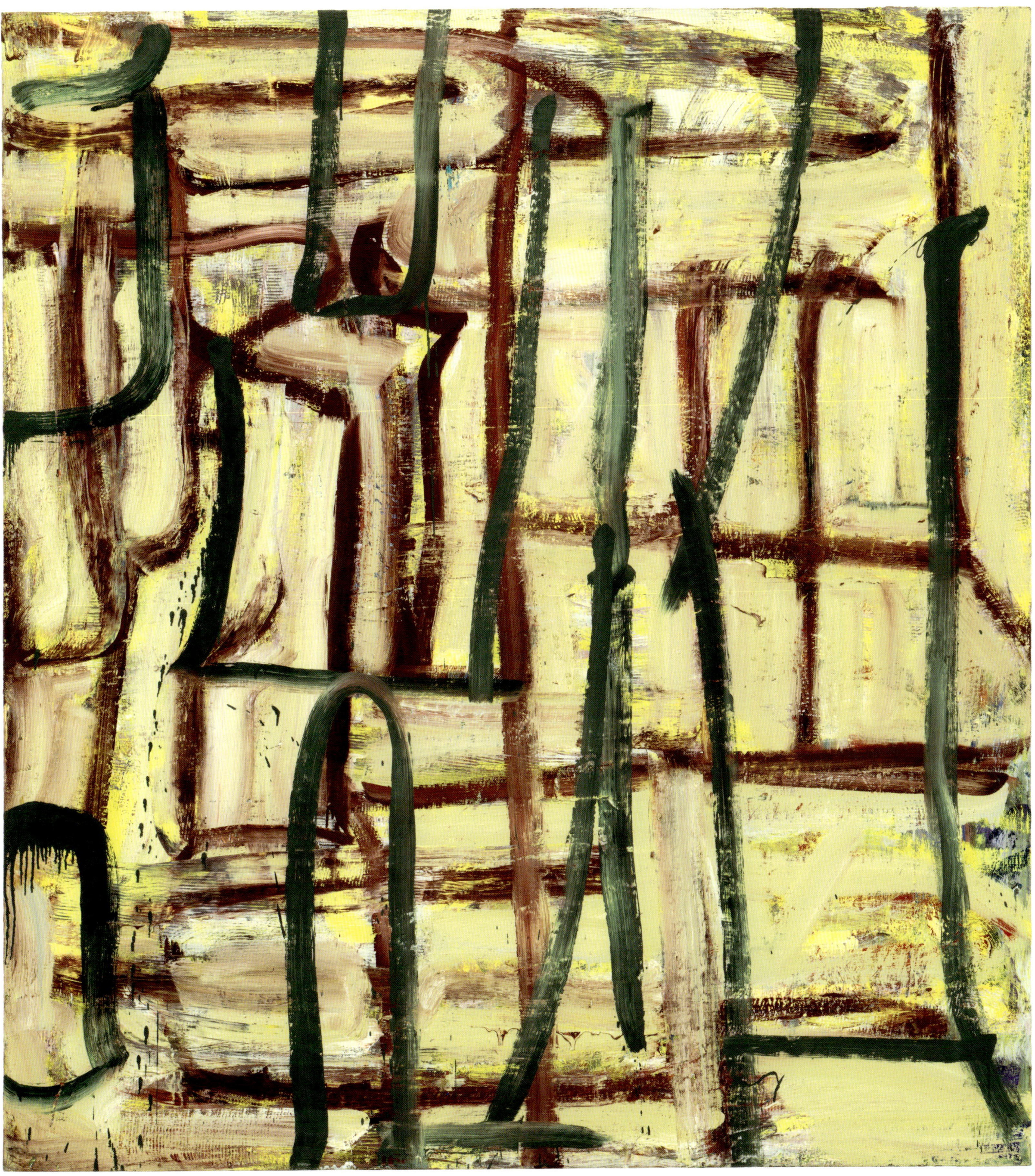

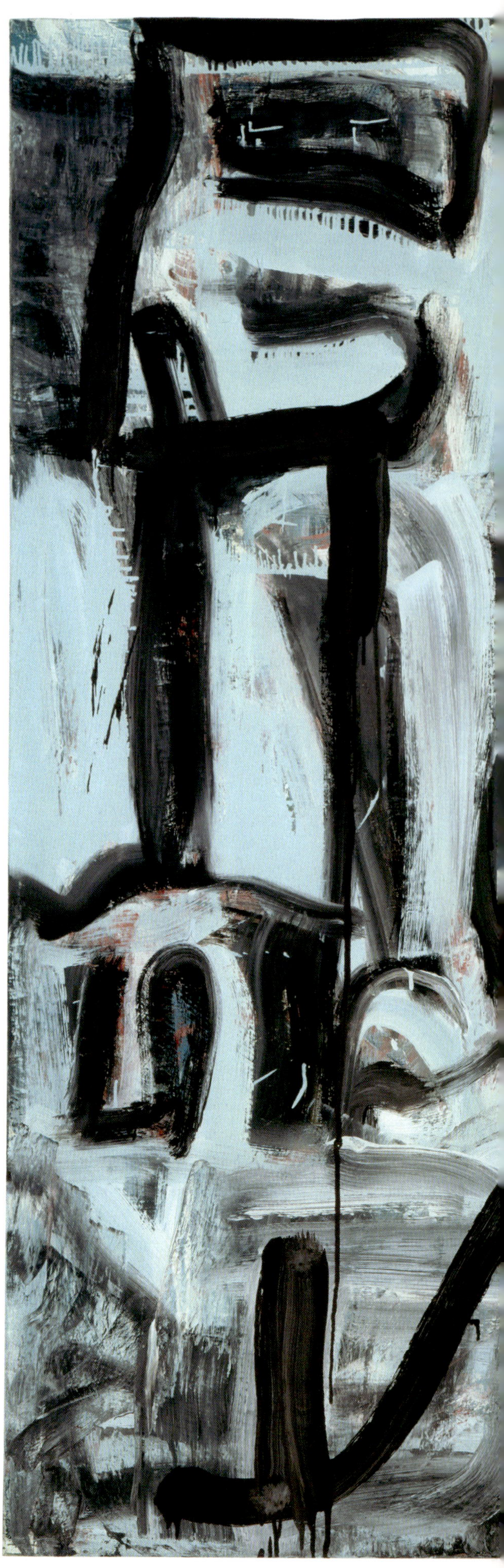

PLATE 78. *The End of a Perfect Day*, 2002. Oil on linen, 72 x 83¾ in. (182.9 x 212.7 cm). Private collection

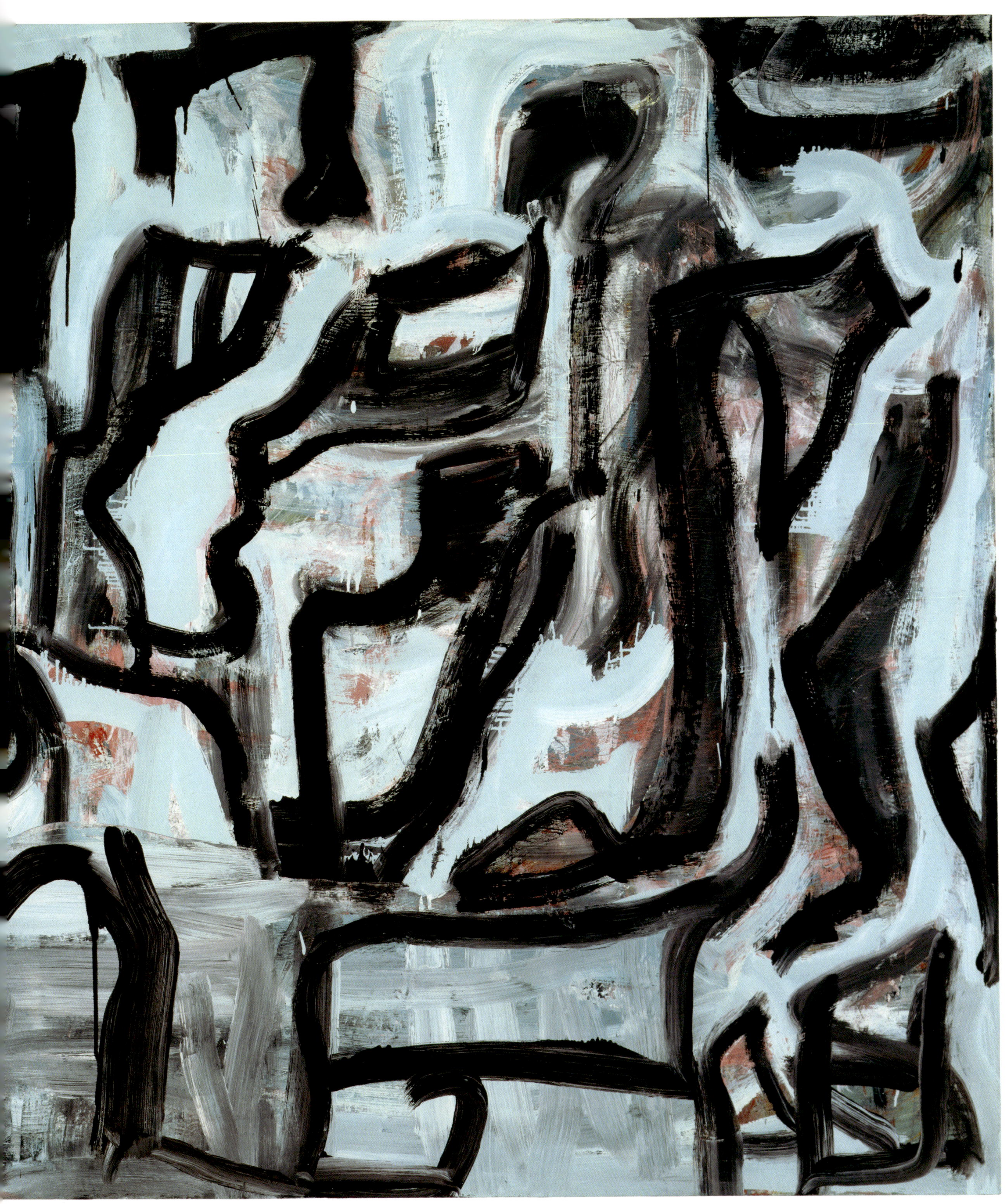

PLATE 79. *The Art of Losing*, 2003. Oil on linen, 80 x 60 in. (203.2 x 152.4 cm)

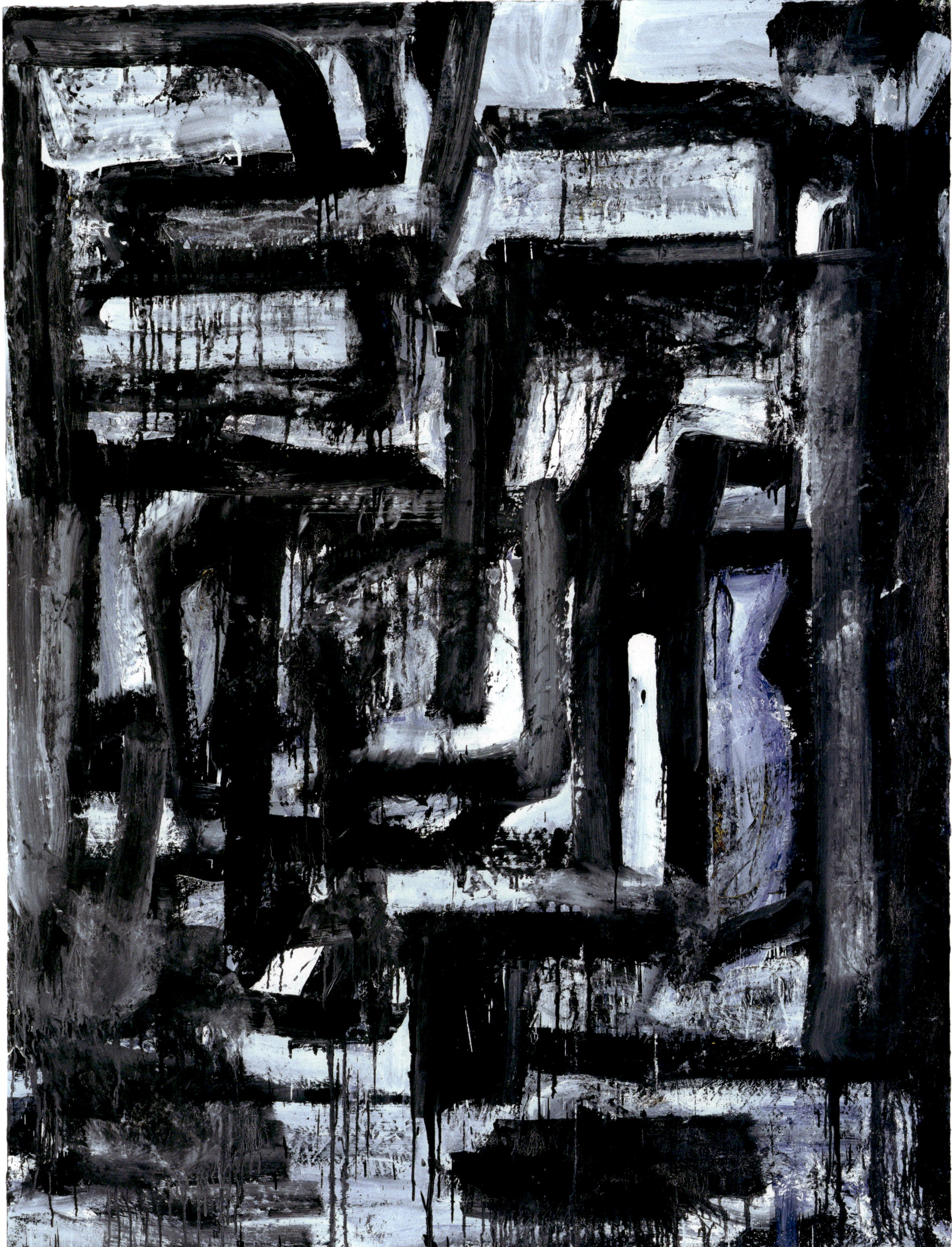

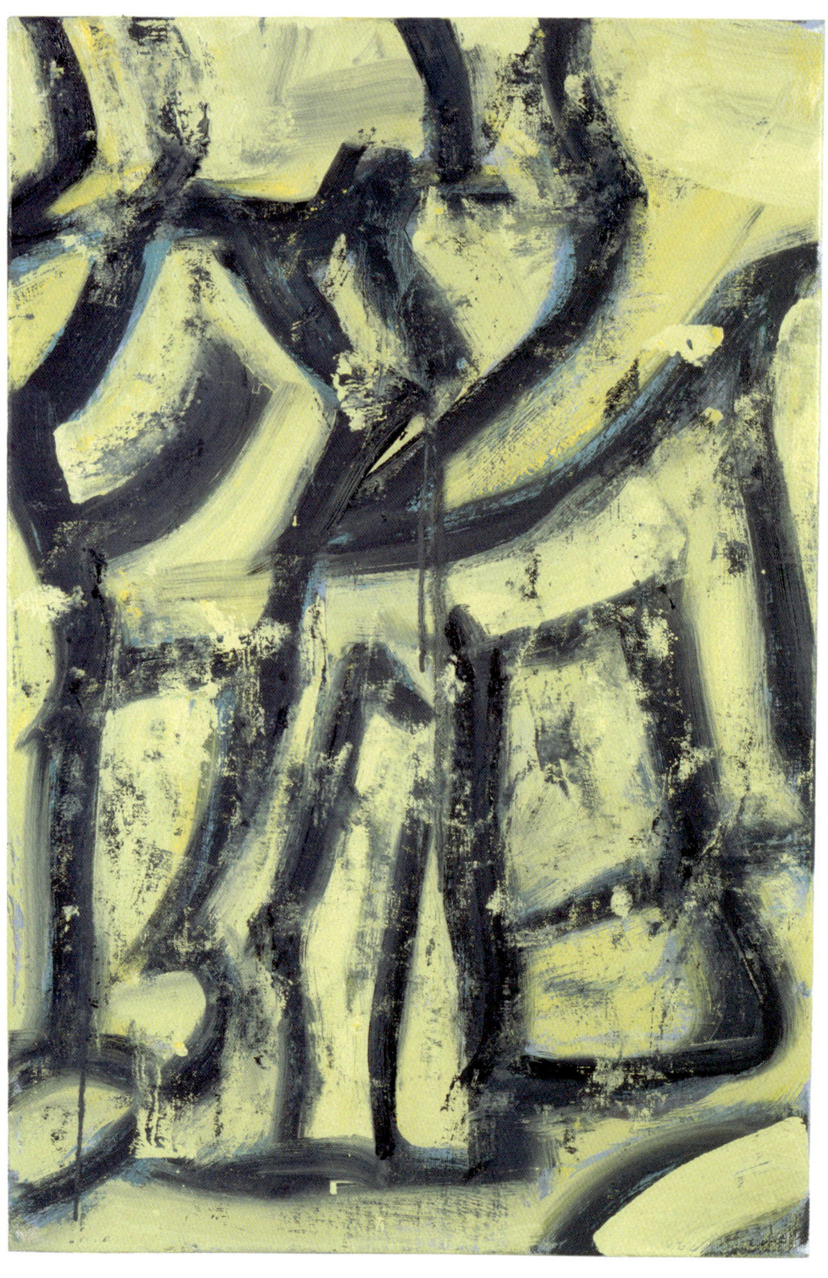

 PLATE 80. *Little Passion*, 2003. Oil on canvas, 40 x 26 in. (101.6 x 66 cm). Collection of Tom Cashin and Jay Johnson, New York

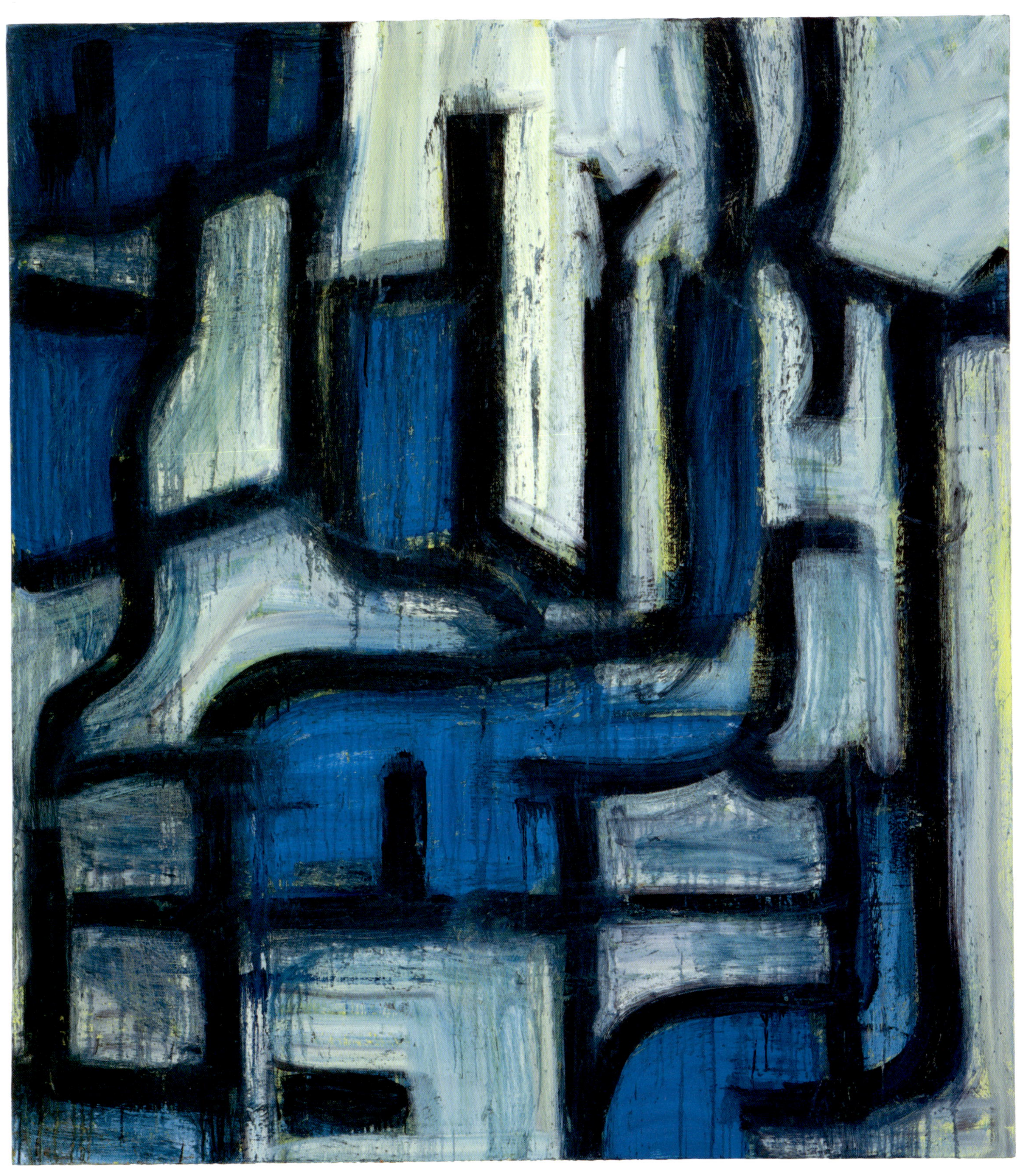

PLATE 81. *Moon and Movies*, 2003. Oil on linen, 66 x 57 in. (167.6 x 144.8 cm). Private collection

PLATE 82. *Perilous Things*, 2003. Oil on linen, 90 x 60 in. (228.6 x 152.4 cm). Private collection

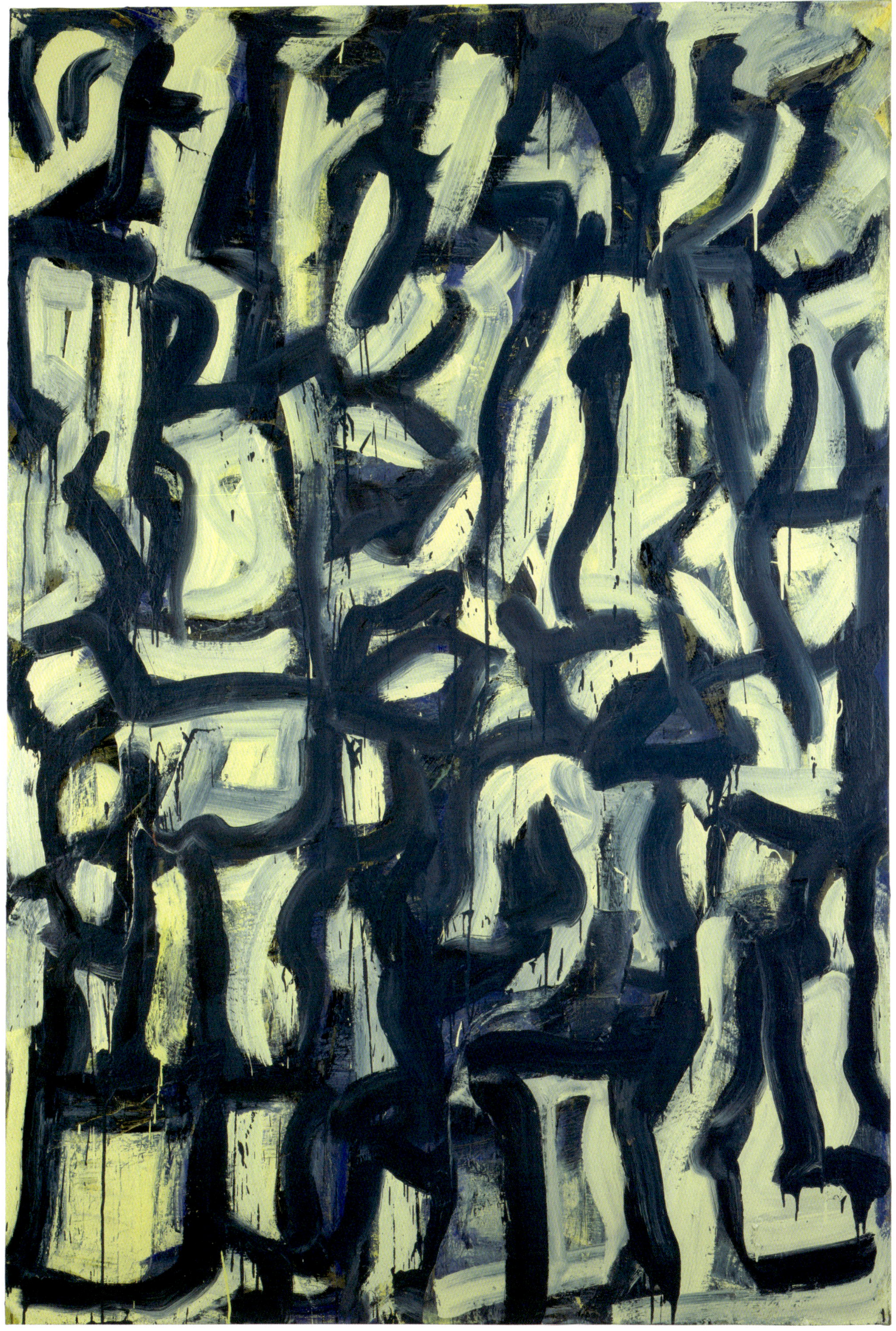

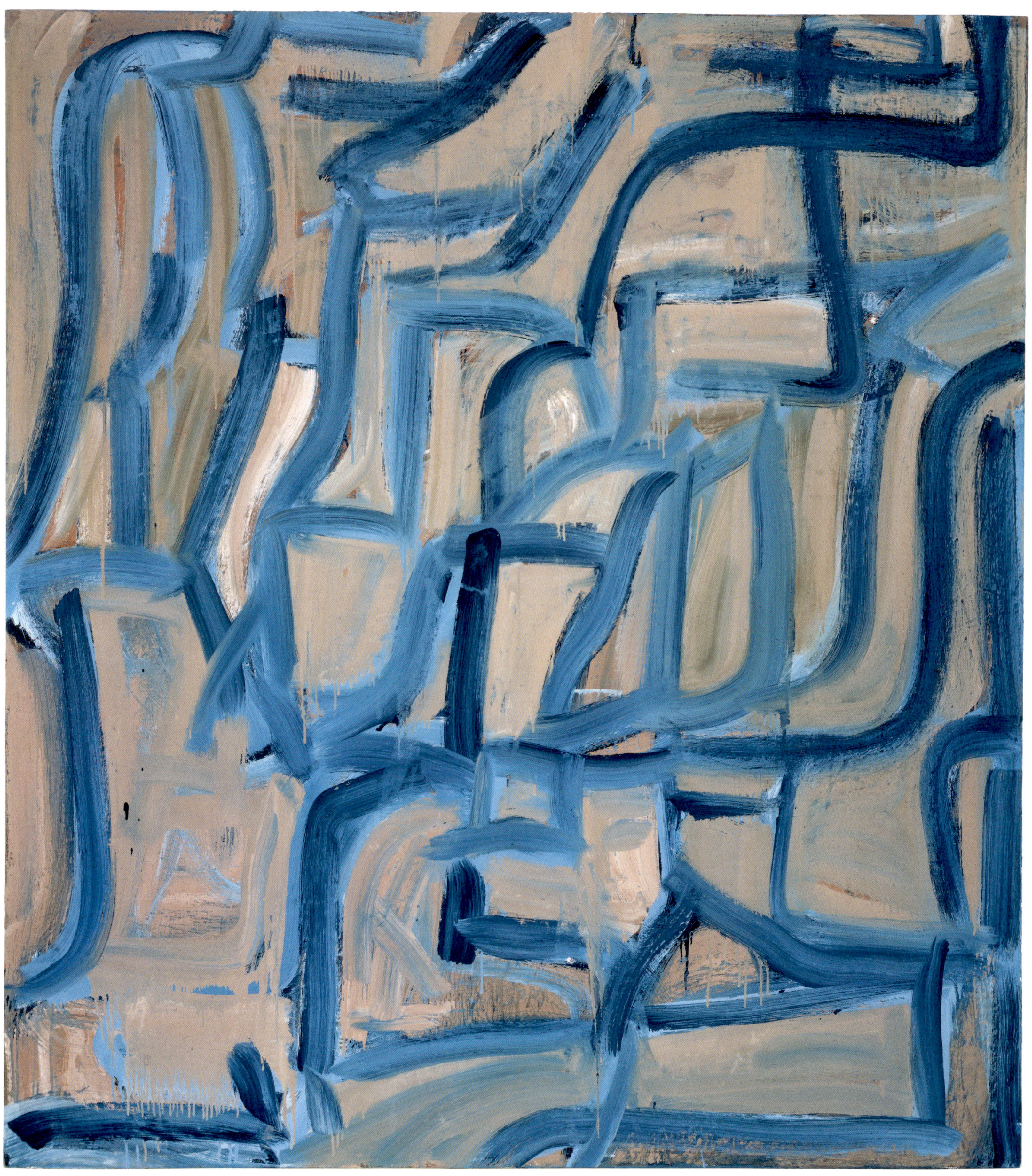

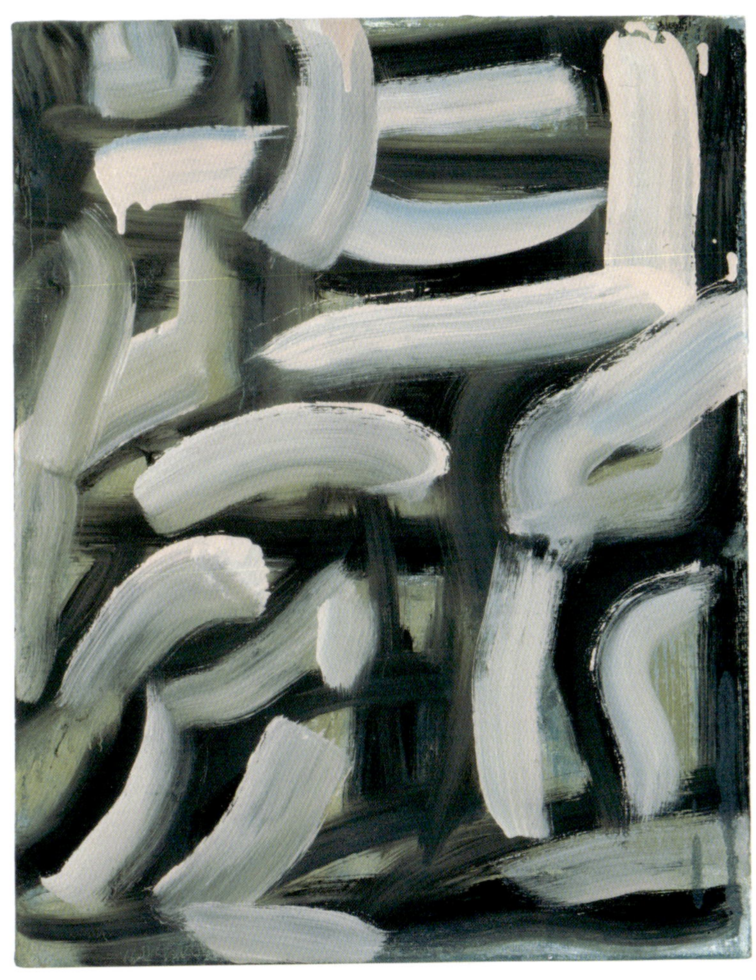

PLATE 83. *Pink and Blue and You*, 2003. Oil on linen, 80 x 70 in. (203.2 x 177.8 cm). Private collection
PLATE 84. *Twenty Three Strokes*, 2003. Oil on linen, 21 x 17 in. (53.3 x 43.2 cm)

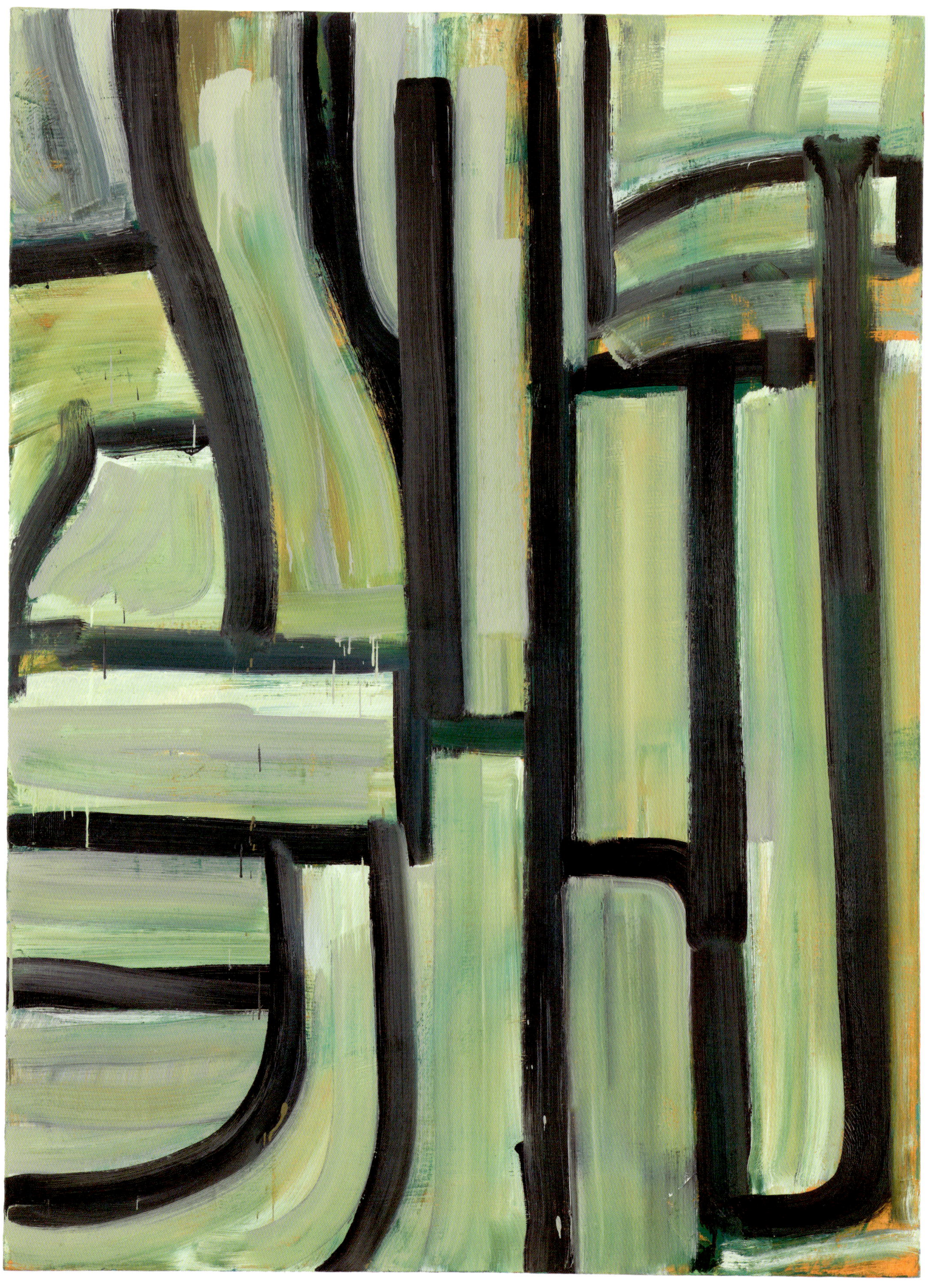

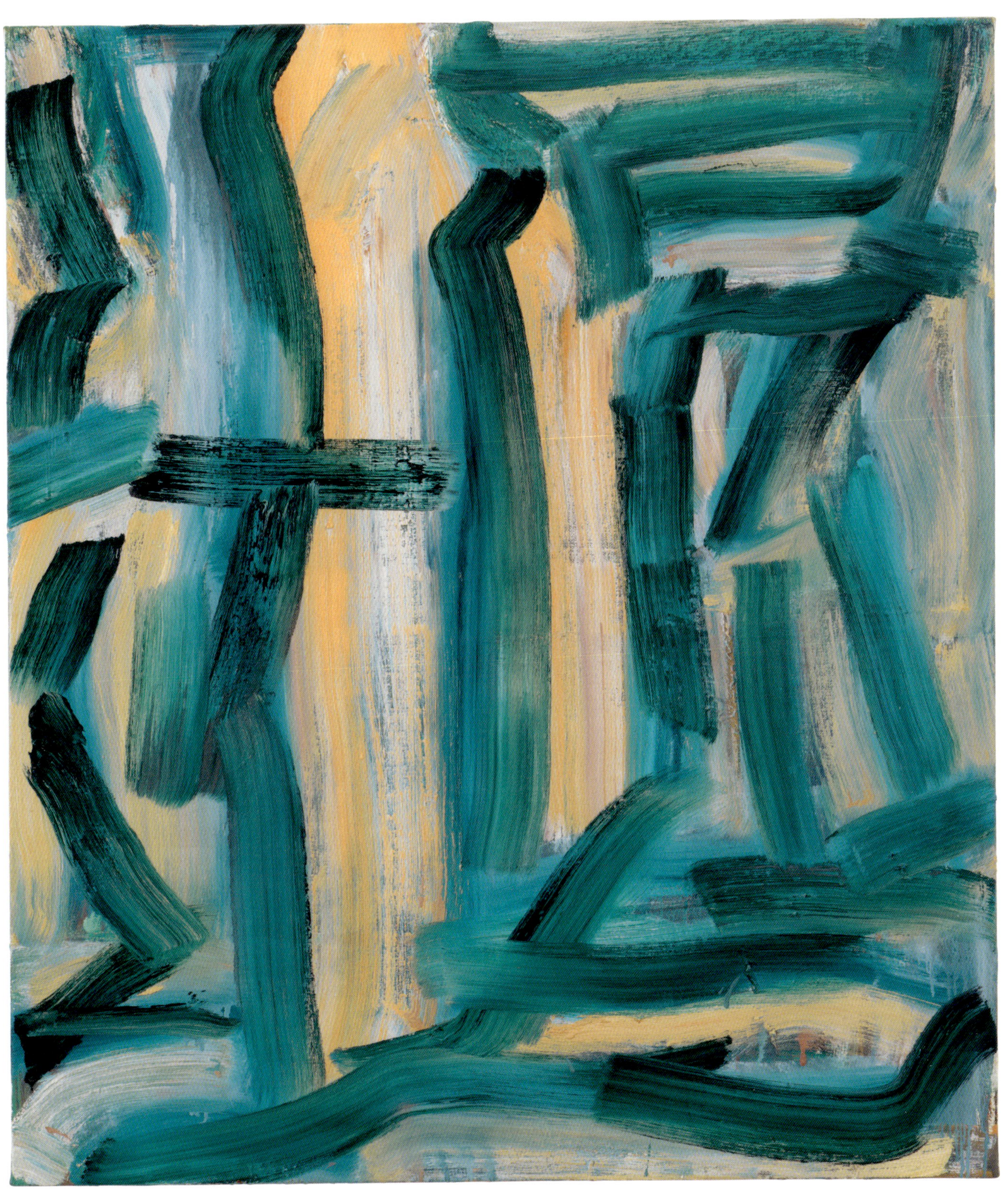

PLATE 85. *Green in the Body*, 2004. Oil on linen, 77 x 55 in. (195.6 x 139.7 cm)
PLATE 86. *Glitter of a Being*, 2005. Oil on jute, 50 x 42¼ in. (127 x 107.3 cm)

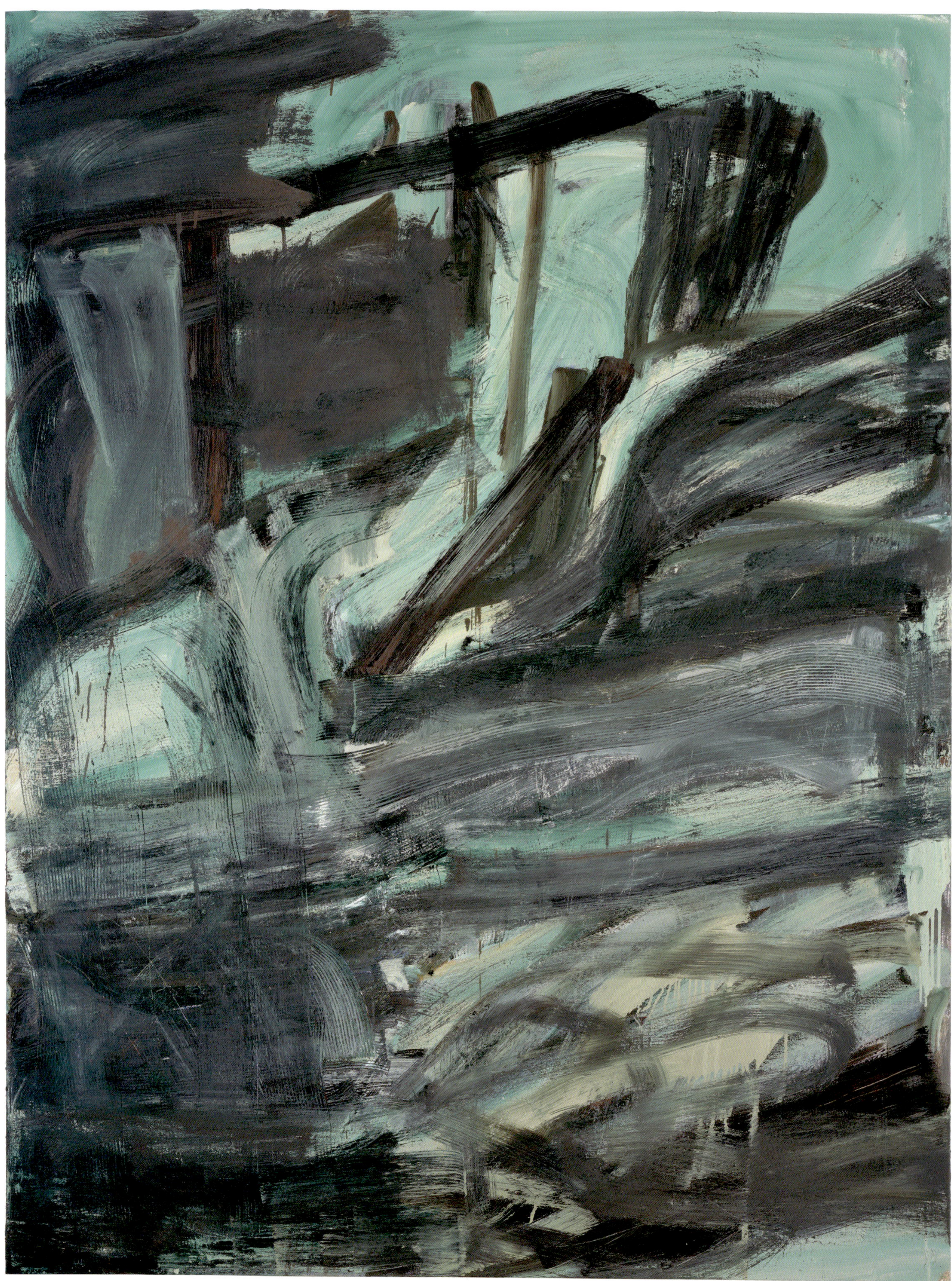

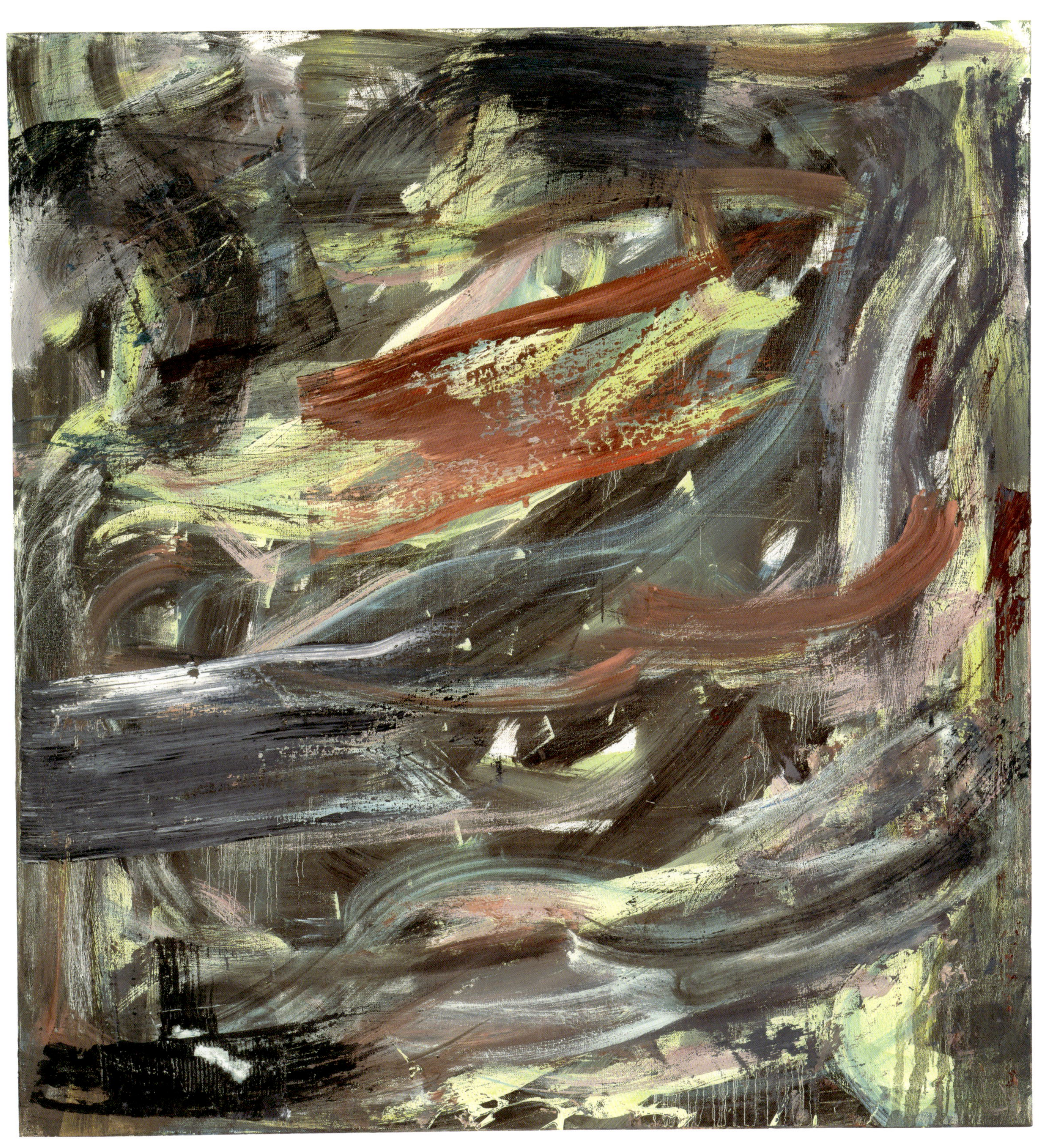

PLATE 87. *Green's Apogee*, 2005. Oil on canvas, 88 x 70 in. (223.5 x 177.8 cm). Hood Museum of Art, Dartmouth College: Purchased through a gift from Mr. and Mrs. Joseph H. Hazen, by exchange, 2013.23
PLATE 88. *Loose Change*, 2005. Oil on canvas, 60 x 55 in. (152.4 x 139.7 cm). The Dicke Collection

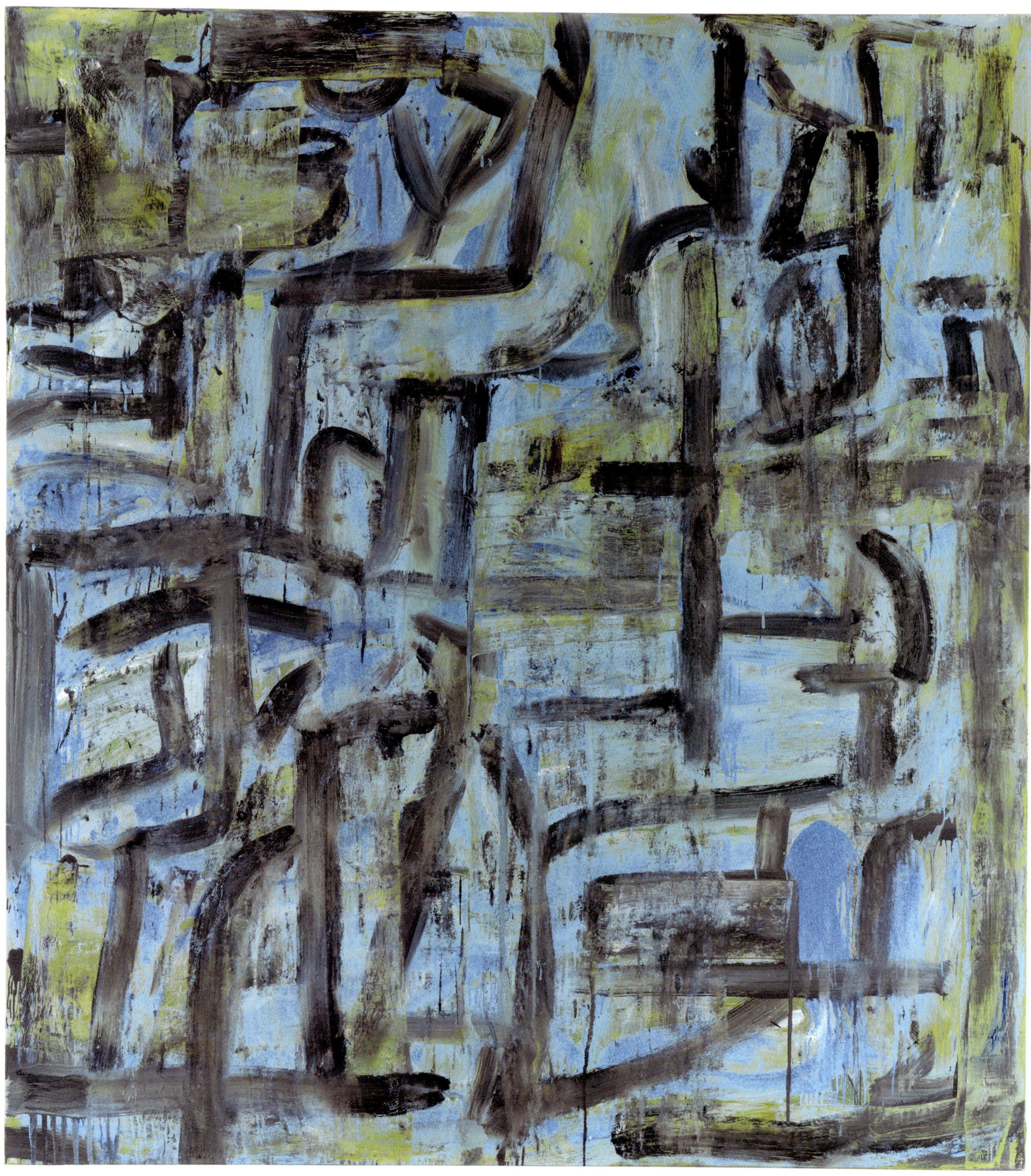

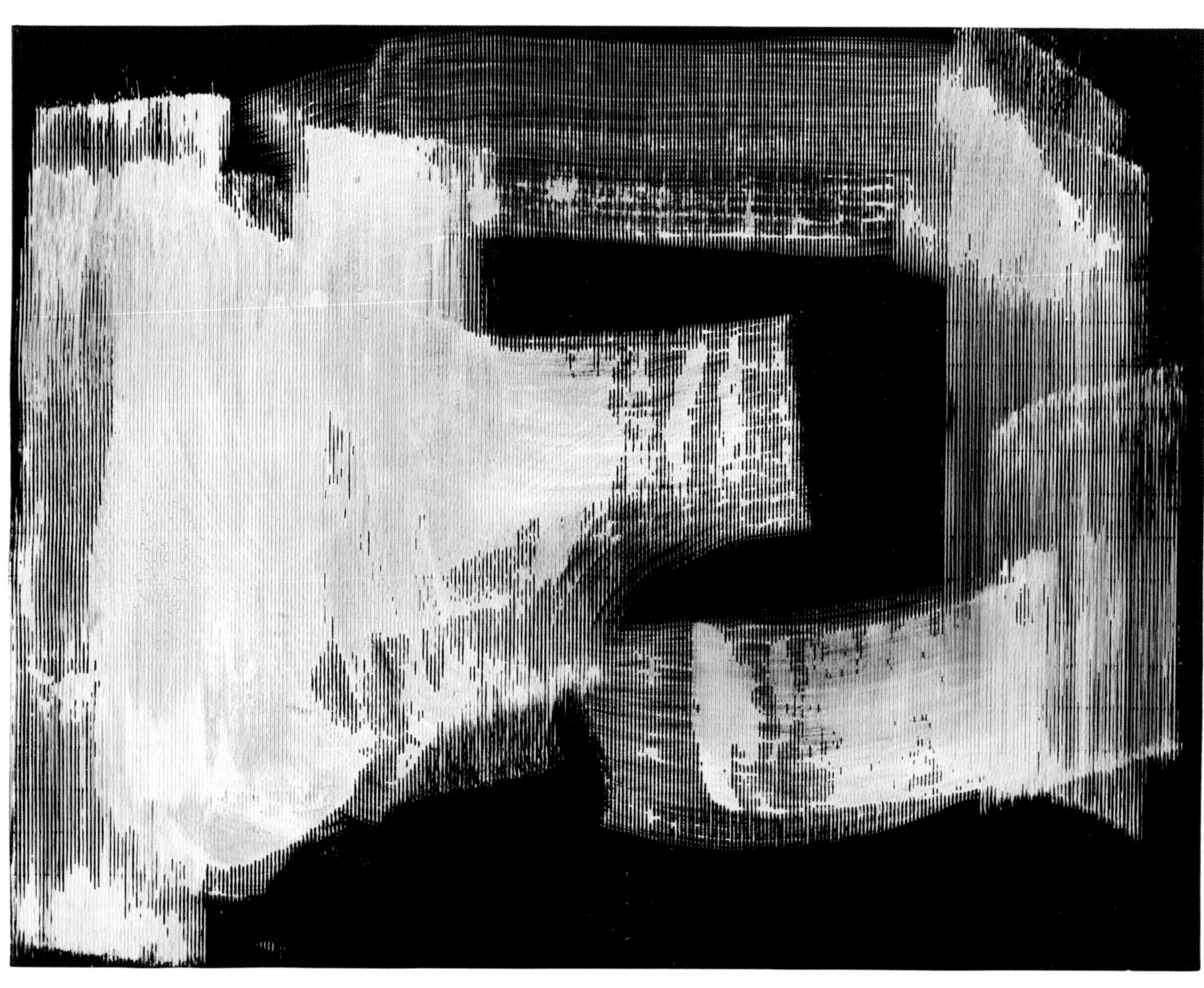

PLATE 89. *Residue of a Gaze*, 2005. Oil on linen, 87¾ x 77 in. (222.9 x 195.6 cm)
PLATE 90. *Untitled*, 2005. Acrylic on corrugated paper, 30½ x 38 in. (77.5 x 96.5 cm)

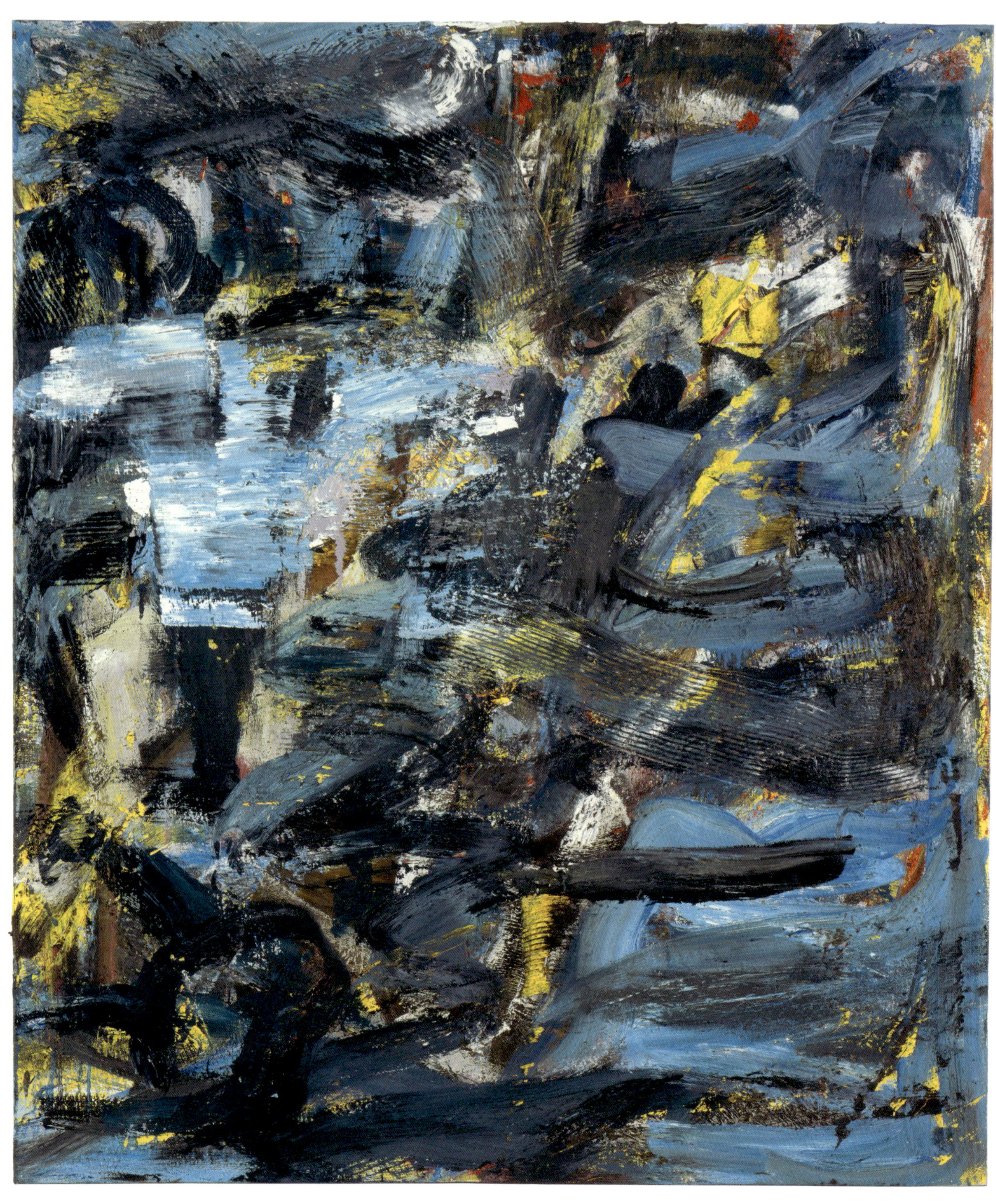

PLATE 91. *A Self That Touches All the Edges*, 2006. Oil on canvas, 50 x 42 in. (127 x 106.7 cm). Private collection

PLATE 92. *Slippery Slope*, 2006. Oil on linen, 88 x 65 in. (223.5 x 165.1 cm)

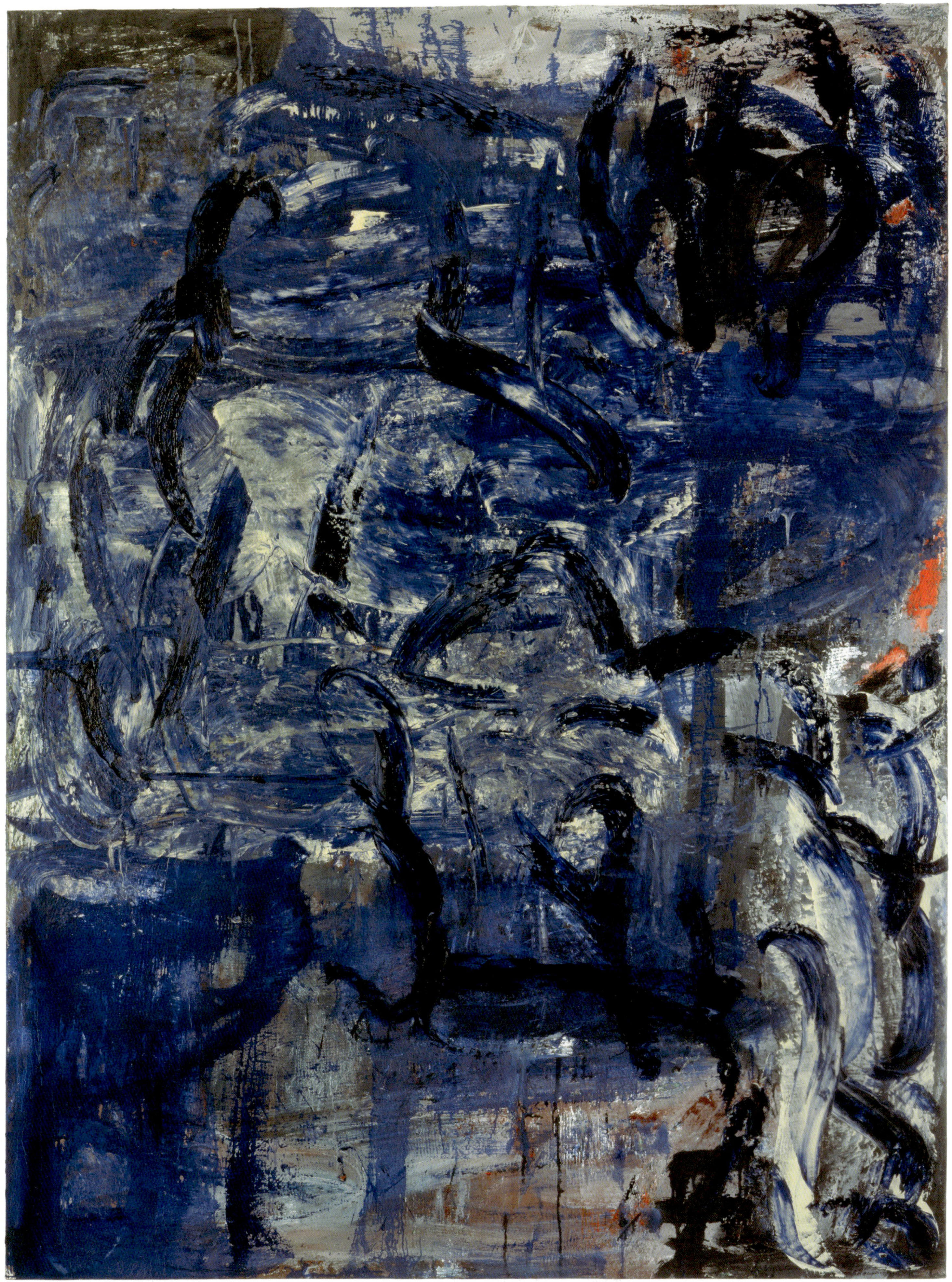

PLATE 93. *Black Dirties*, 2007. Acrylic on canvas, 70 x 48 in. (177.8 x 121.9 cm)

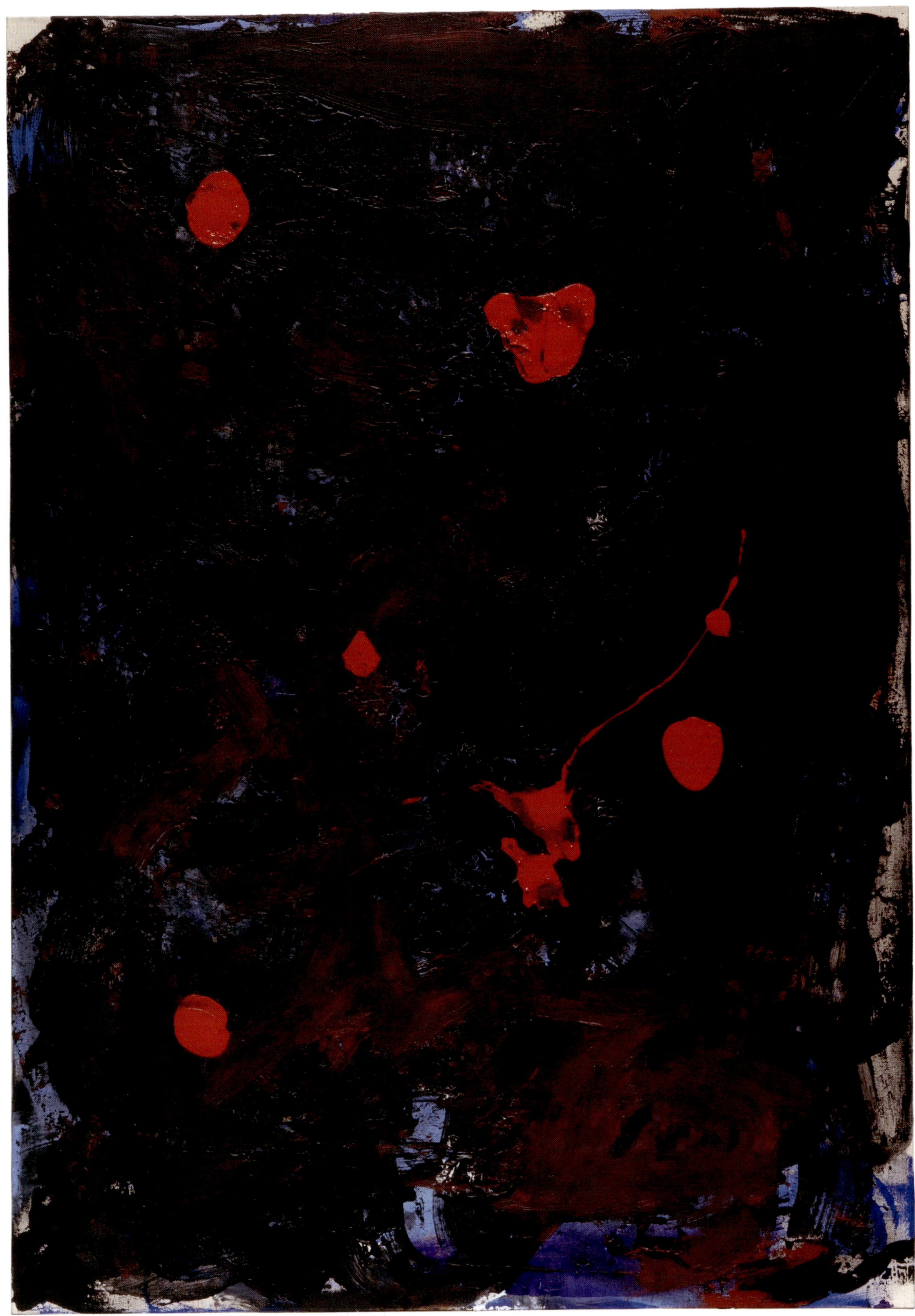

PLATE 94. *Geography*, 2007. Acrylic on canvas, 72 x 65 in. (182.9 x 165.1 cm)

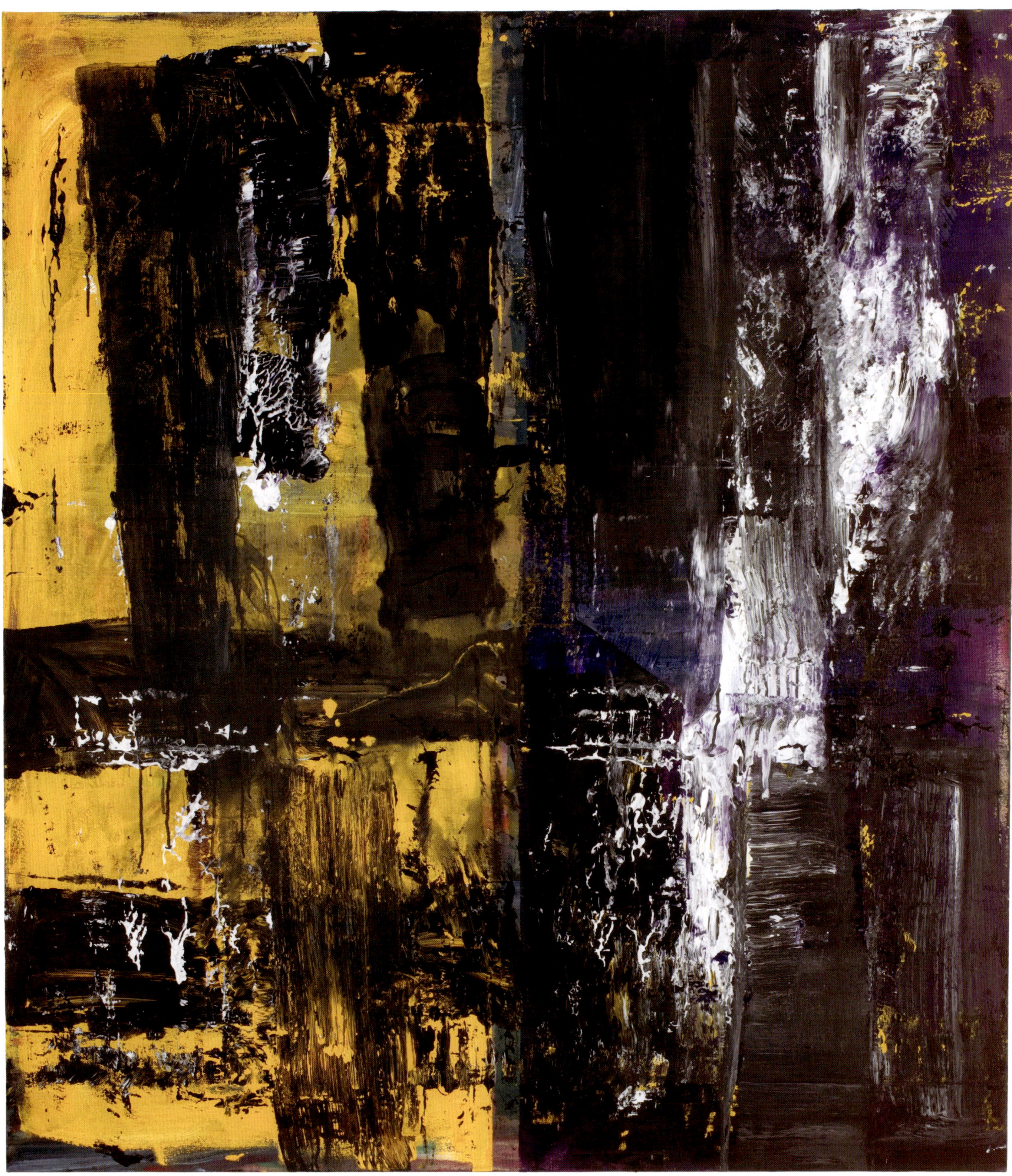

PLATE 95. *Concealing and Revealing*, 2008. Oil on linen, 87¾ x 70 in. (222.9 x 177.8 cm)

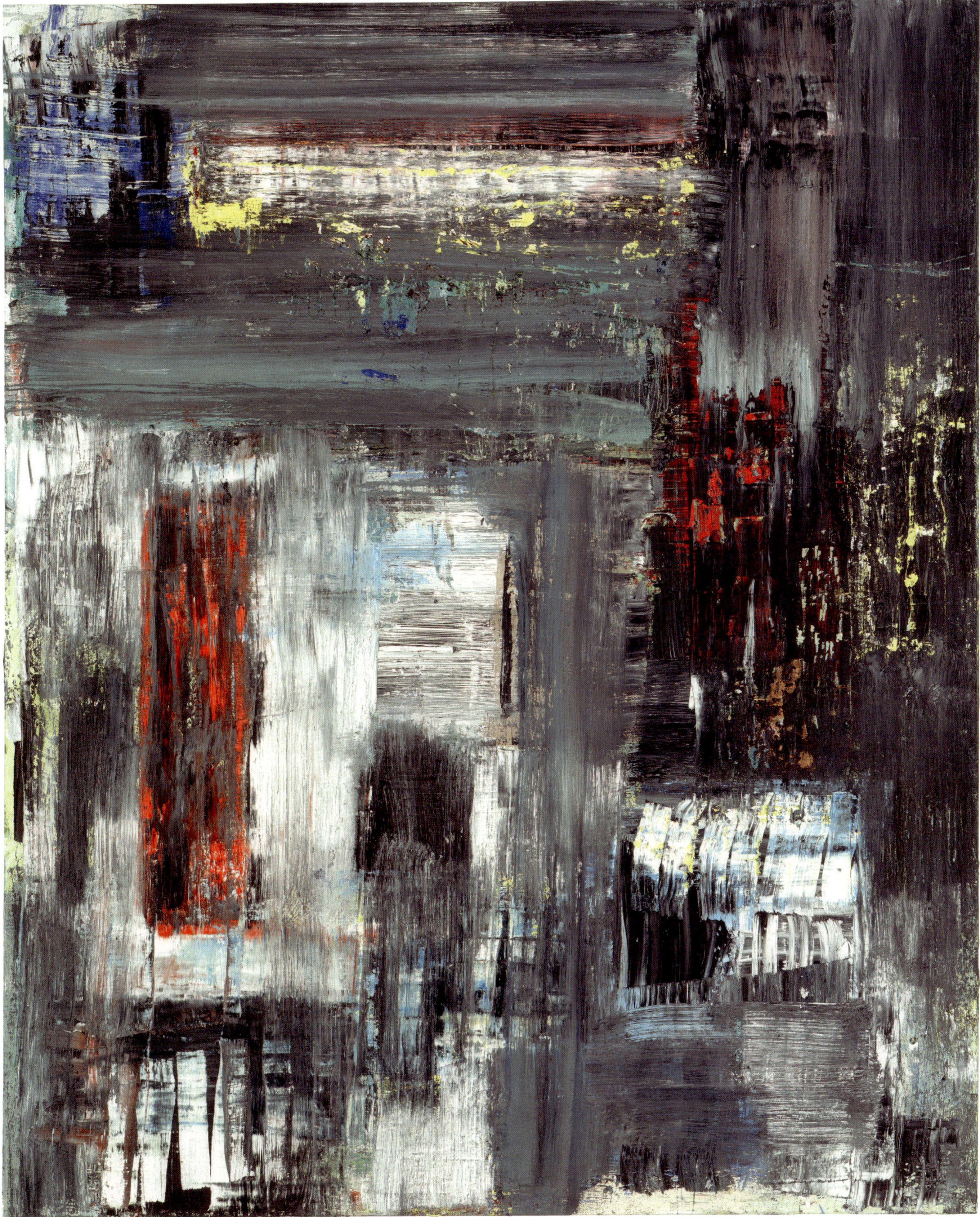

PLATE 96. *Blonde Ambition*, 2009. Collage, graphite, acrylic, sandpaper, and staples, 9⅛ x 11 in. (23.2 x 27.9 cm). Private collection

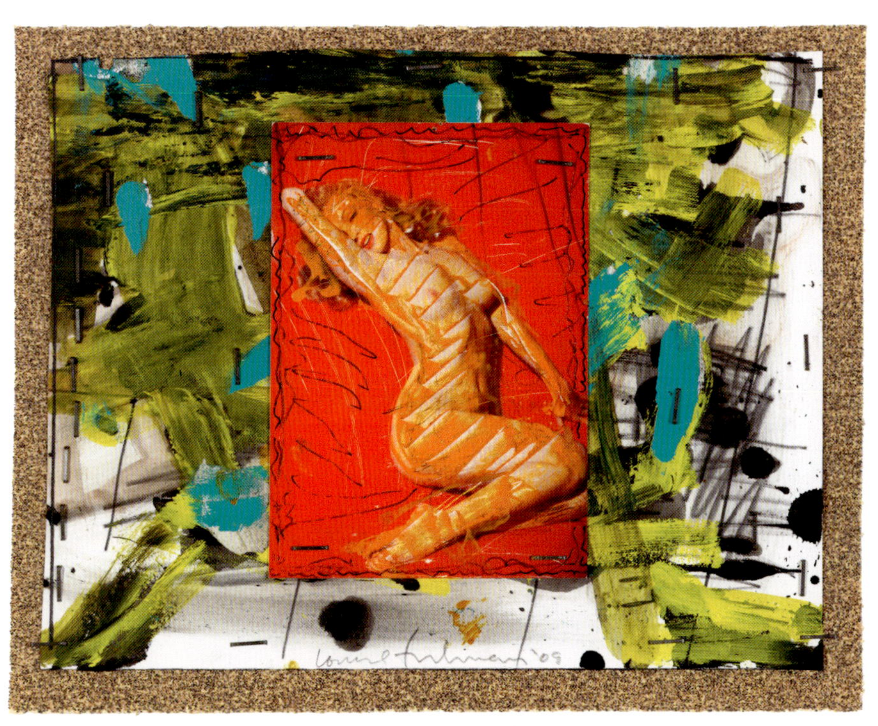

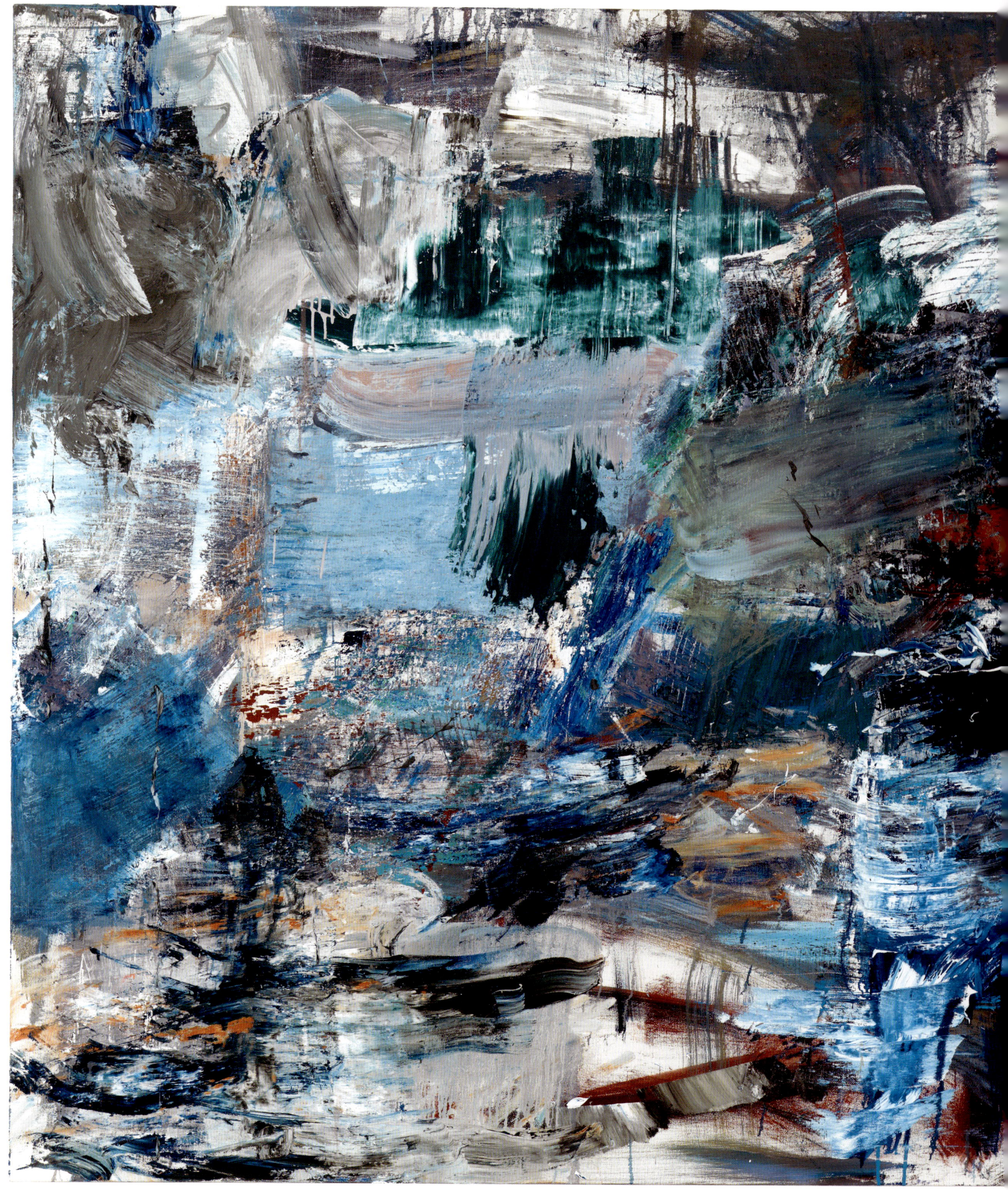

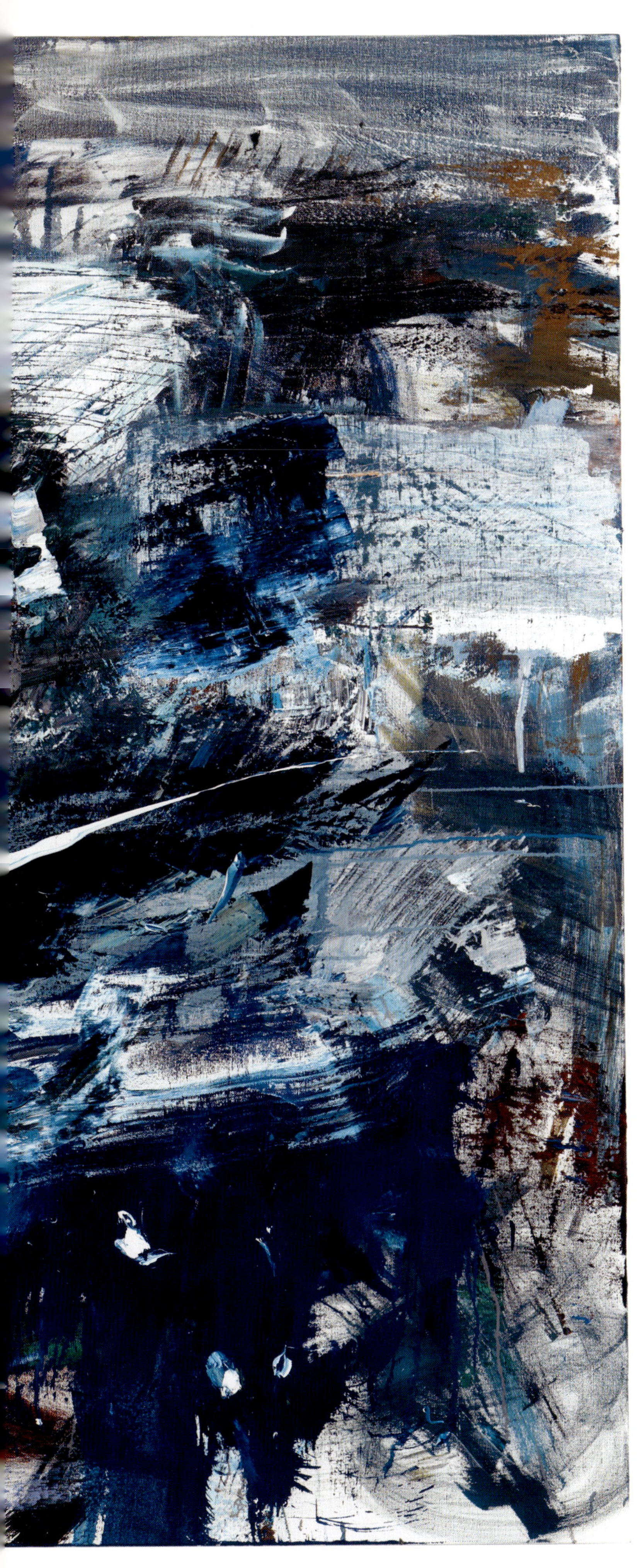

PLATE 97. *Line Drive*, 2010. Oil on linen, 70 x 88 in. (177.8 x 223.5 cm). Private collection

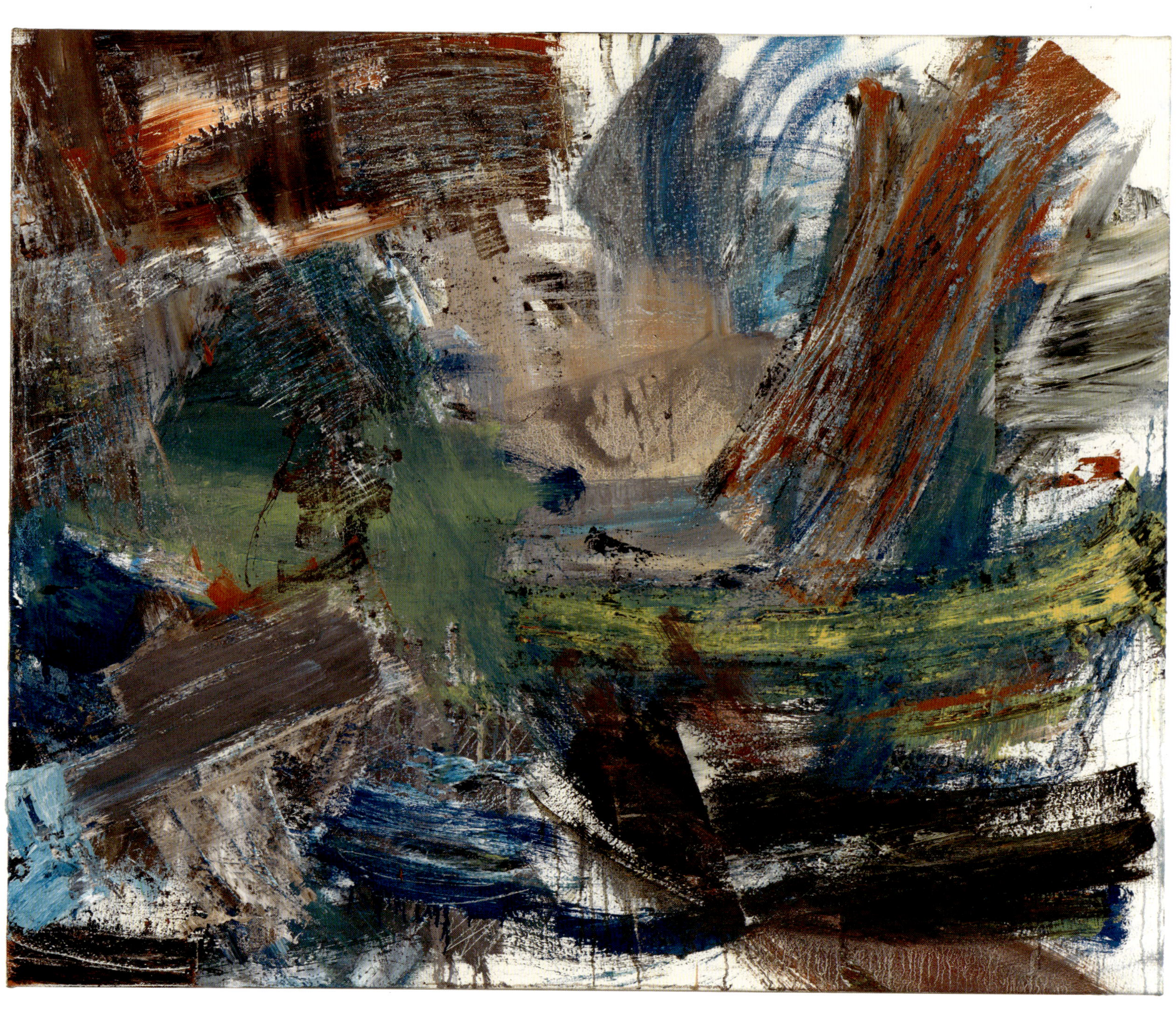

PLATE 98. *Love Lies Sleeping*, 2010. Oil on linen, 42 x 50 in. (106.7 x 127 cm). Private collection

PLATE 99. *Zero at the Bone*, 2010. Oil on linen, 70 x 60 in. (177.8 x 152.4 cm). Collection of Mike De Paola, New York

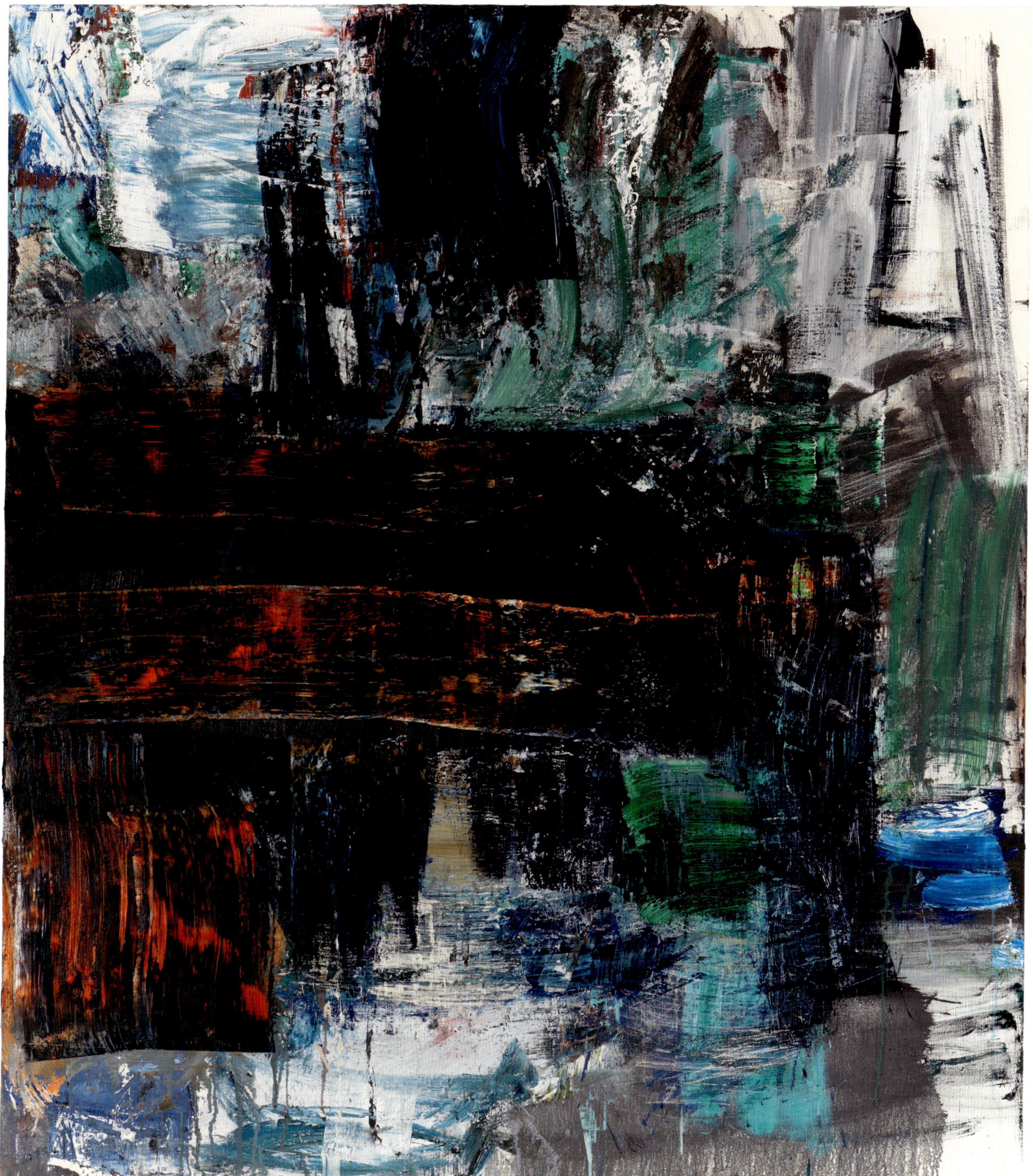

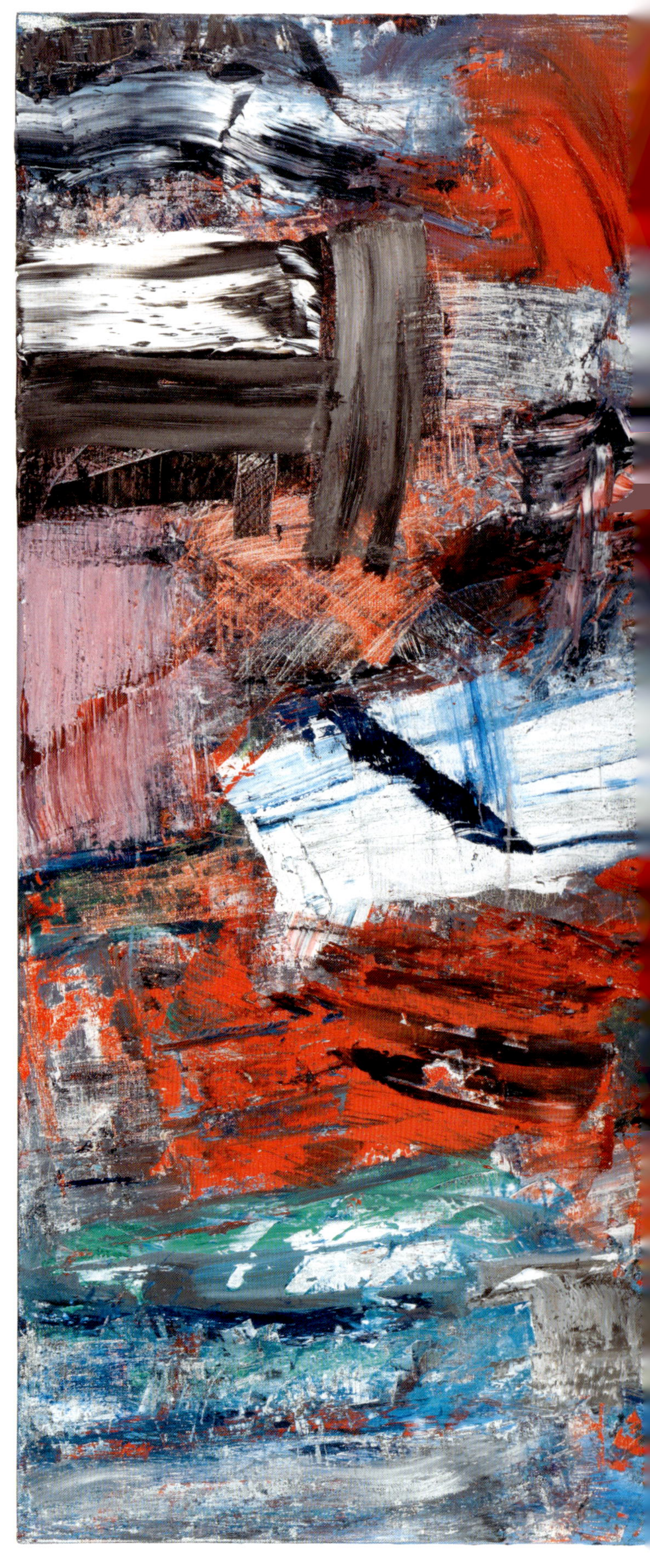

PLATE 100. *Raft of the Medusa*, 2011. Oil on linen, 60 x 80 in. (152.4 x 203.2 cm). Private collection

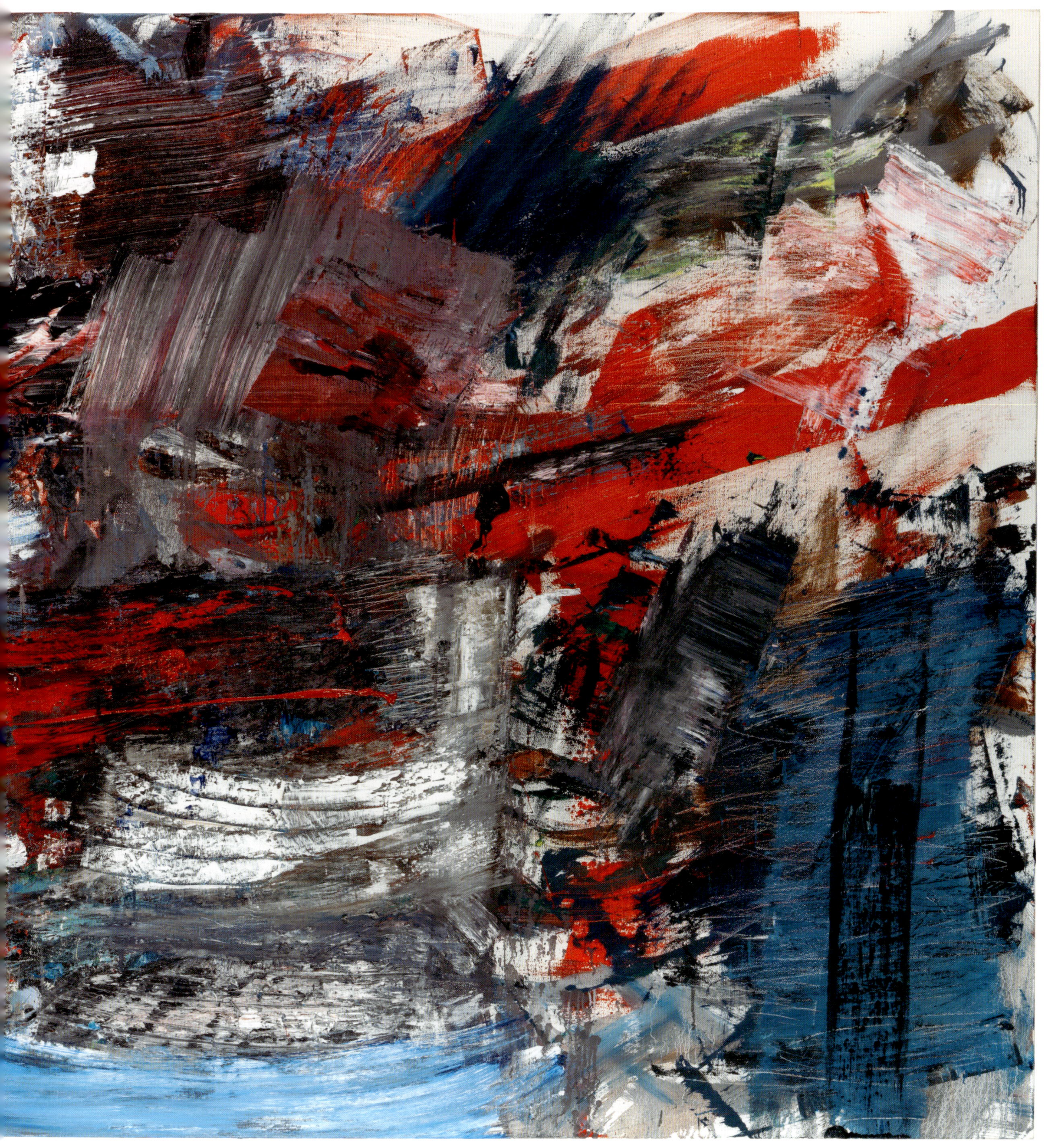

PLATE 101. *Untitled*, 2011. Oil on newspaper, 22 3/16 x 24 1/4 in. (56.4 x 61.6 cm)

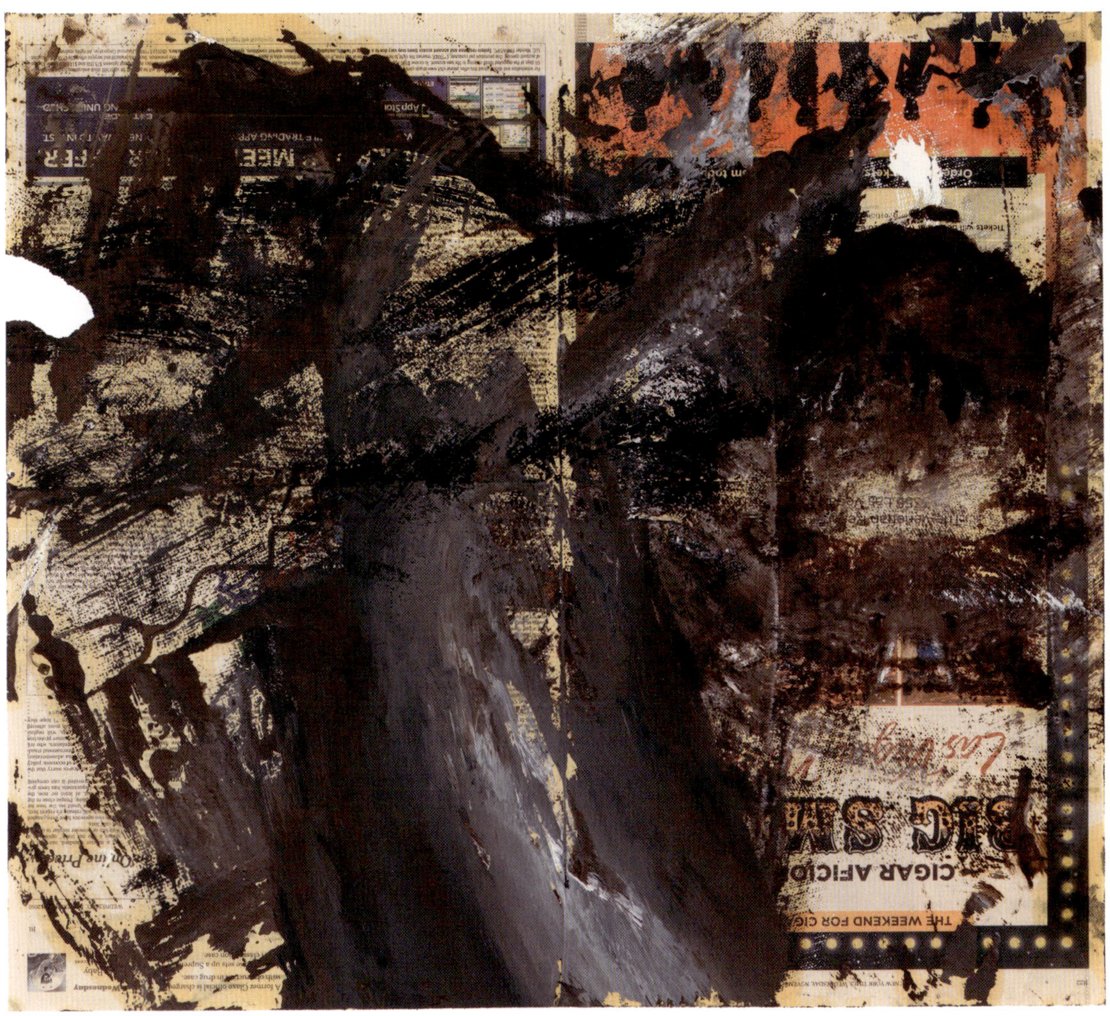

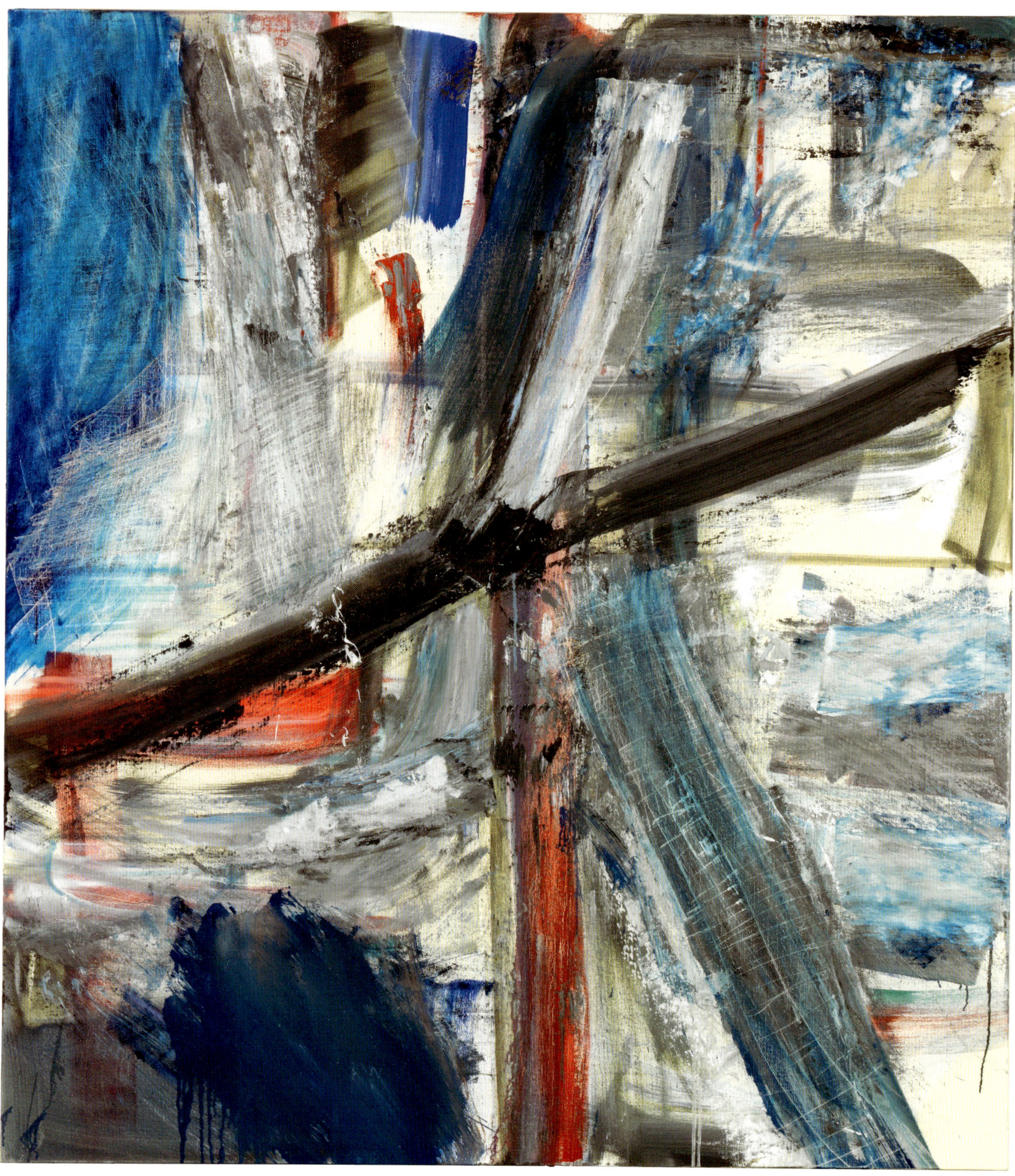

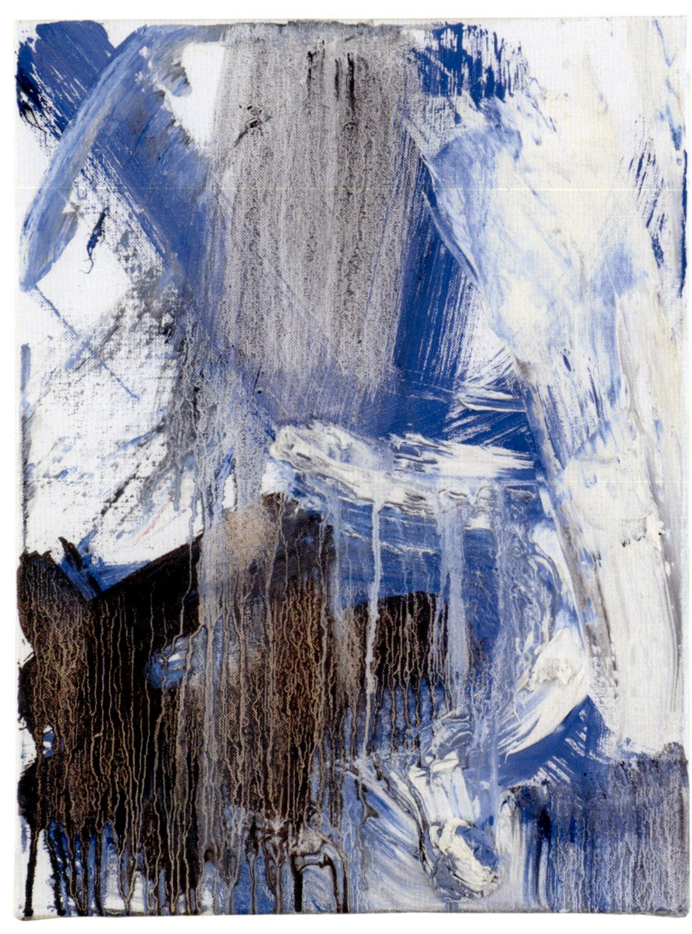

PLATE 102. *Crossing the Rubicon*, 2012. Oil on linen, 66 x 57 in. (167.6 x 144.8 cm).
Collection of James and Janet Kloppenburg
PLATE 103. *Rialto*, 2012. Oil on linen, 16 x 12 in. (40.2 x 30.5 cm)

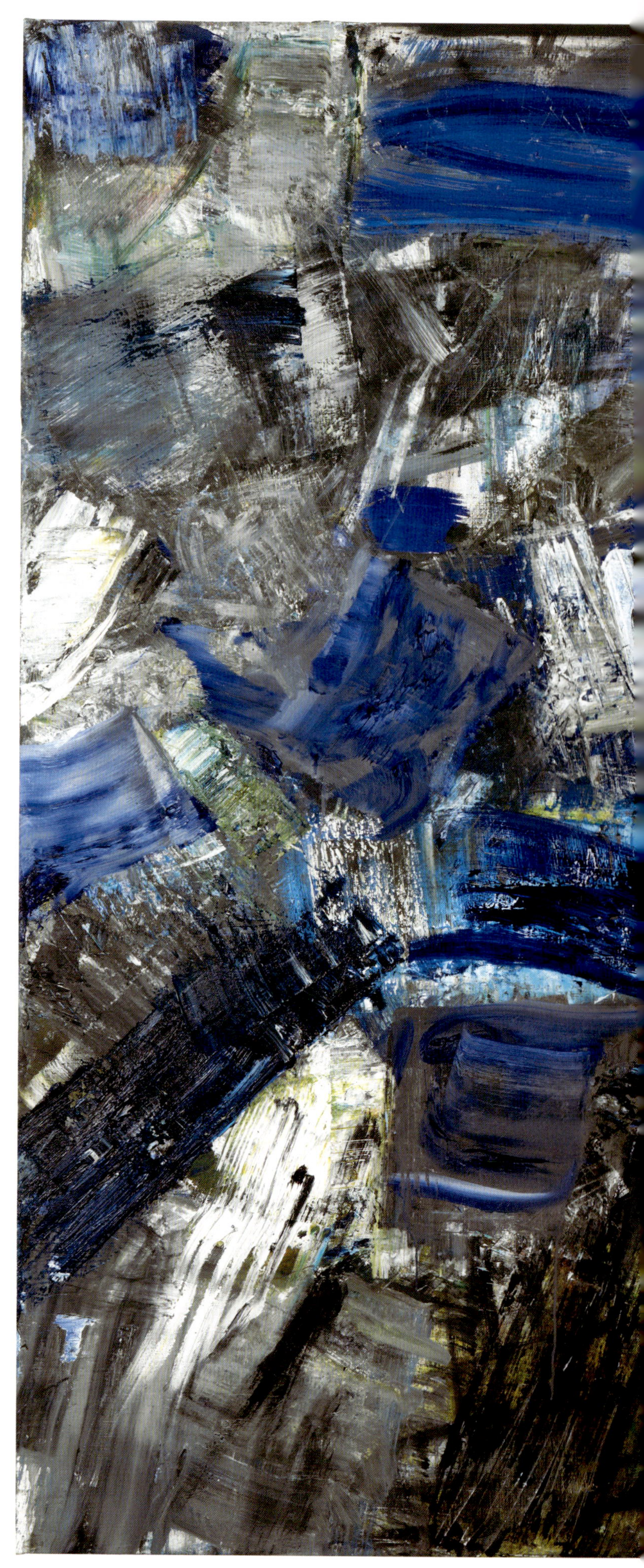

PLATE 104. *The Salt-Wavy Tumult*, 2012. Oil on linen, 70 x 88 in. (177.8 x 223.5 cm). Private collection

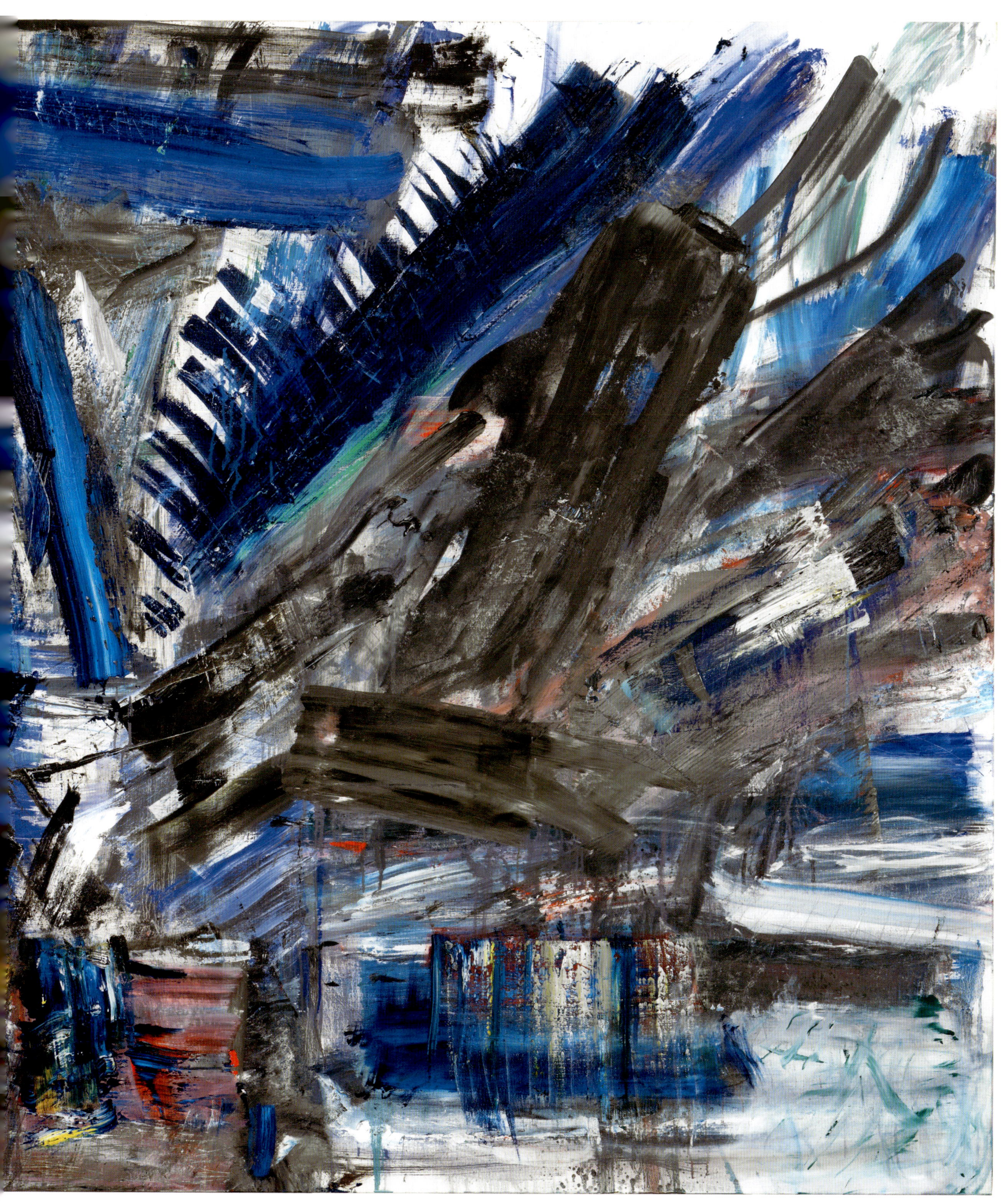

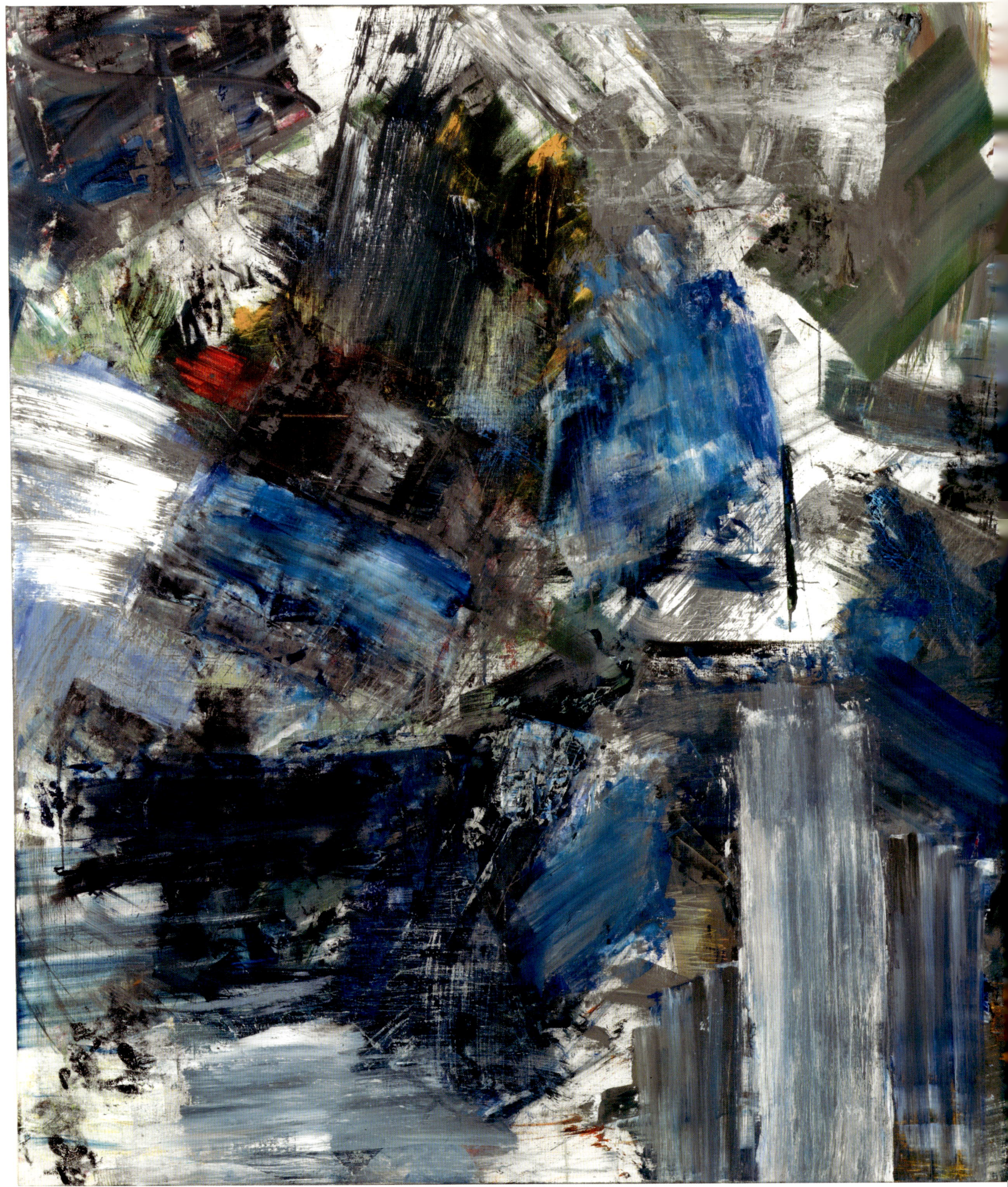

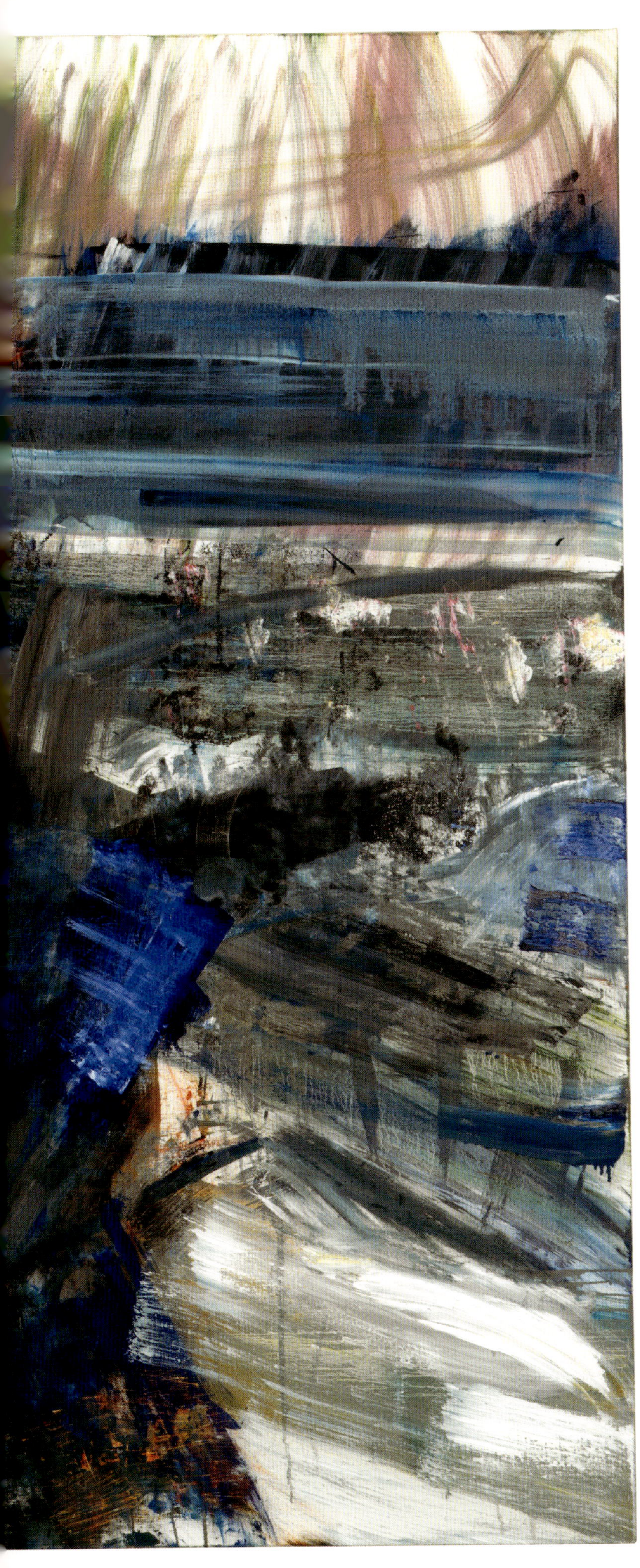

PLATE 105. *Serenissima*, 2012. Oil on linen, 70 x 88 in. (177.8 x 223.5 cm). Collection of Jan and Barry Zubrow, New Jersey

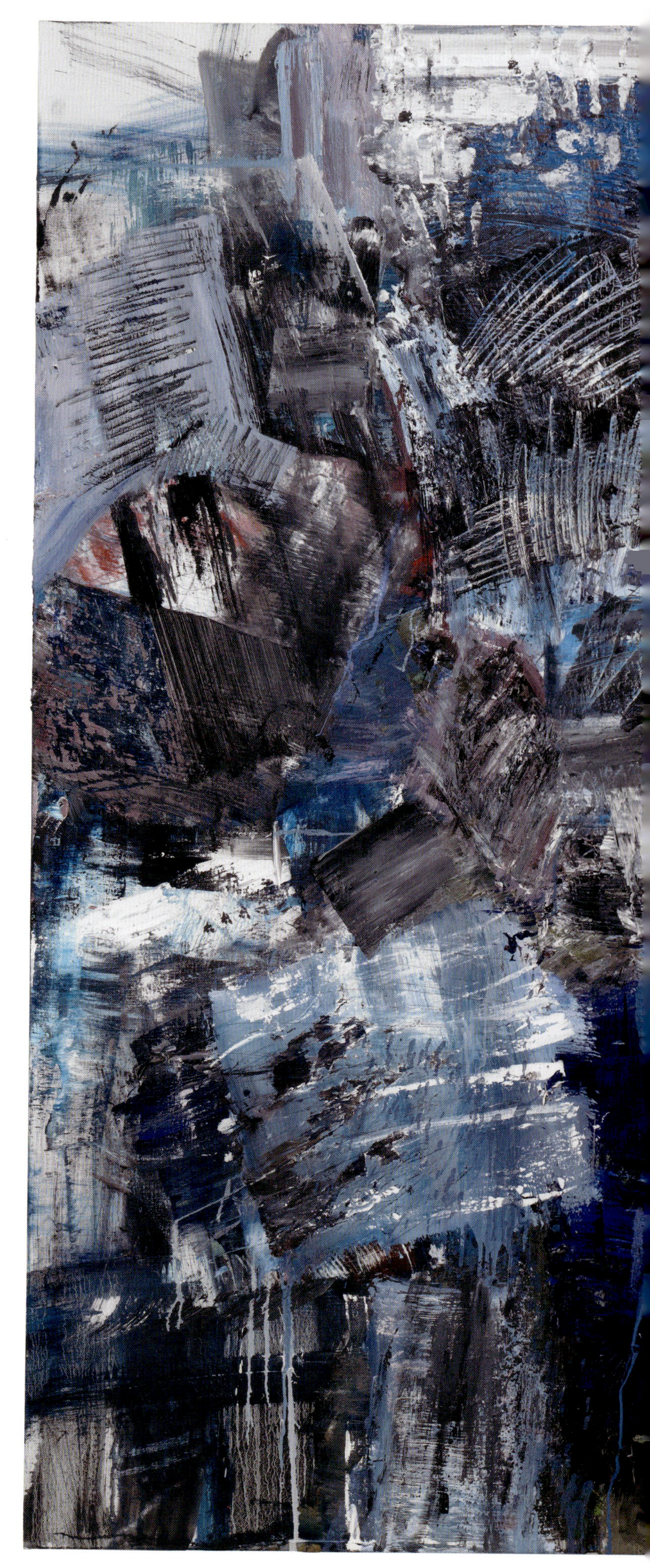

PLATE 106. *9/11 Redux*, 2013. Oil on linen, 70 x 88 in. (177.8 x 223.6 cm). The Forman Family Foundation

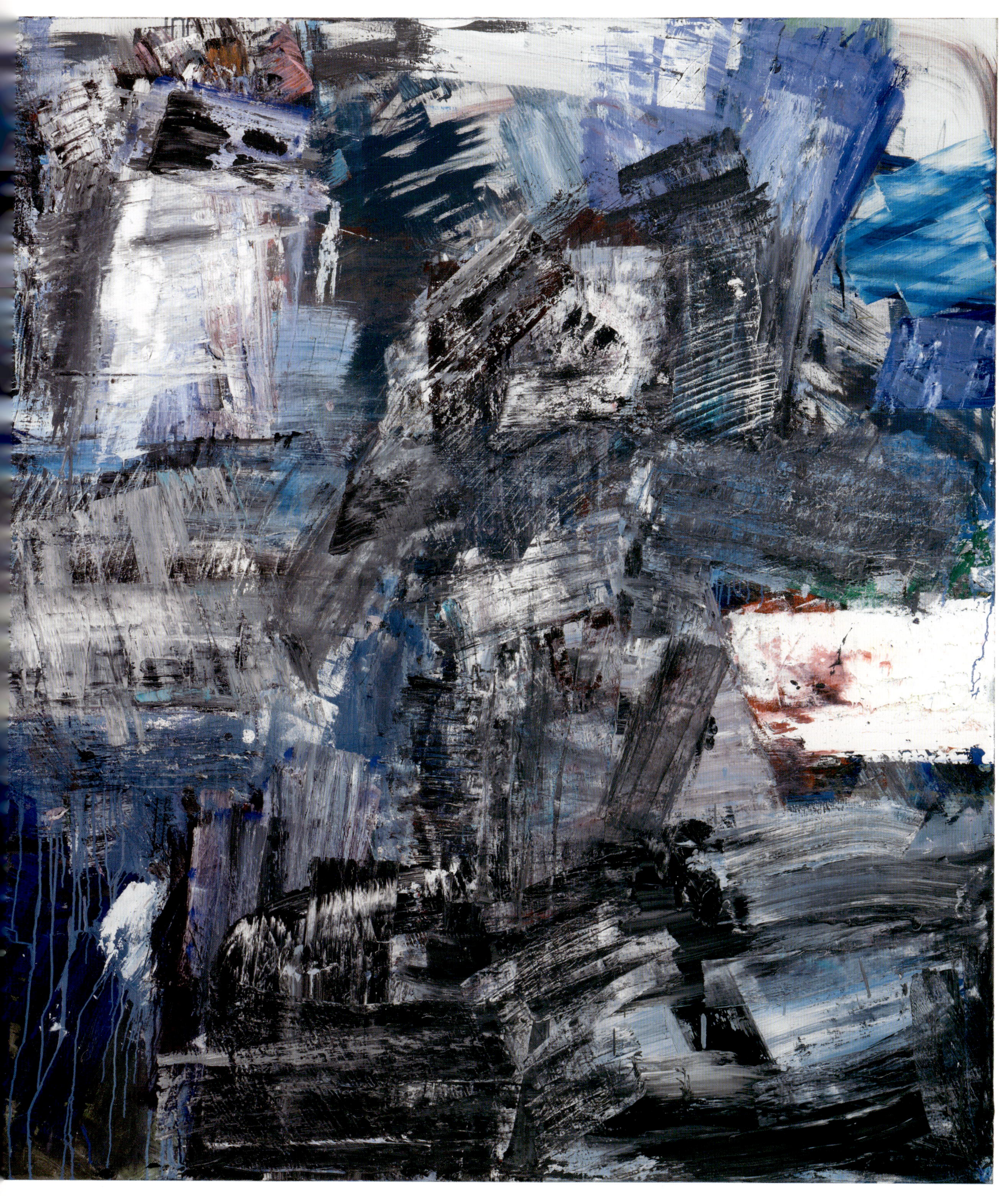

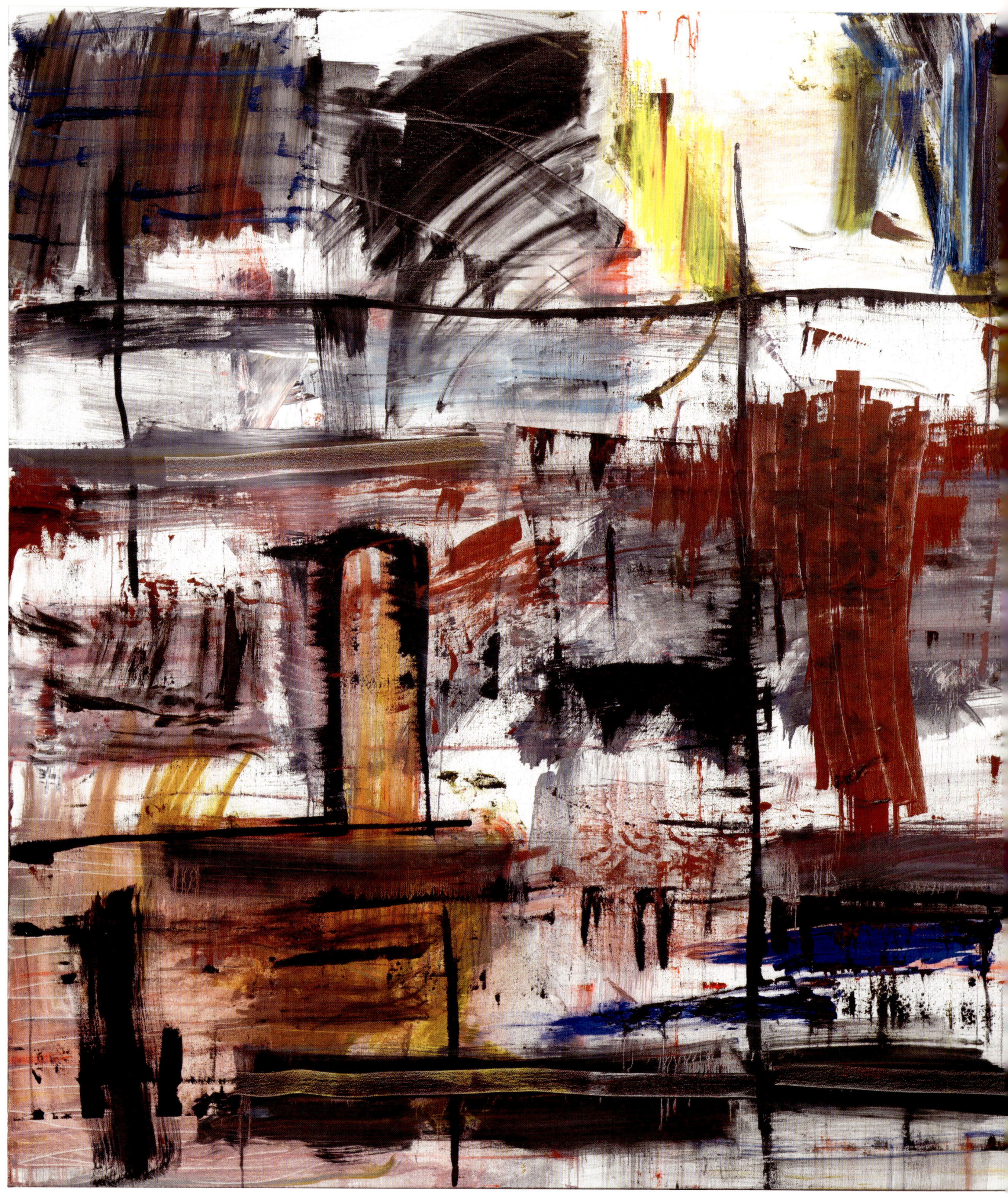

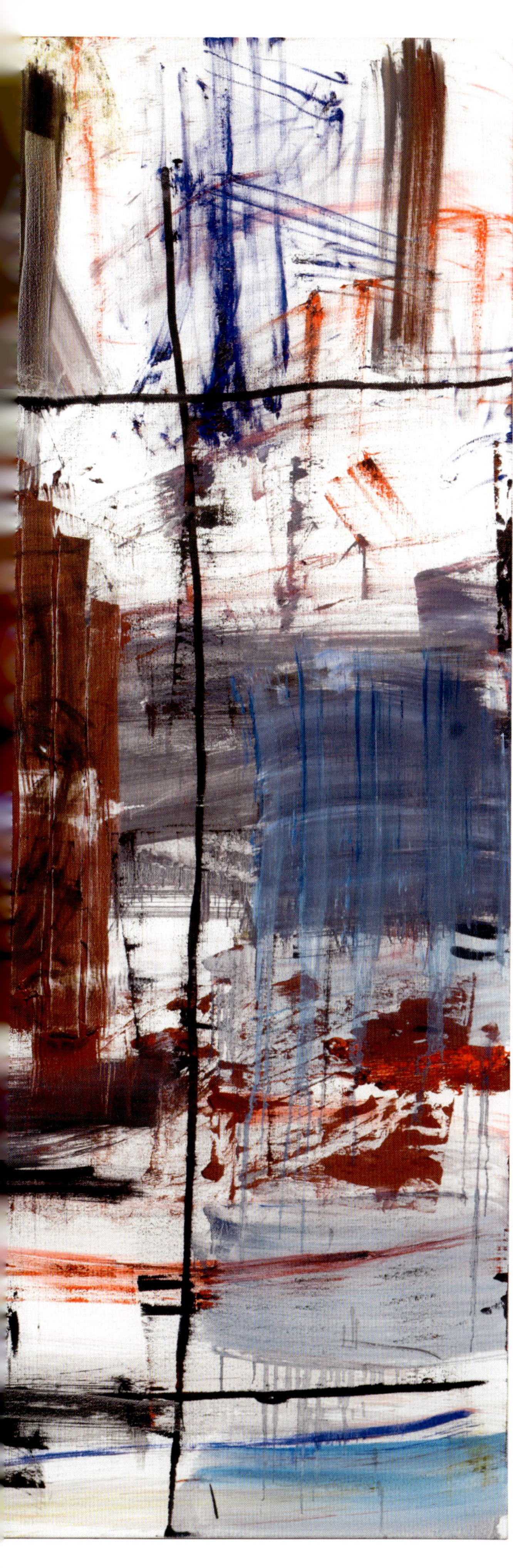

PLATE 107. *Bel Canto*, 2014. Oil on linen, 74 x 88 in. (188 x 223.5 cm)

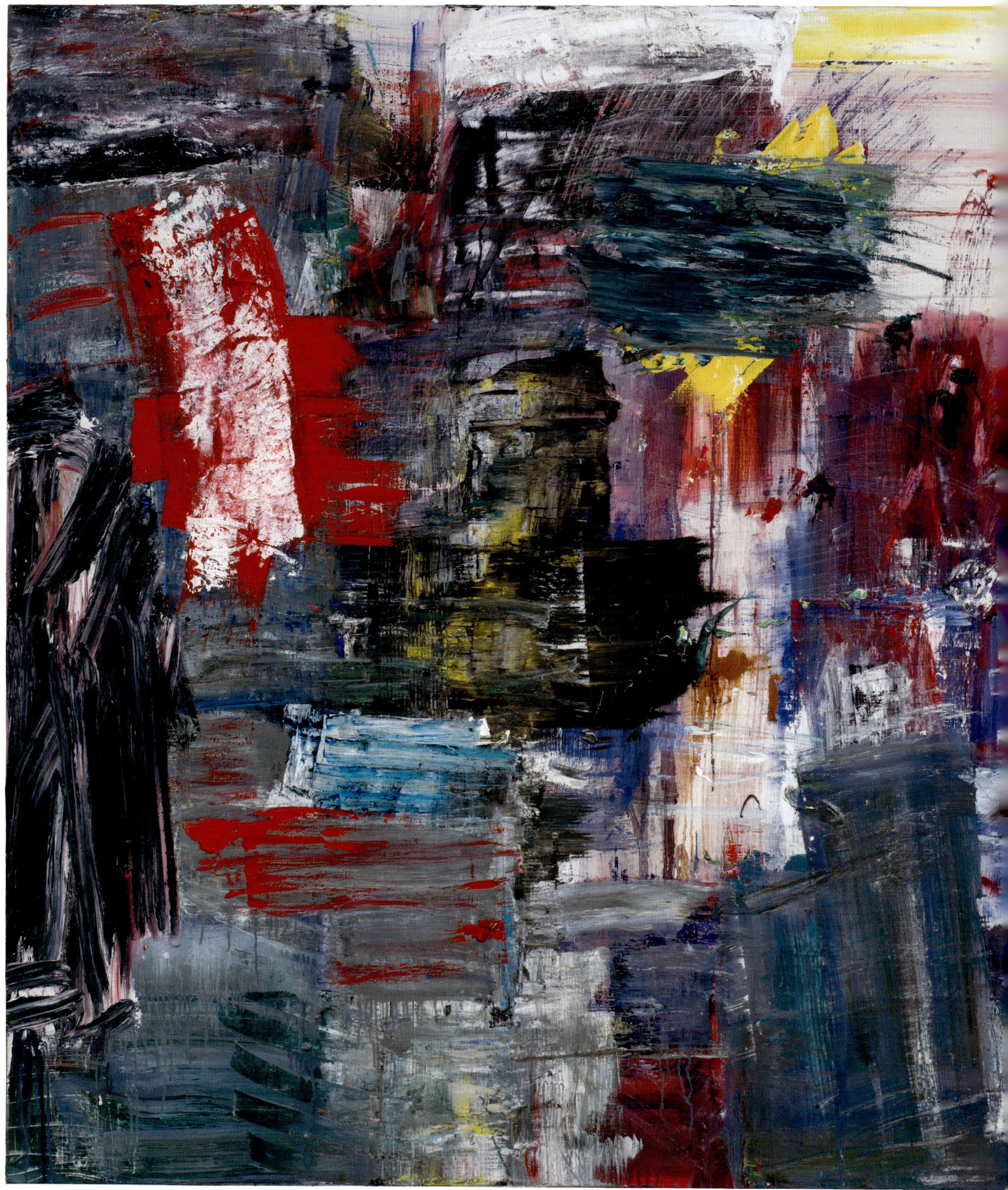

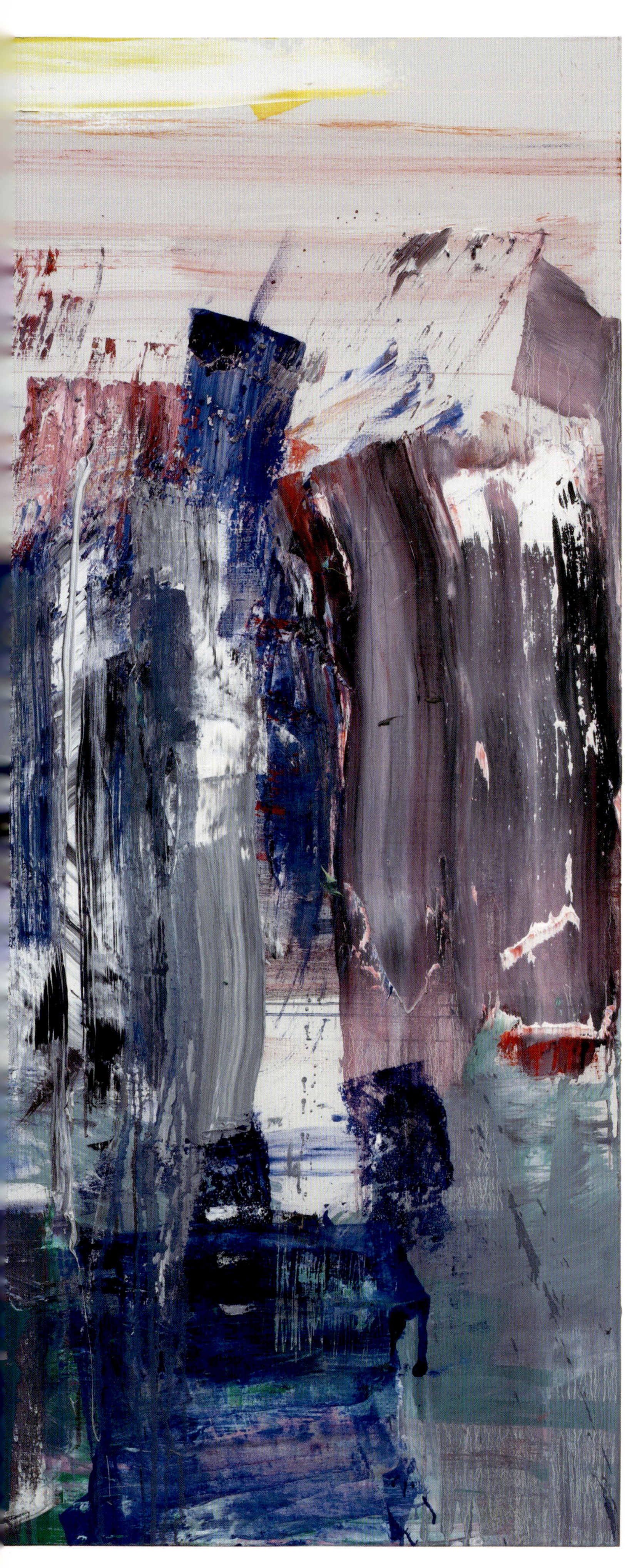

PLATE 108. *For GGG*, 2014. Oil on linen, 70 x 88 in. (177.8 x 223.5 cm). Private collection

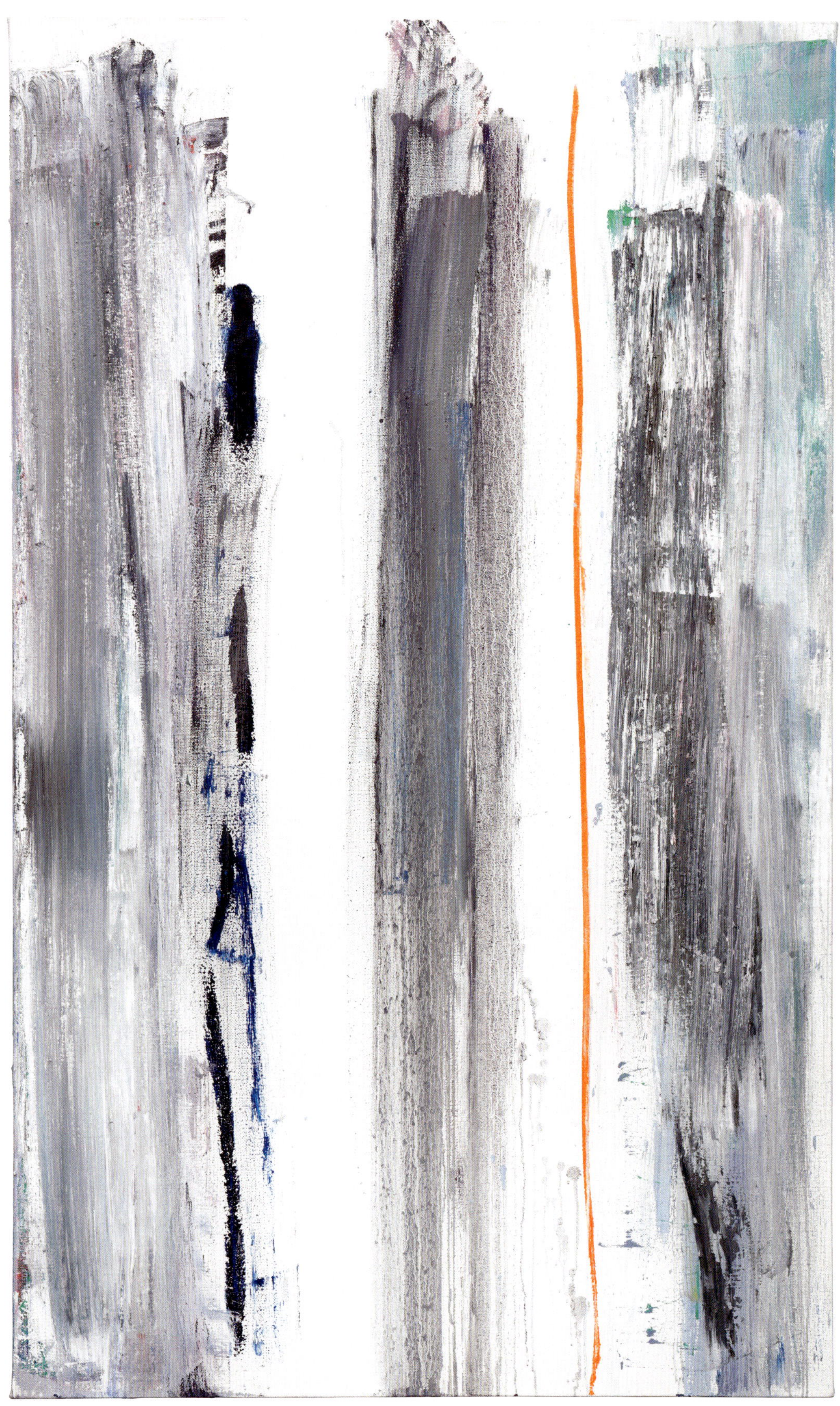

PLATE 109. *Living Forward*, 2014. Oil on linen, 66 x 39 in. (167.6 x 99.1 cm)

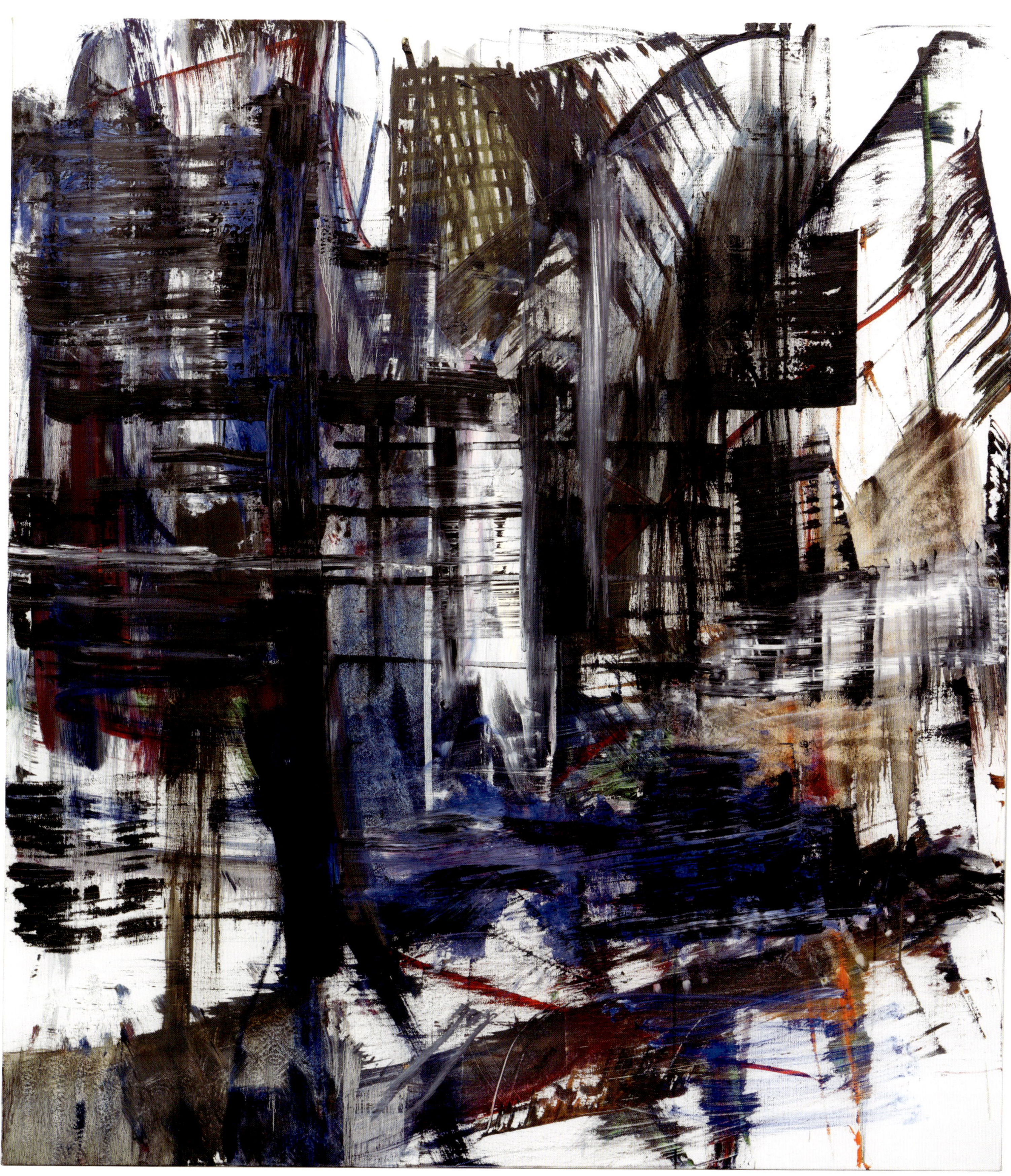

PLATE 110. *Nāmarūpa*, 2014. Oil on linen, 66 x 57 in. (167.6 x 144.8 cm)

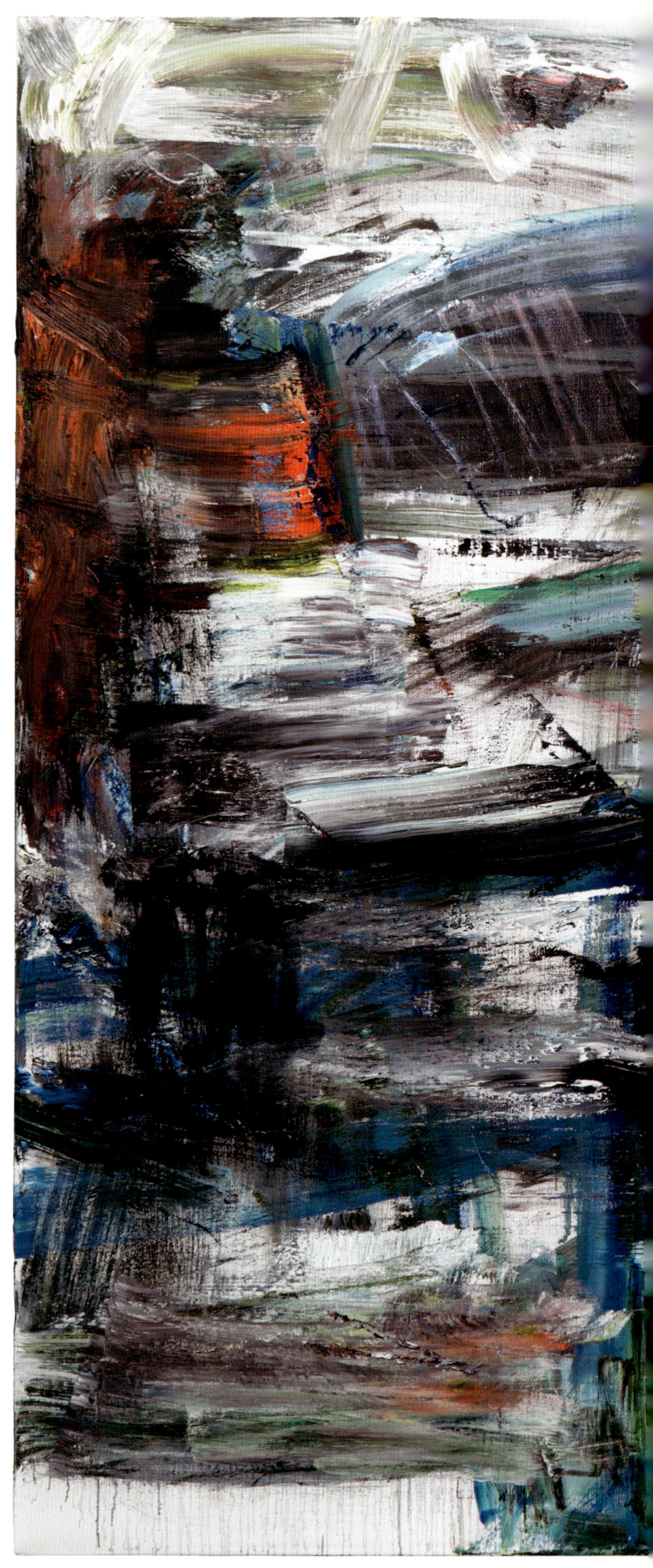

PLATE 111. *Arcanum*, 2015. Oil on linen, 74 x 88 in. (188 x 223.5 cm)

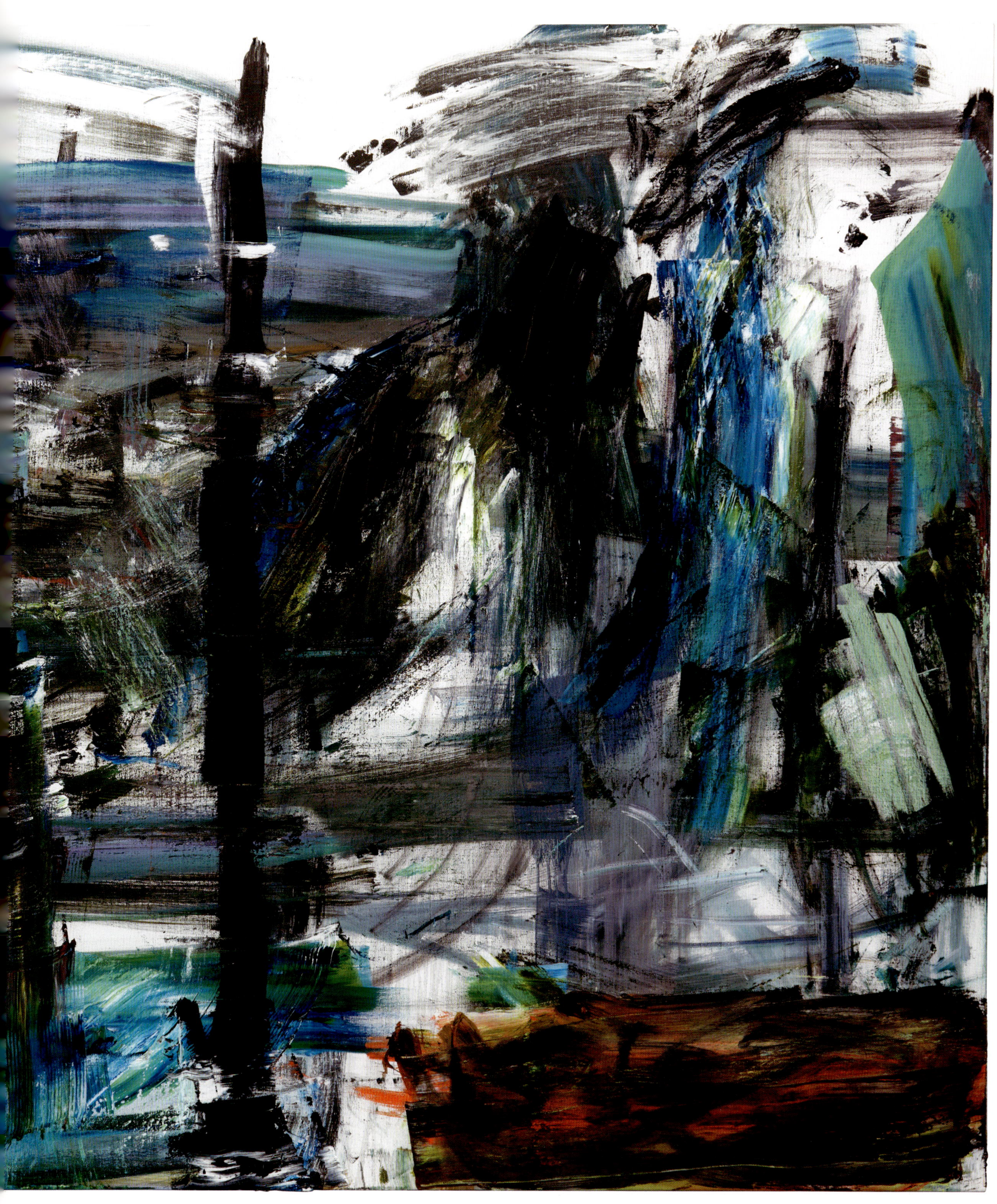

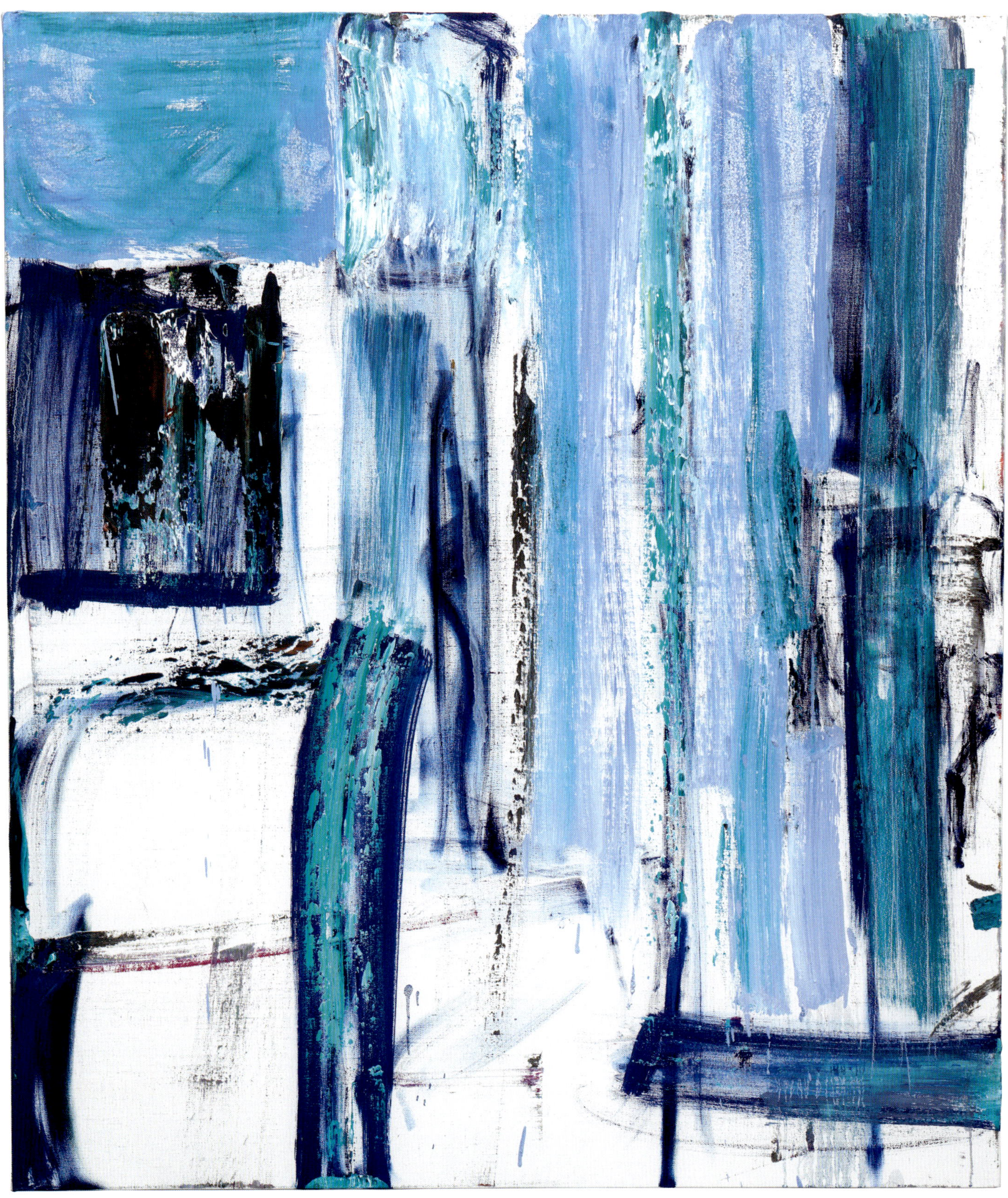

PLATE 112. *Battuto*, 2015. Oil on linen, 60 x 50 in., 152.4 x 127 cm. Private collection

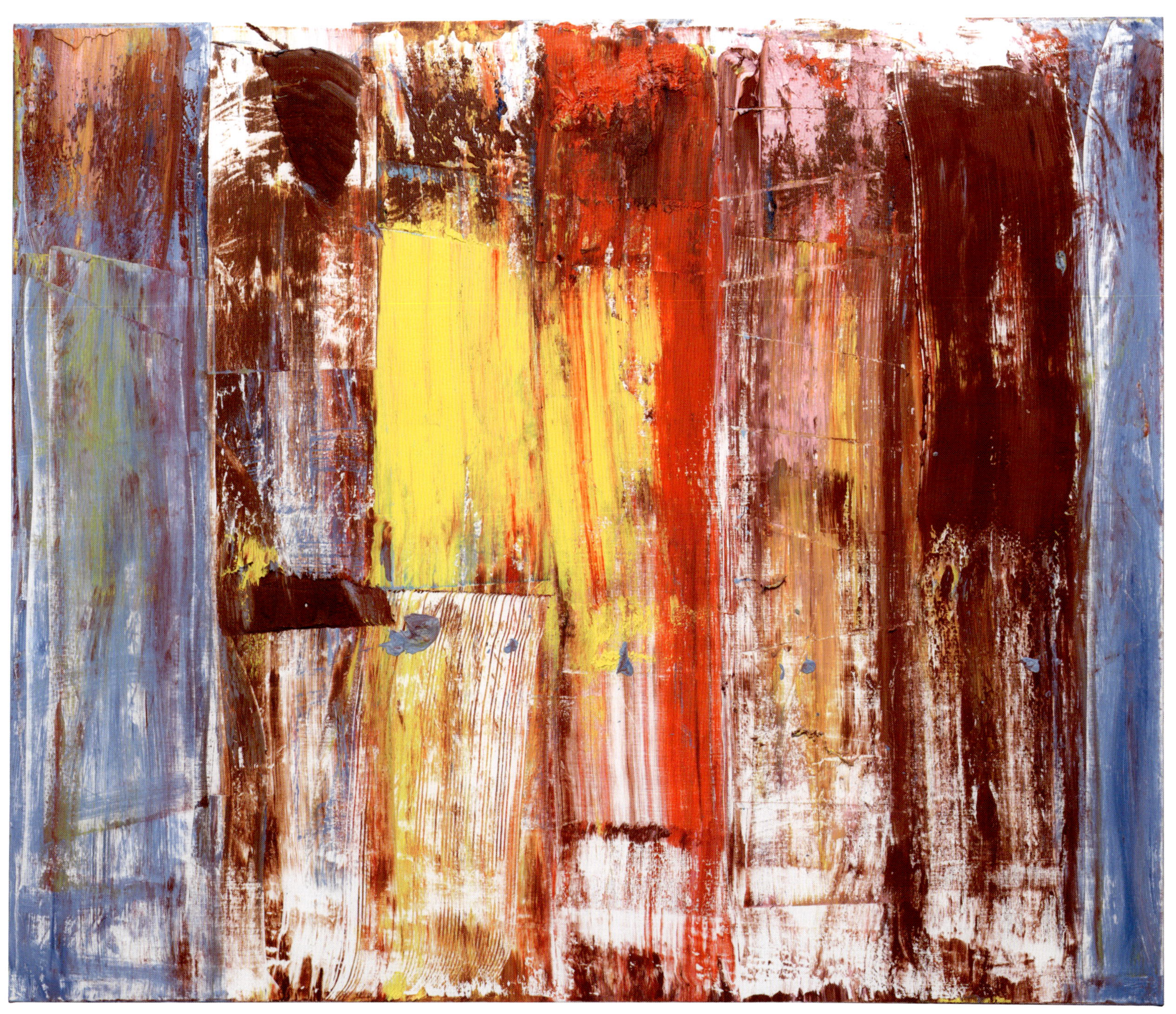

PLATE 113. *Kreisleriana*, 2015. Oil on linen, 57 x 66 in. (144.8 x 167.6 cm)

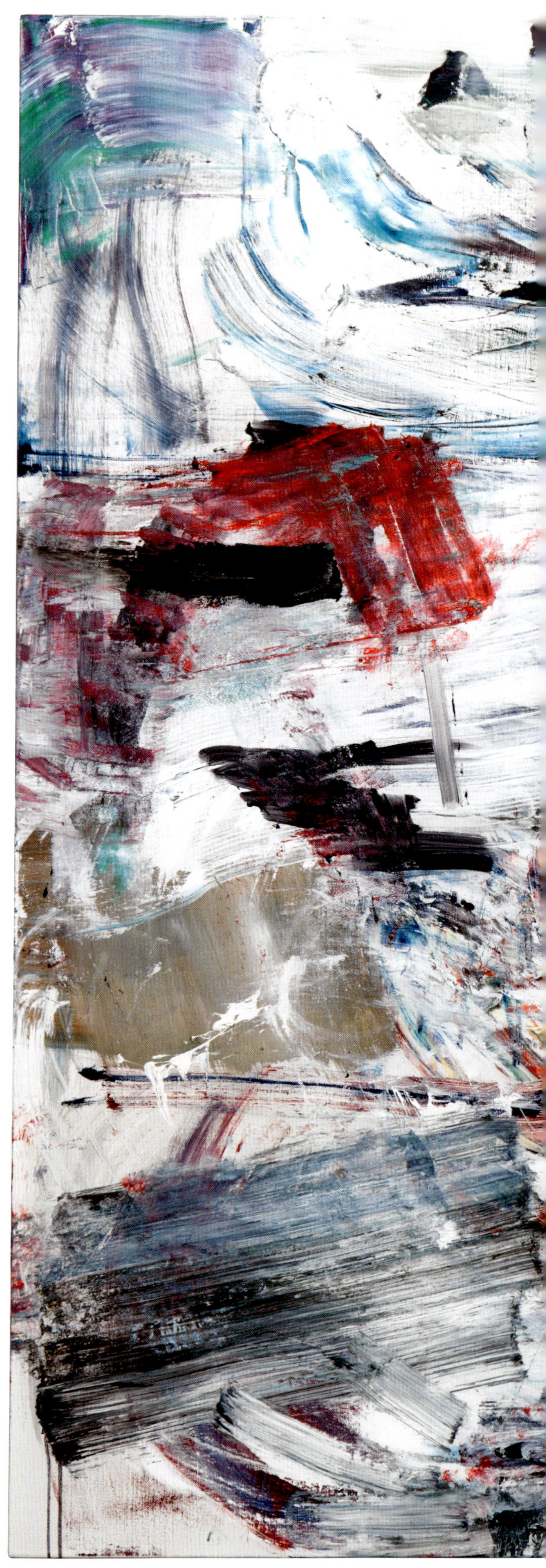

PLATE 114. *Margate*, 2015. Oil on linen, 72 x 88 in. (182.9 x 223.5 cm). Collection of Marc and Jill Fisher, Greenwich, Connecticut

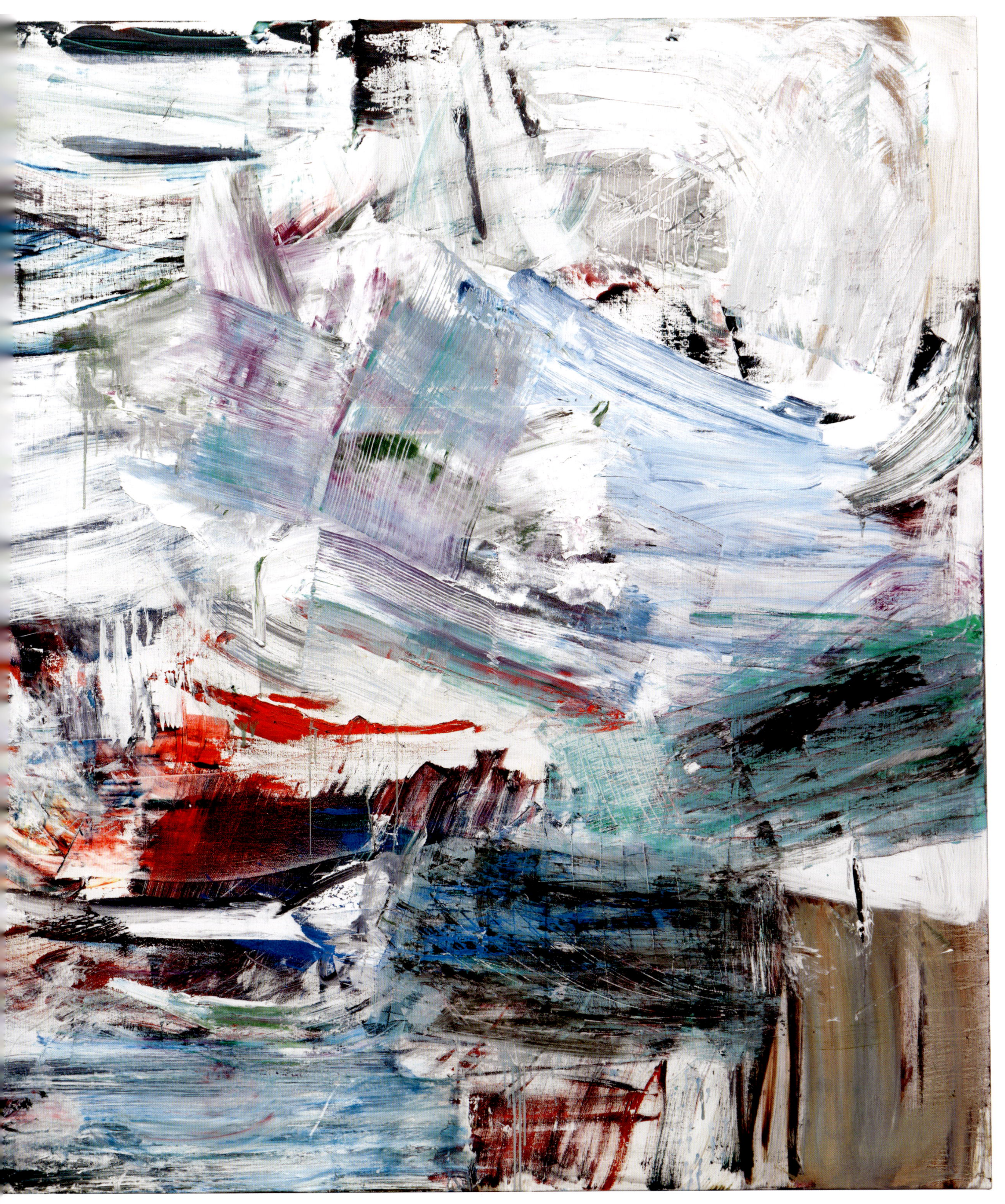

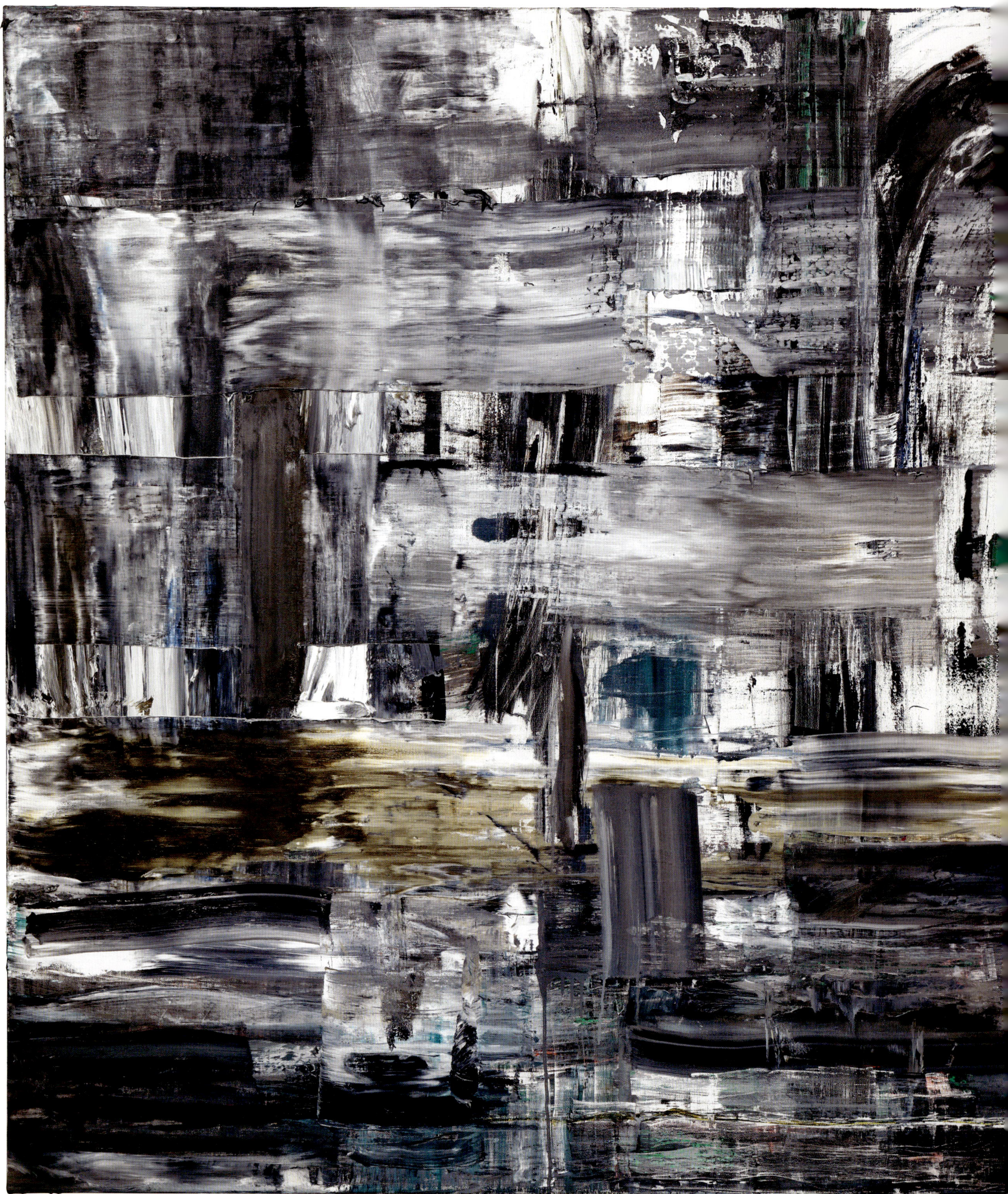

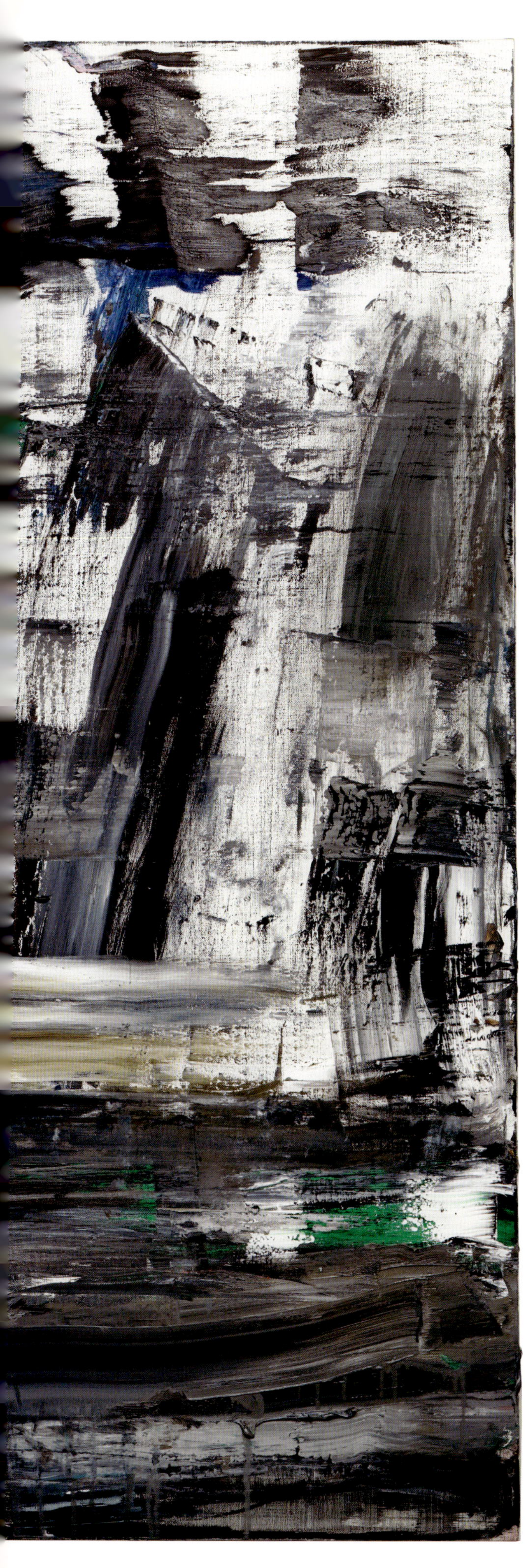

PLATE 115. *Sven Jesper*, 2015. Oil on linen, 74 x 88 in. (188 x 223.5 cm)

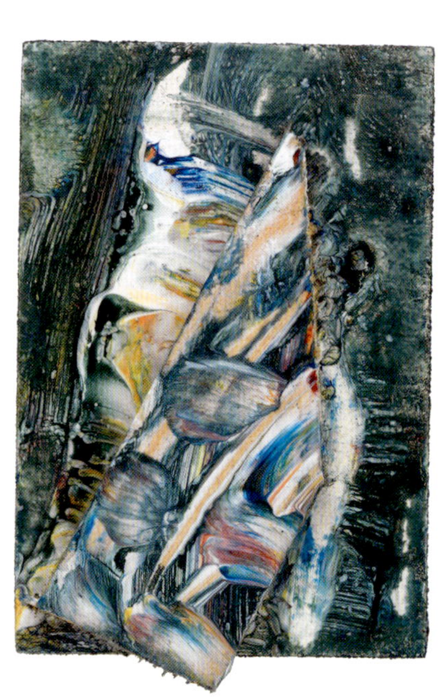

GETTING SMALL WITH LOUISE FISHMAN

INGRID SCHAFFNER

This conversation was held at Louise Fishman's New York studio on June 29, 2015, in advance of the exhibition *Paper Louise Tiny Fishman Rock* that will be held at the Institute of Contemporary Art, University of Pennsylvania, in Philadelphia, April 29–August 14, 2016.

INGRID SCHAFFNER: The three essays in this book make meaty narrative of your major work, in part by drawing extensively on past interviews and conversations. That gives us permission to take this conversation off road, to poke around some lesser-known aspects of your painting, your Philadelphia roots, and your feminist and queer politics. Let's follow the lead of the Institute of Contemporary Art exhibition. Conceived independently from—and running in tandem with—the Neuberger Museum of Art's fifty-year survey, the ICA's *Paper Louise Tiny Fishman Rock* will be more like a studio visit: a chance to see bodies of work that until now have been a mostly private part of your practice.

The installation will present a selection of sketchbooks, miniature paintings, and small sculptures. Not much bigger than two by three inches, the miniatures are as completely realized as full-breadth canvases. The sculptures, some cast in bronze from plaster models, the bulk constructed largely from found objects, are so elemental in form and substance they appear almost geologic. And the books, which are filled with mediums and modes of mark making, burst with narrative drive like Amazon comics rendered abstract. There will also be some very early works, including a self-portrait as a blonde boxer (FIG. 22).

Though surprisingly unlike the large-scale, abstract and gestural paintings for which you are known, these small-scale paintings and sculptural objects are deeply telling distillations of the intimacy and intensity, emotion and physicality, you pack into all of your work. So, Louise, let's get small.

LOUISE FISHMAN: The gloves are off.

INGRID: I want to start by focusing on your early feminist circle by way of a small painting: *Angry Ti-Grace* (FIG. 23). From the Angry Paintings, that are as raw as screams on paper, this work is named for the radical feminist Ti-Grace Atkinson, who was also ICA's unofficial first director. And from what I have researched of the museum's founding history, Ti-Grace had plenty to be angry about! Working as an administrator in the Fine Arts department, she pretty much single-handedly organized ICA's inaugural exhibition in 1963, the first museum survey of the work of Clyfford Still, a big boy of Abstract Expressionism and curmudgeon. He wrote threatening to cancel the show if the catalogue included Atkinson's (very good) essay on his work, because he basically considered her a secretary. Indeed, it was only after she left the job that a full-time director was appointed, a man named Sam Green. Louise, how did you know Ti-Grace Atkinson and her anger?

LOUISE: I didn't know her personally, but she was the best spokesperson for the women's movement and she was 100 percent behind the lesbians. Ti-Grace was the one who was teaching us, even though *we* presented her with the revolution. When she spoke, we got very quiet and really paid attention. We would go off to weekend meetings, seminars, whatever, and everyone would be screaming and yelling because there were all these factions in the women's movement—the lesbians, the socialists, the conservative "feminists," the woman-identified women. Everybody was having trouble. People were taking off their clothes. I remember Rita Mae Brown wandering around taking her shirt off—she was so gorgeous—and everybody was like *oh, I wanna do that*, but nobody else had that body.

OPPOSITE: Louise Fishman, *Untitled*, 2014. Oil and wood collage on board, 3³⁄₁₆ x 2 in. (8.1 x 5.1 cm)

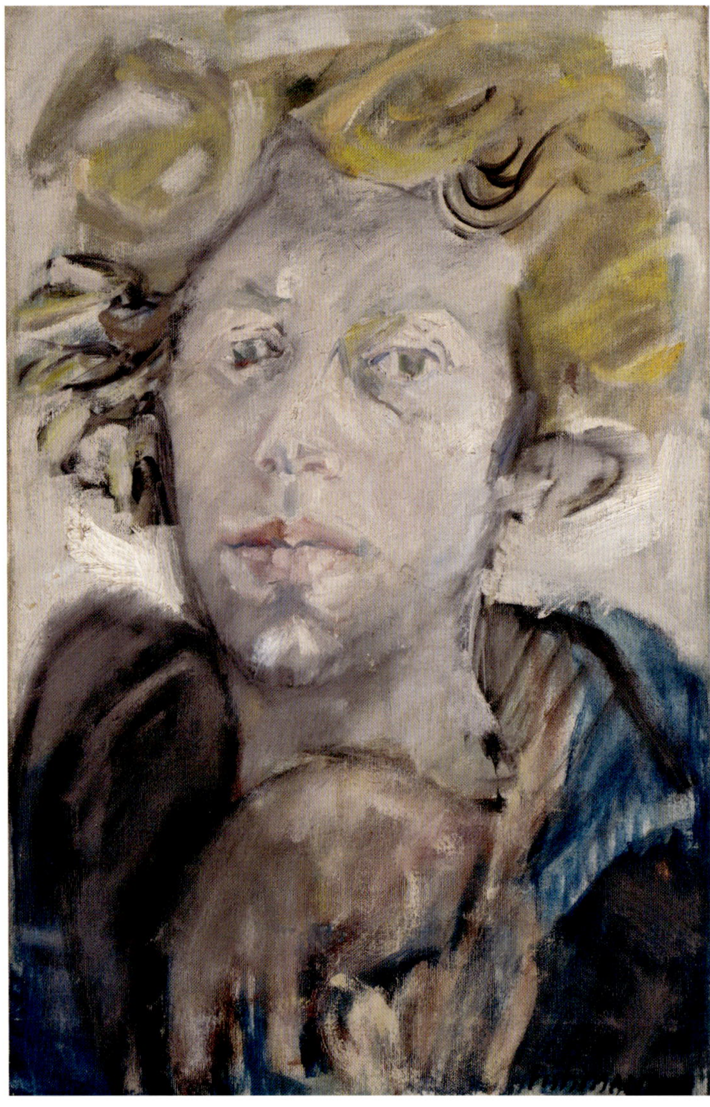

FIGURE 22
Louise Fishman, *Self-Portrait*, 1960
Oil on canvas, 25 x 18 in. (63.5 x 45.7 cm)
Collection of Lynne and Bertram Strieb, Philadelphia

INGRID: It sounds like a very angry and ecstatic time. You've spoken about Jill Johnston—Angry Jill—in similar terms, as an orator for lesbians.

LOUISE: It was a very powerful moment. We all knew we were revolutionaries in a way that had not happened in Western history. Jill and Ti-Grace were both outside of the fury of the movement, but they were the brains.

Jill had a column in *The Village Voice* called "Dance Journal," which I followed from the very beginning because I was interested in dance. When I first came to New York I accidentally walked into a concert by Yvonne Rainer and immediately fell in love with her, her dance, her ideas; she inspired me in every possible way. Jill originally was a dancer with José Limón's studio, but she began writing dance criticism for the *Voice* in 1959. She wrote about Happenings when no one else was. Jill had the ability to touch everything and to say really interesting things. Then the language started shifting: no punctuation, all lowercase, she just started taking tremendous liberties. She became an artist. Everybody was fascinated. Then, of course, she came out in her column, the first person to do so in the media.

INGRID: Jill's archive is managed by her widow, Ingrid Nyeboe, to whom you have been married since 2012. Is there an emblematic "Angry Jill" for you?

LOUISE: I met Jill at several of the little weekend conferences that a group of us who were involved in the movement had at a country house that Jill had bought. She was with Jane O'Wyatt at the time. It was New Year's Eve and I was in a sleeping bag with Esther Newton. Esther had already written *Mother Camp*—the first book on drag queens—terrific book; she later wrote an anthropological study of Cherry Grove. We're still friends. Her partner is Holly Hughes now. Back then, our relationship was on the rocks. Midnight came, everybody was excited. I reached over to kiss Esther and she moved her head away. *POW!* I hit her in the face with my fist. I don't usually hit anybody, but it was New Year's. Everybody kisses everybody. And Jill looked

FIGURE 23
Louise Fishman, *Angry Ti-Grace*, 1973
Acrylic on paper, 26 x 40 in. (66 x 101.6 cm)

at me and she said, "I knew there was more to this relationship than a VW Bug," which is what Esther drove.

INGRID: It sounds like you shocked yourself, Angry Louise. Another woman from the series is the writer Bertha Harris. You are a character in her novel *Lover*.

LOUISE: I *was* Lover. Bertha took an apartment so she could write her novel about having an affair with me in it. We were separated when the book was published, in 1976. Bertha had run off with Charlotte Bunch to Sagaris, the feminist/lesbian think tank. But later, when we were friends again and the book was republished by New York University Press as an important work of lesbian fiction, Bertha wrote a long dedication to me.

INGRID: Angry women are passionate women.

LOUISE: Oh my god, yes. But I was one of the few visual artists in a group of mostly academics and writers. They all kept journals, and I started keeping a journal because I wanted to write, too. The Angry Paintings come out of that desire, using language in a scribbling sort of way.

INGRID: They also break an abstract painter's taboo against words on canvas. There's a strong narrative to the triumphantly feminist title of *Victory Garden of the Amazon Queen* (FIG. 24), one of your abstract paintings on four small pieces of unstretched linen. It looks like a little quilt.

LOUISE: The title refers to the Victory Gardens my parents' generation grew during the war; that painting was in the 1973 Whitney Biennial. The first time Marcia Tucker came for a studio visit was in 1971, and I talked with her about being a lesbian and about my politics and feminism. Apparently I reduced her to tears. Marcia, who may have been going through her own political conversion, didn't include me in the Biennial that year, but for the following Biennial she selected the Amazon Queen Paintings.

INGRID: So, it was your victory.

LOUISE: Using words and bringing narrative into the titles were attempts to communicate in a way that I felt abstract painting was not communicating to the women who were my closest allies and friends.

At a certain point I had to separate from the women's movement and the feminist artists group for which Lucy Lippard was a spokesperson. It seemed like all that these hundreds of women wanted to talk about was their careers and how they couldn't get any shows. After I said I was a lesbian, no one responded, I felt invisible. They were apolitical, really. After a summer of consciousness-raising sessions in 1969 with Carol Gooden, Patsy Norvell, Trisha Brown, and me, I helped form another group with Patsy and artists Harmony Hammond and Sarah Draney, and the anthropologist Elizabeth Weatherford. We went to each other's studios and talked about our work, the problems we were having being women artists, and how to move on, or not. It was very formal consciousness-raising. We accomplished a lot.

INGRID: Is that when you began to question scale in your work?

LOUISE: Franz Kline and Willem de Kooning were big for me—Joan Mitchell too. Then Minimalism came along and I was looking at Sol LeWitt and making hard-edge grid paintings. The group encouraged me to see that everything I was doing as a painter—in terms of scale, gesture, and even using stretched canvas and a paintbrush—was male, and this was problematic. I always hated women's work—growing up first a tomboy, then an athlete, I never sewed. But I wanted to destroy what I had done. So I cut up my paintings and stitched them back together in a woven grid (PL. 6). That was my attempt at making a connection to women's work and craft [laughs]; I even bought a book on stitching and knotting techniques. The scale was small. Some I stained in the bathroom sink. Then I started putting the cut-up canvas paintings in baggies and tacking them to the wall.

INGRID: Were you looking at Eva Hesse's work?

LOUISE: I met Eva Hesse at the Cooper-Hewitt Decorative Arts Library in the Cooper Union building, where I worked. When Eva was attending Cooper Union she had had my job, and she was close friends with the librarian, Edith Adams. When Eva told me she was going to cut her hair, I told her I'm going to cut mine, too. She didn't say she had been diagnosed with a brain tumor. It wasn't until the memorial show at the School of Visual Arts that I really saw her work. I started using liquid rubber in part as an homage to Eva, but also out of a sense of permission (FIG. 25). Her work and my women's group both made me feel like I could do anything I wanted. I may not get to show it, but I can make it. I can make what I want, even paintings on stretched canvas, if I wanted to.

INGRID: Before we move ahead, let's go back to when you were small, Louise. I can see from this childhood drawing (FIG. 26) you were already interested in the grid.

LOUISE: That was done in the early forties when I was around six. The format comes from food coupons. The little figures are the brothers and sisters I would have liked to have had. Each kid has a name: "Fishman," "Fisher,"

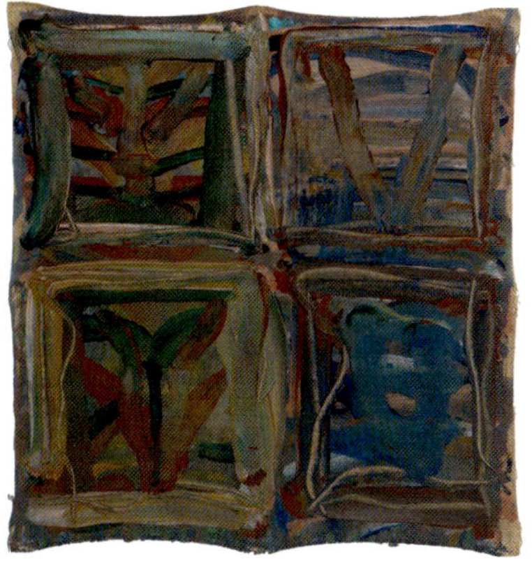
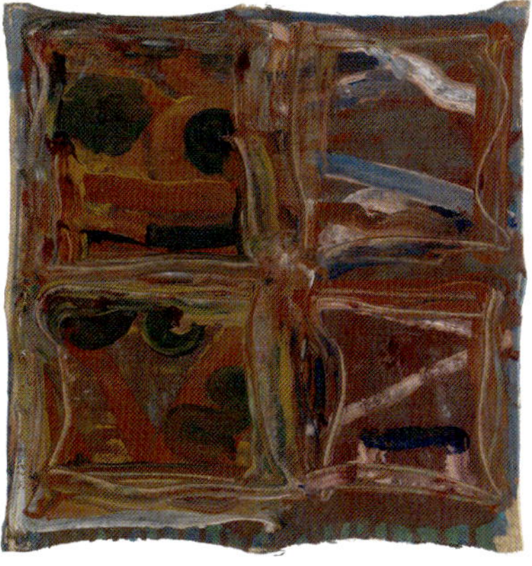
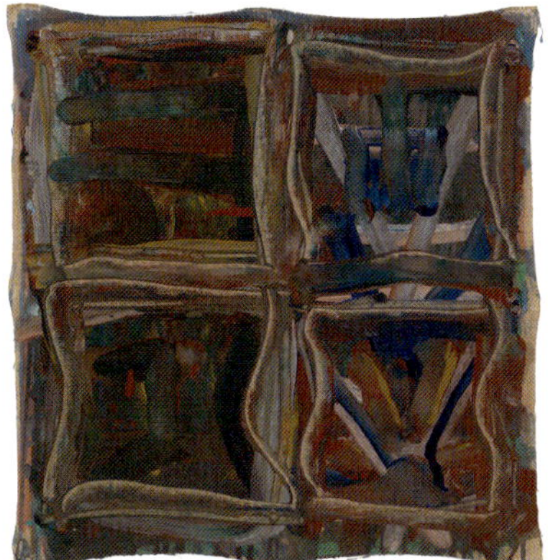
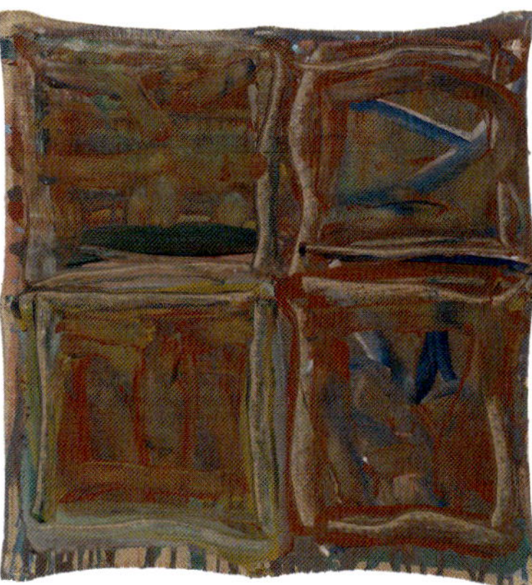

FIGURE 24
Louise Fishman, *Victory Garden of the Amazon* Queen, 1972
Acrylic on linen; four panels, each: 14 x 13 in. (35.6 x 33 cm)

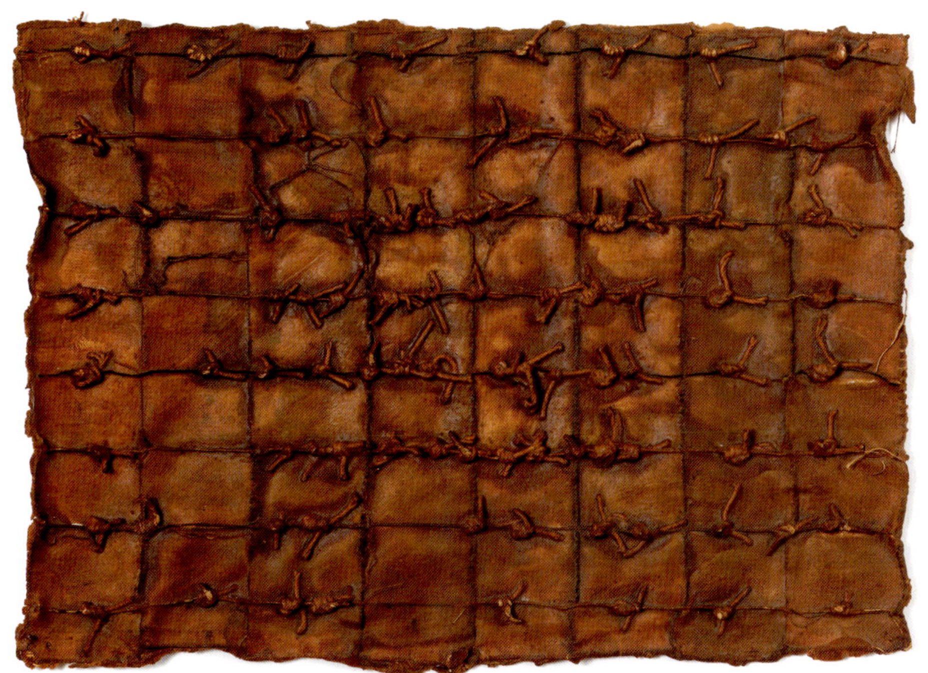

FIGURE 25
Louise Fishman, *Untitled*, 1971
Latex on linen with cotton cord, 15⅝ x 21 in. (39 x 53.3 cm)
Collection of Lynne and Bertram Strieb, Philadelphia

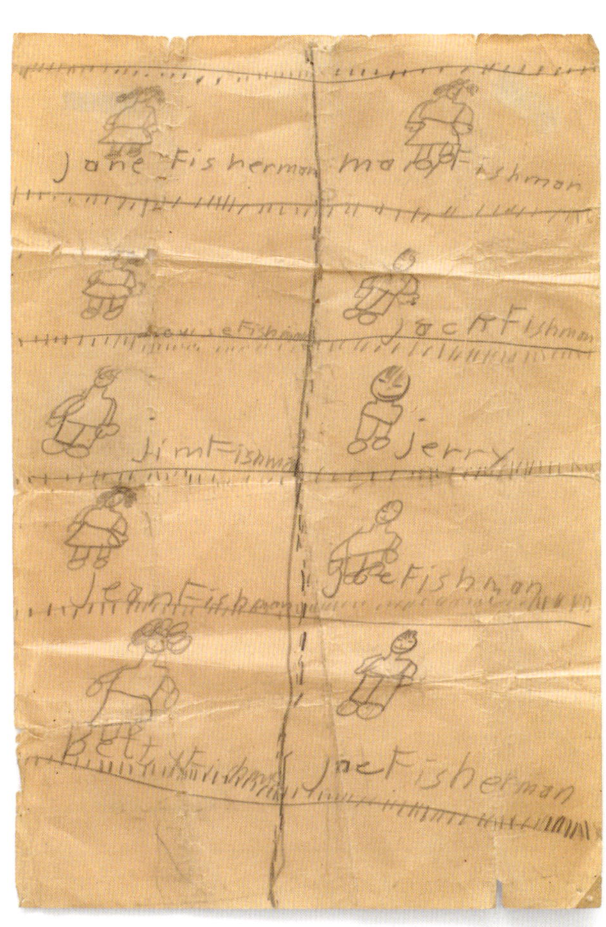

FIGURE 26
Louise Fishman, *Food Coupons for Imaginary Brothers & Sisters*, 1944
Graphite on paper, 8¾ x 6 in. (22.2 x 15.2 cm)

or "Fisherman," because I thought that anyone whose name had the word "fish" in it was a relative of mine. (My mother's maiden name was Fisher.) When my shrink looked at this drawing she pointed to the one child, called "Jerry," that had no arms and said, "I think that's your brother."

INGRID: Philadelphia looms large in your life, making for one of many good reasons for doing this show with you at ICA. You were born, raised, and trained as an artist in Philadelphia. Since you moved to New York in 1965 there have been several exhibitions here keeping steady tabs on your new developments. In 1992 three simultaneous shows were held at the Pennsylvania Academy of the Fine Arts (organized by the incomparable curator and art historian Judith Stein) and the two galleries at Temple University's Tyler School of Art, where you received your BFA and BS in Education. More recently, in 2012 there was the exhibition at the Woodmere Art Museum, *Generations: Louise Fishman, Gertrude Fisher-Fishman, and Razel Kapustin*, honoring a local legacy of women artists. Your aunt, Razel Kapustin, was a professional artist who studied with David Alfaro Siqueiros in New York and was a very important role model for you. Your mother, Gertrude Fisher-Fishman, was a dedicated painter who showed frequently in Philadelphia and Florida. She availed herself of the many opportunities Philadelphia offers its artists, from classes at the Barnes Foundation to membership in the Print, Sketch, and Pen and Pencil Clubs. Both Razel and Gertrude were, I might surmise, Angry Women.

LOUISE: My mother was excited by anything artistic. She loved the Gilded Cage, Philadelphia's first bohemian coffeehouse, where artists and writers—maybe a few queers—drank Earl Grey tea and espressos. Once, she took me along with her to a drawing class at The Print Club, and I was totally disinterested. I was a serious athlete, playing competitively on the Haverford High School girl's basketball team. But the instructor said, "Louise, why don't you do a drawing?" He put a board on an easel and gave me a pencil; they had a nude model, which I'd never been around before. I did a drawing and thought, that looks pretty good. Everybody in the class came over and went *WOW*. My mother, I thought my mother was going have a heart attack. She was showing me what she was doing and suddenly I became the center of it. That was the first time that happened: I thought, *oh, I can draw*.

INGRID: At ICA last year, a group exhibition of artists' emotionally charged correspondence, organized by the queer and feminist art initiative Ridykeulous, included your small five-part *Letter to My Mother about Painting* (1972–73; FIG. 12). It sounds like your mother opened up the field of art to you, yet this painting looks murderous.

LOUISE: I know exactly where the anger came from. When I got that painting into the Whitney Biennial, I thought *look how long it took me to get around to doing this*. I had struggled for years to make sure my mother didn't think I was going be an artist. Even though making art is all I wanted to do and did, I did not want to succeed and I fought every way I could. In a rage, I went into the studio on Mercer Street and put up a piece of paper and wrote "Angry Louise!"

It was so upsetting, I had to turn the paper to face the wall. Then I thought, I'm going to make one for Esther, with whom I was living. So, I made *Angry Esther*. Then I made one for my friend the writer Bertha Harris. I made ones for all of the women in my group, then all the people important to me, like Ti-Grace. Every one of them who came to my studio and saw her painting was really upset. It was as if I'd gotten inside and exposed this anger with which we all identified. They were portraits, somehow, the Angry Paintings, and they had so much power.

INGRID: It's significant, then, what a relatively small and contained body of work it is. Like a powder keg, the Angry Paintings liberated you to pick up a *knife* and start painting again. I'm thinking of that series from the mid-seventies, in which the paint is slathered on disks of Masonite with a blade, then incised. There's even razor blades embedded in the bruise-blue impasto surface of one of them (FIG. 27). These works are sculptural as objects, but your painting in general, its gestures, are full of slashing strokes and cutting physicality. Are you a latent sculptor, Louise?

LOUISE: I would say so. I've had crises at various moments, like in the 1980s when I did that portrait of myself as a man (FIG. 19). I was in my studio on Eighteenth Street and across the street was a chain factory. And it struck me, *what is it I'm doing?* This is not meaningful. Chains have a function. Painting doesn't do anything. It sounds a little bizarre, but I wanted something from my work that was much more concrete.

INGRID: I was interested to come across a trove of early ceramics. Stoneware slab work, not thrown but folded and paddled into vessel forms (FIG. 28).

LOUISE: I was very fortunate when I was at Tyler to study with Rudy Staffel. Learning to use a kick wheel is really hard, which is maybe why I loved doing it, because it was so athletic—all that kicking. Rudy would put his hand gently over yours to show what kind of weight to use.

INGRID: It's nice you can still feel his hand. Though your ceramics, I must say, are the antithesis of Rudy Staffel's porcelain "light catchers."

LOUISE: In graduate school at the University of Illinois, there was a good ceramics teacher and I did mostly hand-built pieces. The desire to move into three-dimensional form has always been there. Early on, I did some woodcarving and a lot of modeling from life in plasticine. One time, when I was studying at the Fleisher Art Memorial, a teacher came over and while he was talking to me—he was nervous—he was touching the clay. "Get your hands off my sculpture," I said. Apparently the faculty had a meeting about me, the woman in the white turtleneck sweater, and how difficult I was. I could be nasty. I remember walking into a jazz bar in Philadelphia to see Nina Simone and saying hello to some people I knew; they later they told me how much I scared them. Really I was just so anxious. I wanted to be Giacometti and that wasn't going to happen. I couldn't afford the materials or the space. I could afford to paint in my parents' basement and that's what I did.

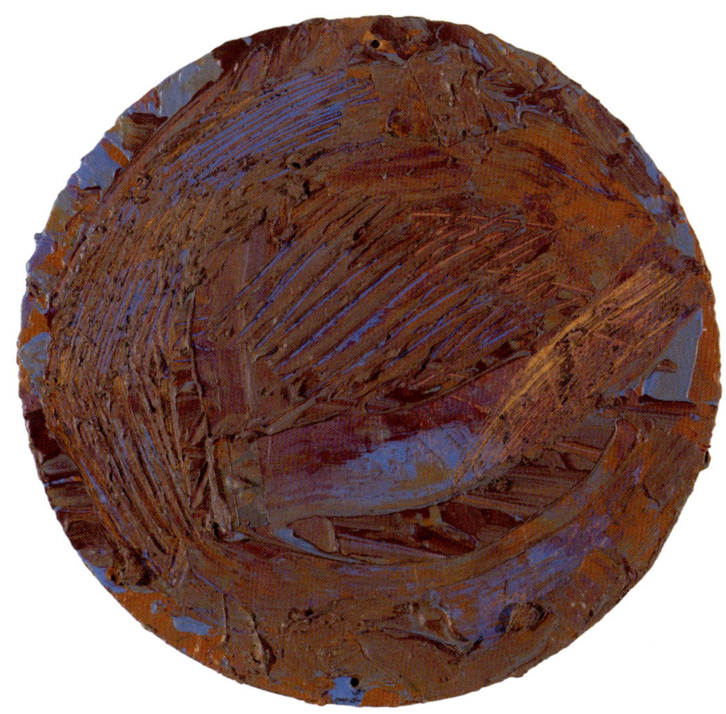

FIGURE 27
Louise Fishman, *Untitled*, 1974
Oil on Masonite with two razor blades, diameter: 11½ in. (29.2 cm)

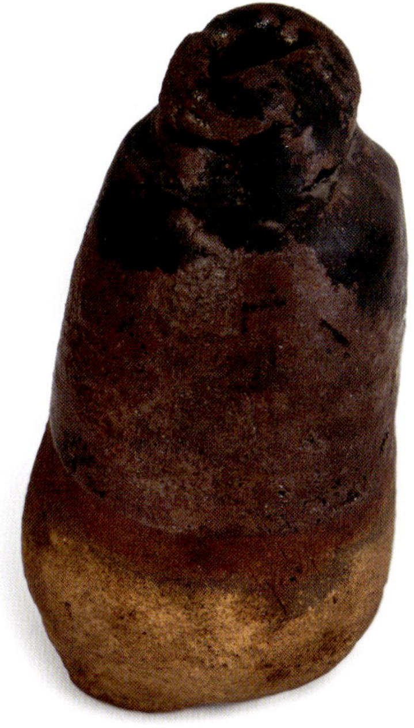

FIGURE 28
Louise Fishman,
Stoneware vase, 1965
Height: 6¼ in. (15.5 cm)
Collection of Lynne and
Bertram Strieb, Philadelphia

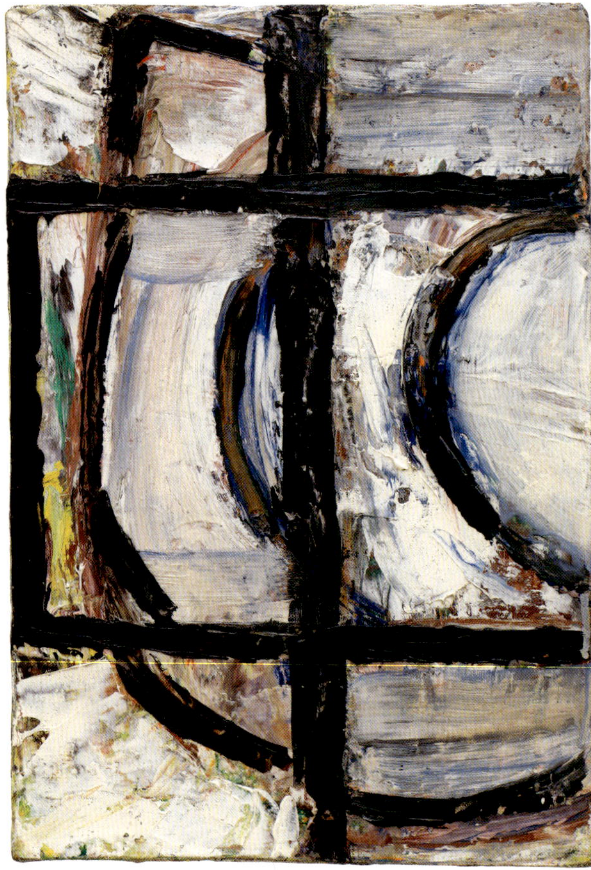

FIGURE 29
Louise Fishman, *MacDowell Series #6 (Hillcrest Barn)*, 1980
Oil on linen, 12 x 8 in. (30.5 x 20.3 cm)

INGRID: When you started painting on canvas again in the late 1970s, how did you approach scale?

LOUISE: Like you said, with a knife! I never used a brush or added any medium. It was very gradual working my way back to oil paint and linen, actually.

INGRID: So the paint itself was slab-like?

LOUISE: Yes, and the work was modest in scale. Then I went to the MacDowell Colony in July 1980 and returned with all of these really little paintings (FIG. 29), based in scale on the predella panels of Duccio's *Maestà* altarpiece, which I saw on my first trip to Italy, in 1979. That was the first time I worked on small paintings. It was also my first time using a curved mark since my student years; up to this point, I was using only horizontal and vertical elements. The miniature paintings that I did thirty years later come out of finding these stunningly small stretched canvases at an art supply store in Berlin, where I was having a show in 2008.

INGRID: What is the relationship between the miniatures and your large paintings?

LOUISE: No matter the size, I think of my works as experiments in scale. I'm always aware of what's happening on the canvas relative to my hands, my arms, my fingers, the stretch of my whole body. There's an athleticism in that, but I also have an interest in diminutive things that are smaller than they're supposed to be.

INGRID: Small things do convey a sense of compression—of being squeezed down in size—that is certainly physical. Also there is the relationship between the miniature and the conceptual, as is so perfectly contained by Marcel Duchamp's *"Museum in a Suitcase."* Likewise, your tiny paintings appear ready-made to exist in the mind's eye, as objects of contemplation. Speaking of Duchamp, let's talk about the explosion in a slat factory—as one wag called his *Nude Descending a Staircase*—that is this stack of painted strips on cardboard and other materials (FIGS. 30, 31).

LOUISE: First let me say how important it was growing up in Philadelphia and seeing Duchamp's *Bride Stripped Bare by Her Bachelors* in the same museum as Rogier van der Weyden's monumental crucifixion with the mourning virgin, Cézanne's bathers, and the work of Mondrian, Rouault, Soutine. As students, we used to climb on Rodin's *Burghers of Calais*. Even before the women's movement, art gave me a sense of freedom and permission that anything was possible. I wasn't imprisoned. And even though I've remained a painter—one who adores paint and the tradition of painting—I think there is the potential to do anything.

The "slats" are from the monoprints I made with Susan Oehme at her print studio in Colorado. They are the plates: scraps of cardboard, mat board, wood, and sandpaper that she had around that I painted and we sent through the press. When the plates turned out to be as interesting as the prints, I kept them.

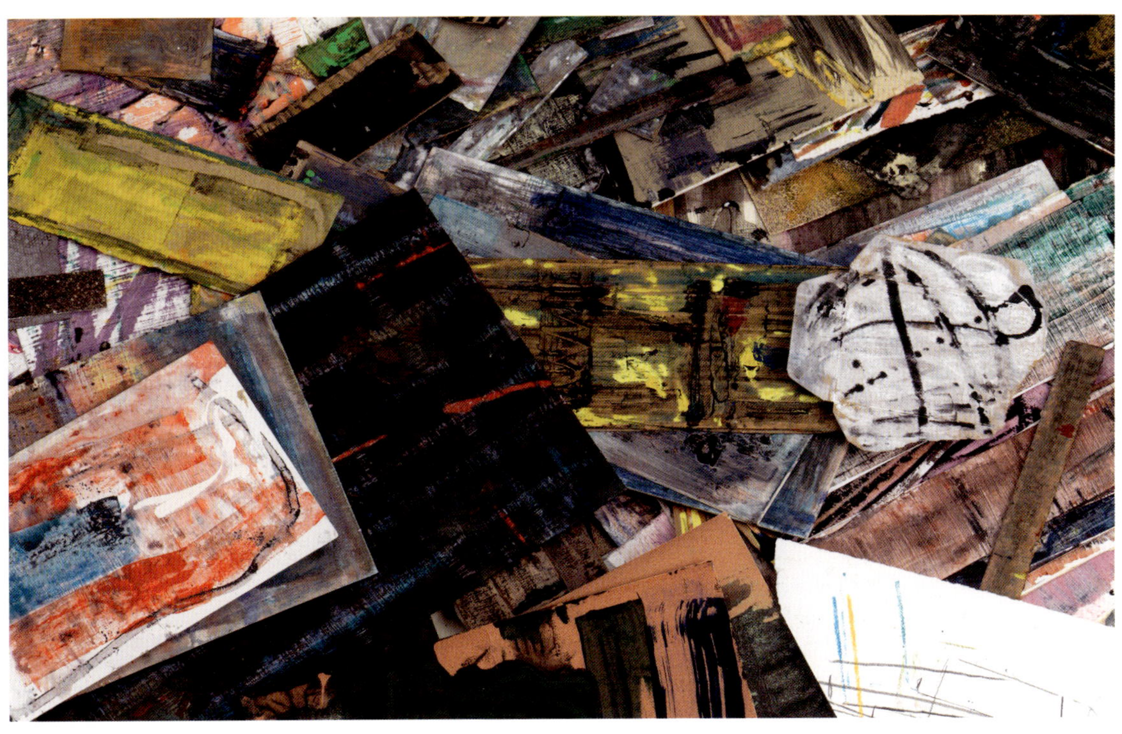

FIGURES 30, 31
Louise Fishman, monoprint plates, various mediums and materials, made at Oehme Graphics, Steamboat Springs, Colorado, in 2011

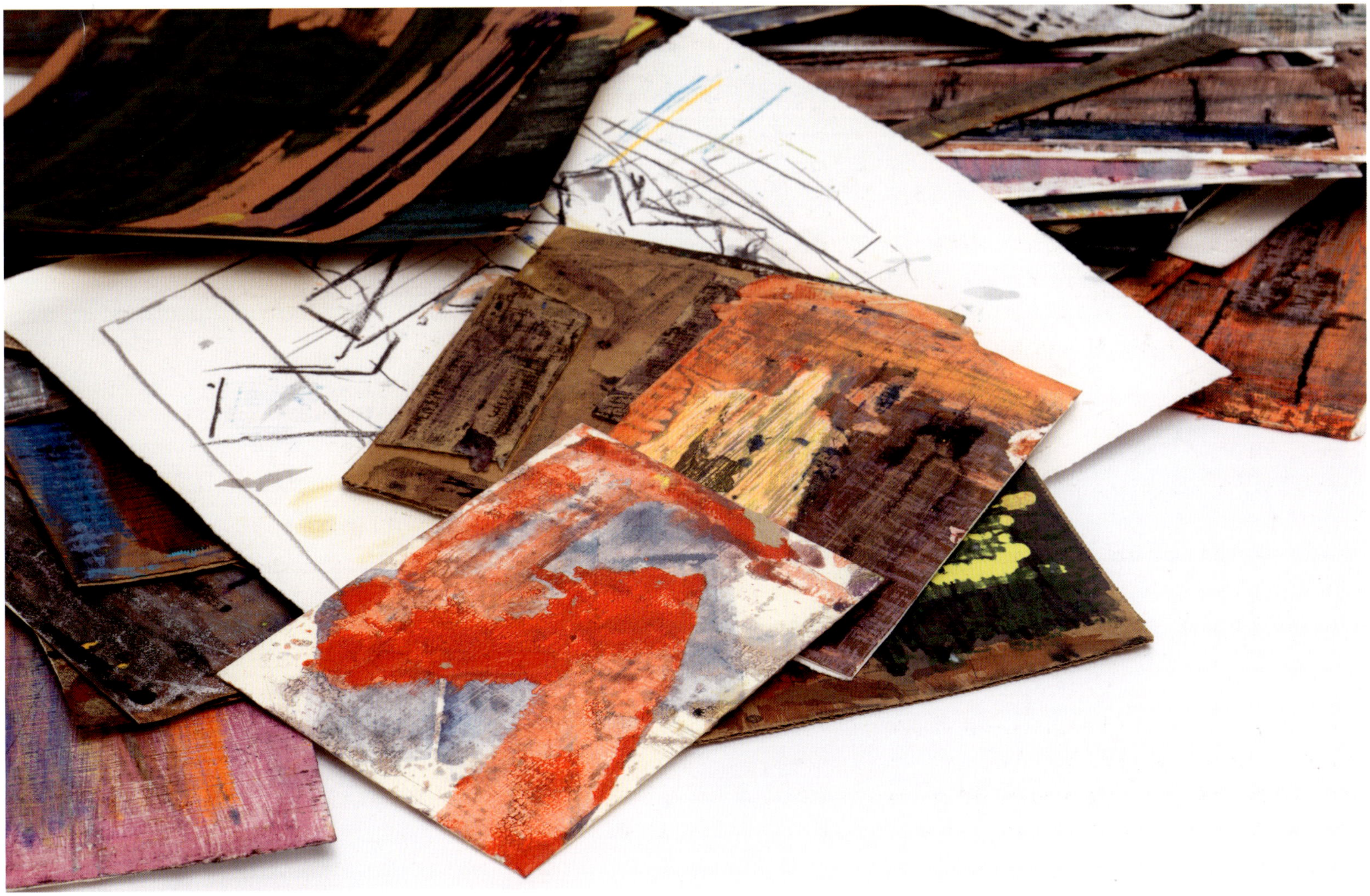

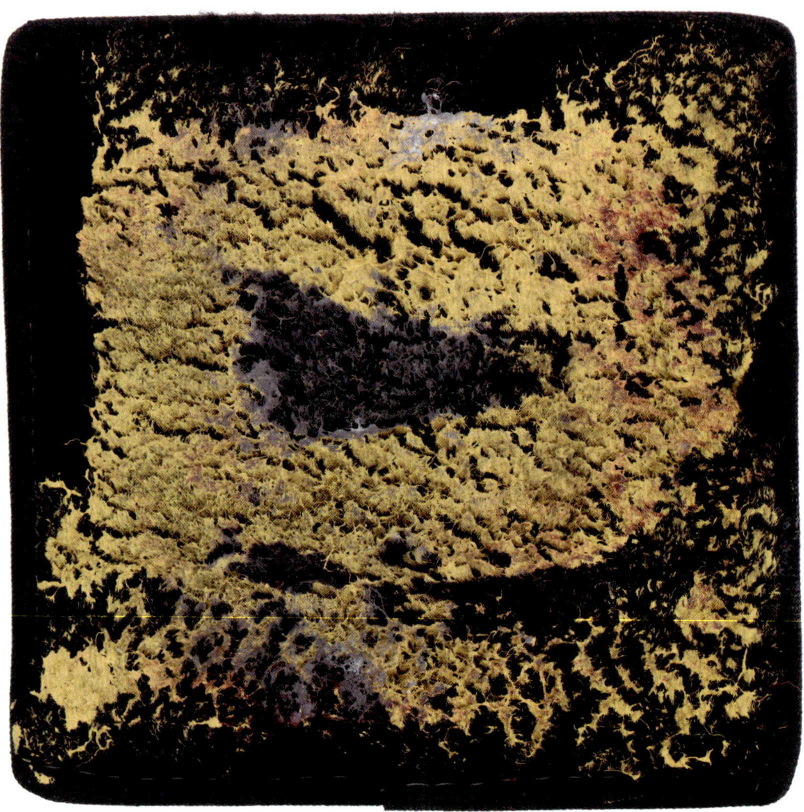

FIGURE 32
Louise Fishman, *Untitled*, 2007
Acrylic on carpet sample, 6⅛ x 6 in. (15.6 x 15.2 cm)

INGRID: Some are very tiny, just shards and slivers. Together they read like an index of painting, mark making, drawing, pigments, and materials that is both astonishingly replete and generative.

LOUISE: It was a terrifically productive moment. I had just begun a relationship with Ingrid Nyeboe. At the end of the two weeks, Susan said, "Louise, you must be in love." She had never seen anyone make so much work.

INGRID: Your work strongly conveys a sense of ethics, in the value of labor, in thrift, in being resourceful, scrappy. Nothing appears to go to waste.

LOUISE: I have paintings on sandpaper that started with scraping down the surface of a canvas and then working back into the sandpaper. I've done the same thing with paper towels. I'm always paying attention to process and scouting for new materials. I used to get a lot of interesting stuff to paint on—squares of Bakelite and rubber, those Masonite circles—on Canal Street.

INGRID: I'm impressed by the carpet samples (FIG. 32). They are such unappealing objects to begin with, yet you've transformed them into such beautifully tactile little paintings that manage to draw extra power by appearing to be messed-up carpet samples only partially redeemed by art.

LOUISE: I made those when I was in residence at Dartmouth College for two months and ran out of linen. But it's true, I would paint on almost anything, including myself if that were viable.

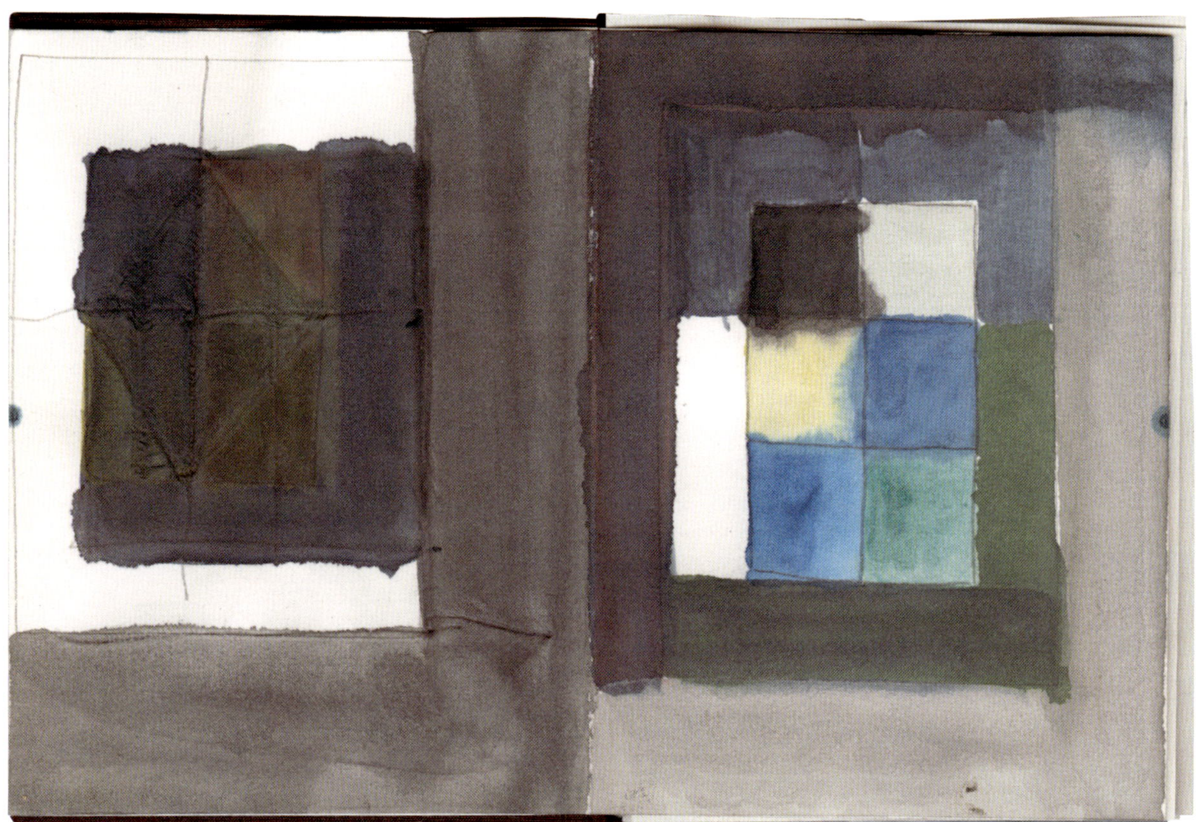

FIGURE 33
Louise Fishman, *Book 1*, 1992
Gouache and graphite on paper (Japanese Leporello Binding), 4⅞ x 3⅝ x 1¼ in. (12.4 x 9.2 x 3.2 cm)

INGRID: Let's talk about the leporellos: such an arcane name for a book with accordion-folded pages. Apparently it was a popular Victorian form of binding for tourist souvenir panoramas.

LOUISE: I still have a little leporello guide to Giotto's frescos in Padua that I bought the first time I went to Italy, in 1979, when I saw the Duccios and realized that I wanted to paint small.

What inspired me to use the leporello form to paint in was learning about a Japanese tradition of carrying these books like passports to be marked at Buddhist pilgrimage sites. I made my first one in 1992 (FIG. 33), after I got back from New Mexico; it has to do with Agnes Martin and scale. I had gone to Galisteo, where she was at the time, because I had the horrible crisis of a fire in my studio. My partner Betsy Crowell and I rented Harmony Hammond's house, and I was a mess.

A couple of remarkable days were spent with Agnes in her studio not saying anything. She sat in her rocking chair and looked at me every once in a while. And I thought, *what's going on here? Oh, she's meditating. I know how to do that.* So I went into my breath and did my meditation. I watched Agnes and listened to her, later, when she showed me drawings and pulled out paintings and talked about her dealer and whatever else artists talk about. It was clear that the work was a meditation for Agnes, a path, and that I could quiet myself down.

Having a fire in your studio is one of the most unhinging experiences an artist can have; everything falls apart. When we got back to upstate New York I started making these books that suddenly made perfect sense. There were little grids and bigger grids, rubbings and blottings. I got interested in transferring the image from one side of the page to the other, because these books can be used in different

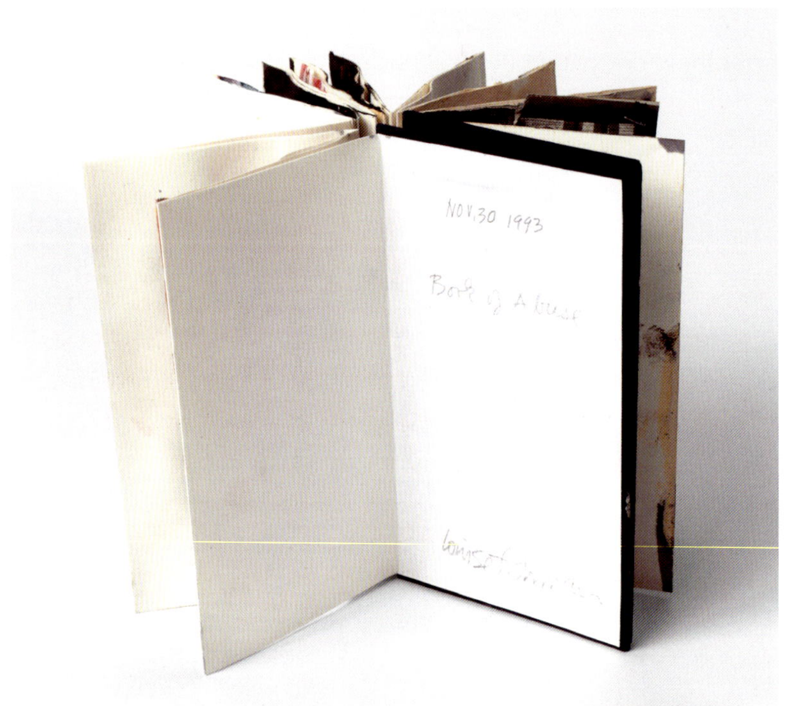

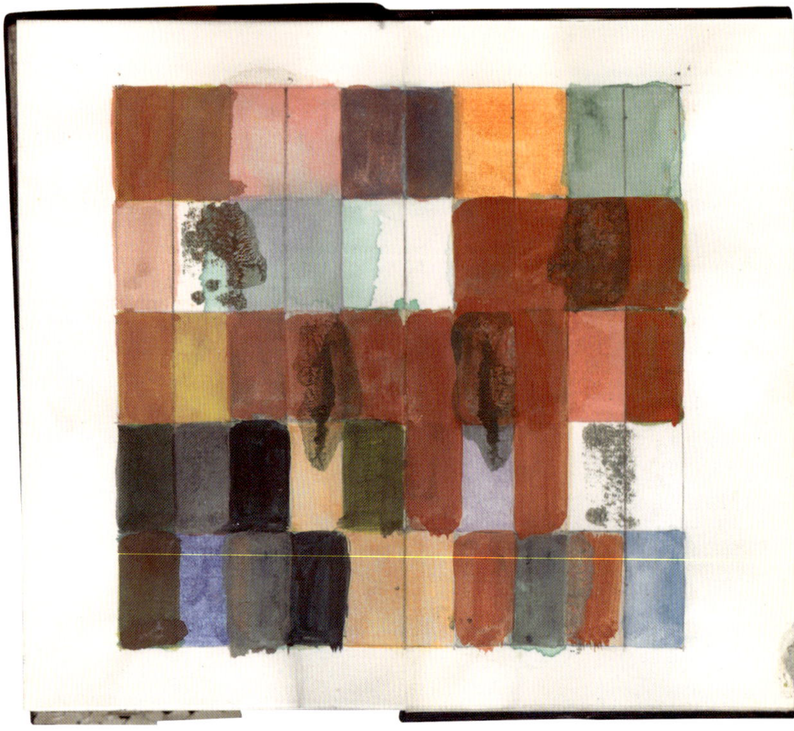

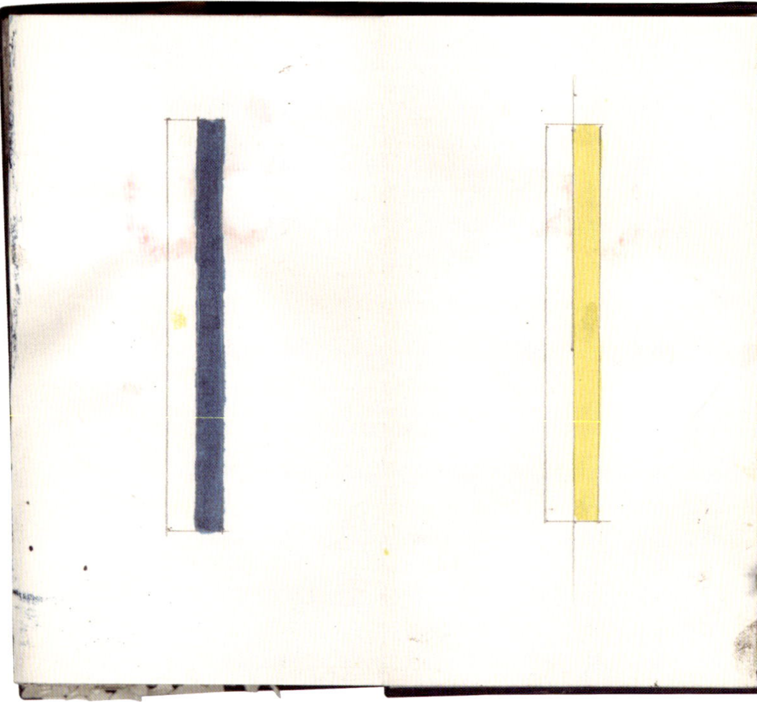

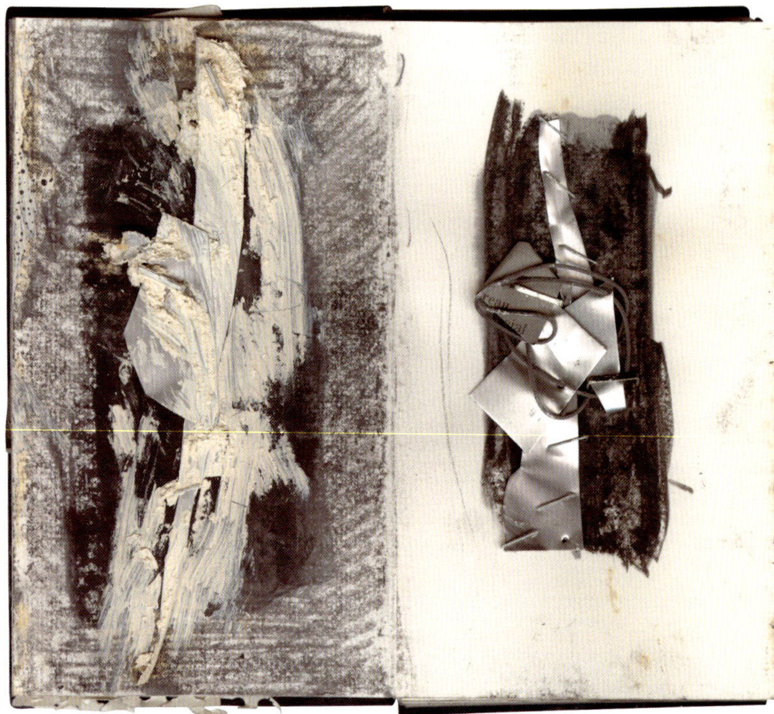

FIGURES 34–37
Louise Fishman, *Book of Abuse*, 1993–94
Acrylic, oil, oil stick, graphite, staples, and wire with aluminum and paper collage on paper (Japanese Leporello Binding), 6⅜ x 3⅝ x 1⅝ in. (16.2 x 9.2 x 4.1 cm)

directions and don't really have a front or back, beginning or end.

INGRID: I'm thinking about your feminist journaling and how these books relate to your early interest in writing. They read in such an interesting way, because they're so episodic. Serene passages of watercolor drawing are interrupted by seismic eruptions of oil paint, metal staples, and built-up accretions of paper and various media (FIGS. 34–37). They're contained, yet volatile; they don't want to be closed—or opened! This one is a crucible of painting so gooey that the pages are protesting as we pull them apart.

LOUISE: I never make drawings for paintings. So I've been surprised at how many ideas that seem to appear on canvas as if from nowhere can actually be found in these little books from years earlier.

INGRID: So we're sitting in your studio with these very sculptural books in front of us, surrounded by objects (FIG. 38). Louise, you're a collector.

LOUISE: It started with Chinese scholars' rocks. In 1985 I saw an exhibition at the China Institute, curated by John Hay—I still have the catalogue, *Kernels of Energy, Bones of Earth: The Rock in Chinese Art*—and my mind was blown. Because not only were these rock formations extraordinary, but their bases had been carved to correspond to their contours. It was the most beautiful melding of one object into another—in total respect of the rock.

So I started learning about scholars' rocks. It never occurred to me that I could own one. But Bernard Lennon, my dealer at the time, knew the sculptor Richard Rosenblum, who was based in Boston and had an incredible rock collection. He told me about a couple of guys who had stands at the flea markets and little antique centers that used to be all over New York. And I started buying, spending $25 or $90 for these beautiful rocks.

INGRID: Aptly, I see a discipline, a form of study. It's very specific what you collect. Besides the scholars' rocks here in the studio, you are a collector of African sculptures, American milking stools, and Venetian glass.

LOUISE: I don't know how disciplined you would consider my collecting if you knew how much stuff I have at home! But they're objects to draw, subjects to study and just have around for their impact. With the African art, which I first started looking at in the University of Pennsylvania Museum of Archeology and Anthropology, what I became interested in were these small-scale pieces, mostly bronzes, some so small I couldn't believe it. There was one African dealer, also at the flea market, who was educating me. Some of what I bought may not have been authentic. It didn't matter. This one piece looks like it has a certain amount of weight, and when you hold it, it's like a feather. That idea amazes me.

INGRID: What special appeal do the other collections have?

LOUISE: The three-legged stools are for milking, but the rest are all work stools. They have all taken on the shape and wear of individual use and work over time. I used to get them at auctions in upstate New York for $5 or $10, but now the antique pickers bid up the prices too high for me to be interested in continuing to collect them. I began collecting the glass after Ingrid and I started spending time in Venice. We may have gone to Murano, but I wasn't that interested until I saw this beautiful piece at a flea market. It was 100 euros, which seemed like a hell of a lot of money, but I bought it. Then I started reading catalogues and found out the period I was interested in was the 1930s to the 1950s. I've gotten a lot of exquisite glass on eBay.

INGRID: Again, there's something about weight: this tiny Carlo Scarpa glass bowl is incredibly heavy.

LOUISE: There are iron filings in the glass, which can contain all kinds of odd materials, like glitter. I've recently made paintings and watercolors inspired by *Spuma de Mare*, a technique that Ercole Barovier invented for getting something decorative to happen inside the glass that makes it look like foam churning up from the sea.

INGRID: That's another correspondence with your work, the elemental nature of these objects. I always feel close to the substance of your materials: the minerality of oil paint, for instance, the malachite of malachite green. On another studio visit you showed me the mortar and pestle you used in 1988 to pulverize the soil you collected at the Pond of Living Ashes at Birkenau for your *Remembrance and Renewal* paintings.

LOUISE: I think all of that has everything to be with being a Jew. My family were Ashkenazim and they were Talmudic scholars. When I was studying Yiddish I went to a lot of old movies. I remember identifying so intensely with this silent film about the golem—the creature made from clay—brought to life to protect the Jews of Prague. Being an American didn't make any difference. I still had that desire for something supernatural that could protect us, protect me.

INGRID: Is that, in part, what painting does: protect you? I'm thinking less about the golem and more about your anger as a material, one that has never been fully transformed by alchemy or anything supernatural, but rather, has been annealed by your art. To anneal is to burn, to make a substance stronger by making it softer, less brittle. To be in your studio now: it's the work that's on fire, not you!

LOUISE: Yes, I am happy being benign Louise. I'm allowing myself much more freedom in the studio. I would have never allowed all that white space of the canvas to be there before. I wanted to give everything a lot of richness, but this is a different story. Now it's about giving reign to what paint does on its own. And I do think there's something magical about painting. Something is *made* out of paint, aside from the purpose it gives my life. You know, I stopped painting to have this knee replacement and I have no idea what's going to happen when I get back to work. I mean, it's a complete mystery.

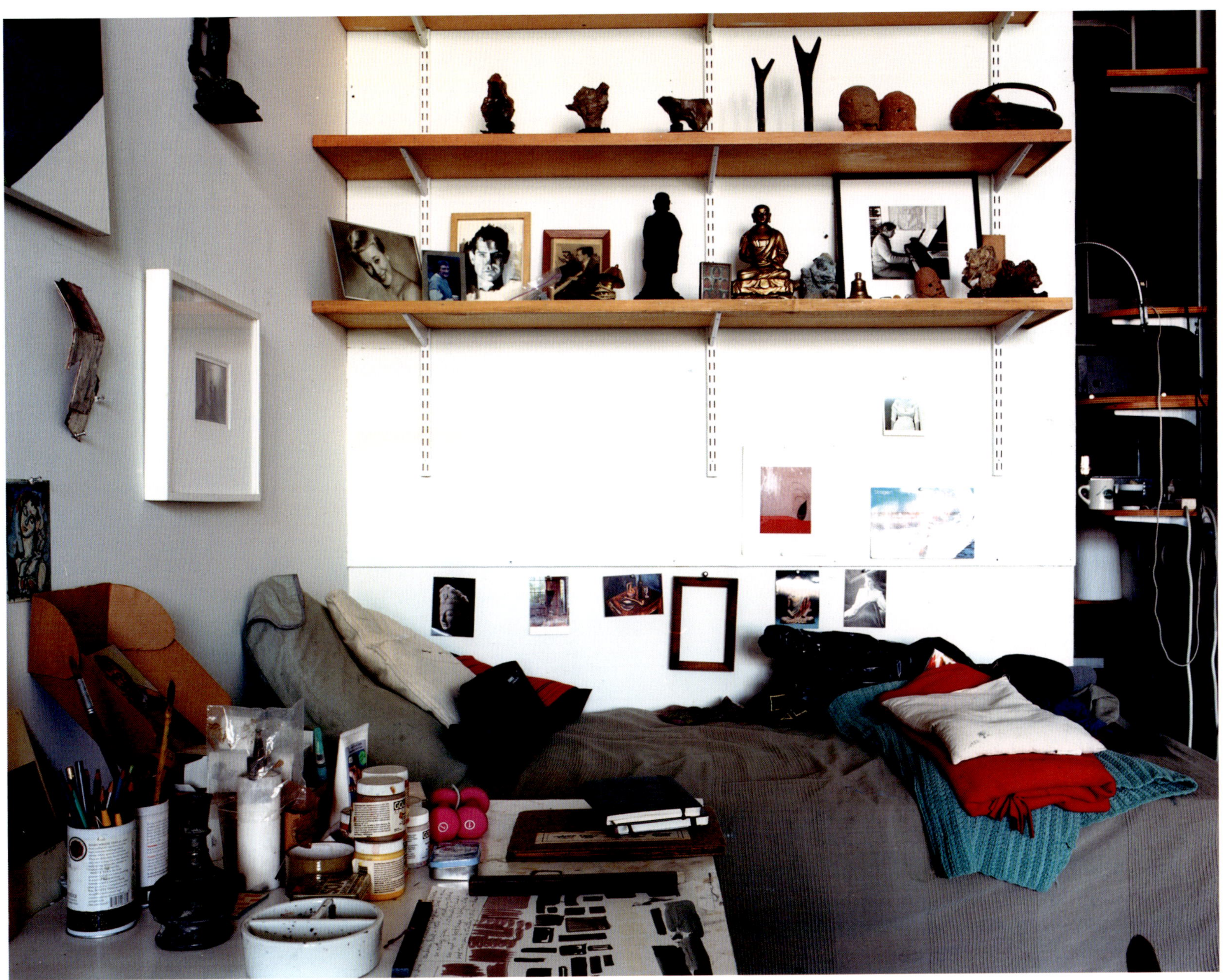

FIGURE 38
Louise Fishman studio, New York, summer 2015. Photograph by Wijnanda Deroo

PLATES IV

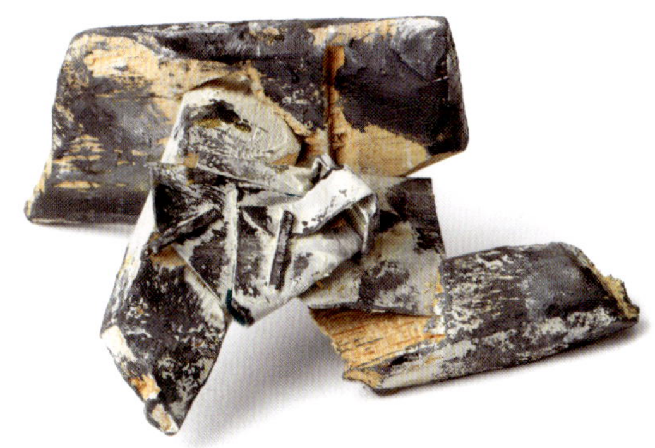

PLATE 116. *Untitled*, 1993–94. Acrylic and staples on wood and aluminum sheet, 1½ x 2¾ x 2½ in. (3.8 x 7 x 6.4 cm)

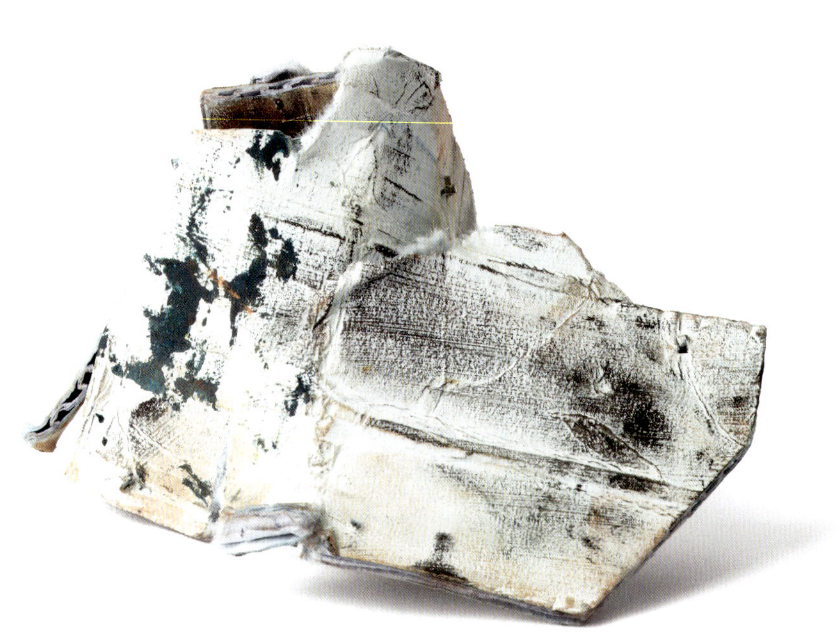

PLATE 117. *Untitled*, 1993–94. Acrylic and staples on aluminum sheet, 3 x 4 x 4½ in. (7.6 x 10.2 x 11.4 cm)

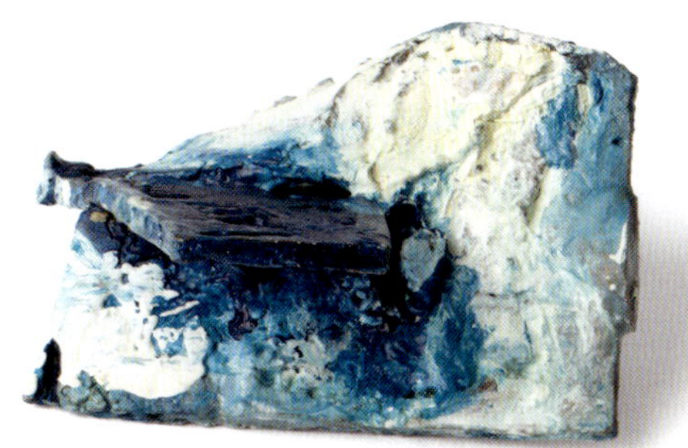

PLATE 118. *Untitled*, 1993–94. Acrylic on bronze, 1½ x 2½ x 3 in. (3.8 x 6.4 x 7.6 cm)

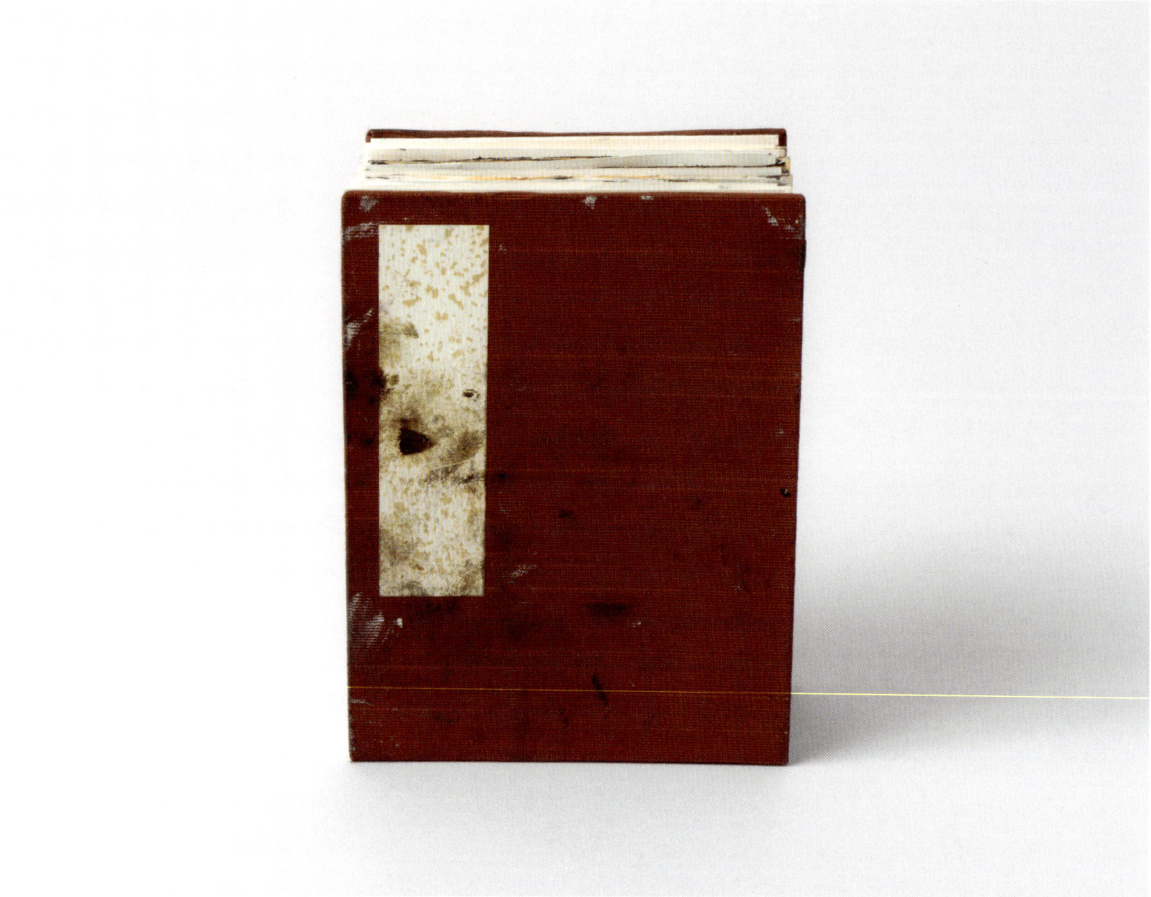

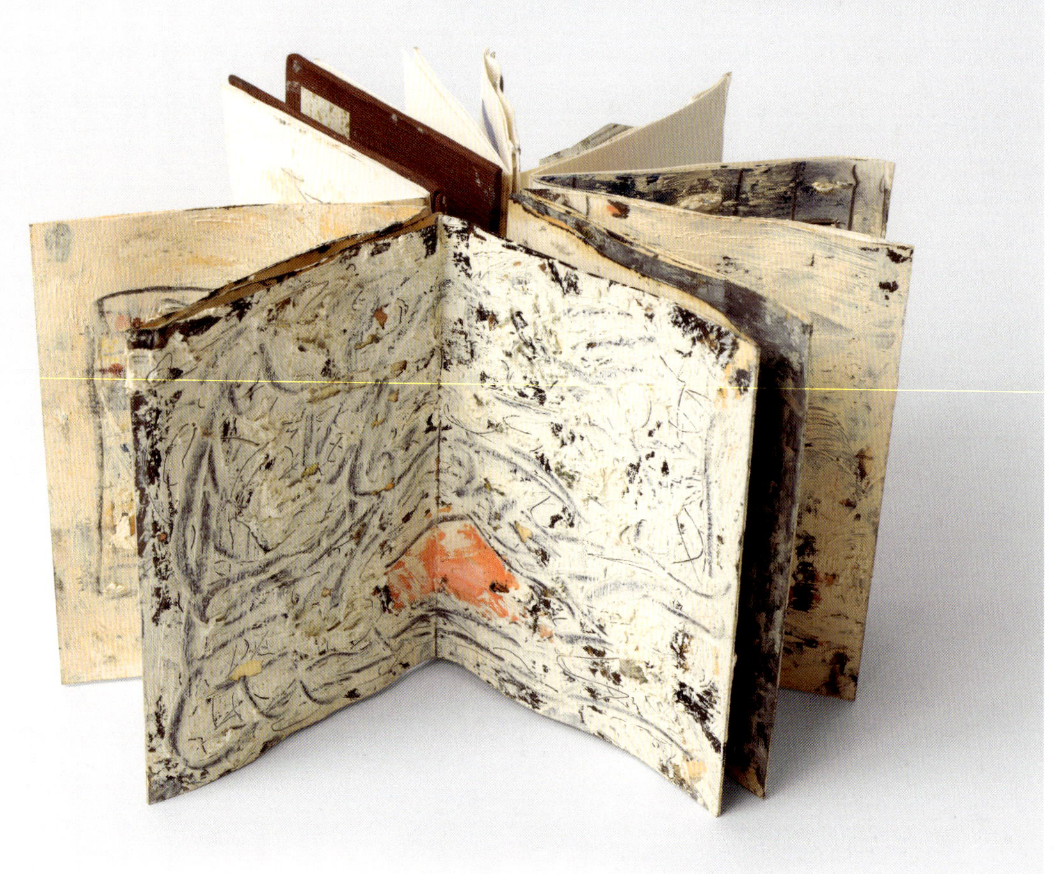

PLATE 119. *Down and Dirty (A Book for Bertha Harris)*, 1994. Oil, gouache, graphite, staples, and paper collage on paper (Japanese

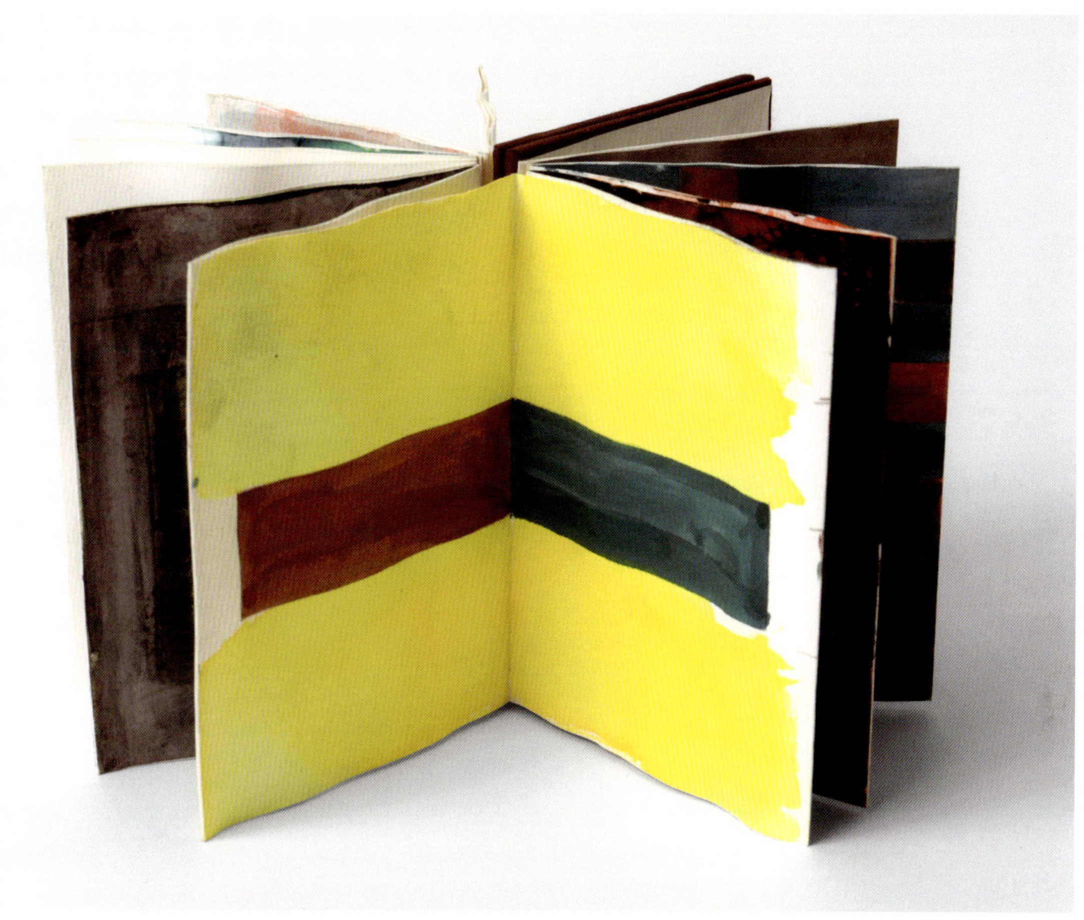

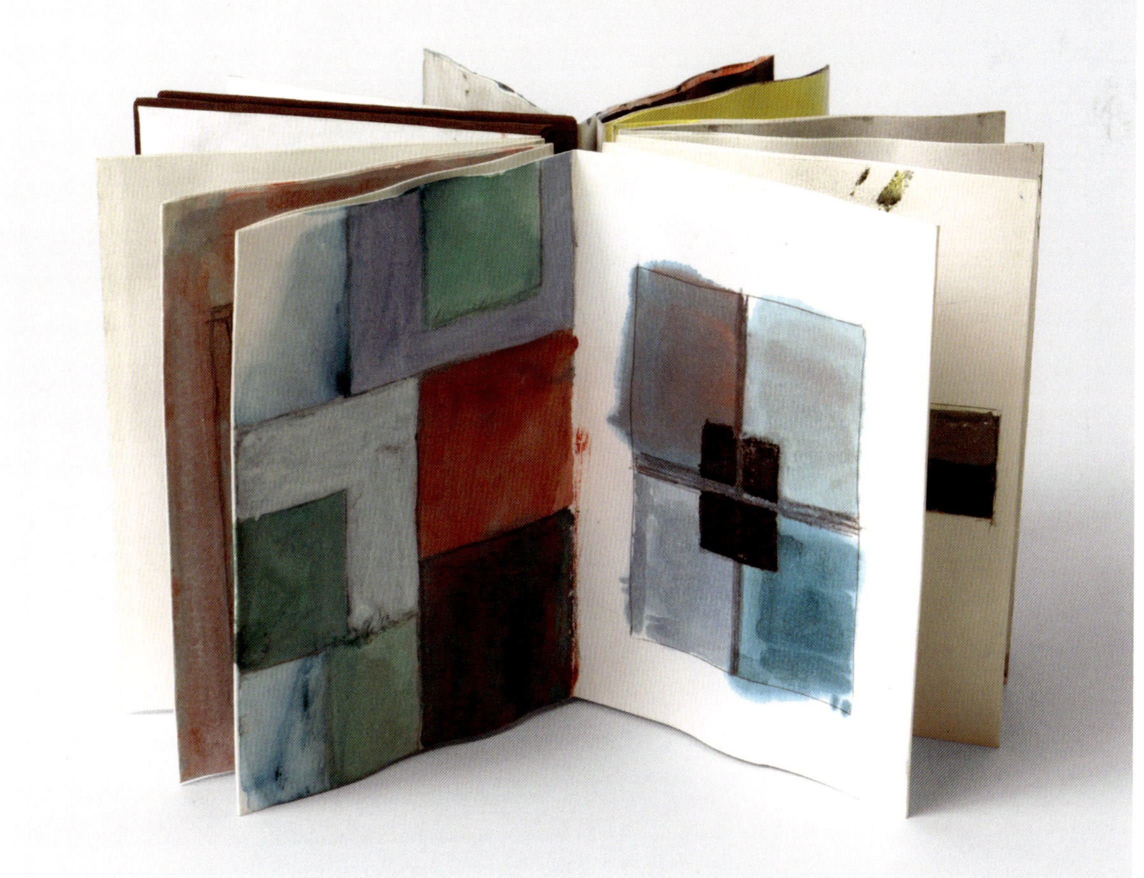

Leporello binding), 4⅞ x 3⅝ x 2 in. (12.4 x 9.2 x 5.1 cm)

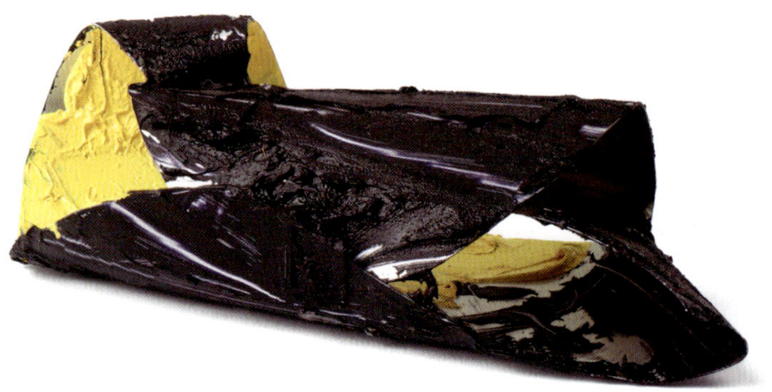

PLATE 120. *Untitled*, 1996. Oil stick and acrylic on aluminum, staples, 1¾ x 6 x 3 in. (4.4 x 15.2 x 7.6 cm)

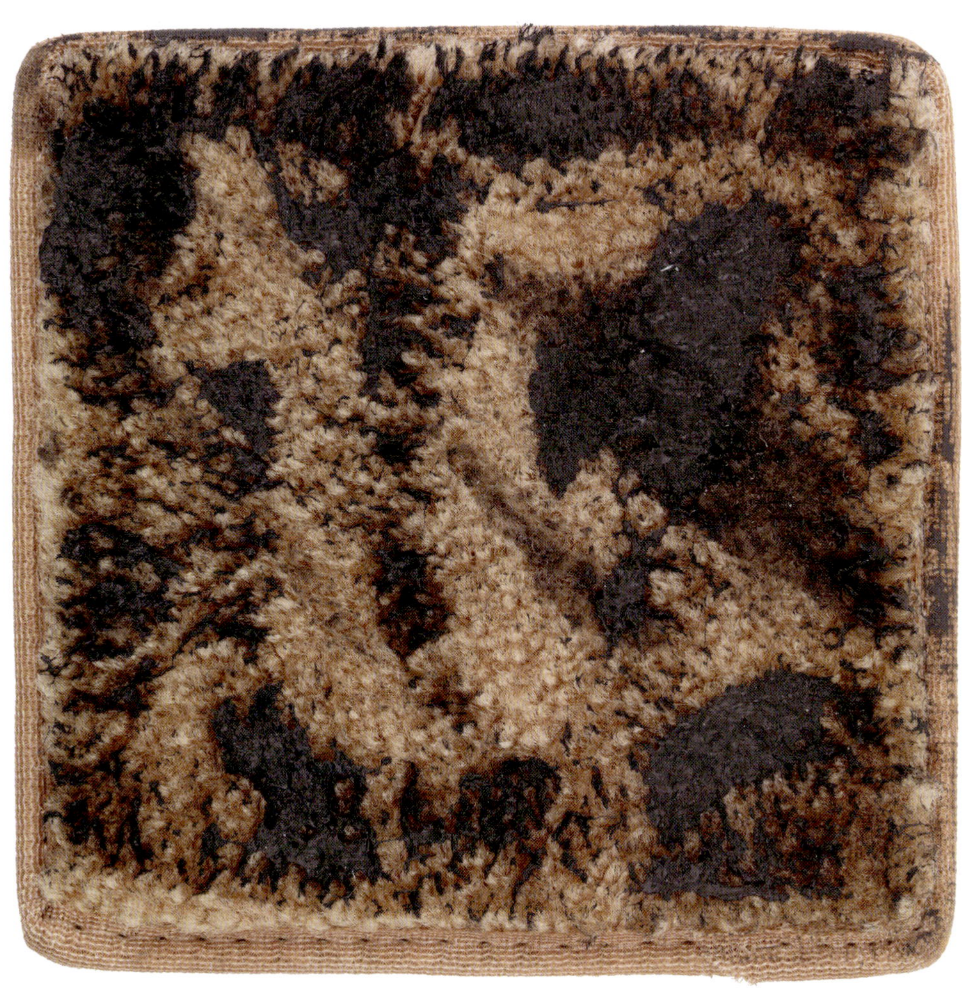

PLATE 121. *Untitled*, 2007. Acrylic on carpet sample, 6⅛ x 6 in. (15.6 x 15.2 cm)

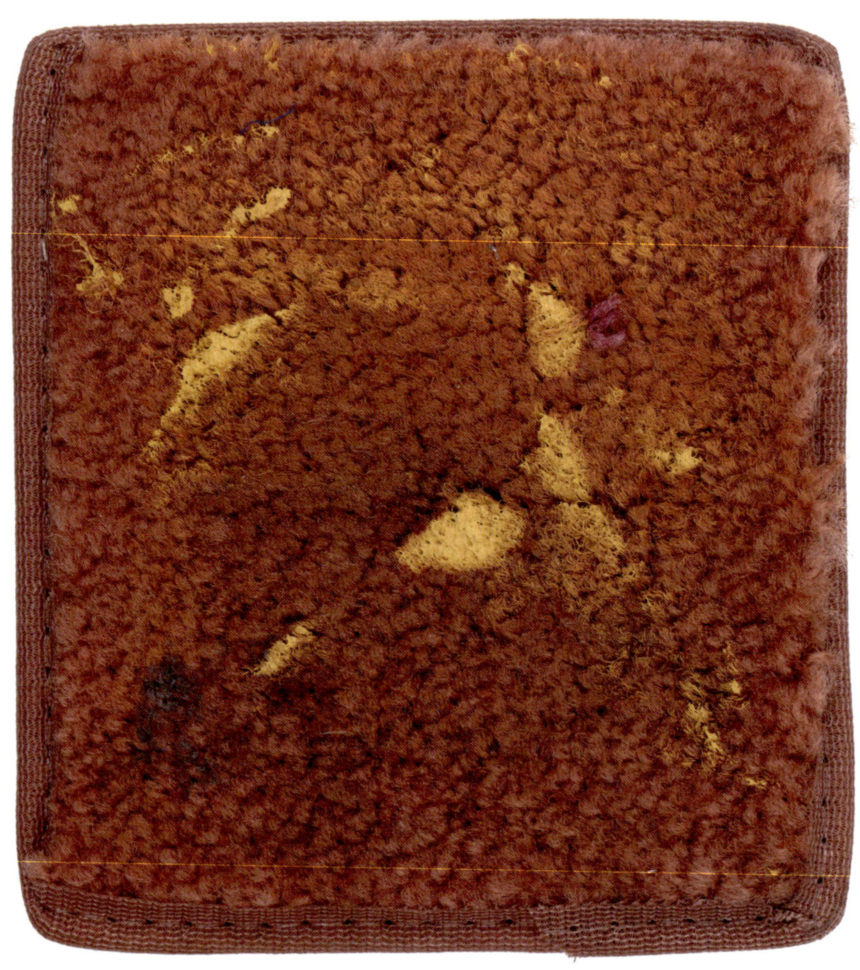

 PLATE 122. *Untitled*, 2007. Acrylic on carpet sample, 6 x 5 5/16 in. (15.2 x 13.5 cm)

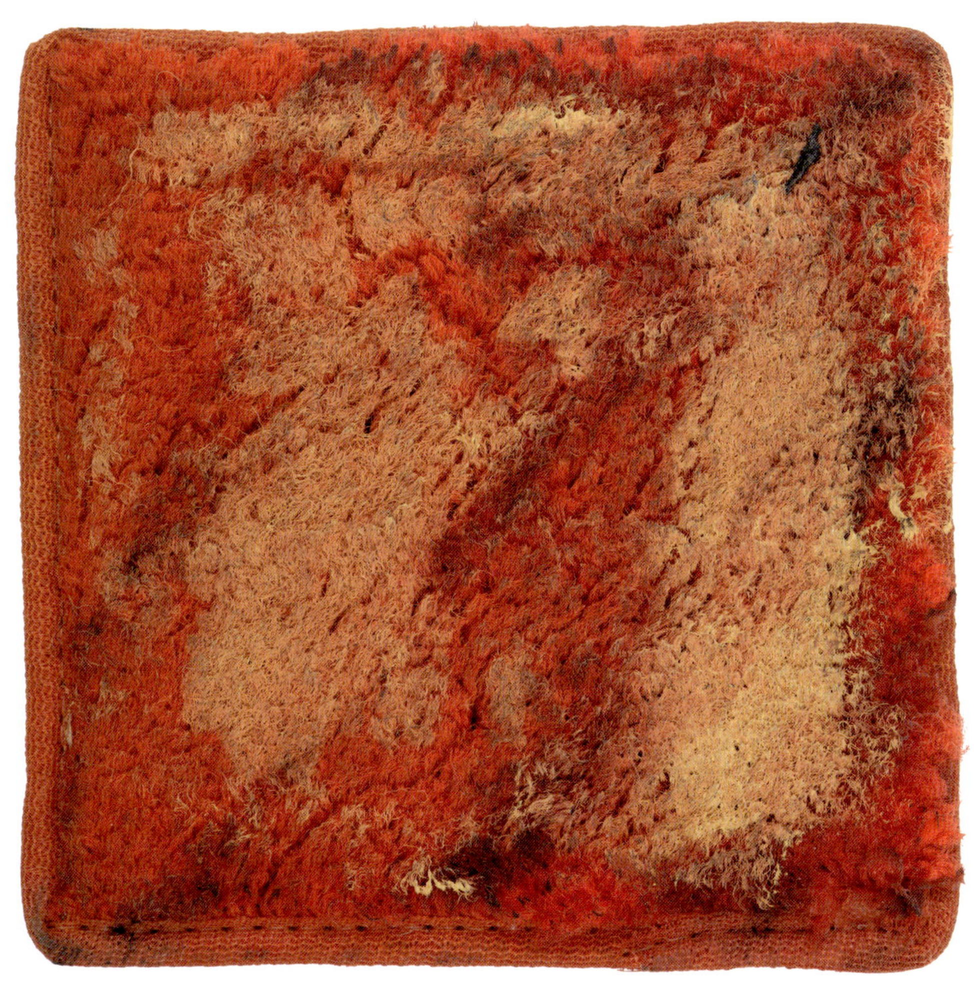

PLATE 123. *Untitled*, 2007. Acrylic on carpet sample, 6⅛ x 6 in. (15.6 x 15.2 cm)

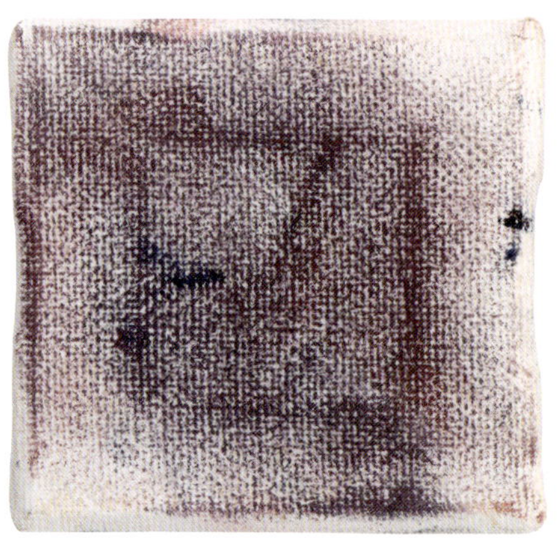

PLATE 124. *Untitled*, 2011. Oil on canvas, 2 x 2 in. (5.1 x 5.1 cm)
PLATE 125. *Untitled*, 2011. Graphite on board, 3 x 2 in. (7.6 x 5.1 cm)

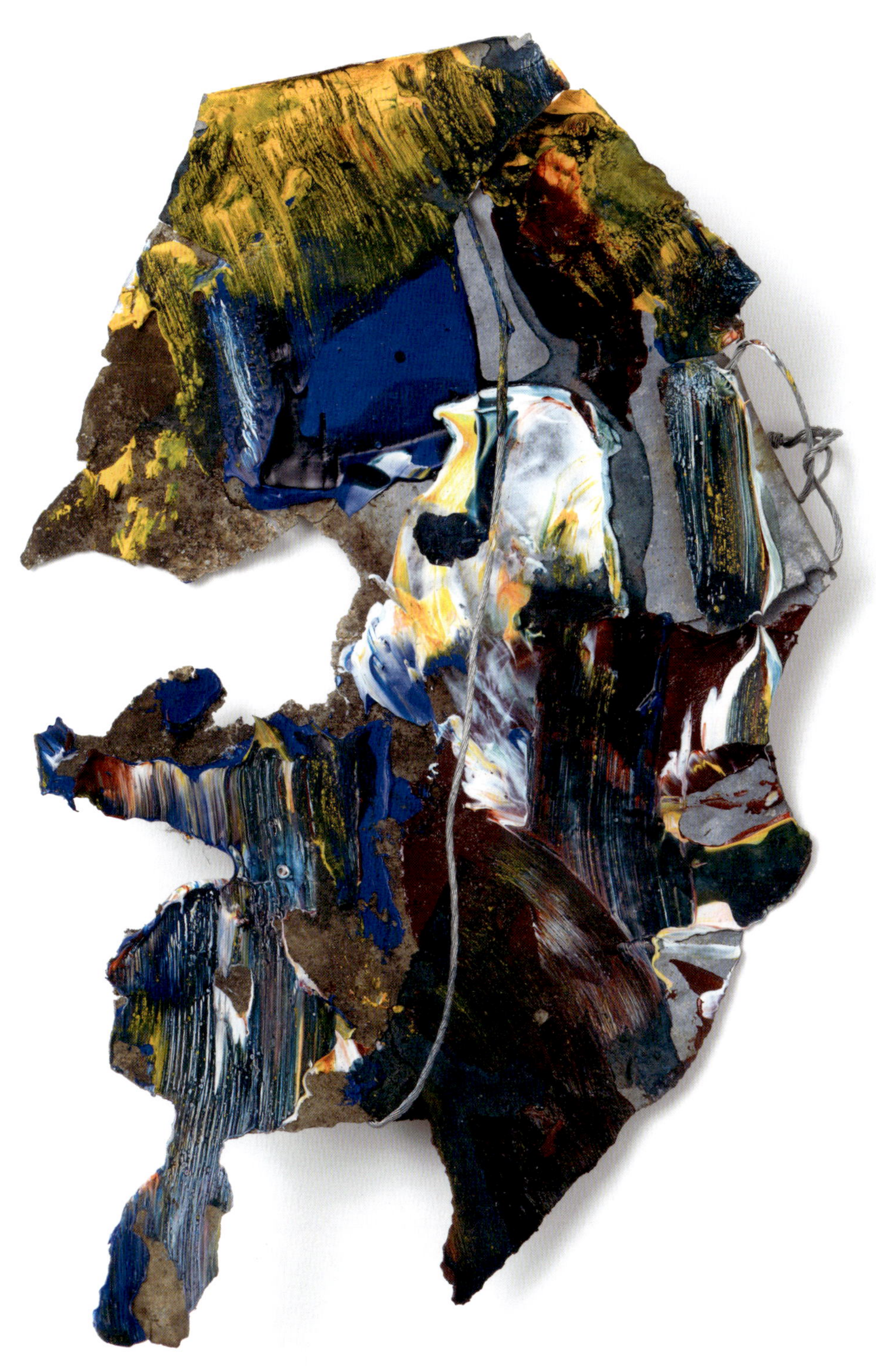

PLATE 126. *Untitled*, 2011. Acrylic on rusted metal with wire, 8¾ x 5¼ x 2 in. (22.2 x 13.3 x 5.1 cm)

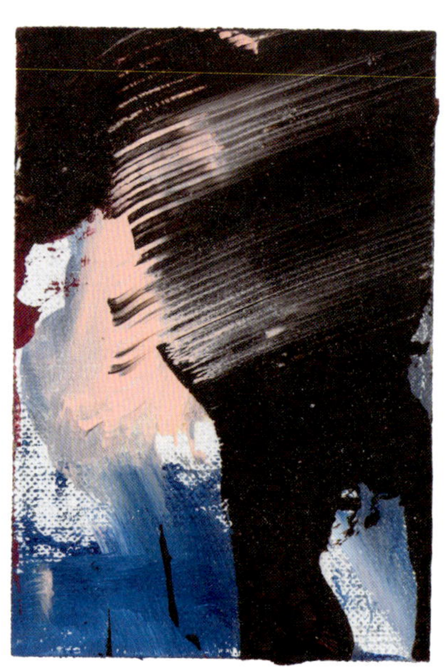

 PLATE 127. *Untitled*, 2014. Oil on board, 3 x 2 in. (7.6 x 5.1 cm)

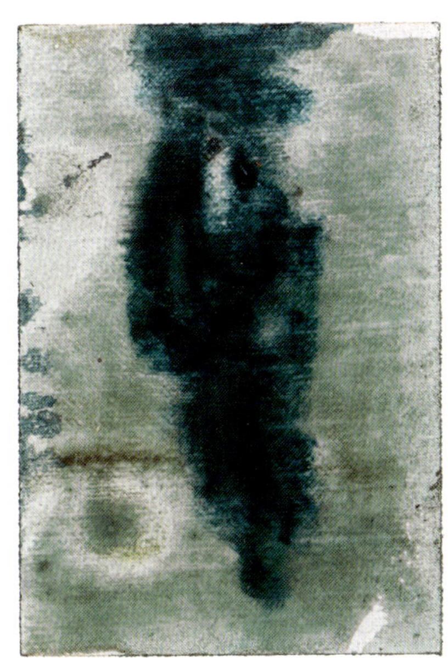

PLATE 128. *Untitled*, 2014. Oil on board, 3 x 2 in. (7.6 x 5.1 cm)

EXHIBITION CHECKLIST

This listing documents the works presented in the exhibition *Louise Fishman: A Retrospective*, Neuberger Museum of Art, Purchase College, SUNY, Purchase, New York (April 3–July 31, 2016). The artwork entries reflect the best information available at the time of publication. All works were exhibited courtesy the artist and Cheim & Read, New York, unless otherwise noted below.

The works presented in *Paper Louise Tiny Fishman Rock*, Institute of Contemporary Art, University of Pennsylvania, Philadelphia (April 29–August 14, 2016), will be composed within the space of the exhibition and are not reflected in this checklist.

In and Out, 1968
Acrylic on canvas
66 x 50 in. (167.6 x 127 cm)
PLATE 1

Untitled, 1968
Gouache and graphite on paper
19 x 17 in. (48.3 x 43.2 cm)
PLATE 2

Untitled, 1970
Acrylic and pastel on canvas
66 x 51 in. (167.6 x129.5 cm)
Collection of Carol A. Calhoun
PLATE 3

Untitled, 1971
Rubber, graphite, string, and staples on tracing paper
14 x 21 in. (35.6 x 53.3 cm)
PLATE 4

Untitled, 1971
Acrylic on canvas with chalk and string
12 x 13½ in. (30.5 x 34.3 cm)
PLATE 5

Angry Djuna, 1973
Acrylic on paper
26 x 40 in. (66 x 101.6 cm)
PLATE 9

Angry Gertrude, 1973
Acrylic on paper
26 x 40 in. (66 x 101.6 cm)
PLATE 10

Angry Jill, 1973
Acrylic on paper
26 x 40 in. (66 x 101.6 cm)
PLATE 11

Angry Louise, 1973
Acrylic on paper
26 x 40 in. (66 x 101.6 cm)
PLATE 12

Angry Marilyn, 1973
Acrylic on paper
26 x 40 in. (66 x 101.6 cm)
PLATE 13

Angry Patsy, 1973
Acrylic on paper
26 x 40 in. (66 x 101.6 cm)
PLATE 14

Angry Paula, 1973
Acrylic on paper
26 x 40 in. (66 x 101.6 cm)
PLATE 15

Angry Razel, 1973
Acrylic on paper
26 x 40 in. (66 x 101.6 cm)
PLATE 16

Angry Radclyffe Hall, 1973
Acrylic on paper
26 x 40 in. (66 x 101.6 cm)
PLATE 17

Untitled, 1973
Oil and staples on paper and cardboard
20 x 16¾ in. (50.8 x 42.5 cm)
PLATE 20

Untitled, 1973
Oil and graphite on cardboard
19 x 19 in. (48.3 x 48.3 cm)
PLATE 21

Caryatid, 1974
Oil and wax on wood
30¼ x 17¼ in. (76.8 x 43.8 cm)
PLATE 23

Untitled, 1975–76
Oil on primed paper
31¼ x 22¾ in. (79.4 x 57.8 cm)
PLATE 25

Ashkenazi, 1978
Oil on linen
32 x 48 in. (81.2 x 122 cm)
PLATE 26

Golem, 1981
Oil on linen
32 x 48 in. (81.3 x 121.9 cm)
The Jewish Museum, New York, Gift of Francine and Samuel Klagsbrun, 1991-56
PLATE 28

Grand Slam, 1985
Oil on canvas
56 x 40 in. (142.2 x101.6 cm)
The Metropolitan Museum of Art, New York, Edith C. Blum Fund, 1986.387
PLATE 30

Headwaters, 1987
Oil on canvas
32 x 17 in. (81.2 x 43 cm)
Private collection
PLATE 35

Stand of Beech, 1987
Oil on linen
65 x 50 in. (165.1 x 127 cm)
PLATE 36

Bitter Herb, 1988
Oil on linen
65 x 45 in. (165.1 x 114.3 cm)
Courtesy of Fernando Luis Alvarez Gallery, Stamford, Connecticut
PLATE 38

Four Questions, 1988
Oil on canvas
65 x 45 in. (165.1 x 114.3 cm)
PLATE 39

Haggadah, 1988
Oil on linen
37 x 50 in. (94 x 127 cm)
Collection of Stuart and Lisa Ginsberg
PLATE 40

Karpas #4, 1988
Oil on linen
32½ x 24 in. (82.6 x 61 cm)
PLATE 41

Untitled, 1989
Oil on paper
31 x 24 in. (78.7 x 61 cm)
PLATE 42

Dybbuk, 1990
Oil on linen
37 x 50 in. (94 x 127 cm)
PLATE 44

Untitled, 1990
Oil on paper
31 x 22¾ in. (78.7 x 57.8 cm)
PLATE 45

Valles Marineris, 1992
Oil on linen
90 x 62 in. (228 x157.5 cm)
PLATE 49

Iron Sharpens Iron, 1993
Oil on linen
110 x 70 in. (279.4 x 177.8 cm)
The Art Institute of Chicago,
gift of Robert Miller and
Sarah Wittenborn Miller
PLATE 50

Blonde Ambition, 1995
Oil on linen
90 x 65 in. (228.6 x165.1 cm)
PLATE 52

Burnt Bridges, 1995
Oil on linen
84 x 61 in. (213.4 x 154.9 cm)
Speyer Family Collection,
New York
PLATE 53

Tossed As It Is Untroubled, 1997
Oil on canvas
30¼ x 20¼ in. (76.8 x 51.4 cm)
Private collection
PLATE 59

Untitled, 1997
Oil and ink on paper
30 x 18 in. (76.2 x 45.7 cm)
PLATE 60

April, 1998
Oil on linen
76 x 46 in. (193 x 116.8 cm)
Collection of John Cheim
PLATE 61

For There She Was, 1998
Oil on linen
76¼ x 82 in. (193.7 x 208.3 cm)
Collection of Romita Shetty
and Nasser Ahmad
PLATE 65

The Sunrise Ruby, 1999
Oil on linen
82 x 75⅞ in. (208.3 x 192.7 cm)
Collection of Martha Macks-Kahn
PLATE 67

Untitled, 1999
Oil and watercolor on paper
23 x 19 in. (58.4 x 48.3 cm)
PLATE 68

Untitled, 1999
Oil on paper
36 x 25 in. (91.4 x 63.5 cm)
PLATE 69

Untitled, 1999
Oil on paper
36 x 25 in. (91.4 x 63.5 cm)
PLATE 70

In Paul's Hands, 2000
Oil on linen
40 x 30½ in. (101.6 x 77.5 cm)
Collection of Thomas Whitridge
PLATE 72

Lesson of the Master, 2000
Oil on linen
30¼ x 18¼ in. (76.8 x 46.4 cm)
Collection of Tracey and
Mark Bilski
PLATE 73

That Iron String, 2000
Oil on linen
38 x 38 in. (96.5 x 96.5 cm)
Collection of Milton and
Sheila Fine
PLATE 75

Untitled, 2001
Oil on paper
30 x 22¼ in. (76.2 x 56.5 cm)
PLATE 76

The Art of Losing, 2003
Oil on linen
80 x 60 in. (203.2 x 152.4 cm)
PLATE 79

Little Passion, 2003
Oil on canvas
40 x 26 in. (101.6 x 66 cm)
Collection of Tom Cashin and
Jay Johnson, New York
PLATE 80

Green in the Body, 2004
Oil on linen
77 x 55 in. (195.6 x 139.7 cm)
PLATE 85

Green's Apogee, 2005
Oil on canvas
88 x 70 in. (223.5 x 177.8 cm)
Hood Museum of Art, Dartmouth
College: Purchased through
a gift from Mr. and Mrs. Joseph
H. Hazen, by exchange, 2013.23.
PLATE 87

Loose Change, 2005
Oil on canvas
60 x 55 in. (152.4 x 139.7 cm)
The Dicke Collection
PLATE 88

Untitled, 2005
Acrylic on corrugated paper
30½ x 38 in. (77.5 x 96.5 cm)
PLATE 90

Slippery Slope, 2006
Oil on linen
88 x 65 in. (223.5 x 165.1 cm)
PLATE 92

Zero at the Bone, 2010
Oil on linen
70 x 60 in. (177.8 x 152.4 cm)
Collection of Mike De Paola,
New York
PLATE 99

Untitled, 2011
Oil on newspaper
22³⁄₁₆ x 24¼ in. (56.4 x 61.6 cm)
PLATE 101

Crossing the Rubicon, 2012
Oil on linen
66 x 57 in. (167.6 x 144.8 cm)
Collection of James and
Janet Kloppenburg
PLATE 102

Serenissima, 2012
Oil on linen
70 x 88 in. (177.8 x 223.5 cm)
Collection of Jan and Barry
Zubrow, New Jersey
PLATE 105

9/11 Redux, 2013
Oil on linen
70 x 88 in. (177.8 x 223.6 cm)
The Forman Family Foundation
PLATE 106

For GGG, 2014
Oil on linen
70 x 88 in. (177.8 x 223.5 cm)
Private collection
PLATE 108

Kreisleriana, 2015
Oil on linen
57 x 56 in. (144.8 x 142.2 cm)
PLATE 113

Margate, 2015
Oil on linen
72 x 88 in. (182.9 x 223.5 cm)
Collection of Marc and Jill Fisher,
Greenwich, Connecticut
PLATE 114

LENDERS TO THE EXHIBITION

LOUISE FISHMAN: A RETROSPECTIVE
NEUBERGER MUSEUM OF ART, PURCHASE COLLEGE, SUNY

Fernando Luis Alvarez Gallery, Stamford, Connecticut
The Art Institute of Chicago
Tracey and Mark Bilski
Carol A. Calhoun
Tom Cashin and Jay Johnson, New York
Cheim & Read, New York
John Cheim
Mike De Paola, New York
The Dicke Collection
Milton and Sheila Fine
Marc and Jill Fisher
Louise Fishman
The Forman Family Foundation
Stuart and Lisa Ginsberg
Hood Museum of Art, Dartmouth College
The Jewish Museum, New York
James and Janet Kloppenburg
Martha Macks-Kahn
The Metropolitan Museum of Art, New York
Romita Shetty and Nasser Ahmad
Speyer Family Collection, New York
Thomas Whitridge
Jan and Barry Zubrow, New Jersey

And several private collectors who wish to remain anonymous

BIOGRAPHY AND SELECTED EXHIBITION HISTORY

COMPILED BY KIMBERLY DETTERBECK

Born 1939 in Philadelphia;
lives and works in New York

EDUCATION

1965
MFA, University of Illinois, Urbana-Champaign

1963
BFA and BS in Education, Tyler School of Art, Temple University, Elkins Park, Pennsylvania

SOLO EXHIBITIONS

2016
Louise Fishman: A Retrospective, Neuberger Museum of Art, Purchase College, SUNY, Purchase, New York. Travels to the Weatherspoon Art Museum, University of North Carolina, Greensboro, in 2017
Paper Louise Tiny Fishman Rock, Institute of Contemporary Art, University of Pennsylvania, Philadelphia

2015
Louise Fishman, Cheim & Read, New York

2014
Louise Fishman: Venice Watercolors, Gallery Nosco, London

2013
Louise Fishman: It's Here-Elsewhere, Goya Contemporary Gallery, Baltimore

2012
Louise Fishman, Cheim & Read, New York
Louise Fishman, John Davis Gallery, New York
Louise Fishman: Five Decades, Jack Tilton Gallery, New York

2010
Louise Fishman, Gallery Paule Anglim, San Francisco

2009
Louise Fishman: Among the Old Masters, The John and Mable Ringling Museum of Art, Sarasota, Florida

2008
Louise Fishman: Between Geometry and Gesture, Galerie Kienzle & Gmeiner, Berlin

2007
Louise Fishman, The Tenacity of Painting: Paintings from 1970 to 2005, Hood Museum of Art, Dartmouth College, Hanover, New Hampshire

2006
Louise Fishman, Cheim & Read, New York

2005
Louise Fishman, Foster-Gwin, San Francisco

2004
Louise Fishman: Recent Work, Manny Silverman Gallery, Los Angeles

2003
Louise Fishman, Cheim & Read, New York

2002
Louise Fishman, Manny Silverman Gallery, Los Angeles

2001
Louise Fishman, Gallery Paule Anglim, San Francisco

2000
Louise Fishman, Cheim & Read, New York

1998
Louise Fishman, Gallery Paule Anglim, San Francisco
Louise Fishman: Recent Paintings and Drawings, Cheim & Read, New York

1996
Louise Fishman: Recent Paintings, Robert Miller Gallery, New York

1995
Small Paintings, Robert Miller Gallery, New York

1994
Small Paintings, 1992–1994, Bianca Lanza Gallery, Miami Beach

1993
Louise Fishman, Robert Miller Gallery, New York

1992
Drawings and Experimental Work, 1971–1992, Tyler Galleries, Tyler School of Art, Temple University, Elkins Park, Pennsylvania
Louise Fishman: Paintings, 1986–1992, Morris Gallery, Pennsylvania Academy of Fine Arts, Philadelphia
Louise Fishman: Small Paintings, Olin Art Gallery, Kenyon College, Gambier, Ohio
Louise Fishman: Small Paintings, 1978–1992, Simon Watson Gallery, New York
Louise Fishman: Small Paintings, 1979–1992, Tyler Galleries, Tyler School of Art, Temple University, Elkins Park, Pennsylvania

1991
Louise Fishman: New Paintings, Lennon, Weinberg, Inc., New York

1989
Louise Fishman: New Paintings 1987–1989, Lennon, Weinberg, Inc., New York
Remembrance and Renewal, Simon Watson Gallery, New York

1986
Louise Fishman: New Paintings, Baskerville & Watson Gallery, New York

1984
Louise Fishman, Baskerville & Watson Gallery, New York

1982
Louise Fishman, John Davis Gallery, Akron, Ohio
Louise Fishman: Recent Work, Oscarsson-Hood Gallery, New York

1980
Louise Fishman: Small Paintings, The MacDowell Colony, July 1980, Oscarsson-Hood Gallery, New York

1979

Louise Fishman, Nancy Hoffman Gallery, New York

Louise Fishman: Five Years, 55 Mercer Gallery, New York

1978

Louise Fishman, United States Department of State, Washington, D.C.

1977

Louise Fishman, Nancy Hoffman Gallery, New York

1976

Louise Fishman, John Doyle Gallery, Chicago

Louise Fishman, University of Rhode Island Art Center, Kingston

1974

Louise Fishman, Nancy Hoffman Gallery, New York

1964

Louise Fishman, Philadelphia Art Alliance

GROUP EXHIBITIONS

2015

Painting 2.0: Expression in the Information Age, Museum Brandhorst, Munich. Travels to the Museum moderner Kunst Stiftung Ludwig Wien, Vienna, in 2016

2014

Whitney Museum of American Art 2014 Biennial Exhibition, Whitney Museum of American Art, New York

2013

Reinventing Abstraction: New York Painting in the 1980s, Cheim & Read, New York

2012

Generations: Louise Fishman, Gertrude Fisher-Fishman, and Razel Kapustin, Woodmere Art Museum, Philadelphia

2011

Abstraction, Albert Merola Gallery, Provincetown, Massachusetts

Dance / Draw, the Institute of Contemporary Art, Boston. Traveled to Grey Art Gallery, New York University, New York, and the Frances Young Tang Teaching Museum and Art Gallery, Skidmore College, Saratoga Springs, New York

Readykeulous: The Hurtful Healer: The Correspondance Issue, Invisible-Exports, New York

Seeing Gertrude Stein: Five Stories, the Contemporary Jewish Museum, San Francisco. Traveled to the National Portrait Gallery, Washington, D.C.

The Women in Our Life: A Fifteen-Year Anniversary Exhibition, Cheim & Read, New York

To the Venetians, Rhode Island School of Design Museum of Art, Providence

2010

Abstraction Revisited, Chelsea Art Museum, New York

Le Tableau: French Abstraction and Its Affinities, Cheim & Read, New York

Painting & Sculpture: To Benefit the Foundation for Contemporary Arts, Lehmann Maupin, New York

Shifting the Gaze: Painting and Feminism, The Jewish Museum, New York

2009

Abstractions by Gallery Artists, Cheim & Read, New York

Before Again: Joan Mitchell, Louise Fishman, Harriet Korman, Melissa Meyer, Jill Moser, Denyse Thomasos, Lennon, Weinberg, Inc., New York

Les Femmes, McClain Gallery, Houston

Propose: Works on Paper from the 1970s, Alexander Gray Associates, New York

2008

Environments and Empires, Rose Art Museum, Brandeis University, Waltham, Massachusetts

MassArt at the Fine Arts Work Center: Faculty and Visiting Artists, Hudson D. Walker Gallery Fine Arts Work Center, Provincetown, Massachusetts

Pretty Ugly, Maccarone Gallery and Gavin Brown's Enterprise, New York

Significant Form, The Persistence of Abstraction, Pushkin State Museum of Fine Arts, Moscow

2007

American Abstract, Maruani & Noirhomme Gallery, Knokke, Belgium

The Fluid Fields: Abstraction and Reference, Tyler Galleries, Tyler School of Art, Temple University, Elkins Park, Pennsylvania

WACK! Art and the Feminist Revolution, the Geffen Contemporary at the Museum of Contemporary Art, Los Angeles. Traveled to the National Museum of Women in the Arts, Washington, D.C.; MoMA P.S. 1, Long Island City, New York; and Vancouver Art Gallery, Vancouver, Canada

2006

High Times, Hard Times: New York Painting 1967–1975, Independent Curators International, New York. Traveled to Weatherspoon Art Museum, University of North Carolina at Greensboro; American University Museum at the Katzen Arts Center, Washington, D.C.; National Academy Museum, New York; Museo Tamayo Arte Contemporáneo, Mexico City; Neue Galerie Graz, Graz, Austria; and ZKM | Center for Art and Media Karlsruhe, Karlsruhe, Germany

The Name of This Show Is Not Gay Art Now, Paul Kasmin Gallery, New York
The New Landscape / The New Still Life: Soutine and Modern Art, Cheim & Read, New York

2005
Contemporary Women Artists: New York, University Art Gallery, Indiana State University, Terre Haute, Indiana
Looking at Words: The Formal Presence of Text in Modern and Contemporary Works on Paper, Andrea Rosen Gallery, New York
Paint, Elizabeth Leach Gallery, Portland, Oregon

2004
Drawing Exhibition, Galerie S 65, Cologne, Germany
New York Abstract Painters: George McNeil / Louise Fishman, Foster-Gwin, San Francisco
Summer Invitational, Nielsen Gallery, Boston
Twelve from Cheim & Read, Fay Gold Gallery, Atlanta

2003
Grisaille, James Graham & Sons, New York
The Invisible Thread: Buddhist Spirit in Contemporary Art, Newhouse Center for Contemporary Art, Snug Harbor Cultural Center, Staten Island
Women's Lines, G Fine Art, Washington, D.C.

2002
177th Annual Exhibition, National Academy of Design, New York
Art Downtown, Wall Street Rising, 48 Wall Street, New York
Nature Found and Made, Chambers Fine Art, New York
Nocturne/Nocturnal, Skoto Gallery, New York
Painting: A Passionate Response, Sixteen American Artists, The Painting Center, New York
Personal and Political: The Women's Art Movement, 1969–1975, Guild Hall Museum, East Hampton, New York
Zenroxy, Von Lintel Gallery, New York

2001
Four Painters, Lindsey Brown, New York
Imaging Judaism / Mining History, Susquehanna Art Museum, Harrisburg, Pennsylvania
Invitational Exhibition of Visual Arts, American Academy of Arts and Letters, New York
Reopening Exhibition, The Lesbian and Gay Community Services Center, New York
Seven Female Visionaries Before Feminism, Mills College Art Museum, Oakland, California
Watercolor: In the Abstract, The Hyde Collection, Glens Falls, New York. Traveled to Michael C. Rockefeller Arts Center Gallery, State University of New York at Fredonia; Butler Institute of American Art, Youngstown, Ohio; Nina Freudenheim, Inc., Buffalo, New York; Ben Shahn Gallery for Visual Arts, William Paterson University, Wayne, New Jersey; Sarah Moody Gallery of Art, University of Alabama, Tuscaloosa

2000
175th Annual Exhibition, National Academy of Design, New York
Painting Abstraction, New York Studio School, New York
The Perpetual Well: Contemporary Art from the Collection of The Jewish Museum, Parrish Art Museum, Southampton, New York
Snapshot, Baltimore Museum of Contemporary Art, Baltimore

1999
Abstraction: Realism, Susquehanna Art Museum, Harrisburg, Pennsylvania
Drawing in the Present Tense, Parsons, the New School for Design, New York
Gestural Abstraction, Hunter College Art Galleries, New York
Severed Ear: The Poetry of Abstraction, Creiger-Dane Gallery, Boston
Walking, Danese, New York

1998
Paintings and Drawings, Rhona Hoffman Gallery, Chicago
Small Paintings, Cheim & Read, New York
Undercurrents and Overtones: Contemporary Abstract Painting, California College of Arts and Crafts Wattis Institute for Contemporary Arts, San Francisco

1997
Abstract Painting, Carrie Haddad Gallery, Hudson, New York
Affinities with the East, Robert Miller Gallery, New York
After the Fall: Aspects of Abstract Painting since 1970, Newhouse Center for Contemporary Art, Snug Harbor Cultural Center, Staten Island
Basically Black and White, Neuberger Museum of Art, Purchase College, State University of New York, Purchase
Convergence, George Billis Gallery, New York
Retreat and Renewal: The Painters and Sculptors of the MacDowell Colony, Currier Gallery of Art, Manchester, Vermont. Traveled to the Equitable Gallery, New York; Wichita Art Museum, Wichita, Kansas; and Fort Wayne Museum of Art, Fort Wayne, Indiana
Voices: The Power of Abstraction, Eighth Floor Gallery, New York

1996
Summer Group Show, Robert Miller Gallery, New York
Transforming the Social Order, Tyler Galleries, Tyler School of Art, Temple University, Elkins Park, Pennsylvania
Women's Work, Greene Naftali, New York

1995
25 Americans: Painting in the '90s, Milwaukee Art Museum
1995 Carnegie International, the Carnegie Museum of Art, Pittsburgh
Artist's Choice: Elizabeth Murray, the Museum of Modern Art, New York
New Faculty, Carpenter Center for the Visual Arts, Harvard University, Cambridge, Massachusetts

1994
46th Annual Academy Purchase Exhibition, American Academy of Arts and Letters, New York
Abstract Works on Paper, Robert Miller Gallery, New York
Consecrations: The Spiritual in Art in the Time of AIDS, Museum of Contemporary Religious Art, Saint Louis University

Couples, Elga Wimmer, New York
Relatively Speaking: Mothers and Daughters in Art, Sweet Briar College, Sweet Briar, Virginia. Traveled to Newhouse Center for Contemporary Art, Snug Harbor Cultural Center, Staten Island; and Rahr West Museum, Manitowoc, Wisconsin
Small and Wet: Abstract Painting and Sculpture, Bernard Toale Gallery, Boston

1993
30th Anniversary Exhibition of Drawings, Leo Castelli Gallery, New York
Art Discovery '93, Cooperstown Art Association and Smithy, Pioneer Gallery, Cooperstown, New York
Drawing the Line Against AIDS, Peggy Guggenheim Collection, Venice, under the aegis of the *45th Venice Biennale*. Traveled to the Solomon R. Guggenheim Museum, New York
The Inaugural Show, The Painting Center, New York
The Linear Image II, Marisa del Re Gallery, New York
Singularities, Blondies Contemporary Art, New York
Soho Abstract–Figurative, Robert Miller Gallery, New York

1992
The Jewish Museum's Masked Ball in Celebration of Purim, The Jewish Museum, New York
Paintings by Martha Diamond, Mary Heilmann, Harriet Korman, Louise Fishman and Bernard Piffaretti, Robert Miller Gallery, New York

1991
Act-Up Benefit, Matthew Marks Gallery, New York
Something Pithier and More Psychological, Simon Watson Gallery, New York
Spring/Summer Exhibition, Part One: Painters, Lennon, Weinberg, Inc., New York
Twentieth-Century Collage, Margo Leavin Gallery, Los Angeles. Traveled to the Centro Cultural Arte Contemporaneo, Polanco, Mexico; and the Musée d'art Moderne et d'art Contemporain, Nice, France

1990
A Group Exhibition, Lennon, Weinberg, Inc., New York
From Earth to Archetype, LedisFlam Gallery, New York
Group Exhibition of Gallery Artists, Lennon, Weinberg, Inc., New York

1989
A Decade of American Drawing 1980–1989, Daniel Weinberg Gallery, Los Angeles
A Group Exhibition, Lennon, Weinberg, Inc., New York
Belief in Paint: Eleven Contemporary Artists, Usdan Gallery, Bennington College, Bennington, Vermont
Fragments of History, Albany Museum of Art, Albany, Georgia
Towards Form, Greenberg Wilson Gallery, New York
Works on Paper, Lennon, Weinberg, Inc., New York

1988
Golem: Danger, Deliverance and Art, The Jewish Museum, New York
Louise Fishman, David Reed, Joan Mitchell, Barbara Toll Fine Arts, New York
Selections from the Edward R. Downe, Jr. Collection, Davis McClain Gallery, Houston

1987
40th Biennial Exhibition of Contemporary American Painting, Corcoran Gallery of Art, Washington, D.C.
Louise Fishman and Andy Spence: Two from the Corcoran, Winston Gallery, Washington, D.C.
Whitney Museum of American Art 1987 Biennial Exhibition, Whitney Museum of American Art, New York

1986
Artists for Pride, Nexus Gallery, Philadelphia
Jewish Themes / Contemporary American Artists II, The Jewish Museum, New York. Traveled to Spertus Museum of Judaica, Chicago, and the National Museum of Jewish History, Philadelphia
Louise Fishman, Hermine Ford and Arthur Cohen, Hofstra University, Hempstead, New York
Spirit Tracks—Big Abstract Drawings, Pratt Manhattan Gallery, Pratt Manhattan, New York, and Pratt Institute Gallery, Brooklyn

1985
An Invitational, Condeso/Lawler, New York
Drawings 1975–1985, Barbara Toll Fine Arts, New York
Fishman / Sanderson, North Carolina Museum of Art, Raleigh
Paintings 1985, Pam Adler Gallery, New York
Painting as Landscape, Parrish Art Museum, Southampton, New York. Traveled to Baxter Art Gallery, Pasadena, California
Twelve Painters and Six Sculptors, Tyler Galleries, Tyler School of Art, Temple University, Elkins Park, Pennsylvania

1984
New Prints since 1980, Philip Johnson Center, Muhlenberg College, Allentown, Pennsylvania
Relief Prints since 1980, Summit Art Center, Summit, New Jersey
Second Nature: Abstract Drawings and Paintings, Procter Art Center, Bard College, Annandale-on-Hudson, New York

1983

Drawing In and Out, Baskerville & Watson Gallery, New York

Painting from the Mind's Eye, Hillwood Art Gallery, Long Island University, Greenvale, New York

Six Painters, Hudson River Museum, Yonkers, New York

1982

Abstract Painting: Substance and Meaning—Painting by Women Artists, New York Chapter of the Women's Caucus for Art, New York

Abstraction, Neuberger Museum of Art, Purchase College, State University of New York, Purchase

Five New York Artists, Usdan Gallery, Bennington College, Bennington, Vermont

Mixing Art and Politics, Randolph Street Gallery, Chicago

Painterly Abstraction, Fort Wayne Museum of Art, Fort Wayne, Indiana

1981

1981 Painting Invitational, Oscarsson-Hood Gallery, New York

CAPS Award Winners in Painting 1980–1981, Procter Art Center, Bard College, Annandale-on-Hudson, New York, and Munson-Williams-Proctor Arts Institute Museum of Art, Utica, New York

CAPS Grantees from Brooklyn, Brooklyn Museum, New York

1980

Inaugural Exhibit, Oscarsson-Hood Gallery, New York

Work on Paper, Mary Boone Gallery, New York

1979

Major New Works, Nancy Hoffman Gallery, New York

1977

Critic's Choice, Joe and Emily Lowe Art Gallery, Syracuse University, Syracuse, New York. Traveled to Munson-Williams-Proctor Arts Institute Museum of Art, Utica, New York

Fifth Anniversary Show, Nancy Hoffman Gallery, New York

Major New Works, Nancy Hoffman Gallery, New York

Nancy Hoffman in Oxford, Miami University, Oxford, Ohio

Paintings That Reveal the Wall, Procter Art Center, Bard College, Annandale-on-Hudson, New York

Preparatory Notes–Thinking Drawings, Part II, 80 Washington Square East Galleries, New York University, New York

1976

Artist '76: A Celebration, Marion Koogler McNay Art Institute, San Antonio, Texas

Paris International Art Fair, Grand Palais, Paris

1975

New York Faculty Exhibition, Procter Art Center, Bard College, Annandale-on-Hudson, New York

1973

A Woman's Group, Nancy Hoffman Gallery, New York

Whitney Museum of American Art 1973 Biennial Exhibition, Whitney Museum of American Art, New York

1972

Open A.I.R., A.I.R. Gallery, New York

Summer Show, Paula Cooper Gallery, New York

1963

National Watercolor and Drawing Exhibition, Pennsylvania Academy of Fine Arts, Philadelphia

FELLOWSHIPS, GRANTS, AND AWARDS

National Academy of Design, Adolph and Clara Obrig Prize for Painting, 2002

National Endowment for the Arts Visual Artists Fellowship, Painting, 1993

Adolph and Esther Gottlieb Foundation General Support Grant, 1986

New York Foundation for the Arts Fellowship in Painting, 1986

National Endowment for the Arts, Visual Artists Fellowship, Painting, 1983

Creative Artists Public Service Program (CAPS) Fellowship in Painting, 1981

MacDowell Colony Visual Artists Fellowship, 1980

John Simon Guggenheim Memorial Foundation Fellowship in Fine Arts, 1979

National Endowment for the Arts, Visual Artists Fellowship, Painting, 1975

Tyler School of Art, Temple University, Bertha Lowenburg Prize for the Senior Woman to Excel in Art, 1975

Tyler School of Art, Temple University, First Painting Prize, Student Exhibit, 1975

Change, Inc., Artists Fellowship, 1974

SELECTED BIBLIOGRAPHY

COMPILED BY KIMBERLY DETTERBECK

ARTICLES

Atkins, Robert. "Goodbye Lesbian / Gay History, Hello Queer Sensibility." *Art Journal* 55, no. 4 (Winter 1996): 80–85.

Burk, Tara. "In Pursuit of the Unspeakable: Heresies' 'Lesbian Art and Artists' Issue, 1977." *Women's Studies Quarterly* 41, no. 3/4 (Fall / Winter 2013): 63–78.

Butler, Sharon. "In Conversation: Louise Fishman with Sharon Butler." *The Brooklyn Rail* (October 2012): 19–21.

Cohen, Cora. "Social Volition." *Bomb* 37 (Fall 1991): 58–65.

Cotter, Holland. "Art after Stonewall: Twelve Artists Interviewed—Louise Fishman." *Art in America* 82, no. 6 (June 1994): 56–66.

Diehl, Carol. "Birds, Beads, and Bannerstones." *ARTnews* 95, no. 7 (Summer 1996): 76–84.

Duncan, Michael. "Queering the Discourse." *Art in America* 83, no. 7 (July 1995): 27–31.

Frank, Priscilla. "Louise Fishman on Fifty Years of Fitting in While Sticking Out." The Huffington Post, September 15, 2012, http://www.huffingtonpost.com/2012/09/11/louise-fishman-show_n_1875067.html.

Franklin, Margery B. "Forging Links in Narratives of Creative Work: Causes, Precursors, and Sources." *Journal of Aesthetic Education* 33, no. 1 (Spring 1999): 72–79.

Gardner, Paul. "Hint: Avoid the Word 'nice'." *ARTnews* 102, no. 11 (December 2003): 110–12.

Goodman, Jonathan. "Louise Fishman," *The Brooklyn Rail* , October 4, 2012, http://www.brooklynrail.org/2012/10/artseen/louise-fishman-artseen.

Hall, L. "Neo-Expressionism: A Richer Fare." *House and Garden* 155, no. 8 (August 1983): 10–13.

Lancaster, C. "Louise Fishman." *Arts Magazine* 56, no. 9 (May 1982): 25.

Landi, Ann. "Artists and Their (Role) Models." *ARTnews* 104, no. 11 (December 2005): 132–35.

______. "When Is an Artwork Finished?" *ARTnews* 113, no. 2 (February 2014): 78–83.

Langer, Cassandra. "The Lavender Menace in Jewish Feminist Art." *Gay & Lesbian Review Worldwide* 18, no. 1 (January / February 2011): 49.

Moyer, Carrie. "A Restless Spirit." *Art in America* 100, no. 9 (October 2012): 128

______. "Zero at the Bone: Louise Fishman Speaks with Carrie Moyer." *Art Journal* 71, no. 4 (Winter 2012): 36–53.

Perl, Jed. "Code Name: Painting." *New Criterion* 12, no. 4 (December 1993): 46–51.

Rand, Archie. "Louise Fishman." *Bomb* 77 (Fall 2001): 42–45.

Ratcliff, Carter, Hayden Herrera, Sarah McFadden, and Joan Simon. "Expressionism Today: An Artists' Symposium." *Art in America* 70, no. 11 (December 1982): 58–75, 139–41.

Saltz, Jerry. "A Year in the Life: Tropic of Painting." *Art in America* 82, no. 10 (October 1994): 90–102.

Schäfer, Magnus. "Malerei nach dem Modernismus" (Painting after Modernism / Canonical Historiography and Recursive Differentiation). *Texte zur Kunst* 22, no. 85 (March 2012): 96–105.

Seidel, Miriam. "Material Imperatives." *Art in America* 81, no. 9 (September 1993): 94–99.

Selengut, Suzanne. "A Jewish Woman's Work." *The Jerusalem Report*, October 25, 2010.

Thompson, Margo Hobbs. "Agreeable Objects and Angry Paintings: 'Female Imagery' in Art by Hannah Wilke and Louise Fishman, 1970–1973." *Genders* 43 (June 2006), http://www.iiav.nl/ezines/IAV_606661/IAV_606661_2010_52/g43_margothompson.html.

Turvey, Lisa. "Louise Fishman." *Artforum International* 51, no. 4 (December 2012): 272–73.

Whitworth, Sarah. "Angry Louise Fishman (Serious)." *Amazon Quarterly* 1 (October 1973): 57–59.

Yau, John. "Drawing a New Line." *Art On Paper* 8, no. 3 (January / February 2004): 56–61.

BOOKS

Broude, Norma, and Mary D. Garrard, eds. *The Power of Feminist Art: The American Movement of the 1970s, History and Impact.* New York: Harry N. Abrams, 1994.

Cottingham, Laura. *Seeing Through the Seventies: Essays on Feminism and Art.* New York: Routledge, 2013.

Franklin, Margery B., and Bernard Kaplan, eds. *Development and the Arts: Critical Perspectives.* Florence, KY: Psychology Press, 2013.

Hammond, Harmony. *Lesbian Art in America: A Contemporary History*. New York: Rizzoli, 2000.

Lord, Catherine, and Richard Meyer. *Art and Queer Culture*, London: Phaidon Press, 2013.

Reed, Christopher. *Art and Homosexuality: A History of Ideas*. New York: Oxford University Press, 2011.

Schor, Mira. A *Decade of Negative Thinking: Essays on Art, Politics, and Daily Life.* Durham, NC: Duke University Press, 2009.

Sirlin, Deanna. *She's Got What It Takes: American Women Artists in Dialogue.* Milan: Charta, 2013.

Taylor, Michael R., and Gerald Auten, eds. *In Residence: Contemporary Artists at Dartmouth.* Hanover, NH: Hood Museum of Art, 2014.

EXHIBITION CATALOGUES

Armstrong, Richard, and Paola Morsiani, eds. *Carnegie International 1995.* Pittsburgh: Carnegie Museum of Art, 1995.

Before Again: Joan Mitchell, Louise Fishman, Harriet Korman, Melissa Meyer, Jill Moser, Denyse Thomasos. New York: Lennon, Weinberg, Inc., 2009.

Brenson, Michael. *Louise Fishman.* Elkins Park, PA: Tyler Galleries, Tyler School of Art, 1993.

Butler, Cornelia, and Lisa Gabrielle Mark, eds. *WACK!: Art and the Feminist Revolution*. Los Angeles: Museum of Contemporary Art, 2007.

Collischan Van Wagner, Judy K. *Painting from the Mind's Eye*. Greenvale, NY: Hillwood Art Gallery, Long Island University, 1983.

Comer, Stuart, Anthony Elms, Michelle Grabner, and Adam D. Weinberg. *Whitney Biennial 2014.* New York: Whitney Museum of American Art, 2014.

Deitcher, David. *Louise Fishman.* New York: Cheim & Read, 2006.

Feldman, Melissa E. *Louise Fishman.* New York: Robert Miller Gallery, 1993.

Flint-Gohlke, Lucy, and Nikki Bruno Clapper, eds. *Creating the New Century: Contemporary Art from the Dicke Collection*. Dayton, OH: Dayton Art Institute, 2011.
Hirsch, Faye. *Louise Fishman: The Tenacity of Painting, Paintings from 1970 to 2005.* Hanover, NH: Dartmouth College, 2007.
Jewish Themes / Contemporary American Artists II. New York: The Jewish Museum, 1986.
Kernan, Nathan. *Louise Fishman*. New York: Cheim & Read, 1998.
Kotik, Charlotta, and Judith Swirsky. *Relatively Speaking: Mothers and Daughters in Art.* New York: Brooklyn Museum, 1994.
Langlykke, Peter. *Six Painters: Gregory Amenoff, Jake Berthot, Howard Buchwald, Louise Fishman, Harry Kramer, Katherine Porter*. Yonkers, NY: Hudson River Museum, 1983.
Molesworth, Helen. *Dance / Draw*. Boston: Institute of Contemporary Art, 2011.
Nelson, Dona. *The Fluid Field: Abstraction and Reference*. Elkins Park, PA: Tyler School of Art, 2007.
Ratcliff, Carter, and Kim Sobel. *Immediacies of the Hand: Recent Abstract Painting in New York.* New York: Hunter College of the City University of New York, 1998.
Rinder, Lawrence. *Undercurrents and Overtones: Contemporary Abstract Painting.* San Francisco: California College of Arts and Crafts Wattis Institute for Contemporary Arts, 1998.
Siegel, Katy, ed. *High Times, Hard Times: New York Painting, 1967–1975*. New York: Independent Curators International, 2006.
Taylor, Simon, and Natalie Ng. *Personal and Political: The Women's Art Movement, 1969–1975.* East Hampton, NY: Guild Hall Museum, 2002.
Wei, Lilly. *After the Fall: Aspects of Abstract Painting since 1970.* Staten Island: Snug Harbor Cultural Center, 1997.
Weinberg, Jill, and Bernard Lennon. *Louise Fishman: Paintings 1987–1989.* New York: Lennon, Weinberg, Inc., 1989.

REPRODUCTION CREDITS

All works by Louise Fishman illustrated in the catalogue are © the artist and reproduced courtesy of Cheim & Read, New York. The following images, identified by page number, are those for which separate or additional credits are due.

Courtesy Albright-Knox Art Gallery / Art Resource, NY: 11. © 2015 Artists Rights Society (ARS), New York: 11, 18. Image © The Barnes Foundation: 18 (right). Photo by Alfredo Dagi Orti / The Art Archive of Art Resource, NY: 19. Photo by Joseph Hyde: 63. Courtesy The Jewish Museum, New York: 56 (bottom). © 2015 Brice Marden / Artists Rights Society (ARS), New York: 50 (bottom). © 2015 Agnes Martin / Artists Rights Society (ARS), New York: 50 (top). Photo by Constance Mensh: 27 (right), 186, 189 (bottom left), 191 (bottom). © Estate of Joan Mitchell: 12. Digital Image © The Museum of Modern Art/Licensed by SCALA / Art Resource, NY: 50 (bottom). © 2015 Bruce Nauman / Artists Rights Society (ARS), New York: 47 (top). Courtesy Tate, London / Art Resource, NY: 20 (left). Additional photography by Brian Buckley

This publication accompanies the concurrent exhibitions *Louise Fishman: A Retrospective*, curated by Helaine Posner and organized by the Neuberger Museum of Art, Purchase College, SUNY; and *Paper Louise Tiny Fishman Rock*, curated by Ingrid Schaffner and organized by the Institute of Contemporary Art, University of Pennsylvania, Philadelphia.

Louise Fishman: A Retrospective
Neuberger Museum of Art
Purchase College, SUNY
April 3–July 31, 2016

Weatherspoon Art Museum
The University of North Carolina at Greensboro
September 30–December 22, 2017

Paper Louise Tiny Fishman Rock
Institute of Contemporary Art
University of Pennsylvania, Philadelphia
April 29–August 14, 2016

Generous support for *Louise Fishman: A Retrospective* has been provided by the National Endowment for the Arts and by Susan and James Dubin. Additional support has been provided by Lauren B. Cramer, Helen Stambler Neuberger and James Neuberger, and Sara and Michelle Vance Waddell. Support is also provided by the Friends of the Neuberger Museum of Art and by the Purchase College Foundation.

Support for *Paper Louise Tiny Fishman Rock* has been provided by the Edna W. Andrade Fund of the Philadelphia Foundation. Additional funding has been provided by Arthur Cohen and Daryl Otte, Marjorie and Michael Levine, Amanda and Andrew Megibow, and Josephine and Christopher Schlank.

ICA is always Free For All.
Free admission is courtesy of Amanda and Glenn Fuhrman.

ICA acknowledges the generous sponsorship of Barbara B. and Theodore R. Aronson for exhibition catalogues. Programming at ICA has been made possible in part by the Emily and Jerry Spiegel Fund to Support Contemporary Culture and Visual Arts and the Lise Spiegel Wilks and Jeffrey Wilks Family Foundation, the Ruth Ivor Foundation, and by Hilarie L. and Mitchell Morgan. Marketing is supported by Pamela Toub Berkman and David J. Berkman and by Lisa A. and Steven A. Tananbaum. Additional funding has been provided by the Horace W. Goldsmith Foundation, the Dietrich Foundation and the Daniel W. Dietrich, II Trust, the Overseers Board for the Institute of Contemporary Art, friends and members of ICA, and the University of Pennsylvania. General operating support is provided, in part, by the Philadelphia Cultural Fund.

ICA receives state arts funding support through a grant from the Pennsylvania Council on the Arts, a state agency funded by the Commonwealth of Pennsylvania and the National Endowment for the Arts, a federal agency. ICA acknowledges Le Méridien Philadelphia as our official Unlock Art™ partner hotel.

Published by the Neuberger Museum of Art, Purchase College, SUNY; Institute of Contemporary Art, University of Pennsylvania; and DelMonico Books • Prestel

Neuberger Museum of Art
Purchase College, SUNY
735 Anderson Hill Road
Purchase, NY 10577
www.neuberger.org

Institute of Contemporary Art
University of Pennsylvania
118 South 36th Street
Philadelphia, PA 19104
www.icaphila.org

DelMonico Books, an imprint of Prestel, a member of Verlagsgruppe Random House GmbH

Prestel Verlag
Neumarkter Strasse 28
81673 Munich
Tel.: +49 89 4136 0
Fax: +49 89 4136 2335

Prestel Publishing Ltd.
14-17 Wells Street
London W1T 3PD
Tel.: +44 20 7323 5004
Fax: +44 20 7323 0271

Prestel Publishing
900 Broadway, Suite 603
New York, NY 10003
Tel.: +1 212 995 2720
Fax: +1 212 995 2733
sales@prestel-usa.com
www.prestel.com

FRONTISPIECE: Detail of *Heavy Is the Root of the Light*, 1997 (pl. 56)
PAGE 4: Detail of *Sven Jesper*, 2015 (pl. 115)
PAGE 9: Monoprint plates, various mediums and materials, made at Oehme Graphics, Steamboat Springs, Colorado, in 2011

Project editor: Ryan Newbanks
Designer: Rita Jules, Miko McGinty Inc.
Copy editor: Amanda Glesmann
Proofreader: Charlotte Blom
Production coordinator: Luke Chase
Printed and bound in China

Library of Congress Cataloging-in-Publication Data
Names: Fishman, Louise, 1939– interviewee. | Moyer, Carrie, 1960– | Posner, Helaine. | Princenthal, Nancy. | Schaffner, Ingrid, interviewer. | Fishman, Louise, 1939– Paintings. Selections. | Neuberger Museum of Art. | University of Pennsylvania. Institute of Contemporary Art.
Title: Louise Fishman / Edited by Helaine Posner ; Essays by Carrie Moyer, Helaine Posner, and Nancy Princenthal ; With an interview by Ingrid Schaffner.
Description: New York : DelMonico Books/Prestel, 2016. | "This publication accompanies the concurrent exhibitions Louise Fishman: A Retrospective, curated by Helaine Posner and organized by the Neuberger Museum of Art, Purchase College, SUNY; and Paper Louise Tiny Fishman Rock, curated by Ingrid Schaffner and organized by the Institute of Contemporary Art, University of Pennsylvania, Philadelphia." | Includes bibliographical references.
Identifiers: LCCN 2015038971 | ISBN 9783791355177
Subjects: LCSH: Fishman, Louise, 1939— Exhibitions.
Classification: LCC ND237.F445 A4 2016 | DDC 759.06/52—dc23
LC record available at http://lccn.loc.gov/2015038971

ISBN 978-3-7913-5517-7

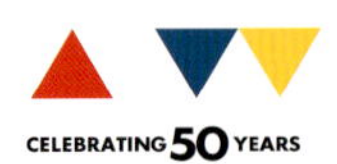

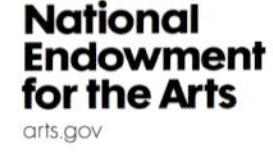

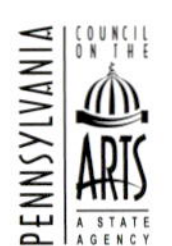

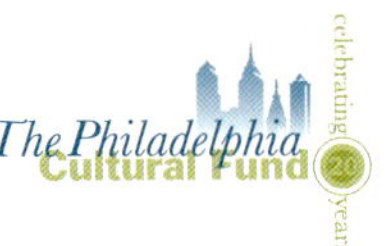

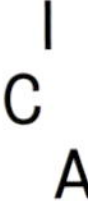

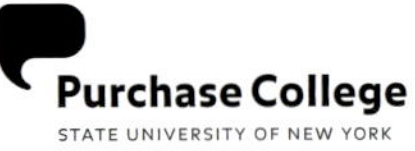